THE HU

Bill Borrows has written for the Guardian, Observer, Sunday Times, Sunday Telegraph, Vogues Hommes International and Maxim magazine among many other publications. He also writes a column for the Daily Mirror. This is his first book.

From the reviews of The Hurricane:

'Bill Borrows' vividly funny and powerful book brings the man and his chaotic times to pulsating life. I couldn't put it down.' Rosie Boycott

'As a vehement anti-snooker merchant, I was astonished to be blown over by The Hurricane. It begins with a gale of expletives, and that's the polite part. As the "turbulent life" of Alex Higgins unfolds (or surges off the rails), it is like watching a train wreck. The man, and the book, pulsate with nervous energy.'
Robert Winder, Books of the Year, New Statesman

'[Borrows] entertainingly portrays the rise and fall of a man who did more than most to popularise the sport... there is no doubt that Higgins was a phenomenon with a near-unbeliev-able story.' Alyson Rudd, Sports Books of the Year, The Times

'This diligently researched and racy biography reveals the twice world champion in all his baffling complexity. It is a tale, compellingly told, of authentic genius fatally under-mined by outlandish and at times obnoxious behaviour'
Clive Everton, Editor, Snooker Scene

'The literary equ   enburg
disasters rolled i   y.'
Neil Drysdale, Sc

'I genuinely e͟██████████████████████t m one sitting, so compelling is the tale of this disturbed genius. … Apart from the harrowing, incredulous and hilarious stories about Higgins, what fascinated me most was the gap between the age-old image snooker likes to present and the truth. … [*The Hurricane*] is a snapshot of reality' Brian Reade, *Daily Mirror*

'Borrows has come up with the goods: a hefty, thorough biography of the billiards legend, flavoured by the reminiscences of those who met or knew him… Great man, great story, great book.' Chris Burke, *Loaded*

'Borrows shows how [Higgins] almost destroyed himself through his addictive, psychotic personality. At times the book almost reads like a script for a horror film… Higgins's obnoxious behaviour is recounted with exasperated relish, including his frequent assaults on girlfriends and other players… for all his monstrous faults, there is also a poignancy about the book, as we watch a unique star end up living like a tramp in a caravan, without friends or money, desperately trying to qualify for tournaments he once dominated.'
Leo McKinstry, Sports Books of the Year, *Sunday Telegraph*

'A reminder of Higgins's wild and wretched ways, but also of his genius' Nick Pitt, Sports Books of the Year, *Sunday Times*

'Higgins' demise from "People's Champion" to alcoholic nuisance makes for well paced and at times jaw-dropping reading… whether you like snooker or not, it's as good a "wild man" story as you're likely to read' *Time Out*

'Alex Higgins created modern snooker and then destroyed himself just to prove it was pointless without him. Cancer, tabloids, fags, models, drinks and inexplicable rage – middle England found it distasteful but middle England has never created anything, so how could it understand a hyper-talented Ulsterman in a concrete auditorium in South Yorkshire threatening to have people shot, and dowsing his genius with drink? This maximum break of a book is proof that shits might not prosper, but they can change the world.' Michael Hodges, Book of the Month, *Maxim*

'Like Gary Sobers, George Best, Ayrton Senna or Muhammed Ali, Higgins was at one with his sport. Unfortunately, he was – and is and has always been, judging by Bill Borrows's unauthorised biography – a complete bastard.' Bryan Appleyard, *New Statesman*

'Sport throws up as many cautionary tales as rock 'n' roll. And if ever there was a case of a great sporting talent pissing on his chips it's two-times world snooker champion, Alex "Hurricane" Higgins. Both lifestyle (fast women, fast drugs and tankers of ale) and style of play (feral, essentially) were anathema to snooker's rulers and they couldn't wait for him to slip in his own vomit. When he did, it was a long and bitter tumble into the gutter. Borrows inevitably fell out with his subject – eventually everybody does – making this an unauthorised account... but it's a compelling tale expertly told.' Andy Fyfe, *Q Magazine*

'Most memories of Alex Higgins are the same it seems – traumatic. His nickname was apt: at the snooker table, and especially away from it, he left a trail of devastation in his wake for 25 years. Bill Borrows catalogues the multiple varieties of vileness perpetrated by a man who comes across as a supremely talented creep. It's hugely entertaining, of course... and a dire warning about the evils of the demon drink.' Chris Maume, *Independent*

'Borrows' book presents a balanced account of an amazing life that has spent more time off than on the rails. At times farcical, at others touching, *The Hurricane* follows Higgins

from his early years in the Belfast ghetto to the height of his success and spectacular fall from grace.'
Scott Birch, *Metro North West*

'A stomach-churning, lung-troubling, no-holds-barred quasi-demonography of the people's hero… Compelling stuff even for those of us who regard seven frames of snooker as seven frames too many' Declan McCormack, *Irish Independent*

'The research is exhaustive and Borrows captures perfectly the early days of snooker as a television sport when it was still making its uneasy way out of social clubs.' *Irish Examiner*

'A riveting chronicle of the adventures of one of the most twisted desperadoes in sport'
Jonathan O' Brien, *Sunday Business Post* (Ireland)

THE HURRICANE

The Turbulent Life & Times of Alex Higgins

BILL BORROWS

ATLANTIC BOOKS
LONDON

For VONDOT.
I can never repay you.

First published in Great Britain in 2002 by Atlantic Books, an imprint of Grove Atlantic Ltd .

This revised paperback edition published by Atlantic Books in 2003.

1 3 5 7 9 8 6 4 2

A CIP catalogue record for this book is available from the British Library.

1 84354 011 8

Printed in Great Britain by Bookmarque Ltd, Croydon, Surrey

Atlantic Books
An imprint of Grove Atlantic Ltd
Ormond House
26–27 Boswell Street
London
WC1N 3JZ

NEW HIGGINS SENSATION

The world of snooker was rocked to its foundations last night when the crowded auditorium of the Sheffield Crucible witnessed amazing scenes involving snooker's bad boy, Mr Alex 'Hurricocaine' Higgins.

Halfway through the first frame, spectators and TV viewers gasped as the veteran Northern Ireland ace and former world champion bent down over the table and deliberately hit a ball.

Said one close observer: 'I couldn't believe my eyes. Alex had been behaving quite normally up until then, missing everything and uttering obscenities, when suddenly he blatantly and without provocation bashed this poor red ball right into the pocket.'

Officials last night refused to comment on Higgins' outrageous behaviour. Said a spokesman for BOWTIE (snooker's governing body): 'We will have to see a video replay of the alleged incident before doing nothing. Mr Higgins knows the score. It's 10–0.'

However, last night Higgins was unrepentant. 'I am what I am. People pay to see me smacking the balls about a bit. They would soon get bored if all I did was to go round head-butting officials and issuing death threats to my opponents.'

Ted Lowe is 108.

PRIVATE EYE, 27 APRIL 1990

CONTENTS

PREFACE TO THE PAPERBACK EDITION

'I can give you the names of a few writers who have tried to finish a biography of Alex Higgins,' a source who wished to remain anonymous told me when I decided to write this book. 'I think one of them had a breakdown. I can't see why you'd want to do it. He hasn't even played for about six years. He's finished.' Jackie Rea, the Irish professional snooker champion for two decades, was similarly unconvinced. He had encouraged Higgins to move to England and make a living from his outrageous talent and had subsequently become a father figure to him. 'I don't know why you're bothering,' he said, 'snooker books never sell'. The determination to write this book was forged from such encouraging beginnings. 'It's not a snooker book,' I told Rea. 'It's the story of a life lived at a frenetic intensity by a remarkable man who refused to give in. It just so happened that he played snooker for a living.' Rea shrugged and put a pinch of snuff up his nose.

Alex Higgins was everywhere when I was growing up in South Manchester in the early 1980s. Not just in the newspapers (although he was certainly there), but in my father's betting shop (he was barred at least twice), in the pub where I did most of my underage drinking, in the centre of Manchester when I decided to take an unscheduled day off school and, most of all, in the stories that made their way in a promiscuous fashion around the area. They would start, typically, with Higgins being asked to leave a licensed premises after insulting a barmaid or another customer. By the time the information had changed hands six or seven times the story would amount to, 'Did you hear about Alex Higgins last night? Apparently he attacked somebody with a chair in the Kenilworth and it took seven police to arrest him.'

He was a folk hero, like Ned Kelly or Dick Turpin, but with one crucial difference: you would hear the story and then, shortly afterwards, actually see the man in the street, en route to another unforgiveable misdemeanour. It felt like being involved in a rolling news story. The press coverage was a mere adjunct, a lick of gloss for the rest of the country. Even when he moved into Delveron House a few miles away, his presence did not diminish. In an area well served by national celebrities, including the cast of the most successful television programme in the country (*Coronation Street*) and international footballers from Manchester City and United, he was still the most talked about. The reason for that is not hard to discern. It is because he did not stay behind the walls and gated-driveway of his luxury property. He went out. Frequently.

He may not have always behaved himself impeccably and he may have been accompanied occasionally by minders (one of whom memorably told a female fan, 'We're not here to look after Alex, we're here to protect the public from him') but he did not live the life of a celebrity as the modern age has come to understand it. He often gave interviews in which he unburdened himself of whatever was troubling him without regard to the consequences; he rarely followed the party line; and he refused to apologize for his lifestyle. All he had to promote was his talent and, later, his sense of grievance. When he was one of the most famous men in the country he could still be seen on public transport or in a 'tired and emotional' state in a nightclub. He could also, just as easily, be found in the local making a nuisance of himself at the end of the bar. When he could pay for a driver and minders he was afforded some protection but when the money dried up he survived through handouts and hustling, just as he had done on the streets of Protestant Belfast in the 1950s and 1960s. He would not, or could not, change.

*

'Once, on a train journey to London, my mother-in-law met a young man who politely asked if she minded if he smoked (it was in the restaurant car),' recalled former *Observer* editor Donald Trelford in his book *Snookered*. 'She noticed that he had a huge wad of fivers in his pocket. When she arrived home she startled everyone with the announcement: "I've just met a snooker player on the train with the most beautiful manners. His name was Higgins. Have you heard of him?"'[1] Although one journalist told me that the only people who like Alex Higgins are those who have never met him, there are exceptions. A chance encounter with the 'Hurricane' can be charming or terrifying, depending upon his mood and relative sobriety, but it is always unforgettable. The people who encountered him most regularly were the men he played against on the circuit but, wrapped as they are in the *omertà* of professional sportsmen and stuck in the groove of repeating well-worn anecdotes, I have also attempted to track down the people who bumped into Alex Higgins in other capacities: friends from his childhood, amateur players, journalists, neighbours, snooker fans, innocent bystanders, witnesses, fellow travellers, friends, former friends and those who just liked to watch him play. He was the 'People's Champion' after all.

I was assisted in this endeavour by several people but specifically by referee John Street, who wrote to tell me about a couple of inaccuracies in the hardback edition and also by Dan Rookwood at the *Guardian* website, who posted an appeal for Higgins related stories on 'the Fiver'. He was overwhelmed with information. A couple of the stories have made it into this paperback. The others involve Alex Higgins throwing darts at a karaoke MC, being comprehensively beaten by a female snooker player before 'offering her outside' and snapping a cue over his knee. Another tale describes his tumble down a flight of stairs at Epsom racecourse on Derby Day. Simon Buller was a student at the time, flipping burgers for some extra cash. 'Higgins stood up and, looking at me with one eye, said "Burger please,"' he remembers.

I thought to myself, 'It's Alex Higgins and he's hammered.' The next minute two coppers came running down the stairs so he scarpered round the back of the van... I saw Alex taking a swing at one of them, missing by about four feet, and then, just as the police were about to get heavy, [he] looked at his watch and started crying. He dropped to his knees and pleaded that they let him back in. As they started to cuff him, Alex turned to me and said, 'Would you please put a bet on for me kind sir?'

Alex Higgins has, on many occasions, behaved disgracefully. He appeared before the World Professional Billiards and Snooker Association (WPBSA) for disciplinary reasons almost as often as the rest of his contemporaries put together, usually with good cause and sometimes not. But there is a side to his story beyond the tabloid front pages that has remained largely unreported. He is estimated to have earned £3 million from snooker yet at one stage in the late 1990s was living in a hotel in Stockport paid for by the WPBSA benevolent fund. Where did his money go? Given his outrageous talent, why did he manage to win only six major titles? What happened the night he won the world championship in 1982? Was he more sinned against than sinner? Where is he now?

I have tried to present the facts with nothing more than brutal honesty. Of the thirty or so people I have interviewed for this book, not one has lacked an opinion. What united them all, vitriolic detractors and fervent supporters alike, was admiration of his ability at the table. He was compared variously to Goya and Mozart (for their artistry and prodigious talent), Chuck Berry (who is credited with creating rock 'n' roll) and Edmund Kean. The last is the most pertinent. Kean was a nineteenth-century actor, womanizer and alcoholic noted as much for his ungovernable behaviour as for his portrayal of Shakespearean villains. He came to the fore in 1814 after playing Shylock with ferocious intensity at the Drury Lane Theatre. It was a breakthrough moment. A small man, he was noted for his facial mobility and became the foremost actor of his generation. The *Encyclopedia Americana* describes him as, 'the greatest proponent of passion in his time'. He toured the United States until he failed to turn up for a show in Boston and word of his unorthodox nature began to spread. In 1825 he was cited as a co-respondent in a divorce case and the following year, on tour in America, he was attacked on and off stage. Several of his performances caused riots. From working class origins, his ascent mirrored his decline. The last years of his life were spent drinking and living a life of excess.[2]

Which is not to say that Alex Higgins is about to die. As he told a television audience of millions in 1991: 'There were lots of bits in the paper about how [I] won't reach 40 but here I am at 42.'[3] He is still here at 54. 'I should be ready for the world championship qualifiers in Harrogate,' he declared soon after the hardback publication of this book. He failed to materialize but was quoted as saying, 'I am quite bored. I have been drinking the black stuff all the time and it does get quite boring so I am going to hit a few balls to give myself a bit of pleasure.'[4] It looked like another curtain call. Then, in February 2003, he turned up for the unofficial Irish Open at the Millennium Forum in Derry. Higgins went down 5–1 to 16 year old Darren Dornan in front of 49 people. His top break was 23 (compiled in the third frame, the only one he managed to win) but there were still flashes of the man who had done so much to drag snooker from the billiard hall and into the front rooms of millions of people. Most notably, there were a couple of audacious shots that ran around the cushions before making an appointment with the intended ball, a pointed observation concerning the lack of a scorer and a prolonged remonstration with the referee about his failure to wear the customary white gloves.

It was not a comeback to treasure but it was a comeback. There will probably be more and that, in a sense, is what attracts me. It is Alex Higgins' refusal to go down and stay down, his survival instinct and his determination to keep on fighting even when there is nothing left to fight for. A famous writer once noted: 'Every great man has his disciples and it is always Judas who writes the biography.'[5] I have never been a disciple of Alex Higgins and this is not a hagiography. Snooker was never my sport (although I boast a top break of 13) but, like millions of others, I knew enough to be thrilled by his ability and charisma.

This is the story of the 'Hurricane'. It does not, necessarily, end here . . .

B. B.,
London,
March 2003.

THANKS

THANKS TO: Laura Alves, Peter Babbage, Tim Birch, Dr John Bourne, Suzy Bramley, Matt Brown, Simon Buller, Catford Academicals, David Chidlow, Warren Clarke, Gemma Cunningham, Daniel Davies, Eunice Duckworth, Steven Gill, Cliff Goodwin, Smyth Harper, John Hindmoor, Robin Flavey, Vanessa Fitton, Stephen Ford, Pete Hackleton, David Hardy, Nick Harper, Smith Harper, Dr David Hempton, Michael Hodges, Jonathan Holford, Simon Kanter, Hilary Lowinger, Arthur Magee, Jim McKenzie, Harry Monk, Trevor Morris, Patrick Mulchrone, Paul Noble, Kath O'Malley, Mark Ranaldi, Dan Rookwood (and everyone else at the Fiver), Jim Shelley, Adrian Silk, John Street, Jem Tovey, Adrian West, Ben Wilson, Phil Wilson. For giving me a break: James Brown, Mike Kelly, Chris Lightbown and Tim Southwell. And, of course, everyone who agreed to be interviewed, those who helped in other ways but who I may have forgotten to include and others who asked or insisted upon anonymity but put up with me anyway. You know who you are.

SPECIAL THANKS: Rodney Dickson, Derek Harbinson, Alan Hart, Paul Hawksbee and Andy Jacobs (at Talksport Radio), Pete Kogoy and Catherine and Graham Stephenson.

THOSE WITHOUT WHOM: Clive Everton, Martin Johnston, Nick Lord, Nicko Milligan, Stephen O'Malley, Matt Tench (the editor of *OSM*), Jon Wilde, my agent Emma Parry, publisher Toby Mundy and everybody at Atlantic Books but specifically the put-upon Clara Farmer, Valerie Duff, Bonnie Chiang and Alice Hunt. E. Stephenson is an angel sent from heaven and S. Queen has all my love always.

ONE

What about that Alex Higgins? . . . He's off his tits. All that money and fame and shit and he's blown the lot. What a fucking way to go. I hope that happens to me. One big fucking blowout. Top.

LIAM GALLAGHER, OASIS (1997)

'I don't fucking care what you think,' railed Alex 'Hurricane' Higgins.

'Really? That's good because I don't care that you don't care what I think.'

'Oh really? Why is that then you fucking prick?'

'Because I don't have to.'

'Fuck off.'

'You fuck off.'

'I'm off.'

'Good.'

As first dates go, I've had better. I'm not sure we both have, but I definitely have. Ostensibly, this was a meeting between a two-time world champion and sporting legend and his potential biographer, set up after weeks of negotiations between mutual friends twice removed and the lure of cold hard cash. The above was how it ended, eight hours later.

There had been a phone call the day before at 10 p.m. I was in London. When I answered it there was no voice, only the kind of background noise you get when someone has accidentally pressed the call button. This, I soon came to appreciate, is the trademark Higgins pause. The only time you don't get it is when you are about to be threatened. And so, a pause and then, 'Hello, is that Bill Borrows?' The voice sounded distant, tremulous and hinted at an urgency behind the slurred words but, for all that, was instantly recognizable.

'It's Alex Higgins here.'

These are four words guaranteed to generate a mild bowel movement in anybody who has mistakenly given the former world snooker champion their telephone number. Higgins keeps a battered handwritten notebook with the names and numbers of such people: ex-managers; ex-friends; people soon to become ex-friends; people who will lend him money; family and emergency contacts. Nobody gives him their number twice but they don't have to because, if they can help Alex Higgins, he will have made a note of it. The book is his lifeline. 'Listen Bill, I'm in a bit of a predicament.' This is a favourite phrase, covering everything from athlete's foot to imminent arrest.

'I've left all my stuff in a little pub . . . golf clubs, a shoulder bag, a carrier bag and another fucking carrier bag. There's a lot of valuable stuff in there you know . . . I've got to find a quieter pub. Call me back in four.' He also has a cue with him in a dirty brown, soft leather cue case but neglects to mention it. Four minutes later. 'Hi Bill, thanks for calling me back. I'm in the best Chinese in Britain,' he shouts, for the benefit of the proprietor of the Pearl City restaurant in Manchester's Chinatown. 'The prices are very reasonable and it's where all the fucking Chinese come, anyway, I'm not going to take the piss you know, I'm sincere, I want you to know I'm sincere, the food will cost between 10 and 20 quid, you know, and I'm going to take it away. Can you pay for it for me?'

His tone of voice contained just the right amount of pathos to preclude inaction but was essentially a mechanism by which Higgins could instantly establish the ground rules of any subsequent relationship. If I refused to pay, he would not meet me. I would be guilty of neglecting him. If I gushed, he would meet me but probably underline my name in his little book as someone he could call and berate at 3 a.m. for some perceived slight. It would also fast-track me onto the shortlist for the position of his next general factotum – his preferred option.

If I agreed to pay with conditions attached, his feral cunning would gauge instantly what he could expect to extract from the relationship in the same way that Albert Pierrepoint, Britain's official hangman until 1956, was supposed to be able to calculate the weight of a condemned man just by shaking his hand. But Higgins does not need physical contact to weigh up what he can get out of any given situation. He can detect the relative worth of any nuance in the same time frame it used to take him to work out which ball he was going to play three shots hence. Which is to say, with preternatural speed.

Of the payment options on offer I went for the third and decided to pay for the Chinese meal (and a hotel for the night) if he would meet me the following day. Higgins' mobile phone was passed over to a waiter at the restaurant but negotiations with three members of staff at the Pearl City revealed that none of them could help Mr Higgins or take credit card bookings over the phone. The mobile, one of eight he would be in temporary possession of throughout the next nine months, was then returned to Higgins, who, possessed by the sudden rage of phosphorous pentoxide coming into contact with water, was incandescent at the injustice of it all. Seconds later he was being wrestled from the premises shouting, 'But I like Chinese' and, oddly, 'What is your VAT number? Tell me your fucking VAT number.'

Ten minutes later: 'Hello Bill, it's Alex again and I'm still in a bit of a predicament.' A general enquiry regarding his precise whereabouts was treated with commendable efficiency (the soon-to-become-familiar 'Shut up you idiot, will you just fucking listen and stop interrupting?'). He continued. 'I've just got to put my feet up. I know it sounds like I've had a few but I haven't really lubricated my throat yet and I need a hotel between £45 and £60 . . . I'm not going there, it's a khazi. When can you get here?' I explained that I was 180 miles away, had no car and no means of getting up to him until the morning. 'What am I going to do?' he asked. Inexplicably, he had managed to get under my guard. I felt guilty and so reassured him that I would try and book him a hotel on the phone and let him know where it was.

Suspecting that his loyalty card for most hotel chains had probably been withdrawn, I opted for the kind of understated opening gambit that the man for whom the room was being booked would find not just alien but also demeaning. The phrase, 'Do you know who he is?' did not pass my lips. It can't if I am to find him a bed tonight. As the writer Gordon Burn once noted, '[Alex Higgins] is probably more unwelcome at more hotels in every part of the globe than any other person in Britain.'[1]

A sample conversation taken at random from any of nearly a dozen calls made that night:

'Hello, reservations.'

'Hello . . . I was just wondering if you have any rooms available?'

'Yes sir, is it for tonight?'

'Yes.'

'And how many rooms?'

'Just the one please, a single.'

'That will be £90 . . . can I have the name please?'

'OK, but it's not for me. It's for Alex Higgins.'

'The snooker player?'

'Er . . . yes.'

'Can you hold the line for a minute?'

'No problem.'

'Hello sir, I've just checked with the duty manager and unfortunately Mr Higgins is no longer welcome here.'

'He's barred?'

'Yes sir, I'm afraid he is.'

'Can I ask why?'

'Well, apparently he was very abusive towards the staff and refused to pay his bar bill.'

'I see.'

Burn was right in 1986 and, more than fifteen years later, he still is. Alex Higgins seems to have systematically targeted every major hotel in the city centre over a sustained period of time and managed to get banned from the lot. That takes real dedication. And so, with no 'Standard', 'Superior' or 'Business Plus' rooms available for Mr Higgins in the city, the only other option was somewhere in the suburbs. The problem was how to get him there. I called a friend.

'Hello Stephen, I need you to do me a massive favour.'

'I can't tonight, it's my first proper night out in weeks.'

'I'm sorry about that but this is a very big favour.'

'What is it?' he asks, his voice raised a pitch higher than is comfortable.

'Right, now it's not as bad as it might initially sound . . .'

'What is it?'

'Don't be like that, it's not that big a deal really, it's just . . .'

'What is it?'

'Can you babysit Alex Higgins until I get up to Manchester tomorrow morning?'

'Alex "Hurricane" Higgins?'

'Yes . . . Hello? . . . Steve, are you still there? . . . Hello, Stephen?'

'What do you mean babysit?'

'You know, just look after him, I'll sort you out with the money tomorrow, I'm coming up first thing.'

'What will it entail?'

'Buying him the odd drink, listening to him, getting him into a hotel. Just looking after him really.'

'It's ten o'clock already . . . is he pissed?'

'No, absolutely not, hasn't touched a drop for a few days. He's in a really good mood.'

Silence.

'All right . . . where is he?'

The 1982 Embassy World Snooker Champion has been out of the limelight for a few years. It is a place where, starved of the oxygen of publicity, Higgins struggles to exist. He is, after all, the self-styled 'People's Champion' and without the People's recognition and the concomitant advantages such status delivers, he is reduced to the status he fears most – that of a working class Irishman, discriminated against and unable to bully or cajole his way to a free bet, drink or interest-free loan. Except that, whether he is the world champion or a borderline down-and-out, Alex Higgins will always be Alex Higgins in the same way that, regardless of credit rating, Monica Lewinsky will always be Monica Lewinsky, George Best will always be George Best and Chuck Berry will always be Chuck Berry.

In the years since he ceased to perform at the highest level Higgins has managed to keep himself in the public domain one way or another. Take this tale from the *Sun* in late July 2001. Headlined, HIGGINS TOOK ME ON TWO HOUR RIDE TO HELL, it told the story of how Higgins, having initially climbed into the taxi for a fifteen-minute ride with a friend into Belfast, suddenly changed his mind after his friend had got out of the car and demanded to be taken to a hotel with a golf course.

'[He] was clearly the worse for wear and was slurring his words,' recalled the English taxi driver.

He said he was on medication but he had clearly had a few drinks as well. I couldn't believe it when he produced a golf course guide and tried to find a hotel. It was obvious that he wasn't going to find anywhere because most of the time he was holding it upside down. When I tried to make suggestions he would order me to shut up and said I should only speak when he asked me a question . . . He started saying that he was Alex Higgins and my job was just to drive and do exactly what he said. [He] was one of my all-time snooker heroes and I could not believe that here he was in my cab calling me a fucking English bastard . . . When I spoke to the base to tell them where I was he snatched the radio off me and shouted: 'I am Alex Higgins. Do you realize who I am?'

At 3 a.m., presumably to the enormous relief of the taxi driver, a hotel was located in Bangor, County Down. As is customary in these situations, the driver then told his passenger what he owed him. Higgins refused to pay. After a heated discussion involving the local constabulary, the former world snooker champion agreed to pay £35 and settle up the rest in the morning. Another taxi driver told a similar story when I was in Belfast researching this book. I soon discovered that everybody in Belfast has got an Alex Higgins story. Peter McKnight, for example, recently wrote to the *Observer Sport Monthly* in response to a 'Where are they now?' feature, which had placed Higgins in a hostel in County Down (although Higgins emphatically denies ever being homeless). 'I don't know exactly where he is,' he explained, 'But he was seen in County Antrim last year. As I heard it, he had borrowed a few quid off the bar owner and had arrived back to make good the repayment of the loan with a holdall full of lobsters.'

But the stories about Higgins are not just restricted to Belfast. They are prevalent anywhere he has stayed for more than a couple of days – although on a projected tour of India in the early 1970s he lasted only twenty-four hours before he was put on the first plane back by his hosts, the Billiards Association and Control Club of India, after drinking to excess, taking off his shirt and lifting up the dhoti of one of the Bombay Gymkhana committee members whilst exclaiming, 'I always wanted to know what you kept up there.' Part of the reason for the sheer number of stories and their recurring themes is that Alex Higgins cannot drive. When he could afford a driver he would be picked up and dropped at the venue but for a large part of his life, from when he first turned professional in the late 1960s until the present day, whenever he has been without a driver he has been criss-crossing Britain on the snooker circuit and getting into trouble on almost every conceivable form of public transport.

He called me on a Wednesday afternoon. There was a pause and then . . .

'Hello is that Bill Borrows? It's Alex Higgins and I'm in a bit of a predicament.'

'Really? Where are you?'

'Carlisle.'

'What are you doing there?'

'Never fucking mind that,' he shouts, before suddenly remembering that he has phoned because he wants something. 'I'm coming back from Dumfries.'

'Right.'

'And I can't afford the ticket to Manchester, can you get it for me?'

'How much is it?'

'I dunno, I'll put you on to the fella behind the desk.'

There is a metallic sound as Alex Higgins passes his phone under the security grille. A concerned voice answers the phone.

'Hello?'

'Hello, I think you have Alex Higgins there.'

'Yes, that's right.'

(A muffled noise comes through the intercom. 'Tell him how much it is and also tell him that I want to go first class.')

'Ignore him, just tell me how much the cheapest fare is to Manchester.'

'It's £35.'

'OK, I'll pay for that. I'm going to give you my credit card details here . . . under no circumstances give Mr Higgins a receipt or anything with my credit card number on . . . do you understand?'

'Yes sir.'

('Tell him it's got to be first class.')

'Ignore him.'

Transaction completed, the phone is passed back to Higgins.

'OK Alex, have you got that?'

He hangs up.

At the time I put his perfunctory tone down to ingratitude. What I did not know was that he was in a state of high anxiety brought about by the proximity of a large Scotsman in a Rangers shirt. This man was, or so Higgins thought, stalking him. I know this because John Hindmoor, a law lecturer from Preston, was on the platform and waiting for the same train. 'I saw Higgins looking at his reflection in a glass door and combing his hair into place. Another couple of people also recognized him and he shook hands with one man and exchanged a few words but he kept staring at this big Scotsman and it was obvious he was quite scared.'

Higgins, wearing stonewashed denim jeans, a tweed jacket and a reddish cravat underneath an open shirt, was carrying a shoulder bag, a carrier bag and his cue case. He had a couple of cuts on his head. 'I thought nothing more about it,' remembers Hindmoor, 'until he came crashing into my carriage with all his stuff banging about. He was still looking behind him when he sat down opposite me. He almost fell into my lap.' Obviously concerned, Higgins' discomfort was heightened as the Rangers fan approached. Hindmoor explained that Alex was not feeling well and asked the man to leave. Which he did.

'He'll come back,' said Higgins, the black dog of depression taking hold, 'They always do.' And then, as he moved over into a seat across the aisle to get a better view of the carriage containing his foe, he announced with a petulant flourish, 'I hate Scotsmen,' and put his head in his hands.

Gradually, as he realized his adversary was not going to come back, he began to relax. The conversation was one-way but not particularly taxing. It consisted of reminiscences about Higgins' life when he lived in Lancashire and used to visit clubs such as the Ace of Spades in Whalley ('I didn't mention the fact that he was notorious for getting cabs and then not paying the drivers because it felt like I was walking on eggshells anyway') and a succession of stories which could not be interrupted. He took a bottle of pre-mixed whisky and soda, drank it and then amused himself by rolling the top down the train and making a gun shape with his fingers and pretending to shoot the Scotsman. As the train pulled in to

Oxford Road Station in Manchester, Hindmoor went to help him on with his bags.

'As I handed him his shoulder bag,' he adds by way of a postscript, 'he looked at me and scowled, "You've forgotten how my bag goes over my shoulder. Very poor memory retention" and then as he was getting off he made a fly remark about my lack of hair and sauntered off mumbling to himself, audibly, "very poor memory retention". Not a thank you or anything. I just thought, "what a very strange man" but then he's more a difficult child really.'[2] John Hindmoor will not be the only member of the public to have arrived at that conclusion after a chance meeting with the 'Hurricane' on his shambolic and seemingly perennial world tour.

Alex Higgins is unwell. He has been unwell for as long as most people can remember. His diet is not something recommended on the pages of *Men's Health* magazine, while his legendary consumption of stimulants (legal and illegal) has probably not helped. 'If he carries on at that rate,' a snooker official remarked of the twenty-three-year-old Irishman at a post-tournament party in 1973, 'He won't even make thirty.' Of course, he did not carry on at that rate – he was just warming up and has since passed thirty, forty and fifty. The BBC have had his obituary taped and recorded for months but, as one of his many former managers once remarked, 'He'll live to be seventy that bastard. They've been writing him off since he started playing. On and off the table, he is a total survivor and he knows it.'

In 1998, however, he had genuine cause for concern. Diagnosed with throat cancer, Higgins became seriously ill and when the paparazzi caught up with him at the funeral of his close friend Oliver Reed a year later, the picture was picked up by everybody. It showed an emaciated Higgins looking down through a pair of half-moon glasses perched imperiously on the end of his nose, his face contorted in a combination of terror and explosive rage. Rage at the indignity and injustice of being photographed at a friend's funeral, and terror at encountering the media while looking so visibly unwell. Alex Higgins takes a great pride in his appearance and the cravat he has adopted is to hide the scars of his throat operation.

It is remarkable then, and also admirable, that he chose to appear on the BBC1 documentary *Tobacco Wars* in July 1999. Described by the Corporation as 'a hard-hitting history of the cigarette', it provided the opportunity for those people who had missed the snapshot of a gaunt and distressed Higgins caught in monochrome to see him in colour and hear him attempt to speak in a halting whisper after forty treatments of radiotherapy and an operation to remove a cancerous lymph node in his neck. Wearing a beige waistcoat over something resembling a dress shirt and then a cravat (tied David Essex style) and weighing less than seven stone, he resembled a grotesque caricature of himself.

Looking into the camera he claimed, with utter conviction, that he felt 'nothing but disgust' for the industry that still sponsors all the major snooker tournaments. 'The tobacco companies and snooker were as thick as thieves,' he continued, warming to his theme. 'Obviously I think that they have got their advertising for a song for twenty-five years. Cigarettes are everywhere in snooker. Freebies everywhere. Most snooker players were given free cigarettes.' It is important to acknowledge that at the time he appeared on the programme he had a court case outstanding against snooker's governing body, the World Professional Billiards and Snooker Association (WPBSA), and would instigate proceedings against the tobacco industry within a fortnight.

But, regardless of his motivation for appearing on the programme, he stole the show. The public was shocked. It was impossible to argue with the man, rasping defiantly, 'I intend to fight this case to the end. It's easy to stop smoking. I have a strong will-power. What chance has cancer against me?'

Given that it is in remission at the time of writing, apparently none. 'I thought you had throat cancer?' asked a perturbed Arthur Magee as he sold him a pouch of Golden Virginia from his Belfast cabin several months after the documentary had been screened. 'I've beaten it,' replied Higgins without a flicker of a smile troubling his lips.[3]

He was back in the public eye. The reasons were not of his choosing but at least people were talking about the 'Hurricane' once more. To a man who, except on rare occasions, has lived his life according to the motto, 'there is no such thing as good publicity', that was something to be cherished. Unlike the next splash. The piece started:

In the semi darkness of an all-night snooker hall, a sad and shabby figure shuffles between the green baize tables. Once he held the world in his palm, a two-time world champion, the best, they said, his sport had ever produced . . . But that was then. Time hasn't been kind to Alex 'Hurricane' Higgins and today the man who elevated snooker to an art form is reduced to playing all-comers for £10 a time in a back-street hall.

The piece, DECLINE OF SNOOKER LEGEND, was written by Patrick Mulchrone and published in the *Mirror* in June 2000. Combined with the picture outside Oliver Reed's funeral and his appearance on *Tobacco Wars*, it was enough to convince the public that Higgins, the biggest name in a sport which in 1984 received 335 hours and thirty-three minutes of scheduled network television coverage (compared with 187 hours and nine minutes of football)[4], was, like the game itself, virtually destitute and near to death. But what Mulchrone probably didn't know – and there is no reason why he should – is that Higgins had started out playing all-comers for money in the Jampot on the Donegal Road in the late 1950s and early 1960s and, despite becoming world champion twice, had never stopped hustling. Even in 1982, after his second world title and while less successful players like Dennis Taylor and John Virgo were fulfilling relatively well-paid exhibition engagements, Higgins, in between even more lucrative exhibition matches at £1,000 to £2,000 a time, was still hustling for £10 here and £20 there in snooker clubs all over Britain.[5]

However, the story surrounding the *Mirror* piece is worth exploring in detail because it demonstrates not only Higgins' relationship with the tabloids but also why he has become so circumspect about every person he meets. The day began with someone tipping off the papers for a nominal amount of money when all he wanted to do was play a bit of snooker and hustle and two days later millions of people had arrived at the conclusion that he deserved pity, something that distresses him greatly. This kind of casual betrayal, repeated countless times over the years, has convinced him that only the paranoid survive but his blithe refusal to accept that he can be outsmarted by 'fucking pressmen' and the money he believes his story is worth keep drawing him back towards the flame where he almost always gets burnt.

Acting on a tip-off phoned into the office, Mulchrone made his way down to a snooker club in the back streets around Strangeways Prison in Manchester. 'We watched him playing and drinking some extraordinary concoction at the bar,' he explains.

My first impression was one of extreme shock because he was so gaunt. He had pallid skin, his cheeks were drawn in, he had thinning hair and his throat was covered by a cravat. He was also wearing what might have once been a garish waistcoat. That said, he was still whizzing around the table as best he could. The frame we saw him play he lost. And so, we were working out what to do, whether we should snatch a picture or try to gain his confidence or whatever.[6]

The press are understandably wary of Higgins and his predilection for sudden and violent outbursts but, eventually deciding upon the latter approach, the journalist and his photographer asked Higgins if he wanted to talk to the paper. For money, obviously.

'He said "yeah" and then tried as best he could to take command of the situation. He asked me to pick up his bag and carry it to my car and then told me to take him to a hotel in town.' The old Albert Pierrepoint treatment. Once ensconced Higgins, assuming that his luck was in, gambled and asked for an 'extraordinary figure'. The paper refused and negotiations commenced. Part of this process involved the newspaper taking Higgins in search of a former friend in a pub in one of the less salubrious parts of the city and then to the home of a female friend. He went in, left the journalist outside for twenty minutes and then reappeared. Financial negotiations, at this point, were still ongoing as were the precise topics for discussion. 'He put a piece of feint-lined notepaper into my hand,' remembers Mulchrone. 'And at the top he had written down my name and telephone numbers and then what he considered to be the terms of our discussion. In capital letters he wrote, "WHO ARE YOU? HOW'S YOUR HEALTH? NORTHERN IRELAND".'

Back at the hotel Higgins ordered champagne and Guinness as the *Mirror* attempted to find a figure he would accept. It proved impossible but, sensing that he had a fantastic exclusive, Mulchrone asked him to sleep on it. The next morning, unsurprisingly, he had not changed his mind. Engaged as he was in legal proceedings against the WPBSA and the tobacco industry, he had calculated the very real benefits of talking to the press but, even at this stage and with 'a substantial amount' of money on the table, he could not override his natural instinct for screwing them for some more. The impulse was not greed. Rather, it was driven by his belief that he was 'owed' for all the papers he had sold for them in the past. Higgins has a keen, although considerably inflated, sense of his own market worth.

Consequently, the *Mirror* snatched a picture of him outside the hotel and the piece went ahead without his cooperation. As Mulchrone now admits, '[The picture] spoke a thousand words for me. I didn't really need to do very much once that picture of him appeared. That told the story . . . it was just an observational piece and I didn't use half the stuff he told me because we agreed we weren't going to talk about that. He was upset when it came out but the man pissed on his own strawberries in an extraordinary way.' In the history of Alex Higgins and interpersonal or professional relationships, this is not a new development.

Back in London, I was still frantically trying to find a hotel that would take him for the night. Although problematic enough, the process was further complicated by Higgins' demands for a hotel with a golf course, his food order ('I've not eaten for three fucking days') and then the need to book somewhere before anyone checked with the duty manager. Using a false name would be futile because when he eventually turned up he would be barred and the whole process would have to start again. I had already received a polite refusal from the last city centre hotel and was actively searching for somewhere in the suburbs, preferably South Manchester where he used to live and might feel at home.

By this stage Stephen O'Malley, the friend I had pressed into a reluctant babysitting role, and a work colleague he had brought along as back-up had made their way to the Circus Tavern. This was the 'little pub' in which Higgins had left most of his worldly possessions. The Circus Tavern is a two-room establishment with a bar the size of a butcher's chopping block. With real fires and an absence of pretension, it has the feel of an Irish country pub despite its location in the centre of Manchester. Consequently, it has a large number of expatriate Irishmen amongst its clientele but not, it would appear, Alex 'Hurricane' Higgins who was in a 'bit of a predicament' somewhere else. Ten minutes later, however, he arrived wearing a fedora (which he took off only once), smoking and demanding both a drink and a place to sit down. He likes to make an entrance.

'I'm looking for O'Malley,' he announced and, satisfied that he had found him and that he would now have somewhere to stay for the night, he began to relax. Fortunately, he approved of my friend's surname ('A good Irish name, I am saved . . . the "Hurricane" is saved') and knew his mother, which was hardly surprising as she is an Irish publican. He ordered himself a drink that he could not pay for and then settled down in the back room. There were three of them, the two men who had driven through the night to deliver the former world snooker champion to the warm embrace of a hotel lobby and the man himself, purging himself of stories from the 1980s and stopping only to damn the casual cruelty of the WPBSA or reminisce about his childhood. Depending upon the subject matter he was, by turns, a charming companion, a snarling bar-room bore or a vulnerable child, sobbing as he talked about his love for his dead mother.

You do not have a conversation with Alex Higgins. You listen and do not interrupt. These were ground rules that a drunken middle-aged interloper who invited himself to sit down at the same table had not taken the opportunity to learn. After a warning for adopting a tone that Higgins considered to be too familiar he subsequently made the fundamental error of interjecting mid-anecdote. There was an uncontrolled explosion. 'Get the fuck out of here,' screamed Higgins as he stood up at the table. The focus of his anger complied almost immediately but the incident had served to disturb whatever temporary truce Higgins had negotiated with the voices inside his head. 'It unsettled Alex, you could tell,' explained O'Malley. Five minutes later he took off his hat, pulled a comb out of his pocket, dipped it in a glass of vodka and orange on the table, stood up and then combed his hair in the mirror over the fireplace. It is always the little things that give it away.

Suddenly there was no light to alleviate the darkness and the subsequent hour spent driving around in a minicab while I attempted to locate a sanctuary cannot have helped. Higgins was becoming paranoid and demanding to know where he was being taken. The taxi driver, who had not recognized the man who had been famous enough to appear on *This is Your Life* and every primetime network chat show for twenty years and even have a *Spitting Image* puppet[7] made in his image, thought he was party to a kidnap. The old man who had just berated him for having a spare tyre in the boot of his car was now cursing and threatening one of the other passengers, telling him that if he said another word he would 'put his snooker cue in his ear and rip his fucking brains out'. Regardless, O'Malley risked his wrath by delivering reassuring stage whispers to the driver until I had located a hotel in a nondescript suburb of South Manchester where Higgins was not *persona non grata*. The duty manager of the Forte Post House, despite the fact that the man about to check in had just pushed the doorman out of the way, welcomed him. The new guest demanded an empty pint glass and a pot of tea and, after sending the white ball around four cushions of the pool table in the bar and just missing the pocket, went to bed in room 271.

All that remained now was for me to meet and strike a deal to write the authorized biography of a man who claimed he had lots to tell, a damaged person who should have had it all but failed to press home the advantage when he had the chance, a man who was denied his career and the money he earned by people he trusted and those he despised, the most exciting player in the world, a self-destructive character but also an inspiring one. A man who got up off the canvas whenever somebody (more often than not himself) or circumstances succeeded in leaving him prone upon it. A man with an unquenchable spirit. A product of his time and upbringing in Protestant Belfast. When I called him at the hotel from Manchester Airport at 9 a.m. the next day, he explained he was tired and asked me to come and see him four hours later with a copy of the *Racing Post* and a pint of 'black and tan' (half-Guinness, half-lager).

The Post House Hotel is a piece of concrete, rain-stained brutalism that owes more to the Eastern Bloc in terms of architectural inspiration than any of the warehouse conversions currently being developed in the centre of Manchester. It is the kind of hotel that Higgins, during the last thirty years of peripatetic existence, would have stayed in thousands of times: en-suite bathroom; tea/coffee facilities; television; lounge bar; free parking; no golf course. I asked at the desk for his room number. The girl behind the desk shot me a look and then told me. I bought him a drink and two for myself and went up to his room. 'Hang on a minute,' he called out before I even knocked on his door. Newspaper under my arm and a tray of drinks in my hand, I already felt like room service. 'You can put them over there,' he said when he finally opened the door. 'Have you got my paper?' All the lights and the television were on.

He was wearing a red cravat but nothing on the upper half of his body, a pair of beige slacks held up by a makeshift belt and, of course, a pair of half-moon glasses halfway down the bridge of his nose. He looked like Max, the English prisoner played by John Hurt in *Midnight Express*. Emaciated, weighing less than seven stone, thinning hair combed back over his head, teeth in a state of disrepair and sores on his upper body, the whole ensemble was nonetheless held together with a vestige of dignity. Although he looked terrible, he was still in better shape than I had been led to believe he might be by his recent media appearances. The room was beyond warm, it was airless and cloying. The smell was of stale tobacco and unwashed clothes.

'Can you ask them to turn the heating down?' he asked. I did but to little effect. The place was a mess, with his belongings (three supermarket carrier bags stuffed with old newspapers, a snooker cue in a leather case, one set of golf clubs – his 'woods' – and two small travel bags) scattered everywhere. There was a copy of *Maxim* magazine on the bed. I am the Editor-at-Large at *Maxim* and he had obviously done his homework.

'Oh, you've seen the magazine then,' I enquired as he expectorated into the bathroom sink. 'No, I've not read it yet,' he answered. He was telling the truth. On picking it up and flicking through it there was a two-inch square missing from one corner and saturated crumbs of yellowish powder trapped between the pages in the spine of the magazine. I noticed there was a bottle of Tipp-Ex at the side of the bed. 'It's so hot in here,' he complained, walking back from the toilet, wiping his mouth with the back of his hand and reaching for a slug of 'black and tan'. The window refused to open. And so, irritated that he could not get his own way, he rocked back on his chair, crossed his legs and put them on the desk, lit a roll-up he had prepared earlier, opened the *Racing Post* and pored over it like an actor looking for a favourable notice in the arts pages while Channel 4 Racing blared in the background. I said nothing. Somehow, he had managed to communicate through an unspoken medium that he was not to be interrupted.

I asked him about when he had tried to become a jockey in the late 1960s at Eddie Reavey's stable in Berkshire but he just responded with a guttural noise from the back of his throat. I asked him who he fancied in the 2.10 at Salisbury but he ignored me. I reminded him that he had been barred from my father's betting shop in Cheadle Hulme for stealing the racing papers from the walls. He suddenly took an interest, wanted to know where the shop was and then suggested we go into Didsbury for a drink. Which we did, via a bookies.

'Can you lend me £50, Bill?'

'Do you mean give you £50?'

'No, lend me £50, and if I win I'll give you the money back.' A good deal in anybody's book.

'I'll go with you fifty-fifty on the winnings.'

'OK, deal.'

'Plus my £50 back.'

'OK,' he snarled, thinking that I might be stitching him up but unable to argue because I had the money. As far as I am aware, the horse is still running and I have still not discounted the possibility that he deliberately put it on a no-hoper in a fit of pique.

Four hours later – after revelations about his childhood (a seemingly cathartic exercise) and his problems coping with the death of his mother; his relationship with his father; his scandalous treatment at the hands of the WPBSA yet again; some libellous comments about the leading lights of his profession; a story involving Oliver Reed and his plans for the future – a single mistimed intervention from me provoked the furious outburst that opened this chapter. It also meant that the already ludicrous figure he was demanding for his cooperation on an authorized biography was automatically doubled. And he was not to be moved. It is part of the reason you are now holding an unauthorized biography in your hands. The other part follows the consideration that being unable to ask questions is a known impediment to the interrogative process. Higgins has already been party to two ghosted autobiographies, one of them in the early 1980s and the other full of boastful introspection at the expense of genuine insight. If I wanted to get close to what has made this unique man so fascinating, an urban myth given human substance, I would have to do it on my own, something I realized the moment he stormed out of the Crown public house.

I called the Post House the next day to see if he had made it back to the hotel. He had but they could not put me through as he had been asked to leave after insulting a guest, racially abusing a member of staff and 'going a bit mad in reception'. A call to his mobile found him in a relatively sunny disposition, as though the argument the day before had never taken place.

'Listen babes,' he said, 'the price stays the same on the book but see what you can do . . . I'm going to be big news again, I'm picking up my cue and I'm going to come back on the Seniors tour and take on those bastards like [Steve] Davis and all the rest of them[8] . . . I'm coming back. And can you do me a favour?'

'What?'

'Can you phone Noel?'

'Noel who?'

'Noel Gallagher, you fucking prick.'

'[Sigh] OK, and . . .'

'Can you tell him I need to borrow one million pounds and that I want to do a book about music with him? Will you tell him that? Get back to me about the money for the book you want to do with me when you've spoken to your publisher.'[9]

TWO

I never eat my dinner
I push away the plate
You can see I'm getting thinner
Because I just can't wait
To get my Mars Bar . . .
It helps me – makes me – work rest and play
It helps me – makes me – work rest and play

THE UNDERTONES, 'MARS BARS', B-SIDE OF 'JIMMY JIMMY'(1979)

'We've got a journalist fella here,' announces Victor, a little too loudly. 'He wants to know about Higgy. Says he's writing a book.' This was in response to my understated request for any information about Alex 'Hurricane' Higgins. I smile, nervously. The rest of the pub stares at me. I am in Belfast, post-ceasefire, on my second visit to the city. We are in a pub off the Donegal Road, round the corner from where Higgins was raised. It is a forbidding one-storey brick-built place with no windows, a small bar and a framed Glasgow Rangers shirt just inside the front door. There is a picture of Billy Graham in the gents. The silent TV in the corner shows the results of the 3.30 from Doncaster. At this time of day the bar is full of the old and the unemployed talking, drinking and ripping up betting slips. The barman has a home-made Ulster Volunteer Force tattoo. This is hardly surprising, since I am in the heart of working class Protestant Belfast, less than five minutes from the Shankill Road.

Everybody else is a regular. It is an area intimidating enough for my Catholic taxi driver to refuse to wait outside. He gave me his mobile number and told me to call him when I wanted picking up.

Victor is in his early sixties, half-pissed and happy. 'You should have been here last night,' he explains, knocking back the Guinness I had just bought him. 'Sandy was in here drinking . . . I've known him for years.' The 'Hurricane' is known as Sandy by his family.

'Alex Higgins was drinking in here last night?'

'No, not Alec, his daddy. I call him Sandy. They don't talk any more, had a big argument about something, but I remember wee Alec since he used to come round to the house selling bits of wood so he could get enough money together to play the snooker. A cheeky wee bastard so he was.' Victor takes another mouthful of the black stuff and polishes off a whisky chaser. 'Fuck of a good player though. I had to stop my boy playing him, he kept losing all his money.' And then he lets go a phlegm-corrupted laugh which rattles up his throat and out of his mouth. 'They used to play in a place round here called the Jampot. It's gone now.'

Elizabeth Higgins had a hard life. Her father had been lost at sea and her mother died at the age of thirty-four. When she was twelve she was left to bring up her siblings in the Belfast of the 1930s. The city, only officially recognized as the capital of Northern Ireland in May 1921, was still coming to terms with partition and the nationalist and Protestant communities were well established in different but adjacent parts of the city. Sectarian hatred was rife but served to foster a keen sense of identity on either side of the divide, as did the grinding poverty. Belfast, like Britain's other great Victorian cities, was in the grip of a post-war recession that kept unemployment at 20 per cent in a good year. The three major industries – shipbuilding, textiles and engineering – were in terminal decline. Harland and Wolff, the world-famous shipyard that had built the *Titanic* in 1911, did not launch a single ship in

1932 or 1933 while Ulster's linen was priced out of the market by cotton and rayon. The desperation was serious enough in 1932 to provoke an outbreak of rioting. It started in the Falls Road area, a Catholic ghetto, before eventually spreading to the Protestant part of East Belfast. It was a difficult time in which to grow up but Elizabeth Higgins possessed the kind of determination such circumstances tended to foster. The Belfast-born poet Louis MacNeice wrote in 'Valediction' (January 1934):

> See Belfast, devout and profane and hard,
> Built on reclaimed mud, hammers playing in the shipyard,
> Time punched with holes like a steel sheet, time
> Hardening the faces, veneering with a grey and speckled rime
> The faces under the shawls and caps:
> This was my mother-city, these my paps.[1]

This was the Belfast in which Alexander 'Sandy' Higgins, the father of the future world snooker champion, also came of age. He had been hit by a lorry as a child and had suffered brain damage that meant that he was unable to read or write. Today he would be described as having 'learning difficulties'. But he was physically fit and able to earn a living as a railway labourer. He would later become a janitor at the Royal Belfast Academical Institution, one of the top schools in the city. 'He was there when I arrived in 1976,' explains former editor of *Loaded* magazine, Derek Harbinson. 'Everyone knew he was Alex Higgins' father but no mention was really made of it by the staff. He was a dapper wee man, always immaculately turned out, and when Alex won anything the kids would cheer whenever he came into the classroom. He never made a big deal about it. He just smiled and got on with it but you could tell he was so proud he might burst into flame at any minute.'[2] Elizabeth Higgins, also known as Lilly, was the cement that held the family together. Higgins still talks about her often, even to comparative strangers and, depending upon his mood, will recount a touching anecdote or begin to weep uncontrollably. He misses her terribly and it is clear that, as her only son, he was doted upon. It is tempting to suggest that he has been searching for this kind of unconditional love, with little success, ever since he left home. As his younger sister Jean confirms, 'He was just mummy's only boy and he could never do anything wrong . . . she knew the girls were alright but worried about him. She loved him to bits.'[3] He does not give Alexander Higgins Senior more than a paragraph in either of his ghostwritten autobiographies, but the love for his mother shines from the page. 'Great lady, my mother,' he said in *Alex Through the Looking Glass*. 'That's where I get my survival instinct from. She was afraid of nothing and no-one . . . I'd back her to find her way across the other side of the world without batting an eyelid. She wore the trousers in our house . . . [Dad] did what he could to help me.'

Alexander Gordon Higgins was born on 18 March 1949 and grew up in a predominantly female household, with his mother, father and three sisters, Isobel, Ann and Jean. They lived in a terraced house in Abingdon Street which had been built for local mill-workers at the turn of the century. The house had escaped the blitz but Belfast was still recovering from an onslaught that had destroyed 3,200 homes and damaged a further 53,000. The government-instituted house building programme included the creation of new estates at Andersontown, Finaghy and Cregagh (where the young George Best grew up). Child mortality rates in Belfast were the worst in the country when Alex Higgins was born. Tuberculosis was rampant and nutrition was poor, not least because rationing was still enforced. Yet it was, according to his sisters, a happy and oblivious childhood in a close-knit community. '[The boys were always] kicking the football and were inclined to make go-karts out of wood and with the wheels off prams,'[4] says his elder sister Ann. As babysitter for both Alex and younger sister Jean whenever their parents went out, she would know.

'We had a different relationship [from that enjoyed by Higgins and his other sisters],' explains Jean. 'As I was the youngest he used to take me on the bus to see our aunties and uncles [in the Shankill Road] on a Sunday and get me up to different things, you know, which I shouldn't have been doing . . . Ann and Isobel were going out with boys at the time and we were in the house the most except when Ann was babysitting us.' Both sisters paint a picture of a loving but unremarkable working class life centred around the perpetual struggle to make ends meet. As a young boy Higgins would go to backyards in the neighbourhood and collect potato peelings (known as 'skins') and other edible detritus, which he would then sell to farmers as pigswill. He would also, as Victor confirmed, sell bundles of firewood door-to-door. Occasionally, he would run to the bookies for his father. This will have been his introduction to the seedy glamour that was the defining characteristic of the billiard halls he would come to frequent. It was also when he made his first acquaintance with gambling on the horses.

He was not particularly popular at Kelvin School. He wasn't really there often enough to make friends. Jackie Thompson was in the same year and, like Higgins, left for the North West of England on the ferry to Holyhead in the late 1960s. 'He wasn't what you would call difficult at school,' he remembers. 'He kept himself to himself really and didn't sort of mix with most of the children. His thing was snooker and most of the lads at school were into football really. He took a lot of stick from one or two people because he was a soft touch. Sometimes people would pick on him and have a go because he was different and always wanting to get back to his snooker. It didn't help that he was so small.' James Wilson was younger than Higgins but lived on Donegal Road. He remembers him but says 'he never stood out in a crowd. He was never known as a "hard man" or humorous or wild or agressive . . . I do not recall anyone saying anything bad or good about him . . . When we used to play street football [he] would always be last picked which irritated him greatly.' Higgins, unlike his contemporary George Best a couple of miles away, knew his future did not lie with a ball at his feet – but that was as much as he did know. Most working class Belfast boys did not spend time worrying about the future. It was already mapped out. Higgins, equally, was not predisposed towards introspection. He knew what he liked and what he didn't – he liked snooker and he didn't like school – and with the hedonistic impulse that would be the engine of his adult life he just went with what he liked. There was no master plan.

His passion for snooker, however, was remarkable for the obsessive nature of his dedication. The game was a popular pastime for working class men and Belfast had four billiard halls by the time Higgins was tall enough to visit one. It was, before he revolutionized the game, a sport like boxing which appealed to both ends of the social spectrum while leaving the middle class cold. David Hempton was born in a more prosperous area of East Belfast. He is three years younger than Higgins and watched him play at the Ulster Hall in the late 1960s. He is now a Professor of History at the University of Boston. 'Certainly as I was growing up I was aware that there were snooker halls around the working class districts of Belfast, not too far from the bars usually,' he explains. 'Although all the stately homes would have a billiards or snooker room, it was a kind of working class sport really. I suppose, once the table has been laid down and if you don't have a terrifically expensive cue then it is quite a cheap game to play, you only have to find the money for the light.' The perpetual scramble for the money to pay for the light was the reason Alex Higgins got up in the early hours of the morning to collect potato peelings. Mary Wallace used to walk past the Jampot on her way to Kelvin School. 'I remember Sandy, or as he was known to most people, "Shitty". He cadged from everyone and would walk with you for at least fifty yards saying, "Go on please lend us a penny, please, go on please." I called him "Shitty" one day and he slapped me hard across the face. I don't think there are many who don't remember him during this era if they had to walk past the Jampot to Kelvin [School].'[5]

The Jampot was just off the Donegal Road and down an

alley next to a row of back-to-backs. It was just behind the Higgins family home. The name of the place referred to the practice of keeping the rent money in a jam jar in the kitchen. The women who despaired of ever seeing their husbands at night called it the Glue Pot, as it often proved impossible to extricate them from the premises. It was run by an elderly Baptist called Harry McMillan and provided everything an adolescent could possibly want (apart from women, who were not welcome). The minimum age at the Jampot was supposed to be fifteen and it took a certain fearlessness to push open the heavy, windowless door and slip into the dark when you were twelve. It amounted to a foray into the forbidden. A large place, about 150 feet long by fifty feet wide with a wooden floor that stank of disinfectant, to the underage players inside was the back-street Belfast equivalent of the Stardust Casino. And the Ratpack, according to Cecil Mason, who was four years older than Higgins and already a regular, were: 'King' Johnson, Bobby 'the Lumberjack', Harry Goldfinger, Billy 'the Trucker' Maxwell, 'Big' George Kirkwood, 'Johnny Easter Egg' and 'Temperamental' Jim Taylor.[6] It was an impossibly glamorous world to the urchins who shuffled past it on their way to school.

As the door shut behind Alex Higgins, the click of the balls, the light slicing through the fug of blue smoke, the men glancing his way and then blanking him in one seamless movement, the etiquette and almost Edwardian ambience seemed a world away from his life in either Abingdon Street or Kelvin School. Even the sound of an old docker spitting into his handkerchief could not dispel the illusion. As his eyes adjusted to the gloom, he took in the baleful glances of the older truants who had already braved the same path. He could sense the imminent violence engendered by the side-betting of men who could ill afford to lose. He absorbed it all. And, to his surprise, was not afraid. After a few more visits it became his second home. His presence was not a problem to the management. Harry McMillan would turn a blind eye if the boys could play and did not disturb his regulars.

Besides, they provided a service, scoring (or 'marking' as it was called) for the older players who would pay them anything between a penny and threepence. Higgins eventually fell into a groove and, at some point after lunchtime, would throw his school bag under one of the fourteen tables in the club and make for number eight. It was on the left as you walked in and was the table where all the action took place and the players gambled for a pound per frame, rather than half a crown. There was a strict hierarchy.

Several hours after he had left for school, one of his sisters would be sent to fetch him home for his evening meal. It would often be Ann. 'I would have said to him to be back for such and such a time before mum and dad came back and, of course, he wasn't so then I had to go looking for him. But I always knew where to get him at the end of the day . . . I remember going up to the Jampot and there was an entry to it that was quite dark. I rapped on the door and said "Is our Sandy there?" The reply came back "No." And I used to say "He is there, I know he is there . . . you better tell him to get home, my mummy's going mad."' The same fascination that had drawn Higgins to the club also drew his younger sister to peer in through the front door on one occasion. 'The men inside chased me because I was disturbing their game,' laughs Jean forty years later.[7] However, despite the fact that everyone knew he was playing snooker for five or six hours a day, the sport was generally held in such low esteem that his talent did not register with his family, teachers or contemporaries at school.

Stewart Love, who taught him mathematics whenever he deigned to turn up, remembers him as 'remarkable for his absence'. There were rumours circulating that a member of the student body was an exceptional snooker player. It never occurred to Love that it might be Alexander Gordon Higgins. 'We used to have a small billiard table in the staff room' remembers Love. 'He went so far as to ask us if he could practise on it in the lunch hours. We wouldn't let him so we were never to see Alex Higgins give an exhibition in the

Kelvin School staff room.'[8] He was considered by his peers to be something of a loner. Consequently, as he was frozen out of team games by a combination of his size and disposition, the solitary pursuit of excellence on the snooker table was an obvious choice. And not least because there was a club within spitting distance of his house, he threw himself into it with every ounce of determination he possessed. It was a kestrel for a knave.[9]

Earning a living as a snooker player was not an option at this time. The last world championship had been in the previous decade and the sport was run as a cartel that did not look favourably upon the young players who may have been able to inject it with some life. This attitude was underpinned by the assumption that there was only a finite amount of money on the snooker circuit and it would be best divided up amongst the people who were already on it. It is the kind of myopic thinking that continues to dog the sport today but also explained the puzzled look on the face of Elizabeth Higgins when a gypsy turned up at her house in the late summer of 1960. According to family legend, the gypsy read her tea leaves and told Mrs Higgins that there was going to be a star in the family. The fact that she may have told the last twenty-five housewives the same thing is not relevant here. 'I was out,' remembers Ann, who had already won talent competitions as a singer.

'Mother said "Oh, that is my Ann," and [the gypsy] said, "No, it's a boy."' The gypsy was insistent but his mother couldn't see it. 'We didn't know anything about snooker,' Ann continues. 'So she just couldn't [see it].' Lack of recognition for his talent at home and school did not worry Higgins. His thirst for that kind of acclaim would come after he first tasted it which, despite his youth, would be very soon.

Life in the Jampot was not easy. His presence was tolerated because he used to score for the older players on table eight. When he had got enough money together for a game, he would then take on anybody who fancied his chances. '[I was in there] morning, noon and night,' he wrote in *'Hurricane' Higgins' Snooker Scrapbook*. 'You'd go in there with your pocket money, two and sixpence or 50p or whatever it was, and lose it. I was a kid, but the older players would take my money, no qualms . . . You might be boiling inside, waiting to play, and there you'd be, scribbling the scores on the back of a cigarette packet. Still, it was a good way to learn. I was watching their mistakes. I was taking it all in.'[10] It was the traditional apprenticeship which Dennis Taylor endured in Coalisland at a place called Gervin's or Jimmy White would later serve in Zan's. Higgins started making a name for himself when he was about thirteen or fourteen. That was when he discovered that he was able to beat the best players on table eight. 'He would come into the billiard hall and right away he ordered himself a five course meal: two Mars bars, a Milky Way and two cokes,' remembers Mason.

It is a practised line but an accurate one. Higgins would use the money his mother gave him for his school dinner to buy a food ticket for Friday lunchtime, reasoning that by that point he would be starving. He would use the rest to pay for time at the Jampot and gamble on his own ability. He had found something he was good at and he enjoyed how winning made him feel. He could also make money by hustling. Jackie Shannon, who would go on to become his teammate at the YMCA, had noted his ability to do this and became one of the first people to invest in his talent. 'I remember one occasion, when Alex was skint as per usual' he explained. I lent [him my pocket money] to play on one of the big tables. We agreed to split the winnings. He turned the 25p into £6.'[11] The men he was able to deprive of their beer and snooker money did not take kindly to losing to a young boy just out of short pants. Predictably enough, the man who gave him the most trouble was 'Temperamental' Jim Taylor. 'He was about nine feet tall,' Higgins recalled in 1981. Taylor used to hit him with the cue if he thought the young prodigy was beginning to humiliate him at the table. '"You lucky little bastard," he'd say' remembered Higgins with something less than affection. 'So before the balls stopped rolling I'd be round the table.'[12] Higgins would later claim that his 'Hurricane' style of play was derived from the need to avoid the violent impulses of the men he was beating with such accomplished ease but it probably had more to do with his state of mind and an overactive metabolism.

Soon, the Jampot's regulars would not play him and he had tired of the competition. He wanted to test himself against better players and, if possible, take money from a new, unsuspecting clientele. His father played at the Canine Club but the prospect of playing under some form of supervision, no matter how limited, did not appeal to him. Besides, Irish amateur champion Maurice Gill and several other highly regarded local players used the Shaftesbury Club on Shaftesbury Square. It did not take long before the players there realized that, even with a handicap, he was adept at taking a sizeable proportion of their wages. Gill, who was eventually three-times Northern Ireland champion and twice all-Ireland champion, soon took notice of the fourteen-year-old prodigy who, even then, would draw a crowd of people to the table whenever he was playing. Higgins liked that. The attractive, all-action style of play he had developed during his apprenticeship at the Jampot was pleasing to the eye and the public acclaim gave him a confidence he had never had when being picked last for street football or being bullied at school. It arrived at just the right time, as he was entering his mid-teens. His mother once heard two people talking in the street about his prowess with a cue which provided further confirmation that he had not been wasting his time. He officially left school in 1964 although he had really left the moment he found the Jampot. The only difference was that he did not have to hide his school bag under the table any more.

The 1960s were just beginning to swing in London. The Beatles released 'Hard Day's Night' in 1964 and performed 'I Want To Hold Your Hand' on the *Ed Sullivan Show* in America. In Belfast the Divis Street riots broke out in the Falls (as the Catholic area of the city was commonly known) after the Royal Ulster Constabulary removed a tricolour from outside a republican office following protests from the Reverend Ian Paisley, Moderator of the Free Presbyterian Church and outspoken opponent of both ecumenism and a united Ireland. The Rolling Stones performed at the Ulster Hall in August 1964. The era of youthful rebellion was soon to be played out in a different way in Belfast.

At fifteen, and with no future that appealed to him, Alex Higgins began to look at his options. He saw an advertisement in the *Belfast Telegraph* for a stable lad at Eddie Reavey's stables in Wantage, Berkshire. Higgins answered it and was taken on. Young Irishmen had crossed the Irish Sea in search of work since the potato famine, but that did not make it any easier for his mother to accept. He had worked as a messenger for the Irish Linen Company straight after leaving school but that afforded few prospects and the industry was on borrowed time. She bought him a new coat and put him on the ferry to Liverpool and then, like so many Irish mothers before and since, went home to cry. He had to leave, there were no opportunities for him in Northern Ireland. The moment is pivotal for another reason. He claims to have had his first drink, half a pint of beer, on the ferry.

Eddie Reavey had made the same journey some years before and felt for those he had left behind. As his widow Jocelyn recalled, he resolved to, 'Get them out of that dreadful place before they become gangsters'.[13] It was a way out that combined two things that Higgins loved, horse racing and gambling. The sport was hugely popular in Belfast across the religious divide. As Professor Hempton recalls of his time in the city, 'I used to work in summer jobs in bread factories and dairies in working class Belfast and there was a tremendous gambling culture in those places. You would see these people working hard all week, earning reasonable, decent sums of money and they would just go and blow it on the horses. And they knew everything about horses, they knew when they rode, who their jockeys were, what their form was. They knew very little about anything else but they were absolute experts on gambling. Of course, many of them lost quite a lot of money on it as well.'

Alex Higgins was no different. Having been introduced to gaming and running bets for his father, he had become immersed in it at the Jampot and the Shaftesbury Club where the regulars, when they were not losing it to him, gave their hard-earned to the bookies instead. Higgins decided he wanted to get involved on the inside. He resolved to become a jockey like his hero Lester Piggott. He had the build for it – at that time he weighed seven stone – but the job required more than a skinny runt who could stay on the back of a horse. A stable lad was, and is, the bottom rung of the ladder and several years away from even becoming an apprentice jockey. He also has to be up at dawn to 'muck out'. These were two elements which were not strong motivating factors for a teenage Belfast boy who resented authority, any hierarchy which did not have him at the pinnacle and menial work that he considered to be beneath him. Shovelling shit at 6 a.m. and taking orders from other teenagers amply qualified on all counts. Reavey, however, was fond of Higgins and overlooked the fights with other stable lads and apprentice jockeys and his distinct lack of application. Higgins was fired six times for various infractions and taken back each time. 'The problem,' explained Jocelyn Reavey, 'was that Alex's ambition was to clean out the local bookmaker and not the stables.'[14]

He might not have enjoyed the work but he had to earn a living. There was still no professional snooker circuit to speak of and, even though the wages at the stables were poor (about thirty-five shillings per week) they were still wages. Higgins eventually stayed nearly two years with Eddie Reavey before being forced to find alternative employment. It was not for disciplinary reasons, remarkably, but because the substitution of regular meals for cans of Coke and Mars Bars had pushed his weight up to ten stone, which is far too heavy for a jockey. He caught the train to London, found a flat in Leytonstone and started playing snooker. There had been few opportunities to play when he was working at the stables but now he picked up a cue again. In order to play, and indeed live, he needed money he secured a job in a paper mill near London Bridge. He began playing four or five hours a day in a club on Windmill Street. It was not exactly practice because there were no tournaments for which to practice and he could hardly launch himself on the exhibition circuit. There were regular money matches, including one with a pianist from the London Philharmonic Orchestra who eventually became so sick of losing that he gave Higgins his cue. But that was all. Money matches and the N98 bus to shift work in a paper mill. His mother, who had been sending him packages of clothes, pleaded with Jocelyn Reavey to take him back but the idea was, in horse-racing parlance, a nonstarter. After nearly a year in London, homesickness eventually got the better of Alex Higgins and he made the return journey to Belfast and moved back in with his parents.

The plan was simple. He would lie in bed until the afternoon, get up, play snooker, gamble, win money, have a drink and then go back to bed. The only complication was that the Belfast he was again calling home was now a far more dangerous place. The UVF firebombed Catholic-owned bars, Unionist headquarters were bombed by the IRA, schools were set on fire, protestors were battered by the police, men were shot in the street and each community withdrew into itself. Staying in bed must have seemed an attractive proposition. When he ventured out he visited his old haunts, the Jampot and the Shaftesbury and occasionally the Crown in the Shankill Road and the Oxford in the city centre. Three years previously the billiard halls had been as close to neutral turf as could be found in Belfast but now the two communities did not mix at all. It was not safe. He renewed his acquaintance with the green baize in Protestant-only clubs, not for reasons of choice but because there was no other option. It was a self-enforced door policy and he did not care for it. 'I came from a Protestant street,' he said. 'But I've no prejudices: I'll play on anybody's table.'[15] The political situation precluded that and he embarked upon the equivalent of a small tour, playing and beating the best players he could find at billiards, snooker or gambling-orientated variants of the game such as 'life pool' or 'sticks'. Money was in such short supply that 'sticks' was often the preferred option as it accommodated up to five players with the loser paying for the table.

Life was relatively easy and it was certainly better than working for a living. But it didn't lead anywhere other than a life spent hustling, drinking and giving money to the bookie. As it turned out, that was pretty much what the future had in store, but on an entirely different level. The reason Higgins was able to reach that level was because he decided to join the snooker league at the Young Men's Christian Association in the winter of 1967. The motivation was part ambition, part sloth. The Mountpottinger YMCA was a ten-minute walk from his house and it meant that rather than travel all over Belfast looking for opponents, they would come to him. It also brought him face to face with a new standard of player. Gambling was expressly forbidden but took place anyway and he was not going to lose a vital income stream. He thrived on and off the table. It was at this point when Ronnie Harper of the *Belfast Telegraph* first came into contact with him. 'I'd been hearing about this whizz-kid from some of the other players and when I saw him play I understood why.' Higgins took to the Belfast and District League and relished the fact that there was almost always a full house at the 'Mount' whenever he played. He had scored for several YMCA players such as Billy Caughey and Tom McBride and knew he had the beating of them. They thought he was just scoring to get the money together for a game but he was memorizing their strengths and weaknesses and learning new shots which he would then practise and improve upon when he was on his own. Now there really was something for which to practise. And he did, five or six hours a day, sometimes more.

He eventually made his first bona fide century break and

then, he claims, immediately followed that with another thirty in the same week. The dam had broken and in January 1968, within six months, he felt ready to enter the Northern Ireland Amateur Championships. He was eighteen. His first opponent was Jackie Holland from West Belfast. Higgins won without breaking sweat. He coasted to the final, albeit with a scare, against Jack Rogers, a former Irish snooker champion from Dun Laoghaire who looked to have him beaten twice. He came back both times and eventually made it through to the final against former champion Maurice Gill, the man he had watched play in the Shaftesbury Club before leaving for the job with Eddie Reavey in Berkshire. He prepared for the contest in what would become a typical fashion and returned from an exhibition in Londonderry the previous night at four in the morning. This time he was in the company of Ronnie Harper. 'I told him he'd never be able to play,' remembers Harper. 'Alex said, "Don't worry, it won't affect me." And it didn't. He produced some marvellous snooker the next day . . . He is a freak of nature.'[16] The 'Mount' was packed and hundreds of people actually had to be turned away from the final. Higgins won 4–1. He took the All-Ireland title the same year after beating Gerry Hanway from Dublin. The trophies were important, even if the silverware for the Northern Ireland Amateur title resembled a huge punchbowl, but the most important consideration at this time was financial. As All-Ireland champion he was guaranteed exhibition games at £20 per night throughout the country, on both sides of the border. One of those games was in Coalisland, County Tyrone, the home of another young amateur called Dennis Taylor.

He had already heard tales of the impetuous young man from the Jampot billiard hall and his remarkable ability with a cue and was able to judge for himself when Higgins turned up at Gervin's to play an exhibition match. He had been to Coalisland before with a rumbustious following from Belfast and, having been beaten by Tommy Walls, complained about the pockets and left without paying for the table. He had, however, also noticed the attractive young woman making tea at the club. It was Taylor's sister, Molly. Higgins told her that he would procure an engagement ring if she went out with him for a month but his offer was not embraced with anything like the enthusiasm he had expected. He subsequently informed her mother that if he could not marry Molly, he would not get married at all. The object of his affections was hiding under the stairs when he called. Eventually, she plucked up the courage to tell him she was unable to see him because she had a boyfriend.

According to Taylor in his autobiography *Frame by Frame*, 'Higgins replied: "I can't fight him myself, but I have friends in Belfast who'll make him a cripple."' He subsequently apologized for this outburst but as Taylor noted, 'Alex is very good at apologising . . . he's had plenty of practice.'[17] The Taylor family took him to the airport but Higgins was not finished. He insisted on carrying Taylor's youngest sister Margaret out on to the tarmac on his shoulders. When the rest of the family were not looking he gave her a letter and told her to give it to Molly and not tell anybody else about it. Margaret dutifully announced that Higgins had given her a letter. Mrs Taylor intercepted the communication and the relationship was over. The relief was tangible. Higgins and Taylor are both from Northern Ireland and almost exact contemporaries but are different in almost every other regard. One is a Protestant and the other a Catholic, one a city boy and the other a country boy, one a flamboyant genius and the other a percentage player, one a playboy and the other a family man. Apart from the fact they come from the same country and had both spent some time working in a paper mill, there was little to connect the two. This did not prevent Higgins from following Taylor, who had already settled in Lancashire, back over the Irish Sea.

John Spencer became the 1969 World Professional Snooker Champion after beating Gary Owen during a match that took one week to finish at the Victoria Hall in London. The sport was not yet tailor-made for television. The total prize money was £3,500. Ten years later the first prize alone was worth almost three times that. Fifteen years later the total prize money was £44,000. After years of stagnation the professional game was beginning to revive. The 1969 championship was contested by eight players including four newcomers: Owen, Spencer, Ray Reardon and Bernard Bennett, who had also opened a well-lit, modern 'snooker centre' in Southampton as opposed to a traditional billiard hall. There was even sponsorship coming into the game. Higgins considered his options but the advantages of becoming a snooker professional as opposed to maintaining his current status were not clear. He would have to move back to the mainland but by this point he had already lived away from home for three years and so the prospect was less daunting. There was only one tournament, which lasted a year, and if you won it you could call yourself world champion but it would entail exclusion from all the amateur events. As he pondered the situation, Bangor-based Dessie Anderson took the Northern Ireland amateur title away from him. It made for a lot more space on the sideboard. But not for long.

Following his performances the previous year, Higgins had turned professional briefly before being reinstated as an amateur and appointed captain of the Mountpottinger YMCA team. He led them into the Players No. 6 UK Team Trophy. It was a tough competition that involved several heats before a team from each of the four home nations could get through to the next round. The Irish champions (Billy Caughey, Jackie Shannon and Higgins) nearly went out to a team from Scotland before qualifying for the final against Penygraig Labour Club from South Wales. The match was to be held at the Bolton Institute of Technology and the sponsors had persuaded John Pulman, officially the world champion from 1957 to 1968 and one of the biggest names in the sport, to present the trophy. Lancashire was a hotbed of snooker, the home of the world champion John Spencer and good crowds could be guaranteed, whichever team got to the final. The title would be decided on an aggregate score basis. Higgins had to decide the running order for the players and opted to go second. The captain's thinking was that, if Caughey could hold his opponent (Welsh amateur champion Terry Parsons), he could score heavily against the Welsh number two. It would also give him a chance to shine against weaker opposition. He had already made a name for himself in snooker circles by scoring two century breaks in the previous rounds and people were keen to see what he could do.

There was a ceremony beforehand during which Higgins presented a local beauty queen with a shillelagh on behalf of the Irish team. Everybody was on their best behaviour. The team from 'the Mount' were accompanied by a couple of officials from the YMCA while the Welsh had organized transport for their raucous supporters. Caughey took a heavy beating and when Higgins came to the table his team were 112 points behind. He started by making a break of 56 against John Shepherd. Twelve minutes later the Irish were in front. The third pairing of Mel Jones and Jackie Shannon was a close affair which Jones just edged to leave the YMCA six ahead on the final black. The ball was on for Jones but he missed and Shannon potted it to secure the title. It was a third major amateur trophy for Higgins. He was beginning to like the way it felt. Vince Laverty, a reporter for the local paper, was in the crowd that afternoon. 'He was quite brilliant,' he remembers, 'He had great flare, great vision and quick thinking . . . the [idea] that he was a good player hadn't gone to his head or anything, he was quite humble about his performance.' Laverty was impressed. He filed his copy and then suggested to his close friend John Spencer that they organize a challenge match. It would be the world champion against this young sensation from Belfast that everybody was talking about. He continues, '[I explained that] it could be a commercially successful [venture] for both of us and on those terms John . . . went ahead and allowed his world championship reputation to be put on the line.'[18]

Laverty wrote to Elizabeth Higgins, explaining that

Spencer would like to play her son and would give him a start of 14. She wrote back saying, 'Alex would be proud to come over as John is his hero.' At this time, Dennis Taylor was back in Ireland for a series of exhibition matches, including several against Higgins (then still All-Ireland champion) and remembers being grilled by him. '[He was] talking to me non-stop, even while the others played at the table . . . he wanted to hear more about the life I was leading in Blackburn and the level of snooker there.'[19] The year in Northern Ireland had begun with a civil rights march attacked by Loyalists at Burntollet Bridge, a riot in Newry, the destruction of a substation in Castlereagh and bomb damage to the Silent Valley water supply which resulted in two thirds of the city going without water. Relocation was on the cards. But first, there was the challenge match with John Spencer. Vince Laverty met Higgins off the boat: 'When I met him . . . he looked a bit of a lost soul really but it didn't take long. As soon as I took him to the billiard hall he was soon in his stride and settled in. We're only talking a matter of half an hour to three quarters of an hour. It was as quick as that . . . we went out for a drink at night and music was playing [in the pub]. Alex immediately jumped up, as soon as he had got a drink, and had a look on the juke box to see what music there was. He put something on, we sat down [but] didn't talk about snooker, he seemed more interested in the music that was on and who the artist was and I just happened to say to him, "Do you like music?" He said "I love music, horses and snooker." And I asked him, "In that order?" He said, "Yes, in that order."'

Higgins returned having earned his fee of £30 for a week of exhibition matches by beating the world champion in front of hundreds of people at several different venues, including a return to the Bolton Institute of Technology. He stayed with Jim Worsley, the Chairman of the Bolton and District Snooker League, who was a friend of Spencer's and had been there the night John Pulman presented Higgins with the trophy for the Players No. 6 UK Team Trophy.

Impressed by what he had seen, he helped arrange the series of games against Spencer for a share of the gate money. 'I remember the match at Dean Conservative Club,' says Spencer. 'I think it catered for about 200. When we got there on the night, Jim met us at the door and said, "God, what a crowd, there must be 400 in." Every seat was taken and they were hanging from the rafters.'[20] Spencer was popular in his own right but people were talking about Alex Higgins and his unorthodox and compelling style of snooker. They remembered him from his last visit to Bolton and gave him an excellent reception everywhere he played. He was getting used to it. He also liked having his picture in the *Belfast Telegraph* and, later that month, in *Snooker Scene*. He had been thinking about turning professional and leaving Belfast for a couple of months. His exhibition games with Spencer and his apparent popularity convinced him that he should take steps to make that happen. The portents were good: snooker was back on television (in the form of *Pot Black*), and the world championship had been reinvigorated by the influx of new talent. Another consideration was that a young man with a snooker cue in a case could be mistaken on the streets of Belfast for an assassin with .22 rifle.

In the late 1960s and early 1970s he decided that Lancashire was, after more consultation with Dennis Taylor, the obvious place to start. Some of the best players in the country lived there and, as (literally) the first port of call for most Irishmen seeking work on the mainland, there was already a huge expat population. He briefly moved in with Jim Worsley but then moved to Blackburn. Clive Everton noted in *The Story of Billiards and Snooker*: 'He was back in Lancashire. Carrying one small suitcase and his cue, he threw out, like a gunfighter in the Old West, his challenge: "I'm a snooker player. I play for money. Who'll play me?"' Higgins denies this and claims that he spent most of his time playing for money with Taylor and Jim Meadowcroft, another local amateur who would subsequently become a professional and then a television commentator. Regardless of its authenticity, it all became part of the mythology that was building up around him. However, he still had no money and moved into a dilapidated flat on Ebony Street in Blackburn. Little more than a squat, it was ready to be demolished. His future manager Jack Leeming takes up the story: 'One week he lived at number 9, number 11, number 13, number 15 and number 17 Ebony Street . . . they were pulling them down and every night, when he went back, one [more] had been pulled down since the morning. He lived in five houses in a week.'[21] Leeming was a bingo tycoon and had met Higgins in the Post Office Club in Blackburn. He played there with Dennis Broderick, a salesman who used to work for a firm of bar fitters and John McLaughlin, another bingo tycoon. They instantly recognized Higgins' talent and, being closely associated with working class culture in a professional capacity, also knew that snooker was in the ascendant. They agreed to act as his agents.

'Between them,' Higgins recalls, 'they found me a more salubrious flat, bought me some new clothes and said: "Right sunshine, here's your chance."'[22] He was a 'probationary' professional again[23] but this time he was on £35 per week wages and £25 per appearance. He was late for his first engagement. Leeming again: 'He was playing against Graham Miles and I went to pick him up at 11 a.m. and he was asleep. I dragged him out of bed. He was getting ready in the car and it took us an hour to get to the venue in Walsall and he made a 100 break in three minutes fifty-five seconds.' He was, by common consent, the fastest player anybody had ever seen. John McLaughlin, who was effectively now his manager, thought he needed a nickname, something a bit showbiz. Higgins fancied 'Alexander the Great'. He was certainly enjoying his near celebrity status and was delighted to learn that his fame had travelled ten miles down the A679 to Accrington, his new base. 'He just blended into snooker in this part of the world,' says Laverty. 'He blended in magnificently.'[24] Eunice Duckworth certainly remembers him as being 'something of a character around the town' but the connotations are not necessarily positive. 'My dad [Ted Kerr] was an A-class referee [in Accrington],' she explains. 'He had a leg amputated when he was twenty-one because he had polio and so he had to officiate on crutches. On one occasion when he was refereeing a match, Alex said, "If you want to referee this match, you are going to have to move around the table much quicker than that." He did apologize to him afterwards but that has always stuck in my mind.'[25]

Roy Duckworth, her husband, encountered him at the Top Working Men's Club on Whalley Road in Clayton-le-Moors (near Accrington): 'The lady who was selling the raffle tickets that night wasn't doing so well so Alex Higgins, thinking he was clever, said, "I'll sell them for you." So he went around expecting everybody to buy them off him and when I said, "I don't want any," he said, "Why not? Do you know who I am?" I just said, "I couldn't care less who you are."' This would become a refrain. The rejoinder would also become familiar in the North of England, at least. Nobody beyond the snooker fraternity knew or cared who the hell he was. That would change but he had yet to see a material return on the investment of his time and effort. His management got him a new place and some more clothes and set about promoting him. The fact that one of these engagements took place at a pensioners' club says more about the status of snooker at that time than it does about the abilities of McLaughlin and Leeming to promote the fastest-rising star in the game. Dennis Taylor was his opponent. The table was not tournament standard. 'There was no way we could say anything,' recalled Taylor in *Natural Break*, a spin-off book designed to cash in on his 1985 world championship success. 'After a quiet opening few shots, Alex . . . thumped this particular [ball] very hard. The white flew off the table and landed at the feet of one of the elderly spectators in the front row. As I turned to look at him,' continued Taylor, 'I just caught a brief little smile on his face and sensed that he had made up his mind to have a little fun with the audience. The next thing I knew he was . . . getting the white to fly off the table on to the laps of the men sitting at the front.'[26] No pension-ers were injured.

Dennis Taylor was still an amateur at this time. He worked for the television rental firm Relayvision during the day and played snooker at night. (He even helped Higgins find a flat and a rental television at a preferential rate.) Taylor was mar-ried. Higgins was single but engaged – in the business of becoming a remorseless professional. Ronnie Harper wrote in the *Belfast Telegraph*: 'Gone is Alex's cheeky little boy atti-tude. He's now a player dedicated to his job, a job that could see him take his place among the great names of British snooker.' Taylor thought he was helping Higgins out, Higgins thought Taylor was working for him. It was nothing personal. Higgins thought everybody worked for him.

'We gave him a fabulous Christmas present,' says Leeming. 'He got a flight ticket home and money to spend on his fam-ily. This was two days before Christmas. He had played in Accrington that night. I went to bed. At about three o'clock in the morning, the phone rings. It's Alex. "Hello," he said, "I am at the Ace of Spades in Whalley." I said, "What are you doing there?" He said, "I'm skint. I've lost it all at roulette . . . Can you pick me up? I've got to get home." He still had his flight ticket but no money. He'd cleared the lot.'

His progress on the table, however, had not gone unno-ticed and his eldest sister Isobel offered to front the £100 entrance fee for the 1971 World Championship. He declined. He didn't think he was ready. He soon would be. His other sisters, Ann and Jean, knew he was good but had no idea that he could play snooker like Eric Clapton could squeeze notes out of a guitar. 'To be honest,' says Ann, 'we didn't know what snooker was about or what it entailed . . . it was something that we just didn't know about so therefore we didn't relate to it. We didn't see how this game could be important to anybody so it really didn't mean a lot to us.'[27] The qualifiers for the 1972 event began in autumn 1970. He scraped the money together himself.

THREE

Champions are made from something they have deep inside them: a desire, a dream, a vision. They have to have last-minute stamina, they have to be a little faster, they have to have the skill and the will. But the will must be stronger than the skill.

MUHAMMAD ALI (1975)

The film of Alex Higgins' life would capture February 1972 like this: underneath the double blanket in the attic room at The Pebbles Hotel, the twenty-two-year-old still had his socks on, a pair of nylon Y-fronts and a stained T-shirt. He looked like a car crash but he felt great. The pomade from his hair was all over the pillow. It was cold and dark and the horizontal plastic switch on the cheap bedside light clicked and clicked again but failed to work. He swore. It was the seventh week of the first miners' strike since 1926, there was a state of emergency and a three-day week. There was no heating in the room, nor was there a carpet. He cursed the miners for not taking a £6 per week pay rise, lit up a Woodbine, scratched his testicles and thought about draining the last mouthful of Guinness from the half-pint pot he had failed to finish the night before. He then remembered that he'd dropped a fag end in it and pulled a face. He had just lost to John Spencer in the final of his first professional tournament, he'd got in at six in the morning, the drizzle outside was leaking through the window frame and Alex Higgins had never felt better.

His only suit lay discarded on the floor, exactly where it had fallen as he struggled out of it during the previous night's blackout. 'Five hundred and fifty fucking quid,' he said to himself through a contorted smile as he tried to squeeze an angry looking spot in the flickering half-light of the candlelit communal bathroom down the hall. Not bad for a couple of days' work, especially when you include £102 for the highest break of the tournament. And he had only just lost to John Spencer, the world champion, by the odd game in seven. His skin-care regime completed, the teeth on his palate (loose and temporarily held in with a rubber band) cleaned, he ran some cold water through his hair and put off having a shave until later. He had definitely made the right decision to become a professional. And now, on the morning of the World Championship final, he was going to be able to prove it to the rest of the world. Suddenly, he remembered Bernard. Where was he?

Bernard was a twenty-stone waiter from Oswaldtwistle, the village in East Lancashire where Higgins was living in a flat above a newsagents arranged by his new managers, Dennis Broderick and Jack Leeming. He was a friend of the 'Hurricane' and had been asked to keep an eye on him. His primary duties were to wake him up and stop their new £35 per week investment from getting into trouble. On this grey Birmingham morning however, Bernard was nowhere to be seen. Walking back into the room as the power cut ended and the lights came back on, he noticed that Bernard's bed was empty. And then he heard him, making his heavy-footed progress up the stairs. 'Morning Higgy,' Bernard called out. He had a copy of the *Daily Mirror* and a *Sporting Life* under his arm.

'I've just been out to get the papers.'

'I can see that.'

'They reckon we've got another few weeks of these power cuts.'

'Give me the *Sporting Life*.'

'There's nothing about the Park Drive [tournament] in

there that I can see,' offered Bernard as he passed the paper over. 'They've not mentioned you.'

'They will do when I become world champion,' said Higgins, flicking through the paper, without looking up.

The film would be shot in black and white, of course.

The 1972 World Professional Snooker Championship final began the day after Spencer had overcome Higgins in the final of the Park Drive £2,000 event in Radcliffe. Unlike the compact format of the one-venue event today, the world title then took place over the period of a year, from March 1971 to February 1972, with the qualifying and subsequent rounds up to the final played all over the country at random intervals. The organization of the game at this time was chaotic, even by the hopelessly amateur standards of the WPBSA. Due to a lack of public interest, from 1958 to 1963 there were no World Championships at all so John Pulman, the 1957 champion, retained the title. In 1964, and for the next four years, a format that revolved around him taking on 'all-comers' (in essence, Fred Davis and Rex Williams with token appearances from non-Brits Eddie Charlton of Australia and Freddie van Rensburg of South Africa) was devised. In 1969, with new sponsorship from Players No. 6 cigarettes and interest from the BBC in staging a thirty-minute, fifteen-week television snooker competition provisionally called *Pot Black*, a more conventional knockout format was introduced for the world championship.

The following year, still sponsored by Players No. 6, the most glittering prize in snooker was contested in April but was then, inexplicably, fought over again in Australia seven months later. This time favouring the 'double elimination' system frequently used in pool to decide the four semi-finalists, the WPBSA also gave its blessing to the decision to use venues around Australia with such tight scheduling that competitors were sometimes compelled to play within hours of arriving at the airport.[1] In 1971, and with no sponsorship in place, the WPBSA presumably just forgot to arrange one (hence Spencer, the winner of the November 1970 title, retaining nominal world champion status). How Laurence Johnston Peter, the co-author of the 1969 bestseller *The Peter Principle: Why Things Always Go Wrong* must have wished that he had taken an interest in snooker. The 'Peter Principle', which revolutionized management theory upon its publication, remains: 'The theory that employees within an organization will advance to their highest level of competence and then be promoted to and remain at a level at which they are incompetent.'[2]

In the case of the world game, the men who constituted the governing body were players who had, largely by virtue of their expertise at the table and the fact that neither snooker nor billiards were regarded as a commercial proposition, been promoted to a position of authority and then sought to stay there. The governing body was a self-serving oligarchy with a small pool of members (just eight when the WPBSA's precursor, the Professional Billiards Players' Association was formed in 1968) and no full-time chief executive to negotiate contracts and promote the game. In 1972, this incompetence manifested itself in the length of the championship; the fact that dates of the rounds before the final were decided on a basis mutually convenient to the protagonists after consultation with their diaries and the financial considerations of the promoter; and that the first day of the world final was scheduled less than twenty-four hours after the conclusion of another event over a hundred miles away. Yet again there was no sponsor. The choice of venue was also less than ideal.

The Selly Park British Legion in Birmingham was a large, one-storey, brick-built social club with hastily improvised tiered seating fashioned from empty beer crates. It has since been demolished. Higgins booked into a guesthouse known as The Pebbles Hotel (which he insisted on referring to as 'The Peebles'). *Belfast Telegraph* reporter Ronnie Harper remembers the room as looking like 'something out of *Rising Damp*'. Harper had been sent to Birmingham in the middle of a national state of emergency brought on by a miners' strike and less than a month after 'Bloody Sunday' to cover an event which merited a day-to-day diary, a picture byline and all necessary expenses. 'It was big news in Belfast all right,' remembers Harper. 'Alex had already got a bit of a name for himself and it was the world final. We thought he could win and people needed cheering up.' Another young journalist, Gordon Burn, was dispatched to write his first piece for the *Sunday Times*. As Clive Everton, the editor of *Snooker Scene*, noted in his definitive history of the game: 'Even Fleet Street sports editors conceded there was a degree of interest in the contest'.[3] There was no television coverage of the matches but, as a direct result of what happened at the Selly Park British Legion, there would be the following year.

And so, Higgins was in a guesthouse with his friend Bernard whilst John Spencer, world champion and established professional, was at the infinitely preferable Strathallan Hotel with his wife. Although The Strathallan actually had carpets, Higgins had not struggled to scrape together the £100 entrance fee and wade through the qualifying rounds in Blackpool to let a power strike, the biting cold and sharing a bedroom with a fat waiter from Oswaldtwistle deflect him from his sense of purpose. Over the last seven months he had backed himself to win the world title at 10/1, 4/1, 2/1 and, more recently, as his progress had been noted, 6/4. The qualifiers were necessary to help reduce eight entrants to two before they joined the eight other players in the competition proper. Other qualifiers included four former amateur champions, Ron Gross, Maurice Parkin, Pat Houlihan and Geoffrey Thompson. Higgins, despite having to be at the table at 10 a.m. when he might have only got to bed a few hours previously, dropped only eight frames in two games (Gross succumbed 16–5 and Parkin 11–3). He was on his way.

Because of the cumbersome organization, Higgins was not scheduled to play in the first round proper until November 1971. His opponent was to be Jackie Rea, the Irish professional champion for the previous two decades and the man who, according to *Belfast Telegraph* reporter Ronnie Harper, had been responsible for Higgins deciding to turn professional. 'I had heard about Higgins from the time when he used to play for the Belfast City YMCA,' explains Harper thirty years later. 'And then I saw him and told Jackie Rea, who was living in the North of England at the time, to get over here and check him out. Jackie was knocked out by what he saw and advised him to pack his bags, leave Northern Ireland and turn professional.' The debt was acknowledged when Higgins admitted, '[Jackie Rea] was a bit of a father figure to me because right from my earliest days, Jack was the only Irishman I knew on the pro-circuit'.[4] Higgins went on to repay the debt by contemptuously pushing past his mentor 19–11 in the first round of the competition proper and then, less than two months later, depriving him of the Irish Professional title that he had held since 1952.

Jackie Rea managed to stick with Higgins for three sessions out of four in the first round of the world championship by using his experience and safety play to frustrate him. Higgins, still flirting with the soubriquet 'Alexander The Great' (he would embrace 'The Hurricane', the *nom de guerre* allocated to him by his first manager John McLaughlin, just before the final with Spencer) relied on his natural potting ability. The older man's guile and cute safety game were not enough. Rea was left behind in the fourth. The new generation were at the gates and demanding to be let in. When, soon after, he also lost his treasured Irish Professional title, Rea told *Snooker Scene*, 'He's a fabulous player when he's going well. When he plays close around the black his cue action is marvellous but with the long ones he throws everything into it. He moves his head, his elbow juts out, he does everything wrong. And yet he knocks them in like nobody's business.' His resignation and genuine astonishment were clear. Next up was John Pulman in the quarter-finals.

Pulman seemed to have been around for ever. By retaining his world title during the wilderness years from 1957 to 1968, he was, along with Fred and Joe Davis, the nearest thing snooker had to an aristocracy. He had been involved in the first round/semi-final of the 1949 World Professional Snooker Championship against Albert Brown at the Leicester Square Hall in London on the same day that Alexander (Sandy) and Elizabeth Higgins, in Belfast, had a baby boy they would christen Alexander Gordon. On that occasion Pulman went on to reach and lose the final. Now, almost twenty-three years later, his task was to be more arduous. Higgins was excited to take him on. 'The quarter-final draw brought me up against one of the game's legends,' smiled the 'Hurricane' years later, 'I remembered the days in the Royal Arcade in Belfast when I used to go into the pub under age to watch Pulman on television. He was my first TV idol.'

Higgins had finally summoned up the courage to introduce himself to Pulman at the quarter-finals of the first 1970 World Championship at the Grimsby Transport Club. The latter was on his way to beating David Taylor 31–20 in the quarter-finals. Until that time, Higgins held his opponent in the kind of awe reserved for television celebrities and had always called him 'Mr Pulman' on the circuit. At the bar of the Grimsby Transport Club between sessions, Pulman said, 'Call me John,' and, although Higgins was later to cross him on several occasions and subsequently came to resent him, he never forgot that small courtesy. That said, he paid scant attention to reputation. 'Here was a living legend standing at the same table as me,' Higgins recalled. 'It was a thrilling feeling but I wasn't overawed because I had this supreme belief in myself. I'd already worked out my battle plan. These were percentage players and I figured the best way to beat them was to go for the jugular . . . attack with brute force and scare them to death.' He destroyed Pulman 31–23.

It was his most satisfying victory to date and, despite the fact that his parents did not own a phone, he still managed to get news of his great 'scalp' back to East Belfast. He then awoke in the lobby of a hotel in Morecambe at 5.30 a.m. The

Lancashire seaside town had been the venue for the quarter-final and, as he came round from a night of straight vodkas, his tie long since discarded and his shirt open, he found the elegantly dressed Pulman, diamond and onyx cufflinks on his shirt and buttons on his waistcoat still fastened, sitting looking at him, drinking whisky and water. Higgins might not have recognized the look at the time but, again, it was a mixture of contempt and disquiet. Just who was this young Irishman and how could he play like that? Those who did not already know were about to find out.

The semi-final was scheduled to be played in Bolton but, because the players had to find a mutually convenient time, it was rescheduled three times. Higgins was to meet Rex Williams, the world professional billiards champion. He was an ambitious man who had been responsible for reviving the world championship in 1964 (primarily in order to challenge John Pulman for the title) and also for re-forming the professional association. Williams, the chairman of the governing body and a busy man with financial interests away from the table, could not easily accommodate the young pretender to the crown. Higgins suspected gamesmanship and was irritated by having to cancel lucrative engagements and exhibitions to suit Rex Williams' diary. There would be run-ins throughout his career with the chairman of the WPBSA but, on a personal level, this was the beginning of a deep and mutual antipathy. Higgins was also on a cut of the gate money at the well-attended Bolton Co-Operative Hall, the venue for the eventual game, but would say later: 'All I made out of the semi-final of the world championship was £68 for the week [i.e. the length of the contest] . . . I've never been quite sure who was to blame. I swore it would never happen again.'

He was determined to punish Williams for the delay in arranging a date. There was also disdain for a man who, despite beating Ray Reardon in the quarter-final, was clearly a billiards player first and a snooker player second. Once again, the twenty-two-year-old, uncomfortable in his dress suit and eager to get the job done, had to overcome a dapper old professional who wanted nothing more than to halt him in his tracks. Higgins resolved to blow him off the table with his explosive potting game. It did not work. Williams, with the patience necessary for billiards, almost won. In the first two days Higgins lost nine frames in succession and it was not until the fifth session, after he stopped playing to the gallery and concentrated on winning, that he drew level. In the final session he went ahead 30–28. But Williams came back at 30–30 and then forged a 20-point lead in the decider before missing a relatively simple blue. That was it. Both players knew Higgins was going to win. Williams would later confess ruefully: 'That blue could have changed the direction of both our careers.' And he was right. Higgins was going onwards and upwards and looking forward to the world championship final against John Spencer.

There was a momentum building. Having beaten Williams by taking the last of sixty-one frames, Higgins went on to take Jackie Rea's Irish title and easily overcome Ray Reardon in a match at Sheffield City Hall. John Spencer, likewise, was feeling good about himself. Four years previously, he had become the first new snooker professional since 1951 (soon to be followed by Reardon and Gary Owen). Since then, the thirty-seven-year-old Lancastrian had won two world titles, reached the semi-final of another and started to win other tournaments in between. He was also earning £14 a night on the exhibition circuit, a dramatic increase on the money he had made as a wages clerk at a cash and carry. He was the reigning world champion, had dispatched two more of the old guard (Fred Davis and Eddie Charlton) on his way to his second consecutive final and had just beaten Alex in the Park Drive £2,000. Spencer knew he had the beating of Higgins. 'His style of play wasn't what I would call professional,' he says now. 'It was very exciting and he had probably the quickest snooker brain in the game but, as a player, I did not fear him.' He had, after all, won seven of their eleven previous meetings.

*

After putting away a breakfast of tinned spaghetti before Bernard could get his hands on it, Alex 'Hurricane' Higgins made the most of the electricity to have a shave by artificial light and then went across the road to the venue. It smelled of old men, cigarette smoke and spilt beer. It reminded him of the Jampot and he felt immediately at home. There were a few punters in there who had already paid their 50p entrance fee, people rendered idle by the three-day week, but Higgins had come to practise and he put in nearly three hours while there was still light over the table. It felt right and he lost count of the number of cigarettes that burned down in the ashtray while he sped around the table potting balls, a blur on a time-lapse photograph. He would brook no interruptions but for Bernard coming back from the bookies with the results, and two well-wishers were told to leave him 'a-fucking-lone'. As John Spencer, his wife and a friend got ready for the first afternoon session of the 1972 World Professional Snooker Championship, the Selly Park British Legion began to fill up. And then, once it was full, the rush started.

It was not standing room only. There was no room left to stand. 'It was incredible,' remembers Spencer. 'It wasn't much to look at but the atmosphere was unbelievable. They were packed in there . . . they were sat on beer crates, radiators, anything that was available. There must have been over 500 in there.' Clive Everton was filing his first snooker copy for a series of national newspapers and got as close to the action as he could. There was very little natural daylight and he had only the light from above the table, blurred through a fug of cigarette smoke, to help him write his dispatches. Higgins received a remarkable ovation, as did the reigning world champion but, as Everton recalls, 'They were really there to see Higgins.' They were his people and the sound of glasses being put down and picked up again and a general level of noise that would never be permitted at the Crucible was a constant. Sweat and condensation ran down the walls. Spectators, despite having access to five-minute intermission toilet breaks, wandered around the table as Spencer and Higgins were taking their shots. It was chaos. And it suited the challenger more than the champion.

There was a contrast in styles, but only in as much as every other professional had a style different to Higgins'. He had little regard for playing safe in any aspect of his life but, at this stage, particularly in regard to his snooker. He could slow it down and put his opponents in difficulty but Spencer's problem was how to play his cultivated safety game. Almost wherever he left the cue ball, Higgins would inevitably try a pot. It unsettled him. Spencer was an elegant player who could also play quickly, but Higgins was something else. 'People thought he was rash,' says Spencer. 'But I played him so many times and I didn't often see him take on the wrong shot. He was so quick at teeing. People would think he had rushed this shot or that shot but he was what I would call a snooker brain. If you have got a snooker brain you are probably three shots ahead and that's how Alex was. He was a complete natural.' Higgins agreed. He had already backed himself with more than £1,000.

The opening frames were like the first rounds of a big fight, with each opponent jabbing and using light combinations rather than trying to land a big right or left. By the third frame they had settled into their respective grooves with Higgins potting as fast as he could and Spencer not far behind. 'It was brilliant snooker,' says Everton. 'Brilliant. And the crowd loved it.' At the end of the first day, after one afternoon and one evening session (ticket price for the latter, 75p), they were level. Spencer went back to his hotel and Higgins went back for the supper his landlady had left in the kitchen for him at The Pebbles. The next day was much the same but for the fact that Spencer won the first three frames and it took all day for Higgins to get back to within two games of him. It finished 13–11 in favour of the champion. The news was buried on page 23 of the *Guardian* in the 'Sport in brief' column, just above the news that Australia had pulled out of the show-jumping events in the Munich Olympics.

Unmoved, Higgins was still practising until the last moment and by the end of the Wednesday evening session – the halfway stage – they were tied at 18–18. Gordon Burn noted:

The snooker establishment appears increasingly apprehensive. There are rumbles. 'He hits the bottle some, you know.' 'I tell you what'll be his downfall – girls. They can twist him round their little fingers' . . . 'Sitting playing cards, gambling for money right in front of people. What way is that for a professional to behave? No class. And he'll always be the same.'[5]

The apprehension of the 'establishment' would not have eased at the end of Thursday afternoon, which saw both players locked at 21–21. After the evening session, that afternoon must, even now, feel like it belonged to a different era. Like the last high tea on the veranda as the sun finally set on the British Empire.

Spencer, normally unflappable, had not been happy since the Wednesday evening session. He had been stuck in a lift with his wife for half an hour during a power cut and involved in a minor car crash on the way to the venue then lost his cool completely in the final frame of the day when referee Jim Thorpe, who was not officiating in an ideal championship environment, called a pink ball foul and awarded six points to Higgins. This was despite the fact that Spencer had been playing for, and had seemed to hit, a red. Ronnie Harper, in his world championship diary for the *Belfast Telegraph*, wrote:

Spencer was amazed and threw both hands up in the air. The crowd immediately sided with the champion but, despite Spencer's protests, the referee's decision stood. Even after the session was over, a furious world champion spent almost 40 minutes arguing with the referee . . . I wasn't surprised in the least by Spencer's reaction. His temper had been on the boil throughout the evening session.[6]

In such a fraught state, the indiscipline of the crowd, the inadequate emergency generator powering the light above the table and the refusal of his opponent to lie down must have played on Spencer's mind. 'Not really,' he says now, without conviction. He was concerned enough at the time to demand that 'linesmen' be appointed to assist the referee. Higgins, the beginnings of a smile held in check, raised no objections.

He had played Spencer in the final of the Park Drive £2,000 and would soon play him in a best of seventy–five frame challenge match in Radcliffe. He was getting to know the way Spencer played. Every weakness he revealed went down in Higgins' memory. He would soon be approached by commentator and snooker grandee 'Whispering' Ted Lowe to appear on a new television programme dedicated to snooker called *Pot Black*. He met Lowe in a hotel in Manchester to discuss it. It was over an hour each way but it was too big an opportunity to turn down. *Pot Black* offered Higgins television exposure, an exponential increase in public awareness of him and the chance to increase his fee for exhibition appearances. An afternoon in the hotel bar cost him his six-frame lead when he got back to Radcliffe and helped Spencer to race six frames in front. Higgins pulled the difference back to level going into the final game. Spencer offered to make it the best of three which Higgins, sensing fear seep from the pores of his opponent, rejected.

On the fourth day of the 1972 World Snooker Championship final, Spencer just about held it together for the first session but then, in the evening, Higgins clicked and whitewashed the champion 6–0 to go into a 27–21 lead. The referee could not re-spot the colours quick enough. Harper again: 'As one very contented fan put it on his way out of the hall, "Just who is the world champion?" . . . And it's very much on the cards that Spencer will soon be changing the bill-head at the top of his personal notepaper.' Everton wrote in *Snooker Scene*, 'Higgins opened up as if he was playing a light-hearted knockabout as pots flew in from every conceivable angle.'[7] If Spencer needed a sign from above it came in the final frame: as Higgins sank a black with premeditated violence the generator groaned, packed in and plunged the room into darkness. Relishing the drama and unperturbed by the blackout, he went on to win the frame 115–5. It was the kind of frame that those who were privileged to witness it (and the match was not covered on television) will never forget. Higgins was, like his hero Muhammad Ali, making those who had reservations about his boasting and posturing begin to re-evaluate. Suddenly, he seemed less like a braggart and more like a prophet.

Even so, he could not carry on at that pace and Spencer pulled back two frames. But, by the end of Friday, Higgins needed only five frames for the title while Spencer needed thirteen. The *Belfast Telegraph* believed that Higgins was on the cusp of a huge upset but reported that he looked jaded and went on: 'This week has been one of the most hectic in his short career. Almost every day he has spent hours in between sessions being interviewed by press and television reporters.'[8] The interviews for local television news were nothing compared to the late nights at the Selly Park Tavern (next to The Pebbles) or the early mornings spent coming back from La Dolce Vita in the city centre before being woken with a slap by Bernard four hours later. In fact, precisely what happened in the early hours of Saturday morning. With victory so close, they had both moved into the Strathallan but gambled away all their spending money and had to borrow the taxi fare home.

Higgins took the first frame of the day. Spencer, no doubt drawing upon the advice John Pulman had given him never to look at the scoreboard, hit back with three (including an impressive 123–0 whitewash in the second). It was now 33–31 and Higgins needed four more frames to become the youngest ever professional world snooker champion and the only man to win it at the first attempt. He took the first two at 96–18 and 88–14, just edged the next and then, in the final frame, made a break of 94 (his biggest of the match) and another of 46 to take the title. The twelfth and final session took just fifteen minutes and the crowd reacted as you might expect. The 'Hurricane' had won 37–31.

Higgins calculated his winnings (significantly more than the £480 prize money) and wondered what he might expect to earn in the next year. If Spencer was claiming £12,000, he was sure he could double that. When John Pulman presented him with the trophy, the former champion told the crowd: 'You've got to give the kid credit because he's hardly had a shot for three frames and then Spencer makes two negligible mistakes and he's snapped up the two frames to go back four in front.'

That would be the last time 'the kid' got any credit from the men who ran the game. On his way to the final he had disposed of (in order) the second-longest-serving professional in the game, a man who had held the world snooker title from the year the USSR launched a dog into space until someone in America put the Bee Gees on network television, the chairman of the governing body and then, in the final, the first player since 1951 to be vetted and then accepted into the closed shop of professional snooker. If Higgins had set out to cause more trouble, distress and discord it would scarcely have been possible. And that was simply on the table. He was the wedding guest nobody wanted but who had invited himself anyway, goosed one of the bridesmaids, molested the groom's mother and also succeeded in taking the bride home with him. Or, in his own words: 'I think [the 1972 World Championship] was the coming of the saviour: myself.'

FOUR

hurricane *n*. **1**. a severe, often destructive storm **2**. a wind of force 12 or above on the Beaufort scale **3**. anything acting like such a wind.

COLLINS ENGLISH DICTIONARY (THIRD EDITION, 1991)

The new world champion awoke later than planned. Bernard should have slapped his face at 8.30 a.m. and dragged him down to breakfast but Higgins, having returned from a nightclub and climbed into bed three hours earlier, was out for the count. So was Bernard. Besides, after a week of nervous tension and heavy drinking, they were both due a lie-in. The trophy, in essence a large spittoon with a gap on the plinth where his name was about to be engraved, sat on the table opposite. It was next to an empty bottle of Asti Spumante and a discarded packet of Panatella cigars. As yet another power cut ended, the black and white television he and Bernard had taken from the lounge the previous evening and deposited in the corner of the room warmed into life. He did not know if he had made the news because he had slept right through it. With the sound turned right down, the television relayed pictures of Richard Nixon and Chairman Mao smiling and shaking hands somewhere in China. Higgins wondered if, now he was champion of the entire world, he would ever meet Chairman Mao. Probably, he reckoned. In the next bed, less than five feet away, Bernard broke wind audibly. It would turn out to be a more accurate analysis of the next few years.

But for the time being, the 'Hurricane' (the press had run with the name and he had eventually taken to it himself) was in a nice hotel room, he had his 'valet' with him and his management had promised him the world. There was already talk of a three-month tour of Australia and a series of matches against Eddie Charlton and John Pulman and a trip to Bombay. In less than twelve hours, he would be in Dublin to take on former world professional snooker champion Ray Reardon in an exhibition match at the Gresham Hotel. At that moment he liked the sound of the word 'former'. He would soon come to hate it. Straight after the final he had disappeared into the only public phone box in the Selly Park British Legion and spent £5 in loose change telling his mother and sisters what he was about to tell the gentlemen of the fourth estate: 'I want to make world history by achieving things I have never done before,' he told the press. 'I shall be world champion for five or six years and then when I'm thirty I'll retire.' It seemed feasible. 'I'm very good at this game,' he carried on, 'and I'm going to make a lot of money playing it. That's a fact.' There were not many in attendance who doubted him.

After his return from Dublin he played a mid-week exhibition at a Staffordshire miners' club. Mike Langley, billed as the 'Talk of Sport' in the *Sunday People* was shadowing him for a piece in his weekly column. He called it, ALL MUMS PLEASE START HERE . . . And then continued:

Traffic lights in Oswaldtwistle are said to be honouring 'Hurricane' Higgins by going red–black–red since he brought the world snooker title to the little Lancashire mill-town a week ago. Higgins, 22, and first name Alex, has founded a career on a misspent youth. He's the lad all our mums warned us against becoming.

HE DRINKS: Campari and soda ('I've had six today,' he said at tea) and halves of bitter.

HE SMOKES: 80 a day, he estimates, in filter tips.

HE'S HUSTLED: 'For months I took up to £15 a week off a post card dealer from Haringey – and all the time he was giving me a seven start.'

HE GAMBLES: He's no stranger to card schools or to snooker betting . . . And as a former apprentice with Berkshire trainer Eddie Reavey, he knows the horses too.[1]

Higgins turned on the style for his Fleet Street stalker. One of the thirteen frames he played ended in six minutes and a local butcher from Lower Gornal was crushed by a break of 109 in three minutes and fifty-three seconds. Langley concluded, 'In a profession recently regarded as an elderly closed-shop, the "Hurricane" is a refreshing breeze, the needed ticket-seller and a living proof that mum doesn't always know best.' The pay-off line might need revision, but the rest stands. It was his first real taste of national newspaper gossip column coverage and the first indication that Alex Higgins was permitting himself, on what he imagined to be his own terms, to become public property. First thing on Sunday morning he went out to buy the paper and hated the piece. It did not tally with his self-image. He thought it made him sound low-rent. He had, however, succeeded in dredging snooker from out of the 'Sport in Brief' ghetto and into the main body of the paper. Soon, he would complete the job and put both himself and his sport on the front page. In early summer 1972 he would also appear on television in a half-hour documentary called *Hurricane Higgins*, which did for Higgins and snooker what the series *Boiling Point* did for Gordon Ramsay and contemporary British cuisine twenty-five years later.

The programme, made by Thames TV, featured his first manager John McLaughlin in one of his bingo halls explaining, 'Alex has only three vices – drinking, gambling and women,' but was remarkable for the bleak portrayal of the loneliness of the professional snooker player. It opened with a close-up of Higgins in a dodgem at a funfair in Lancashire and closed with him unsuccessfully trying to elicit a kiss from a girl on a Ferris wheel. In between these scenes he was filmed waiting on empty station platforms with his cue case, making a break of 104 against John Spencer at Wallasey Town Hall and playing in exhibition matches at a variety of unsalubrious, smoke-filled venues. Higgins reckoned, '[The programme makers] deliberately set out to show the seedy side of snooker.' He neglected to mention that John Morgan, the writer and narrator, had successfully diverted the attentions of the local police during the filming of the programme after several of the usual drunken, late-night escapades involving his quarry. A blind eye was usually turned in exchange for a commitment to play an exhibition at the police club at a future date. Whatever their intentions, Morgan and director Christopher Goddard captured the pathos at the heart of their subject. Goddard was later quoted as saying: 'What I think we show is that there is no real glamour in the life Alex leads. I think at the end of the film, a lot of people will say, "Poor sod."'[2]

The documentary was critically well-received and reached twenty-fifth place in the joint ITV/BBC ratings for that week. Nancy Banks-Smith, then, as now, the *Guardian* TV critic, wrote, 'For some time I thought Hurricane Higgins was a bullfighter. I still feel he was a bullfighter and changed when I wasn't looking.'[3] The young Alex Higgins, ridiculous with cocky pride, certainly had some of a matador's bravado. But there was also something childlike about him. This was most apparent when he was asked in the programme about the billiard room Welsh bingo tycoon Dan Tobin maintained in his back garden in the Vale of Neath. Higgins was there to play Spencer again. 'It's a marvellous place, it's got everything you really want,' he says of the glorified scout hut that provided free beer, snooker and chicken and chips to the lucky few invited through its doors.

Morgan asks him, 'What does it have that you really want?'

'It's got a beautiful view,' gushes Higgins. 'It's got three bedrooms in case you're stuck and it's got a snooker room which is one of the best in the country. I'd like to have a place like that . . . everything about the house is so fantastic it's untrue, plus the fact that it's not like a mansion, it's just right.'

'What's wrong with having a mansion?' Morgan wants to know.

'Well, I mean, you have to check up every night to see if there are burglars in the twenty-two bedrooms, it would be a bit tedious and I wouldn't really fancy that. And I wouldn't want to have a wife with about fifteen servants knocking about, you wouldn't get a lot of privacy . . . no it's not for me that, I would just like a house like this, you know, really nice.'[4]

He was driven to the Staffordshire miners' club for the exhibition reported in the *Sunday People* by Jim Meadowcroft, a former driving instructor and one of the three professionals based in East Lancashire. Higgins and future world champion Dennis Taylor were the others. They were were known locally as the 'Three Musketeers' and spent hours practising and playing together. Meadowcroft had also become Higgins' 'chauffeur' in the same way that Bernard had become his 'valet'. The world champion might not have wanted a mansion but he was taking on staff, usually unpaid. It was done with an irresistible combination of charm, vulnerability and his propensity for verbal and physical pyrotechnics. Consequently, Meadowcroft spent a substantial amount of time with the 'Hurricane' and saw the man divorced from the crowds and journalists who had started to hang on his every word. 'I drove over to pick him up for a practice session one day,' he remembered later, 'and found him slumped in an armchair like an old man. I've never reminded him of the incident and I don't suppose he will even remember it. But, at 22, the king of snooker looked for all the world as if his career had finished, not just started.'[5]

Soon after winning the 1972 World Championship Higgins left the flat over the newsagents in Oswaldtwistle and moved into lodgings in Accrington which, with his brief residence in the Ebony Street squat and several other residences in the East Lancashire area, engendered a sense of dislocation to compound the homesickness familiar to thousands of expat Irishmen across the water. But it was not all gloom. He was now earning £50 per exhibition and looking forward to visiting Australia. It would be the first time he had ever left Britain. The tour had been organized by John Pulman, the man he had vanquished in the quarter-finals. Pulman knew that Higgins, as world champion, would be a popular draw on the other side of the world. As a warm-up for that event they were scheduled to play an exhibition match back at the Selly Park British Legion in Birmingham. Higgins, delayed while trying to organize the passport he had only just realized he would need to board the plane to Australia, missed the train and had to hitch his way to the venue with a French couple. He eventually arrived one hour late and checked into the Strathallan Hotel. World champions do not stay in 'The Peebles'. He checked his cue, the prized Burwat Champion, into the porter's lodge. It had not cost much but it felt perfect.

A cue is an extension of the player's arm and attracts a certain superstition amongst the people who earn their living by their mastery of it. As Paul Newman says of his pool stick in *The Hustler*, 'It's got nerves in it. It's a piece of wood, got nerves in it.' A good cue, which is to say one that feels precisely right, is venerated by professionals with the devotion reserved in other cultures for the preserved body parts of dead saints. Even Higgins, an unapologetic iconoclast in almost every other regard, defers to the supernatural potency of the right cue. John Spencer is generally considered to have lost his edge after his cue, one he had rescued from a foot of water in the basement of a derelict club and fixed with a six-inch nail, was broken into four pieces in a car crash. He had it repaired but, despite subsequently winning the title in 1977 with a two-piece cue, was never able to achieve the same level of consistency. In 1989, during the Grand Prix at Reading, Stephen Hendry had his favourite cue stolen from a practice room at the Ramada Hotel. It originally cost £30 and was bought for him by his father from an Edinburgh sports shop. A £10,000 reward was immediately offered for information leading to its recovery and then paid when it was found at the roadside the next day and taken to a police station. He has since won seven world championships with it.

In the unmade film of Higgins' life and to give dramatic emphasis to little more than a clumsy stumble, the moment when a hotel porter at the Strathallan Hotel stood on his Burwat Champion and snapped it would be shot in a fast-edit with ear-splitting sound. He has since described it as 'Like losing an arm or a leg.' His record immediately afterwards suggested that he might have had a point. The circumstances surrounding its fracture remain uncertain. He has often said that a porter trod on it by mistake but he has also been known to recount a slightly different version of events: 'My snooker cue travelled [to the Selly Park British Legion] in one of those black tin cases' he wrote in *Alex Through the Looking Glass*. 'Pulman sent his friend round in a big Vanden Plas to collect me from the hotel. I sent the cue on ahead and . . . when I took [it] out the end was hanging off. The priceless weapon had fallen down the seat of the car and been caught in the door.' Whatever the reason, he was without the cue he had used since he was seventeen.[6] He played on with it that night, making the damage more difficult to repair with each shot. He felt the cue which had won the world championship die in his hands. Pulman won 19–14.

As it explained in the front of his new passport, 'Her Britannic Majesty's Secretary of State requests and requires in the Name of Her Majesty all those whom it may concern . . . afford the bearer such assistance and protection as may be necessary.' On his first trip outside Britain, the bearer of this particular passport was going to be in need of all the assistance and protection Her Majesty's Name could muster.[7] Higgins first set foot on foreign soil in Singapore where a three-day stopover had been scheduled to accommodate an exhibition of a game called hexapool played, as the name suggests, on a six-sided table. It had three pockets and three baulk areas and a crowd of 3,000 turned up to watch the new world champion struggle with the unusual format. From there he travelled to Australia which was, as he remembered it years later, 'A real playground for me because my hell-raising reputation hadn't caught up with me then. They were good days. Sydney in the seventies was similar to London in the sixties . . . a bit behind but a swinging city full of women, money and massive gamblers. That suited me down to the ground.'[8]

Sydney at that time was not the cosmospolitan Olympic city it is now. The most famous landmark and symbol of its remarkable economic and cultural emergence, the Opera House, had not even been completed. Rather than being the busiest performing arts centre in the world, which it is today, the area it now occupies was just a building site at one end of King's Cross, the red-light district that backs onto it. The tourist board boasts that the area has a 'proud and diverse community' and, indeed, thirty years ago it was where the snooker tables, brothels and gambling dens were to be found. Consequently, it was the natural habitat for a young man from the back streets of Belfast on his first sojourn abroad. Higgins loved Sydney and, particularly, 'The Cross'. He began to frequent an illegal casino called Carlisle House which also had a snooker room on the top floor. The club was owned by Joe Taylor, someone who might be euphemistically referred to as a 'well-connected businessman'. It did not take long for the young Irishman to get on the wrong side of him.

The 'Hurricane' had been hustling a respected old professional called Norman Squires. After giving him a start of 65 each time, he had gone three frames ahead before an argument erupted about the nature of the handicapping system. Higgins reached boiling point in less time than it took him to pot a long red and referred disparagingly to Squires as a 'no-hoper'. This did not go down well. During the ensuing furore, a large man with all the gentility of the unapologetically violent politely asked the world champion to calm down. Higgins responded with enough choice invective to facilitate his swift exit from the premises at the hands of two robust doormen. He instantly regretted his intemperate behaviour when he was told the man he had insulted was Joe Taylor. Even Higgins, who had been in Sydney for what seemed like five minutes, had heard of Joe Taylor. As Higgins remembers it, he sat in the gutter and scribbled out an apology on a piece of notepaper. Legend has it that he was also encouraged to write an apology to Norman Squires on a sheet of toilet paper. Whatever the truth, he was forgiven and readmitted.

He loved the informality of Australia and the generosity of spirit exhibited by its inhabitants. Particularly the women. Higgins had a succession of Australian girlfriends and within two years would be married to one of them, but the nature of his job, the constant travel and late nights, and his personality precluded settling down at this point. He was single and enjoying himself too much. 'It's the same with the birdos,' he told the *Daily Mirror* at the time, drawing a typically modest comparison between his world-class ability on a snooker table and his prowess in a king-size bed. 'I know I've got a reputation like George Best. Well it's true. And I've found it helps being a world champion, especially at snooker. I always tell them I'm a great potter and they know what I mean.'[9] In the meantime he was due to meet another girlfriend, Liz Kendal, on the way back from another trip to Australia. He first encountered her at Churchill's nightclub in London and some papers had speculated that they were engaged to be married. That was not the case but he liked Ms Kendal enough to arrange a rendezvous with her in Bombay where he was due to play a series of prestigious expenses-only exhibition matches. It was a brilliant plan with just one fatal flaw: Alex Higgins.

He drank too much before and during the match. 'I played Indian champion Girish Parikh on a dreadful table and made a 109 break with my first hit,' he later remarked. Somebody then offered a cash prize for a century break. This infuriated Higgins who felt he deserved the money having just achieved such a feat. 'The temperature in there was way over 100 degrees so I stripped off my shirt, knowing it would upset them,' he said later.[10] He is less revealing about the incident with the dhoti belonging to one of the Bombay Gymkhana committee but R.K. Vissanji, the Vice-chairman of the Billiards Association and Control Council of India told *The Times of India*, 'During the 25 years of my association with the game, I have never seen such disgraceful behaviour.' Higgins was asked by his hosts to return to Britain immediately, although he claims he arrived at the same decision independently. He met Liz Kendal at Bombay Airport, kissed her and said, 'Babe, it's good to see you – we're leaving on the next flight.'

News of his Indian mutiny reached Britain before Higgins. The snooker hierarchy, already uneasy at the prospect of ill-disciplined young men like the current world champion beating them on the table and stealing their limelight off it, took a dim view. Higgins was fined £200. Drinking and gambling were by no means anathema to the older professionals who ran the game, but it was their belief that the sport should project the same formal image of evening dress and deference which had hitherto prevented the general public from embracing it. The maintenance of the status quo was, and remains, a defining characteristic of the closed shop. This was not the view of Alex Higgins. He refused to answer to anyone, least of all those he could beat on the table. In this respect (and several others), he shared something with Billy Mitchell, a bibulous Edwardian billiards player, who travelled to South Africa for a testimonial arranged by a group of enthusiasts and created so much mayhem that another group clubbed together to send him home. Mitchell also arrived at a venue to play Cecil Harverson on one historic occasion.

'They were both so far gone,' records Clive Everton, 'that their first attempt to hit an object ball was an abject failure. "There will now be a short interval", declared the harassed promoter, thus bringing to an end the shortest session on record.'[11]

If Lou Reed was taking a walk on the wild side in 1972 then Alex Higgins was right beside him, with a hustle here and a hustle there. The 'Hurricane' was finally living the life he believed was his by right. He had started to put on weight and the beginnings of a double chin were visible just below his wispy sideburns and collar-length hair. The slicked-down and combed-into-place choirboy cut he had favoured a year previously had been replaced by an unruly fringe as worn by his namesake 'Alex', played by Malcolm McDowell, in *A Clockwork Orange* (usually without the mascara and the bowler hat). He may have also borrowed a little from the behaviour of Anthony Burgess' anti-hero. As world champion, he was escorted from the table at an exhibition match in Ilfracombe after attempting to spear a voluble member of the public with his cue. He later put the outburst down to his decision to give up smoking. A couple of months later he turned up for a game with Ray Reardon at Sheffield City Hall, with a black eye – the only visible sign of a beating which had put him in hospital the night before. 'Somebody just walked over and punched me,' he said. 'No reason. Jealousy probably.'[12] Probably not. He beat Reardon with room to spare on that occasion.

All Higgins needed was the licence to misbehave and being world champion had stamped his papers and seemed to allow him to do just that. But his form was suffering. The drinking and gambling had been constants in his adult life and so were not really a distraction. But he had discovered a whole new group of 'friends' through his new-found fame and notoriety and they were capable of leading him astray. They could be male or female but they were entranced by his sudden celebrity. They were people who owned 'fashionable' boutiques, snooker groupies, prominent local businessmen on the make, would-be jet-setters who owned nothing more than a speedboat they had found in the classified ads of a regional evening paper, bingo tycoons (again), scrubbers, strumpets and hustlers. John Spencer noted the development.

There were so many hangers-on, he never had to move,' he remembers thirty years later. 'They would go and get him a drink, everything was done for him, but he attracted the wrong type of person. And as time went on it got worse and worse. I remember once we were playing an exhibition in Accrington. [When it finished] we decided to go out and were walking down the street on the way to a nightclub when we saw a panda car. Alex just walked out in front of it and held his arm up. He told the policeman where we were going and asked him to give us a lift. He honestly expected him to drive us to the club. The policeman told him what to do, obviously, but that is how the hangers-on had got him thinking.

There was more trouble with Spencer in Hartlepool when Higgins refused to finish an exhibition match because the lighting in the hall was too bright. In Middlesbrough, he refused to play at all. Spencer again: '[The promoter] came up to my hotel at about 2 p.m. and said, "We're in trouble, Higgins won't play". I can't remember the reason he'd given but I said, "Oh well, forget it." The evening paper came out with the headline "Alex Higgins refuses to play". Which is why Alex had done it [to get his name in the paper]. Anyway, at about six o'clock the promoter came in and said, "We're all right John, he's agreed to play". I said, "That's fine, but if he's playing I'm not . . . I don't think the public should be treated like this. If you go with him I won't be there."' Higgins left. It was a sell-out and so Spencer agreed to play seven of the club members, give them a generous start and forfeit his fee if he was beaten. He told the crowd what had happened and explained that anyone who was not happy could have their money back. Only two people asked for, and received, a refund. 'I said, "Alex Higgins agreed to play eventually but I don't think the public should be treated this way and I have refused to play him." It brought the place down that but I know that if Alex had come across to the club at that moment, what I had just said would not have mattered at all. They would have still brought the place down just because of Alex.' He carries on, 'That's why I had to get rid of him before we got to the club because I knew nothing I said would have mattered if Alex had walked in, there would have been a big roar and that would have been it.' Spencer maintains that this was the moment Higgins adopted him as a mentor ('He realized he couldn't mess about with me').

By this time Higgins was on course to hit his target of £20,000 for the year and was earning almost ten times the national wage.[13] However, the loss of his cue, a transparent loneliness and homesickness for his family in Belfast (a city at that time tearing itself apart),[14] the attentions of hangers-on and the collateral damage inflicted by his lifestyle ensured that he was not at the top of his game throughout much of his first year as world champion. As David Taylor, the Manchester hairdresser turned snooker professional, remarked, 'I don't think he leads the ideal life for a top snooker player. But I wouldn't dream of giving him advice.'

Higgins had played John Spencer on almost thirty occasions since the 1972 World Championship. In the final of the Park Drive £2,000 and in front of a capacity crowd at Belle Vue, Manchester he was beaten by him for the sixth consecutive occasion, including a pulsating game at Radcliffe Town Hall which he lost 38–37. In the month before the defence of his world title, he lost almost every match he played, including three against fellow professional Gary Owen, another to amateur international Mark Wildman (5–1) and a 3–0 whitewash for £500 after conceding a start of 40 to a club player in London. Jim Williams, the man who had promoted the 1972 finals in Birmingham, reflected on the eve of the 1973 event in Manchester, 'I don't think there is any doubt that he has come to the top too quickly . . . [losing his title] would be the best thing that could happen to him. By losing the championship he would have to start his apprenticeship all over again and this would release him from the pressures he now finds himself under.' Even Higgins, seldom his own sternest critic, admitted, 'I'm terrible at the moment but I think I'll be OK for the championships.' He had had his hair cut specially.

FIVE

He's a lonely forgotten man desperate to prove he's alive.

PROMOTIONAL TAGLINE FOR THE FILM *TAXI DRIVER* (1976)

Two forces had collided in 1972 to put snooker back on the map. The 'Hurricane' was the most remarkable but the advent of colour television, which had first been broadcast on the new BBC2 station on 1 July 1967, was the other. Initially, colour was available only in certain regions but by 1972 the coverage had expanded and 17 per cent of households were able to boast a colour television in the front room. Snooker, with the green baize, white cue ball and seven other colours, was tailor-made for the medium. Three years previously, a producer at the BBC called Phillip Lewis had asked snooker impresario Ted Lowe, formerly the manager of the Leicester Square Hall venue, to devise a thirty-minute programme to run for eight weeks which featured the sport. Lowe has since described *Pot Black* in a peculiar way, as 'a chink of light at the end of a very dark and long snooker tunnel.'[1] After the *Hurricane Higgins* documentary had brought the sport to an even wider audience three years later, *Snooker Scene* described *Pot Black* as, 'The most important single influence in selling snooker to the general public.'

The first programme was screened on 23 July 1969 and offered the players who appeared on it nationwide exposure and therefore the ability to charge more for exhibition matches, which was at that time still the only way a professional could earn a living. It was shot in colour but was viewed by the majority in black and white (the confusion which gave rise to Lowe's famous commentary, 'For those of you watching in black and white, the pink is behind the green.') The idea was simple: two groups of four invitation-only professionals played each other in a one-frame, round-robin tournament. Eventually, the top two in each group qualified for the semi-finals which were recorded in a four-day period in Birmingham between Christmas and New Year. The format was flawed in that one frame was not enough to test the ability of the players but at least snooker was back on the box. It had not been featured on television since the early 1950s when Joe and Fred Davis had been in early middle age. Ray Reardon won the inaugural title followed by John Spencer in 1970 and 1971.

Lowe, who takes only half the credit for sowing 'the seed of snooker's astounding popularity on television', had already invited Higgins to participate in the next series of *Pot Black*. There were so few professionals at this stage that nobody was excluded. After he had won the world title, it was impossible to ignore him. A million people were estimated to have watched the first series but, by the time Higgins became involved, the figure had trebled. However much the pairing might sound like the name of an upmarket gentleman's out-fitters, Higgins and Lowe were cut from radically different cloth. Lowe was brought up in the quiet racing town of Lambourn in Berkshire and had a respect for tradition. Higgins was not and did not. Lowe and two BBC executives, Jim Dumigham and Reginald Perrin were, as Ted Lowe put it, 'mainly responsible' for choosing the eight professionals. They were soon to regret extending that invitation to Higgins.

'I did not realize what sort of headache I had let myself in for,' Lowe repented years later. '[He] was beaten in his first frame and immediately protested against the whole system of *Pot Black*, declaring forcibly how crazy it was to decide a match on one frame. He also objected strongly at having to wait around for television producers, directors and crew, and did not like cameras at this stage. He told me bluntly that he did not intend to hang around any more for this particular series. With fifteen matches still to be filmed, the powers-that-be became very annoyed with the "Hurricane's" attitude . . .'[2] Higgins stormed off the set. Lowe spent a long evening in a Birmingham hotel room with Higgins trying to convince him to finish the remaining games. He eventually succeeded but the mutual antipathy was genuine. Gordon Burn wrote, 'Ted personally got Alex Higgins banned from *Pot Black* for five years, for threatening to walk out . . . and for other behaviour unbecoming of a sportsman and a gentleman.'[3] In Lowe's eyes this could have included having three girls, who he described as 'black as the ace of spades, straight off the streets of Birmingham', in his dressing room.[4] Unfortunately, however, his behaviour had alarmed the people who were attempting to portray snooker as something other than a game that thrived in dimly lit snooker halls and gambling dens like the Jampot.

If the game was to attract major sponsorship and capitalize upon its popularity with the viewing public, those in charge knew it had to shed the image that gave rise to the old saw, coined by the nineteenth-century economist Herbert Spencer, that dexterity at 'games of skill' was the sign of a 'misspent youth'. Snooker needed to be civilized, smart and controlled. These were not adjectives often used in connection with the world champion.

'I was the one who peed in the changing room sink because the toilets were too far away,' recalled Higgins. 'It's all the respect the show deserved.'

He did not receive another invitation to appear until 1978 and even then, only following a vigorous campaign in the form of letters to the BBC and the popular press. This in turn elicited the following response from Reginald Perrin in the pages of *Snooker Scene*: '. . . accusations such as "banned", "punished" and "vendetta" are not accepted by this office as possessing validity'.[5] The invitation-only nature of the programme makes this difficult to believe.

Acting as agents for the tobacco concern Gallaher, Peter West and Patrick Nally had already brought Park Drive cigarettes and snooker together. After the capacity crowd at the 1973 Park Drive £2,000 they realized that the sport and its star turn, the 'Hurricane', were ripe for commercial exploitation. West was a television commentator and an urbane compère whilst Nally was an ideas man in the relatively fresh world of public relations. They both recognized that snooker needed completely repackaging and the world championship reorganizing if the sport was to realize its potential. Under the direction of Snooker Promotions, as the West-Nally enterprise was known, the haphazard, year-long world championship format of the previous year was curtailed and, with the sponsorship of Park Drive and £8,000 in prize money, the event was streamlined. It would now be contested in one venue – The City Exhibition Halls, Manchester – with eight tables and play taking place simultaneously. Crucially, the final stages would be filmed, for the first time, by the BBC.

'We stopped at a little pub,' recalled Alan Birstall, a friend of Higgins' from Oswaldtwistle. 'And the landlord said, "Will you sign this for me so I can put it in the pub?" and handed him some document that Alex duly signed as "World Professional Snooker Champion 1972" before adding, "If you like I'll put 1973, 1974, 1975 and 1976." That was Alex.'[6] More specifically, that was Alex in 1972. A year later he had changed managers again and, in a more formal arrangement that necessitated the signing of contracts, linked up with West and Nally. It made perfect sense for both parties. Higgins was the new commodity driving the publicity for the game and they were the commodity brokers selling the game to the sponsors. The relationship, brought to a premature end by the non-attendance of the commodity at several exhibition matches and behaviour likely to ward off potential and existing sponsors, lasted just long enough for Patrick Nally to introduce Higgins to a new wardrobe. The traditional and well-worn black evening suit he had transported from squat to flat to house and around the country was replaced, in the argot of the time, by 'flash gear' including white pants, red and green outfits, with waistcoats to match and a range of hats. The WPBSA was not impressed and fined him £100 for wearing a green evening suit at one event. 'They think I'm supposed to play the game looking like a tailor's dummy,' he answered back, 'What I wear on my back is my business.' This was technically incorrect. He was also fined again for playing in a pair of braces, a fedora, an open waistcoat and without a tie. He would subsequently challenge the WPBSA's strict dress code by producing a doctor's note detailing the painful symptoms of *sycosis barbae*, a skin condition like shaving rash, which he claimed was aggravated by wearing a tie. Ted Lowe was outraged.

For the defence of his title in Manchester (as a 3/1 second favourite to Spencer at 9/4) he signalled his intent in the first match by turning up twenty-two minutes late and wearing a pair of white Oxford bags. He claimed he had been caught in traffic and, instantly choosing attack as the best form of defence, complained about the unauthorized use of his image on a cigarette advertisement at the venue. It cut no ice with tournament organizer Bruce Donkin who issued a stern reprimand (with the usual £100 fine to follow). Higgins apologized to the crowd for his behaviour but they were not in the mood to forgive. Typically, 'he won the crowd over within five minutes with a dazzling break of 78'[7] and went on to beat Pat Houlihan 16–3. It seemed as though, despite the lack of confidence in his replacement cue and the vicissitudes of the previous twelve months, he was on course to blow away any obstacle in his path. Fred Davis was next. An eight times former world champion, Davis was a teetotal non-smoker who had turned professional in 1930. Higgins considered the draw a bye into the semi-finals. He was too cocky by half. Davis went 14–12 ahead but, after a farcical interlude in which rain stopped play (a leak in the roof had to be repaired before the game could continue), Davis missed a pink that would have left him needing only one frame for victory. Higgins won the next four to move into the semi-finals but it was a measure of how his game had suffered that he nearly went out at this early stage. Davis later reckoned that 'the initial impact [of his arrival on the scene] is gone . . . opponents are more accustomed to his play and this tends to make it more difficult for Alex.'[8] This was underlined by Eddie Charlton's comprehensive 23–9 demolition of Higgins in the semi-finals.

Another worrying sign for Higgins was the re-emergence of former policeman Ray Reardon as the man to beat. As PC184 he had received a commendation for disarming a man with a shotgun and, as a pre-championship 9/1 shot, was used to overcoming difficult situations. He had already pulled back a 19–12 deficit to beat John Spencer 23–22 in the deciding frame of the semi-final.

They had been playing to a half-empty arena until the arrival of spectators from the unexpectedly brief Higgins–Charlton game. The influx of people, and therefore atmosphere, helped Reardon to raise his game – his temperament for the big occasion being demonstrated by the fact that in the thirty matches he played in the world championships between 1970 and 1978 he won twenty-seven and lost only three. John Spencer, it seemed, was in danger of being eclipsed by Reardon. As was Higgins himself. Television cameras were introduced for the final and, distracted by the glare of the lights, Reardon managed to lose a 27–25 lead. He demanded that two huge arc lights be turned off and went on to beat Eddie Charlton 38–32.

By nature a possessive man, Higgins did not appreciate losing his title and, unable to accept that he had just been beaten, put it down to the loss of his cue. Others were less traumatized by the turn of events. John Pulman probably spoke for most of the established professionals when he remarked that he was glad Higgins had been beaten because he was 'dragging the game down'. It was a comment that was as indicative of the feelings Higgins had inspired in his year as world champion as it was of the inability of the old guard to recognize the positive things he had brought to the game. Higgins would have to wait twenty months before he won another title. In the meantime he had two objectives: to carry on living in the style to which he had become accustomed, and to rebuild his game to the standard which would ensure he could carry on living in the style to which he had become accustomed. He had not played his way out of East Belfast just to go straight back on the next ferry. The first objective was easily achieved. He was still big box office and even snooker promoter Jim Williams, the man who had staged the 1972 World Championship and cautioned Higgins that his private life was getting out of control, went on the record as saying, 'I would be pleased to put him on in a match with or without his title.' The immediate priority, however, was the redevelopment of his game.

With his instinct for self-preservation to the fore, he had already started. Rex Williams reflected on his defeat at the hands of Higgins in 1972, 'In some ways I was unlucky that Alex played John Pulman in the previous round because he learned so much about safety during that match. Before then he relied on his outstanding potting and break-building but [Pulman] was a tremendous safety player and Alex realized he would have to match him to get the better of him, and that's what he did.' [9]

Unlike the players who had been coached to play safety or took to it as just another extension of their personality, Higgins was learning a new dimension to his game in competition conditions against some of its best practitioners. Even more remarkably for a man often perceived as inflexible in situations that are not of his choosing, he was having to suppress his own temperament to embrace this new method of playing. He was learning to curb his natural inclination to play to the gallery at every opportunity.

After the 'Rumble in the Jungle' heavyweight title fight between George Foreman and Muhammad Ali in October

Alex Higgins is on the front row, bottom left. The look would subsequently be appropriated by Sid Vicious.

Right: With his mother, Elizabeth, his father, Alexander, and the Amateur Northern Ireland Championship trophy. He has just turned 18.
(*Mirrorpix*)

World champion John Spencer and Higgins at the Park Drive 2000, the week before the title changed hands. (*Trevor Smith*)

The mid-1970s, when six hours practice a day was still possible. And enjoyable. (*Trevor Smith*)

A relaxed Alex Higgins during his first reign as champion. (*Express Newspapers*)

Left: Reconciled with girlfriend Lynn Robbins after the dramatic 'Spitfire' court case in Plymouth. (*Express Newspapers*)

Below: Alex Higgins and Lynn Robbins marry in Wilmslow, Cheshire in January 1980. Higgins almost missed the wedding. (*PA Photos*)

The 1976 world championship final against Ray Reardon in Manchester, the year before the tournament moved to the Crucible. (*Trevor Smith*)

Crowd pleasing, Higgins-style. (*Trevor Smith*)

Left: Higgins cleans the ball during the 1980 world championship final with Cliff Thorburn. He would subsequently be banned from doing this. (*Trevor Smith*)

Below: The hustlers. Higgins and Thorburn clashed many times, sometimes physically. (*Trevor Smith*)

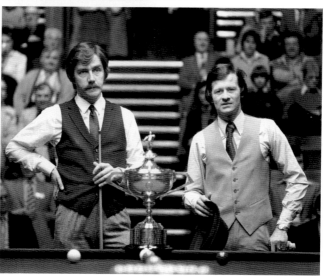

'Resting' in a nursing home in September 1981. Within a year he would be world champion once more. (*Mirrorpix*)

1974, Higgins began to justify his new style of play with reference to the rope-a-dope tactic. As demonstrated to devastating effect by Ali, this involved soaking up punishment by lying on the ropes and waiting for the opportune moment to strike back with precision and speed. It was devised when it occurred to the former World Heavyweight Champion that raw ability would not be enough to beat the younger and more destructive George Foreman. As Norman Mailer remembered it for the Oscar-nominated documentary film *When We Were Kings*, Ali's performance was shocking and totally unexpected. 'He went into rope-a-dope . . . a lot of people at that time thought the fight was over.' George Plimpton, ringside with Mailer in Zaire, was equally astonished. 'You don't go to the ropes . . . he just looked as though he had to cave in.'[10] Although not devised for one opponent or one particular match, the analogy was apposite and did not flatter Higgins. As Ali went to the ropes, Higgins went to the cushions.

Angela Patmore, a Fulbright scholar who ghosted Higgins' first autobiography in 1981 and also wrote a seminal book on the pressures faced by sportsmen,[11] maintains: 'All spectator sports are an experiment. They are set up so people can buy tickets and come and watch what happens to other people under pressure, that's all it is. Professional sportsmen think it's all to do with their skills but, in fact, when they get in the arena they meet opponents who have more or less the same skill and so their skill cancels each other out. What is left is this sort of psychological edge, the ability to produce the goods under pressure.' Higgins knew that if he was to deliver the goods he needed to add safety to his game. He was aided in this endeavour by something Patmore describes as, '[Being able to] look at the table with his eye like the shutter of a camera . . . he could see a picture of the game and tell you what shots have to be played and he could see it instantaneously.'[12]

The process of learning a defensive style not only contradicted his modus operandi, it offended his ego. It was as painful as Ali soaking up a pounding from sparring partner Larry Holmes in an effort to train his body to withstand the punishment Foreman was about to inflict. And it took a long time. West and Nally, their Snooker Promotions outfit flourishing, organized two snooker evenings in London at the Café Royal in 1973 and 1974. Ladbrokes were brought in to sponsor a ranking list whilst Norwich Union agreed to put their name to the main event at the Piccadilly Hotel. Although it was officially an 'open' and therefore a magnet for ambitious amateurs, the professionals dominated. After beating Dennis Taylor and then Cliff Thorburn, Higgins was easily beaten 8–2 by John Spencer in the semi-final. The next year, he lost again at the same stage to Ray Reardon. In the meantime the young Irishman who had done so much to breathe life into the game had been beaten in the Canadian Open by Dennis Taylor and had crashed out of the 1974 Park Drive World Championship to a sexagenarian recovering from his second heart attack.

Fred Davis, the man who had pushed Higgins all the way in the 1973 quarter-final, beat him 15–14 at Belle Vue, Manchester, after Higgins had been leading 13–9. The collapse was prompted by a controversial refereeing decision from Jim Thorpe. Higgins, lending it disproportionate weight, still refers to it as 'The Push Stroke Affair.'[13] 'I was in the middle of a 32 break and looking at an easy blue' he has said. 'I'd got up close to the blue and probably, had I used the rest, I'd have potted the blue anyway and Thorpe wouldn't have thought of fouling me. But I'm good at stretching.'[14] The referee called a push stroke and awarded Davis five points. Higgins protested forcefully, telling Thorpe he should 'read the fucking rule book' but, immune to such delicate persuasion, the referee refused to change his mind. The 'Hurricane's' concentration broken, the old master dispatched him 15–14.

In the press conference after the match, Higgins berated the sponsors, the referee and anybody else who came to mind. Outbursts of this kind became familiar at press conferences (or to any other kind of captive audience) as Higgins struggled to deal with defeat and the cyclical build-ups of internal tension that often accompanied a failure on the table. On this occasion, it concluded with the disconsolate former world champion challenging a journalist to a fight. Soon after, West and Nally and Snooker Promotions severed their ties with Higgins. Although Higgins won the Watney's £1,000 Open in December there was no doubt that 1974 was a plague year on the table. Off it he managed to get married to Cara Hasler.

Higgins refused to let Angela Patmore mention his first wife in the autobiography she ghosted for him in 1981. He had copy approval and, despite her coaxing, was adamant that he did not want to talk about it. 'I told him it should go in,' she shrugs, 'but couldn't do anything about it. He had only recently married Lynn so that could have had something to do with it.'[15] Five years later Hasler was granted just over a page in his second autobiography *Alex Through the Looking Glass*. He had met her on a blind date arranged by the racing writer Phil Wilson while on his first trip to Australia. 'I was very friendly with Cara's dad, Baden Hasler,' explains Wilson. 'He was a prominent racehorse trainer and very well respected and, through my job I'd got to know the family. Cara and her sister were often at the races and were both very good-looking. When I became good mates with Alex I introduced them.' Higgins recalled, 'As soon as I saw her my head was turned. She was very glamorous with an irresistible personality.'

Wilson had first met Higgins in a bar at a racecourse and remembers that they 'clicked' straight away. 'He was almost schoolboyish but you could instantly tell that he was very sharp and a good judge of a horse. He could weigh up the worth of a horse just by looking at it in the paddock. We got talking and even though I was older than him we still had a lot in common.' The bond was cemented at racecourses all over New South Wales where negligible drinking and driving restrictions (there were no breathalysers) meant that in between tournaments Higgins and Wilson and a couple of other friends would take off to Canterbury Park or Wyong racecourses and gamble and drink until the early hours. 'We'd often get back at 2.30 a.m.,' remembers Wilson, 'And I had to be at work at five the next morning. It was a great time but very demanding and the only time Alex and I argued was when he wanted to go somewhere but I had to go home. If I'd carried on at that rate I'd have been divorced in six months but he was a young man and still single.'[16] He would remain so for two years but in the meantime maintained an on–off relationship with Cara Hasler which could be characterized as 'on' when he was with her and 'off' when he was elsewhere.

Back in Australia in 1974 Cara had 'talked him' into marrying her and, as the incurable romantic put it later, 'I hadn't got the heart "to do a runner."' The wedding was held on 11 April 1975 at St Edmond's Chapel in Darling Point, an upmarket suburb of Sydney, and was attended by, among others, Ray Reardon. The two men rarely socialized away from the snooker circuit but, as he explains now, 'I was just out there really and went along to sort of represent snooker. It was a nice wedding from what I remember but I did not go to the do afterwards.' Higgins behaved impeccably throughout. 'He had a big smile on his face,' says Wilson. 'We left the wedding and went to the wedding breakfast but after three hours he and Cara left and said they were going to a party hosted by Elton John at The Sebel Town House Hotel.' Whilst there he bumped into Keith Moon and the rest of The Who who had just finished filming the rock opera *Tommy* with Oliver Reed. Within a matter of months, Moon and Reed had the idea of putting Higgins on the West End stage in a play called *The Dinner Party*.

'We were going to have a dinner table on stage and then invite a restaurant around to serve dinner,' explained Reed later. 'Keith would invite his friends and I would invite my friends. There would be telephones on the tables, and upstairs, in the shape of an Easter egg, would be a snooker table. And we'd have Alex Higgins and people like that playing snooker, and us eating, and people coming on and off, and waiters serving. Five people from the audience would be invited to join us every night. Everybody in the audience would have a little pair of opera glasses. That would be it. The poster would read: "Have you been to *The Dinner Party*?"'[17] The idea was first mooted in the press in July 1974 and finance was seriously discussed but the show never made it off the drawing board. The world never had the opportunity to witness Reed, Moon and Higgins all on stage at the same time. It would have been an extremely short run however, since the after-show party alone would have made the chances of a second night highly unlikely.

In the meantime, with his theatrical career on hold, Higgins continued his snooker tour of Australia. Phil Wilson used to see him whenever he came over to Sydney and remembers the 'Hurricane' practising in Tattersall's club. 'He might have been spending more time at the track but he never went off his snooker,' recalls Wilson. 'We were going out for a drink once and went past a snooker club, a dodgy-looking place, and he went in and played a five-minute frame by himself just because he loved the game. Then he said, "Come on Phil, we're off."'[18] Others, like sports reporter Les Wheeler, later to become the Sports Editor of the *Sydney Morning Herald*, remember the newly married Higgins in a different light at this time. In the early hours of the morning, after losing a session to Eddie Charlton in a match that was scheduled to last a week, Higgins asked Wheeler if he could still get access to the wires (i.e. the means of transmitting a story). 'Yeah,' replied Wheeler, 'But what is there to say?'

'I'm retiring, Les, I'm going to give up snooker and take up table tennis.' He was deadly serious.

'And you want me to file that story tonight?'

'Yeah, get a message out and tell them the "Hurricane's" blown himself out.'

'I tell you what, Alex,' counselled Wheeler, 'I'll ask you

again in the morning and if you still want me to wire that story, I will.'[19] When Higgins awoke he had changed his mind. It amounts to his first recorded threat to quit the game. There would, of course, be many more.

As Higgins indulged himself, Ray Reardon took the opportunity to reclaim his world title and sucessfully defend it. He also appeared in the finals of the 1974 Norwich Union Open and the inaugural Benson and Hedges Masters at the West Centre Hotel in Fulham. He was beaten in both by John Spencer who appeared, in the absence of a serious challenge from Higgins, to be renewing his rivalry for recognition as the best player in the world with the man who had beaten him in the English Amateur Championship final in 1964. Gallaher, who owned both the Park Drive and Benson and Hedges brands, had been seduced by West and Nally into promoting another event. It was a remarkable achievement by Higgins' former management team, especially considering that they had decided to scale back their involvement in snooker. They had become disillusioned after their problematic relationship with the 'Hurricane' and the reaction of the WPBSA to their plans for an international tournament circuit which they presented immediately after the successful 1974 World Championships. The project was rebuffed with characteristic myopia and arrogance. Clive Everton wrote: 'What the company had achieved for snooker became a matter not for gratitude but envy, jealousy and distrust.'[20] When institutionalized incompetence and occasional corruption are added to that list, it represents a reasonable summary of the guiding principles then practised by the governing body of world snooker. It is unrealistic, if not preposterous, to expect one organization to act as both management and trade union. West and Nally, with their degree of professionalism, were clearly surplus to requirements.

The Benson and Hedges Masters was a qualified success with a less than capacity knife-edge final between Spencer and Reardon settled on the re-spotting of the black. Alex

Higgins did not prosper at all, going out at the quarter-final stage to Rex Williams. He was to dominate the event in the late 1970s and early 1980s, reaching the final every year from 1978 to 1981, but in 1975 he was struggling and his only notable success that year was victory in the Canadian Open at the National Exhibition Centre in Toronto. However, if his game was still in a state of transition, his behaviour was not. Terry Griffiths, eighteen months older than Higgins but, at this stage, still an amateur and a collector for Pearl Insurance, organized an exhibition featuring himself and the former World Champion at the Drill Hall in Llanelli in 1975.

He sold 400 tickets – a sell-out – and organized sponsorship from a local brewery. The Welsh amateur snooker champion then had the temerity to win. Higgins had been drinking and after the final frame turned to the referee, in full view of the guests and sponsors Griffiths had invited, and stuck two fingers up at him.

He then made his way to the 'sponsor's room' and began to act in an over-familiar way with Griffiths' sister-in-law. Her husband, predictably, took exception and demanded to know what was going on. Higgins swung a punch, which missed, and connected with a friend of the alarmed host. 'All of a sudden a ruck developed,' recalled Griffiths in his autobiography. 'Alex picked up a bottle from the table and said, "Come on then" . . . I ran straight at [him] to break it up although will freely admit that I was very frightened. The whole night was ruined.' The following day, a subdued Griffiths went to find Higgins. He had been his idol since 1972 and it is difficult to appreciate the feelings of despondency, fear and regret he must have experienced as he walked into the club at Pontardulais, a few miles up the road, to see Higgins. He continues, 'I saw Alex reading the newspaper . . . He glanced up briefly [but] Alex never looks at you and he just could not face me. To him I was a nobody and that disgusted me. He could have stood up and said, "Sorry about last night, Terry. I got carried away." It would have been forgotten . . . but from that day on, although he has always had my respect on the table, he never had it off the table.'[21] The 'Hurricane's' reputation on the snooker circuit was becoming poisonous.

Away from the world of professional snooker however, and relaxed in the company of others, he was cultivating another reputation entirely. Val Mutch was the stewardess at the Eccles Central Conservative Club when Alex Higgins came to visit. 'He came to play a few games of snooker with the members and my daughter happened to be sat in the lounge doing her homework. She would have been about 11 at the time. Alex sat down next to her and asked what she was doing. On being told she was doing an essay about snooker he promptly started to help her and gave her an autograph . . . when I apologized about the noise from the bar while he was playing, he told me not to worry as it didn't bother him. My husband actually scored six against him, which he is very proud about. He thrashed everyone he played that night. As you can probably appreciate, my family and I have only good memories of Alex.'[22]

Following the decision by West and Nally to withdraw from the front line of professional snooker promotion, the 1975 world professional championships were without a sponsor. Guaranteed prize money of £18,900, however, ensured that the bid to host the event in Australia went to Eddie Charlton Promotions – the suggestion of which had helped West and Nally to scale down their involvement in the first place. Higgins, one of the top players in the world, was not invited to compete but opted to pay his own passage. The most important competition in the snooker calender was to be staged in various locations all over Australia but the draw was made contrary to WPBSA conditions. As Everton noted in *The Story of Billiards and Snooker*, 'It did not escape the attentions of the cognoscenti that not only Reardon and Spencer but Higgins were all in the opposite half of the draw to the promoter.' That is to say, Eddie Charlton. A former member of the Australian surfing championship team and talented at cricket, athletics and boxing, Charlton had carried the Olympic torch on the way to the stadium in Melbourne in 1956. However, he was never a fully paid-up member of the Alex Higgins fan club. The feeling was mutual. It is hard to conceive of two more different individuals – one, a sporting all-rounder who forged a career for himself on the snooker table with a dogged playing style which wore opponents down and the other, an instinctive genius who took on impossible shots, made crowds feel alive and made and lost over £2 million. Charlton chose snooker, snooker chose Higgins. After beating David Taylor 15–2 and then Rex Williams 19–12, he lost to Reardon 19–14 in the semi-final. 'Alex always gave me too much respect,' says Reardon now. 'That's why I kept beating him.' And he chuckles.

Reardon was reluctant to talk at first. 'Look,' he said, 'I've said it all before. There are loads of people who have written books on him, I don't see the point. I've done so many of them, all you talk about is him, it's pathetic.' It is a Sunday night and it is difficult not to conjure up an image of him stood by the phone, probably under a set of stairs, as a pair of lamb chops start to burn and weld themselves to the bottom of a pan. 'I don't know why you bother,' he sighs. 'I'm not really interested.' But, of course, he is. He told the producers of a documentary less than a year ago, '[Higgins] made you feel uneasy in your seat somehow . . . he put you on edge because it was all action . . . his lips would be twitching, his nose would be twitching, he had a different type of bridge [in which] he held . . . a cue in his hand while one finger sort of pointed down. That was different and, of course, every time he played a shot he always tapped the table.'[23] Higgins did not always tap the table. He did that only when he was winning (or 'cruising' as he preferred to call it). Once persuaded to hold forth Reardon found it difficult not to drop into his Higgins routine. This recalls the time Reardon was beaten by Higgins when the latter had a black eye, but Reardon's favourite quote refers to the ability of the 1972 World Champion to make the cue ball do anything he wanted. 'He has tried,' said Reardon, 'every kind of side [on the ball] but suicide.' It is a statement that is not entirely true.

The final of the 1975 World Championship was held at Nunawading Basketball Stadium. Although Reardon beat Charlton 31–30 in the last frame of an absorbing game, the sport was going backwards, from a sponsored, professional televised event in an exhibition hall to an unsatisfactory kind of challenge match half-arranged for the benefit of participants on the other side of the world. In purely commercial terms (and despite the prize money), it was just not a good idea. The men who ran the game were as startled by the success of their sport as the decision-makers at the BBC. Snooker needed to capitalize upon the arrival of colour television and the fascinating battle between the new generation and the established order. Alex 'Hurricane' Higgins was perfectly cast as the rebel with a cause. Maurice Hayes believed he was the man to do that. He was wrong and was last seen ten years ago driving a taxi in Canada.

In 1976, however, Hayes seemed to have established himself and his promotions and management company, 'Q' Promotions. As well as his position as head of 'Q' Promotions, Hayes was also vice-chairman of the amateur game's ruling body. He was managing Graham Miles, Bill Werbeniuk and amateurs John Virgo and Willie Thorne before he made Higgins an offer he did not want to refuse. Higgins signed on the dotted line and was billed as 'The New Alex "Hurricane" Higgins'. For several days, it seemed Hayes had a point. A stopover mini-tour of New Zealand on the way to the Canadian Open failed to result in temporary incarceration or significant controversy of any kind. Presumably convinced that he was some kind of alchemist, Hayes soon signed John Spencer, Cliff Thorburn and Dennis Taylor and helped to convince Embassy cigarettes to sponsor the 1976 World Championships with a record first prize of £6,000. It would be his lasting contribution to the game of snooker.

Given the success of the single-location 1974 tournament,

it seemed a peculiar decision to locate one half of the draw at Middlesbrough Town Hall and the other, plus the final, at Wythenshawe Forum in South Manchester. It was, it transpired, just another example of the organizational inadequacy of 'Q' Promotions, an operation which was also developing a reputation for booking its contracted players for exhibitions without actually telling them. This happened on a couple of occasions with Higgins and, through no fault of his own, resulted in him receiving unwarranted bad press. Unsurprisingly, the 1976 Embassy World Championship was not a resounding success although it did prove that the 'Hurricane' was still a force to be reckoned with. His marriage to Cara might have been struggling and his off-the-table lifestyle chaotic but he had successfully laid the foundations of a new safety game to compensate for the diminution of his ability to sink the outrageous long pot. He was also break-building with greater consistency. Earlier in 1976 he had whitewashed Willie Thorne 10–0 at the Leicester YMCA with a break of 146 which included a freeball on the brown with all the reds remaining. Taking brown as his 'extra' red, and by trying harder to retain black ball position, Higgins could probably have made more than 147. Reardon had noticed the improvement and warned: 'People don't appreciate what a great safety player he is . . . he doesn't pot as well as he did in the year he won and he doesn't have the same inspiration but he's always dangerous.'

In truth, however, Ray Reardon was the dangerous one. He had just claimed the £2,000 first prize for the Benson and Hedges Masters (Higgins had been easily beaten by Graham Miles 4–1 in the quarter-finals). He was chasing a fourth consecutive world title and enjoyed a markedly easier draw than Higgins but the conditions at Middlesbrough Town Hall were far from satisfactory. The world champion had to deal with non-tournament standard tables and an undisciplined crowd which left and arrived at inopportune moments, but did not allow anything to get in the way of his regal procession to the final at the Wythenshawe Forum. John Dunning, Dennis Taylor and Perrie Mans were destroyed with casual abandon. All Reardon needed was a red carpet. Higgins did not have it so easy. In the first round he faced Cliff Thorburn, the Canadian snooker champion and pool-hall hustler who began commuting to England in 1973. He had seen footage of the Reardon–Charlton world final in that year and had decided to turn professional. He would soon develop a fervent dislike for the 'Hurricane' while Higgins would later christen him 'the Grinder' in recognition of his less than flamboyant playing style.

There was room for only one natural born hustler. Thorburn recalled in his autobiography *Playing for Keeps*, 'Higgins was in London at this time and somehow he asked me if I wanted to play snooker for a fiver a game. He said he'd give me a 40 start. Being the gentleman I am, I only took 28. I don't think he won a game. All I remember is Higgins at the top of some stairs, I'm running down the stairs, I still haven't been paid and he's got a ball in his hand, threatening to throw it at me.'[24]

There would be more violent confrontations between the two in the next few years but, on a table with pockets larger than standard size, Thorburn went into a 14–12 lead in the first round before Higgins, riding his luck, won the next three frames in succession to go through. He would meet John Spencer, his great rival and the man who had humiliated him 5–0 in the televised Benson and Hedges Irish Masters a few weeks previously, in the next round. Again, it went to the last frame and again, with a noisy and partisan crowd on his side, Higgins won. The semi-final matched him against Eddie Charlton, the man who ended his title defence in 1973 and placed him in a far more difficult half of the draw when promoting the event in Australia. Higgins was tested to the full but his new safety game was more than a match for Charlton's brand of effective but joyless attrition snooker. Higgins booked a place in the final with a 20–18 win. He felt the title was within his reach. Reardon had to decamp from

Middlesbrough to Manchester. Higgins had an unorthodox and unruly band of supporters yearning for him to win. In fact, after entrusting the local turf accountant with their wages for the week, most of them needed him to win.

It looked like a good bet. Higgins had already endured three severe tests of character. What he had not reckoned upon, however, was the testing examination the three previous rounds had made of his stamina. That he was exhausted is evidenced by the publicity pictures taken before the final. Higgins and Reardon are mugging with four players from the unsuccessful 1976 FA Cup Final Manchester United squad at the Forum. Higgins looks immaculate with a white on black daisy motif running down the front of his white dress shirt and is even wearing a bow tie and smiling but his eyes seem shot. He looks, for the first time, suddenly older. Like a man in the company of men and no longer an ingénu. Reardon won five consecutive frames to go 8–5 ahead before complaining about the glare from the TV lights (again) and, the following day, the run of the table when 10–9 behind. He had every right to complain but Higgins, highly suspicious of his motives, went on to reflect, 'I was a bit silly at the time, a bit too easy-going. I had every right to say . . . "This is the table we've elected to play on and I don't want this table touched." If I'd stuck to my guns they wouldn't have touched it. But like a fool I let him have his own way.' With his mental equilibrium already troubled, a wrong call by referee Bill Timms destroyed any chance Higgins may have had of winning a second title. At 15–11 he needlessly opted to play a red left-handed and missed. Had he potted it, Reardon would have been left needing snookers. The champion cleared up and after Timms was replaced by John Williams (supposedly after falling ill but probably as the result of another altercation, this time with Reardon) went on to establish an unassailable 24–15 advantage going into the final day. From that moment Higgins had no way back and lost three of the next four frames and the final.

The film *Taxi Driver* was released in America in the same

month. The film featured Robert de Niro as Travis Bickle, a vulnerable working class stereotype with suspect taste in recreation wear and work clothes. Regardless of both, he chooses to spend his waking hours in an environment surrounded by hustlers and people on the fringes of civilized society. He is attracted to it. A wounded man constantly raging against injustice and capable of routine acts of explosive violence and random kindness, he ultimately seeks a kind of redemption which nobody can provide. If Alex Higgins, still married to a woman on the other side of the world and with a child he seemed reluctant to acknowledge, failed to recognize the type and could not disagree more with the fucked-up declaration of the lead character, 'I don't believe that one should devote his life to morbid self-attention. I believe that someone should become a person, like other people' he will still have appreciated the line, 'Shit . . . I'm waiting for the sun to shine.' He would not have to wait long.

SIX

To alcohol! The cause of, and solution to, all of life's problems.

HOMER J. SIMPSON

The sun hardly stopped shining in 1976. By 31 May a drought had been declared as the reservoirs of Britain began to run dry. Some days it even refused to rain on Alex Higgins. However, given the nature of the man, there could be no real respite from intermittent showers, unexpected downpours and dangerous electrical storms. The first of these was the collapse of 'Q' Promotions. It folded a few weeks after overextending itself during the 1976 World Championship. In the course of the year Higgins would link up with the late Del Simmons and his International Snooker Agency (ISA). Simmons was a bear of a man who would come to manage his affairs, rescue him frequently from actual bodily harm, sometimes effect it and generally put up with his temperament in one capacity or another for the next ten years. In the meantime, however, Higgins was looking after himself. He gained a measure of revenge for his world title defeat against Ray Reardon (and a positive boost to his confidence) by beating him in the Canadian Club Tournament in Leeds and would shortly qualify for the final of the Canadian Open, where he would lose 17–9 to John Spencer. He was once again making the finals of major competitions.

He could not, however, be expected to excel in tournaments that had been effectively gerrymandered, like the 1975 World Championships in Australia or the 1976 World Professional Matchplay Championship. Both were promoted by Eddie Charlton Promotions out of Hurstville, New South Wales and while the world championship could just about be legitimately staged in Australia, the latter event was a much stranger affair. Presumably given the name by the same person who came up with the marketing concept for Chessington World of Adventures, the event was a sixteen-man international tournament in Melbourne which was granted recognition by the governing body.

Clive Everton, in *The Story of Billiards and Snooker*, described it thus:

One of the WPBSA's mistakes was to approve a so-called World Professional Matchplay Championship . . . Charlton beat Reardon to win it and financially the players did well out of it but the indiscriminate application of the word 'world' to a tournament which was no more than a pale carbon copy of the genuine championship was no more than an exploitation of the Australian public and, in the dilution of the authentic article and confusion which was sown among the unknowledgable as to who was the real world champion, a disservice to the game.[1]

Higgins went out two rounds before the final to expat Irishman Paddy Morgan.

The older generation of established snooker professionals faced a paradox: playing or organizing an event featuring Alex Higgins was a fast track to snooker gold because he attracted the paying public and the imagination of the media. The downside was that on his day he was good enough to beat anyone in the world (specifically including the promoter and the various members of the governing body) and could also be an extremely difficult man to accommodate. A letter, dated 18 May 1976, from Eddie Charlton Promotions begins, 'Dear Alex'. After detailing the 'great response' he had received from New Zealand regarding a possible tour involving both players, the letter went on, in terms so patronizing and dictatorial he could have written a papal encyclical. He insisted that Higgins continued to build up a 'good reputation' and suggested that he allow Charlton to organise his appearances in Australia and 'don't do, or go into, anything I do not agree with.' Charlton, with no contractual relationship with Higgins or any method of persuasion other than by excluding him from any tours that might be to his financial advantage, was not bluffing. He had already neglected to invite him to the 1975 World Championships (although, naturally, Higgins paid his own way there). Charlton did not like the fact that Higgins had also agreed to play in a pool tournament in Sydney without asking his permission and counselled him against such a course of action.

Higgins, with the insistence of Eddie Charlton that he build up a good reputation clearly at the forefront of his mind, succeeded in getting himself arrested and kept in custody for thirty-six hours after damaging two doors at the house of an ex-girlfriend when entry was denied (the magistrate, granting an absolute discharge, noted that the offence arose out of a mixture of 'alcohol and passion'). Higgins may have eventually taken part in the World Matchplay event but, with another delicious two-fingered salute, stayed in Australia to play in the pool tournament. And won.

Back in England, the remorseless drag of the modern snooker professional was already a way of life for Alex Higgins. It amounted to exhibitions in clubs, the occasional tournament, travelling all over the country like a convict on the run and late nights in cheap hotels. He was widely recognized (something he generally liked when he was sober), people wanted to buy him drinks (he let them), they asked for his autograph (it depended upon what mood he was in), but he was always under pressure to get somewhere by a certain time.

Reliant upon public transport and a network of friends he

considered and treated like chauffeurs, he developed a reputation for being unreliable. Thomas White had heard the rumours and, after booking him for a charity exhibition match at the United Services Club in Balham in 1976, took the precaution of paying promising amateur Willie Thorne £40 to turn up just in case the 'Hurricane' failed to make it (the insurance for a no-show cost exactly the same amount as Thorne). He had nothing to worry about. Alex Higgins turned up on time, behaved like a gentleman and lost to White's fourteen-year-old son James.

'You get loads of promising kids,' smiled Higgins to Tom White before he left. 'Some are more promising than others. Some burn out. But one like Jimmy shines.'

'From that day,' Jimmy White recalled in his autobiography *Behind the White Ball*, 'Alex used to get in touch with Dad and say, "Tom, I'm playing in Southend, could you get Jimmy down here? He can take over when I have a rest." To be invited to play with Alex Higgins on a regular basis was like a dream come true . . . [he] would take me to one side and explain the terms in his high, light, Belfast brogue.' Higgins would let him play, and invariably beat, half a dozen people for money during the interval in any exhibition he might be playing. White would normally make around £10 for a night's work depending upon how many lambs he could slaughter in the time allowed. It helped develop his fast playing style. 'Alex played with me and one or two of the other promising kids, using us as sparring partners,' he carried on.

'Once dad was thanking Alex for the experience, I overheard [him] reply, "This is someone out of the ordinary. Young Jimmy shows promise and I like the person as well as the player. He's a nice kid."'[2]

In terms of both upbringing and playing style, Higgins saw much that he recognized.

A young man who had less in common with the 'Hurricane' was the 1976 National U-19 Billiards Champion. Five years older than White, Steve Davis was the product of a close-knit working class family from Plumstead in South East

London and had first picked up a cue in the year Higgins arrived in Lancashire on the ferry from Belfast. He was being groomed by his mother for a 'proper' job in banking or accountancy but his father had noted his ability at the table and was encouraging him to play regularly at Plumstead Common Working Men's Club. Looking for a more difficult challenge, he soon found his way north of the river to Romford and one of the Luciana snooker halls. The chain of seventeen halls had been bought in 1974 by Kendall House Investments. The company was owned by a sandy-haired twenty-five-year-old entrepreneur called Barry Hearn. When Davis decided to enter a Luciana tournament he had seen advertised in a snooker magazine, Hearn, having already been tipped off by top Essex amateur Vic Harris, stopped by to take a look at the gawky kid with red hair and regulation working class uniform of cheap shirt, polyester jumper and colour uncoordinated slacks. 'There's no way I thought he was a champion,' Hearn told *Observer* editor Donald Trelford ten years later for his book *Snookered*. Davis also failed to recognize that the moment represented a seismic shift in his prospects, although he was to note with hindsight, 'As soon as [Hearn] walked through the door, Providence smiled on me.' Davis was not to turn professional for a further two years, although Hearn paid for players like Higgins to travel south from his new home in Salford to take him on.

'It was a great grounding and great fun,' says Davis twenty years later. 'I once played Alex Higgins in a best of sixty-five [frame] match over four days and he refused to turn up for the last day. He was really doing it because I had him under it. I used to beat everybody there. It was the start of a new breed.' It certainly was. Higgins was the father. 'I first remember seeing him whilst watching the *Nationwide* TV programme in the early seventies,' recalls Davis during a break from commentating on the 2001 UK Championships for the BBC. 'He had just won the world championship and I had just started taking an interest in snooker. And there he was in this white tank top, with Sue Lawley, knocking a few balls

around . . . he was ahead of his time in some respects . . .
[When I first played him] it was an exhibition to Alex but it
was a match to me. That was my first introduction to the
"Hurricane" and the turmoil that he brought.'[3] It was as
nothing compared to the turmoil the arrival of Steve Davis
brought the 'Hurricane'.

Predictably enough, other areas of his life were also in a
familiar state of upheaval in the second half of the 1970s. His
'long distance international affair' (as he occasionally
referred to his marriage) was unravelling. Cara Higgins, who
now lives in the prosperous Rose Bay suburb of Sydney, will
say nothing about it other than to comment, 'That is all in
the past now, it is a closed chapter and I don't want to talk
about it. He's got on with his life and I've got on with mine.'
She had no option. Alex Higgins had provided her with a
child, Christel. According to a friend of Cara's he has only
seen the child once, when she was aged three or four, and has
not acknowledged her existence in either authorised autobiography. When he appeared on *This is Your Life* in 1980, no
mention was made of Christel or Cara Higgins. Eamonn
Andrews, the genial host of the programme, closed the show
with the words:

There is a special someone who has brought a calm to the life of
"Hurricane" Higgins and this programme would not be complete
without her . . . here she is, your two-month-old daughter, Lauren
[waves of applause] . . . Alex Higgins, this is your life.

It was, it now transpires, just one of his lives, a fact to which
an ex-wife and a three-year-old daughter in Australia could
have attested. Cara Higgins, a devout Catholic, was divorced
by Higgins in 1979 and has never remarried.

As his wife coped with a baby, Alex Higgins was preparing for
the 1977 Benson and Hedges Masters at the New London
Theatre, Drury Lane. After making the finals of the 1976

Embassy World Championships and the Canadian Open of the same year and beating Reardon in another Benson and Hedges event at Leopardstown Race Club in the Republic of Ireland, he had every reason to believe he was in with an excellent chance of taking the £2,000 first prize. Despite a plush new city centre venue in London, a larger and more enthusiastic crowd and opponents including the South African Perrie Mans (overcome without difficulty) and 33/1 rank outsider Doug Mountjoy, it was not to be. A former miner with the physiognomy of a middleweight boxer, Mountjoy had been the 1968 Welsh amateur champion and then claimed the title again in 1976. This made him eligible to represent Wales in the world amateur championships in Johannesburg. He won and turned professional as soon as he returned home. Two months later he was brought into the Benson and Hedges Masters as a late entrant.

Mountjoy made quite an impression. With his shoulder-length hair, his white dress shirt and velveteen bow tie carefully packaged into a low-slung three-button waistcoat, he looked like Detective Inspector Jack Regan at a sportsman's dinner. In his first professional tournament he swept aside John Pulman and Fred Davis but was not expected to beat Higgins. He eased past him 5–3 and then went on to trumpet his arrival on the professional scene by beating Ray Reardon, his third world champion in a week, after a dramatic finish on the final pink of the last frame. Higgins was not disconsolate. He hated being beaten but Reardon had also lost and his mind was beginning to focus on the world championships. It was part ego and part necessity.

In an attempt to ring-fence their peculiar confraternity, the WPBSA had opted to organize the official rankings entirely on the basis of results achieved in the three previous world championships irrespective of performances in any intervening tournaments – a situation that clearly discriminated against newcomers to the professional ranks and which served to protect the position of those who sat in judgement on their peers.[4] The governing body, more by luck than judgement, was also able to announce the continuing sponsorship of the world championships by Embassy in early 1977. Following the undignified affair in Manchester and Middlesbrough the previous year, Embassy were ready to walk away but for the intervention of minor player and sports entrepreneur Mike Watterson. His wife had been to see a play at the Crucible Theatre in Sheffield and upon her return mentioned to him that the venue would be perfect for the sport. She was right. The world championships are still held there today.

A theatre-in-the-round with room for two tables divided by a false wall covered in expensive pink-coloured flock wallpaper, with guaranteed and increased television coverage and something approaching a professional organization to promote it, Embassy agreed to put their name to the world championships for a second year. There was £17,000 prize money at stake and Higgins, as he boasted four years later in *'Hurricane' Higgins' Snooker Scrapbook*, thought he was a certainty for the 1977 world championships. 'I felt good,' he said. 'I was playing more convincingly than for a long time, I was seeded two and . . . I'd turned the corner.' He went out in the first round to Doug Mountjoy after the Welshman sank a superb black in the final frame which ran all the way along the rail before dropping into the pocket like a ten-inch putt. Higgins claimed his concentration had been broken when, as he was about to play a shot on the black, somebody called out that the scores were wrong. The someone was right. There was a discrepancy. But it was immaterial and only of the order of a couple of points. Higgins missed the black. Mountjoy potted it. The Welshman was beaten in the next round by Dennis Taylor but the first world championship at the Crucible Theatre was largely notable for the performance of Cliff Thorburn, who progressed to the final before being beaten by John Spencer.

The final death knell for the marriage between Alexander Gordon Higgins and Cara Hasler sounded in a nightclub owned by George Best just off Albert Square in city centre Manchester. Higgins was a frequent visitor to Oscars and instantly recognizable for, among other things, his unortho-dox fashion sense which on this occasion included an Australian-style bush hat complete with corks. He was also wearing an old raincoat. He spotted a young woman with whom he had enjoyed a complicated romantic entanglement a year previously, and approached the table. His 'old flame' was sitting with a group of people including Best who, it almost goes without saying, was chatting to an attractive young blonde woman. Lynn Robbins was a twenty-three-year-old secretary who worked for Servisair at Manchester Airport and bore an astonishing resemblance to Higgins' younger sis-ter Jean. It was, however, something else that served to divert his attention. It was a purely chemical response. She looked fantastic and, crucially, was determined to ignore him. Lynn Robbins was separated from her husband and had heard all about Higgins from the friend seated next to her. She had been led to believe he would expect her to clean the house and never take her out. She had resolved to treat him with the contempt she thought he deserved and turned her back on him. When it was her turn to buy a round of drinks and Higgins jumped in to order a large vodka and tonic she told him to get his own. Like so many men who find themselves in this situation, it was an irresistible come-on and he decided to persist with the chase.

Eventually, he discovered where Ms Robbins worked and, after dispatching his hapless ex-girlfriend to order a taxi, asked her out on a date. She refused. However, by judicious use of that most precious and rare Higgins resource, charm, he finally managed to persuade the two women to share his cab. They were intent upon visiting a discotheque. The for-mer world snooker champion, temporarily tiring of the strug-gle, jumped out of the taxi when it stopped at the lights. He had elicited the information he needed and called her at work for several days until, impressed by his determination, she finally agreed to meet him for a meal. They arranged to go to a restaurant in Manchester's Chinatown and so, as Higgins could not drive, a rendezvous was arranged at Potters snooker club which was managed by one of his best friends, Geoff Lomas. Lynn Robbins turned up dressed ready for a night on the town. Higgins was wearing a pair of too-short jeans and a jumper that had seen better days. His new girlfriend threatened to leave immediately. It is possible he was testing the water to see what he could get away with – the Albert Pierrepoint treatment. There was, it transpired, not much of a margin to work within and he made a grovelling apology.

In the next hour they visited six clubs in each of which he ordered her a vodka. They then moved on to Chinatown where Higgins promised to teach her how to use chopsticks. He was playing to the gallery and, to impress her, was about to demonstrate what he could do with hand-to-eye coordination and two pieces of balsa-wood. He could not know that using chopsticks was an art in which she was already more proficient than him. He soon did and it irked him. Her avowed intent to be deliberately unmoved about anything he said or did irritated him further. Didn't she know who he was? He was Alex Higgins. The night ended in the early hours of the morning in the Press Club, a members-only bar situated in the basement of a building off Deansgate and the venue of choice for celebrities and drinkers seeking relative anonymity and an extremely late licence. Ms Robbins arrived home some time after the milkman and the postman had called. The next day Higgins called her father, who happened to be a keen snooker fan, and declared undying love for his daughter. Her father's precise thoughts at that time are unrecorded but it is believed that they were not synonymous with 'that's got to be the best news I've ever heard'.

Within two months, by application of that erratic charm, he was a lodger at the family home of his new girlfriend. He enjoyed the refuge from extended periods of time in his own company and was quartered in the spare room in a nice house in South Manchester. In the stolen days between exhibitions, tournaments and lost weekends he managed to stay there for two years. There were other girls, as he has subsequently admitted, but 'nothing important'. Lynn, aware of life on the 'circuit', drove him whenever she could, from London to Scotland and everywhere in between. Occasionally, if he felt inclined, she would join him on a foreign assignment. As she confessed in *Alex Through the Looking Glass*, 'It sounded romantic when he phoned me from Trinidad where he was on a snooker trip and said he'd arranged a ticket for me to join him.' It was the rainy season and a threat from Higgins to return home was only withdrawn when the sponsors organized a transfer from the low-rent accommodation in which the players were expected to stay to the Holiday Inn, followed by five days on the neighbouring island of Tobago. He had his uses.

'Keep in the swim' was the name of an animated public information film designed to prevent the general populace from drowning. It was first shown in 1972, the year the 'Hurricane' became world champion, and featured a sporting all-rounder who 'kept losing [his] birds' because he couldn't swim.

The well-meant campaign had obviously bypassed Alex Higgins. Fortunately for him, his latest 'bird' thought it was outrageously funny that he could not swim. A state of mind not obviously challenged by his decision to tie one end of a piece of rope around his waist and the other to a palm tree before wading out into the Caribbean. Whatever Alex Higgins brought to the relationship, Lynn Robbins brought common sense. She did not care much for the game of snooker but she knew enough to know that just because Higgins had not been invited to the Pontins professional tournament in Prestatyn it did not mean that he could not enter the Pontins Open. She persuaded him that it was a good idea.

The event was not as small-time as the name might suggest. It had been a regular fixture on the snooker calendar since

1974 and was popular with everyone involved with the game. The professionals invited to play were the same ones who had been invited by Ted Lowe (among others) to appear in *Pot Black*. Hence the absence of Alex Higgins. Lowe was also a consultant to Sir Fred Pontin's holiday camp empire. There were two events, a professional tournament that involved eight invited players and was largely for the benefit of the holidaymakers, and the Pontins Open, in which the eight professionals would join twenty-four survivors from the original list of entrants in competition for a £1,500 first prize. Higgins, effectively excluded from the professional competition by Lowe[5] and encouraged by the new element of stability in his life, was drawn in group 14 of an 864-person qualifying competition that included youngsters, veterans, pub, club and professional-standard amateur players. As a professional, Higgins had to concede 21 points per frame and play on non-tournament standard tables upstairs in the sports complex. His sisters Jean and Ann came over from Belfast to offer their support. Everyone who witnessed his defiant performance still talks about it. It was the 'Hurricane' at his back-against-the-wall best, spitting resentment and destroying anybody who dared to get in his way.

In a peculiar arrangement, the winner was calculated after a two-frame aggregate score (Higgins was, therefore, effectively, conceding a 42-point advantage). In his second match he trailed a talented amateur from Manchester called Billy Kelly by 104 points with just four reds remaining in the first frame. By the end of the second he had beaten him 133–121. From there he went on to beat the rest of the non-professional opposition to secure a meeting with Ray Reardon in the quarter-finals of the competition proper. Having only recently lost his world title, Reardon was at a low ebb. Higgins punished him 4–0 and then went on to beat Fred Davis by the same score in the next round. Higgins was sharing a cabin with Conleth Dunne, a promoter from Dublin who went on to open a club called Tramps on West 21st Street in New York. Dunne caught him one morning hiding behind the curtains with a carving knife. When asked what he was doing Higgins explained that, having put bread on the veranda for the birds, he was trying to refine his killer instinct.

Refinement was the last thing his killer instinct needed. As he said himself, 'I was snorting fire . . . it was the venom in me. I was deadly. And, of course, in the final I played a shy little boy called Griffiths.'[6]

Terry Griffiths, the man he had embarrassed at an exhibition in Llanelli two years previously and still an amateur, was clearly overawed. There were over 2,000 snooker players and holidaymakers packed in to watch the final. It was tight and chaotic and reminiscent of the Selly Park British Legion, with the players unable to even take a toilet break because of the weight of numbers. Griffiths was playing on home turf but the sense of injustice that had fired Higgins to play his most devastating snooker for months inspired the crowd. For once, they wanted the professional to beat the amateur and he loved it as the hall rang out with the chant 'Higgins! Higgins! Higgins!' Before the game Higgins asked his opponent if he wanted to split the prize money. There was £2,000 in the kitty (including £500 for second prize) and Griffiths agreed. They were playing for pride and, after ending the first afternoon 3–3, Higgins went on to win 7–4 during the evening session. Jimmy White, who was in the audience, described the result as 'lifting the roof off'.

This was the essence of the self-styled 'People's Champion', a young man prepared to take on the establishment and those who would exclude him and beat them. Audiences responded to it. Terry Griffiths was just in the wrong place at the wrong time. At the prize-giving Higgins suppressed his natural inclination to rant about the situation and fell into a kind of dignified silence as the crowd demanded to know, 'What about *Pot Black*?' – a reference to his exclusion from the television series. Griffiths, later to become a board member of the WPBSA, wrote in his autobiography: 'My view of [*Pot Black*], I think, stems from this time. It actually dictated what happened to a player's future. I never liked the scene; it was a closed shop, without a shadow of a doubt. You got on *Pot Black* if the odd place became available. And you got it by favours rather than ability.' Ted Lowe was in the audience at Prestatyn and Alex Higgins received an invitation to appear in the next series of the show.

Higgins felt good. He had a new girlfriend and was living in a family environment for the first time since leaving Belfast. His form had also reappeared. Two days after returning from the Pontins Open he broke the world record for the fastest maximum break: allegedly in four minutes and fourty-two seconds at Potters snooker club in Manchester. He almost had another 147 on the same night but just missed the black and, having signed for Del Simmons and the ISA organization, was in high spirits as he travelled to Toronto for the Canadian Open a few months later. It was one of his favourite events and he had entered it every year since the inaugural tournament in 1974. This was the year that eighteen-year-old Kirk Stevens, then still an amateur, made his debut in a major event. He had been playing money matches since he was fifteen but when he heard that Alex Higgins was in his home town he turned up at the Canadian National Exhibition Centre (CNE) expecting to meet an immaculate, well-dressed snooker professional. Higgins was not at the venue and Stevens was redirected to a pool hall in the city centre. When he got there he found Higgins and his opponent playing snooker in their underpants. They were, it transpired, playing for each other's trousers.

The 1977 Canadian Open was not held in the usual venue but in a huge blue-and-white striped marquee. The heat was stifling and the flies, probably attracted by the animals at the adjacent circus, were almost as irritating as the noise from the steel band that played non-stop throughout the tournament. When it was not intolerably hot, it rained. The conditions were far from ideal but the gauche Kirk Stevens made it to the last sixteen before losing to Ray Reardon, while Higgins beat John Spencer in the final to take the $6,000 cheque. Canada appealed to the 'Hurricane'. He responded to the dramatic scenery and wide open spaces, and he had always wanted to see Niagara Falls. He is rumoured to have got his opportunity during one Canadian Open, when a heavily beaten opponent mentioned that he was going there with his family the following day. Higgins asked if he could tag along. There are slightly different versions of this story and no names to put with it, so it may be apocryphal but it is certainly worth repeating if only to demonstrate the essence of the Higgins legend. Almost everybody wants to believe anything remotely attributable to him.

It is only a two-hour drive to Niagara Falls from Toronto and his vanquished opponent and his wife and an indeterminate number of offspring were at the three-quarter point of the journey in a station wagon when Higgins announced that he was thirsty and needed a pint. It was 10 a.m. They left the highway and found a small roadside restaurant which served food and alcohol and also kept two pool tables which, after 'breakfast', were pressed into service. As his lift explained the rules of eight ball to Higgins, a local who had been paying close attention to the proceedings offered to take on either of the two out-of-towners for a dollar a game, first to seven. 'OK,' fired back Higgins, 'But make it $10 a game, I don't think I can get interested for a buck.' The local grinned but warned, 'It's your money. House rules . . . you only have to call the eight ball' (which is to say, you have to nominate the pocket in which you intend to pot the last ball before you strike it). They tossed a coin, Higgins won and opted to break first. A stripe went down. He looked up and nominated the top right-hand pocket for the eight ball. 'You don't have to call the eight ball until you've sunk all of your stripes,' advised the local. 'Nonsense,' replied Higgins, 'Eight ball in the top right.' He potted all the stripes without pausing for breath and then sank the eight ball in the top right-hand pocket. He did the same in the next six games before thanking his hapless victim, taking $70 in rolled bills from him, putting the lot behind the bar and declaring, 'The drinks are on the house.' As the story goes, 'He left waving to the locals like a queen at a fucking parade.' The man likes to make a memorable exit as much as a grand entrance.

The International Snooker Agency run by Del Simmons was a professional enough business but was complicated by the management structure. Simmons had set up the company after booking John Spencer to play an event and being astonished at the relatively poor remuneration for the top professionals and the haphazard way in which their activities were organized. Simmons knew Spencer from the golf course. They were both very keen players and competed on the Pro-Am circuit with such mainstream television comedy staples as Jimmy Tarbuck and Bruce Forsyth. Simmons had business interests with Sean Connery and former England captain Bobby Moore and when he approached Spencer with the idea for a new kind of management company for snooker professionals, the former world champion agreed straight away. Simmons and Spencer brought in Ray Reardon and all three became directors of ISA. Then they signed Alex Higgins. 'We took Alex on,' remembers Spencer with an intake of breath. 'He approached Del, he told me and I just said "Yeah, go ahead." Del was managing him and sorting out the bookings and things like that. I was just a partner really and didn't have any say in things. I didn't want to bother, you know. I just left it all to him.' Technically, Spencer and Reardon were now involved in the management of Alex Higgins, which lent a certain frisson to encounters on and off the table between the most popular client on the books and the directors of the company that acted as his management.

It was not to become an issue in the immediate future and Higgins had other things on his mind. He knew he had to capitalize upon his sudden return to form and the next major fixture in the calendar was the Mike Watterson-promoted UK championship, sponsored by Super Crystalate, a leading manufacturer of snooker balls. Held at the

Blackpool Tower Circus in December, the event disappointed in terms of crowd attendance but provided a number of amazing upsets. Higgins was the only established player in the last four alongside Patsy Fagan and new professionals John Virgo and Doug Mountjoy. Fagan went on to eclipse Mountjoy for the £2,000 first prize in the final and then doubled that a fortnight later by beating both Spencer and Higgins in the Dry Blackthorn Cup at Wembley Conference Centre. The 'Hurricane' was becoming a victim of his own success as younger players and new professionals, inspired by the trail he had blazed since 1972, began to appear on the scene and beat him. But he still had an edge in the run-up to the 1978 Embassy World Championship and claimed the Benson and Hedges title by overcoming Cliff Thorburn in the final. In classic Higgins style, with no tie to restrict him and all caution thrown to the wind, he then destroyed Dennis Taylor 21–7 in the defence of his Irish title at a packed Ulster Hall. His lack of a tie, justified by a medical technicality, was symbolic of his rejection of the strictures of authority. It meant he was in charge and playing by a different set of rules to the common herd. Once again he felt confident about winning back his world title and once again his confidence was misplaced.

Despite his preparation and the relative stability of his home life, he went out in the first round for the second year in succession. This time it was Patsy Fagan who rained on his parade. Higgins had seemed to be on the brink of winning the match several times but, after some typically flamboyant and reckless play when in a commanding position, he allowed Fagan to win on the pink in the final frame. His confidence was dictating terms to his hard-won safety game. It was edge of the seat stuff and the audience, both at the Crucible and the four million people watching the BBC's extended coverage, loved it. In the crowd, a young fan of Higgins with bone marrow disease, Tony Metcalf, collapsed after enduring the tension of the final few frames.

Higgins' defeat meant another agonizing wait before he

could claim the thing he desired most – the right to call himself the best player in the world. He already insisted that this was the case and, generously, even brought Ray Reardon into the equation claiming, 'There's nobody else in it [apart from us two]' but with the trophy in his hands nobody could dispute it. It was that simple. Before he could take possession of it, however, he had to endure the grind and flux of his professional life. It often drove him to the brink of despair. In May that year his frustration spilled over in an exhibition against Graham Miles in Caerphilly. As Miles went up to collect the £500 winner's cheque Higgins called him a 'jammy bald bugger' and was caught off guard as his normally mild-mannered opponent turned round and swung a punch at him. The punch missed but Higgins fell into the audience who were, by this stage, in a state of collective shock. Back in the dressing room Higgins and Miles started fighting again and had to be separated by bouncers. A joint statement issued the next day said, 'Both players have been heavily fined and censured and the incident reported to the Professional Players' Association.' They had to open a new file for Graham Miles – Higgins already had his own filing cabinet.

It was this catalogue of misbehaviour which Eddie Charlton cited whilst refusing to invite Higgins to the 1979 World Matchplay Championship in Melbourne. His letter of two years previously had included that fairly unambiguous warning, 'What I do insist on Alex, is that you continue to build up a good reputation.' This was not something that Higgins had tried conspicuously to do and, consequently, along with other unspecified 'incidents' that were alleged to have occurred during the 1976 World Matchplay event, he was the only top player not to receive an invitation. The WPBSA committee refused to sanction Charlton's attempts to stage the tournament in 1977 but, with $35,000 of prize money at stake, had agreed in April 1978 to once more devalue the currency of the label 'world' and lend it to Eddie Charlton. 'I'm very unhappy about it,' commented Higgins. 'I'll have to consider what to do. It's what you do on the table that counts, not what you do off.' As he already knew, this was not actually the case but he was not much exercised as organizational difficulties precluded the event from taking place.

The tail end of 1978 was financially rewarding for Higgin but ultimately frustrating. He went out at the semi-final stage in both the Canadian Open (having just scraped through against Steve Davis 9–8 in the previous round) and the UK championship (beaten by David Taylor who went on to reach his first major final after a decade of professional snooker) which was now sponsored by Coral Racing and had a new home at the Preston Guild Hall – later to be the scene of the most infamous episode in the whole canon of Higgins-related bad behaviour. That said, the business with the 'Spitfire Girl' and the subsequent court case that put him on the front page of the *Sun* cannot be far behind.

It began innocuously enough, after ten days on the road and an exhibition in Plymouth. In the mood for a drink, Higgins started with whisky and repaired to the Ace of Clubs nightclub where a short, attractive blonde woman in a long black lurex dress and stilettos caught his eye. She was twenty-one and he was three weeks away from his thirtieth birthday. A conversation ensued during which he convinced Mrs Wendy Dring, a young woman who looked like a mobile hair-dresser who had applied her make-up in a very dark room, to accompany him to the Olympic casino. He lost most of the money he had on him and then cashed a cheque for £650, which he then proceeded to hand back to the cashier in increasingly large increments via the croupiers at both the roulette and the poker tables. He had been in better moods.

The pair then made their haphazard way back to the Holiday Inn where Higgins had already secured a room. Only two people know exactly what happened next but Mrs Dring was certainly thrown out of the hotel room after an incident amounting to something more than a scuffle. She was wearing a black bra and had a towel wrapped round her waist. There is no debate that Higgins spent a considerable amount of time hunched over the hotel phone trying to cancel his cheque for £650 as his new lady friend scratched his back in a comforting manner and attempted to kiss him. Suddenly, she maintained, he went 'haywire'. From this point until the arrival of the police, the stories differ. Mrs Dring told the court,

I was sitting on a chair beside the bed . . . I was moaning because he had stopped the cheque and I was with him and didn't want to be involved. . . . there was quite a bit of kissing but no sexual intercourse. Then he threw a whisky bottle at me . . . I never said anything to really upset him and make him violent. He was shouting and hitting me and I was trying to hit him back . . . I was kicking and biting and screaming and he was pulling my hair very hard. Complete patches were pulled out . . . I bit him in the leg and was hitting him with a shoe . . . he was on top of me. A knife just appeared in his hand. It looked as though he was going to stick me with it.

This is at variance with Higgins' account. 'She was scratching my back for about forty minutes while I was making phone calls,' he began, establishing some common ground. 'But she kept saying she wanted her money. When I spoke of £20 or £30 she suddenly denied being a prostitute.' In court Mrs Dring denied both being a prostitute and also saying, 'If you want me in the cot it will cost you money. I'm very expensive.' After admitting a conviction for an assault on a policeman four years previously, she responded to the prompting of Higgins' defence counsel about whether she was a 'little spitfire' with the answer, 'Yes, if I'm hit I will hit back.' That gave the tabloids the Second World War fighter aircraft reference they had been groping for and the headline factory went into overdrive – 'HURRICANE AND HIS SPITFIRE' (*Sun*) 'HURRICANE HIGGINS AND THE BACK-SCRATCHING SPITFIRE GIRL' (*Daily Mail*) and 'HURRICANE v SPITFIRE' (*Daily Mirror*). Higgins, for his part, rejected the assertion he had thrown a bottle of whisky at her with the jury-disarming response, 'The Irish and Scots respect whisky, they don't throw it about' and then went on to claim he had acted in self-defence. 'I was very frightened,' he confessed. 'I had no intention of hurting her. I would say I saved myself from injury that night.' The jury of nine men and three women, after advice from Recorder Lionel Jervis to treat Mrs Dring's testimony with 'great care,' took less than forty minutes to see his side of the story and cleared him of assaulting her. Lynn Robbins probably took a while longer.

By this time Higgins and his fiancée were living in a house in Burnage. People there still remember with something approaching reverence the 'house where Alex Higgins lived with the triangle-shaped windows'. In court, he delivered a heart-rending attempt at a soliloquy, 'After being on the road for about ten days or so,' he began, 'I am ashamed to say that, missing the young lady I love, who shall remain nameless, I felt I probably needed some female companionship.' The faux-chivalry worked and he was found not guilty of causing actual bodily harm. After the verdict, the errant boyfriend and his forgiving partner (who remained nameless no longer) were pictured outside their house in a style rendered risible several years later by adulterous politicians. Lynn Robbins looked angelic in a simple white dress with a plunging neckline and a clean-shaven Higgins seemed contrite and uneasy kissing his girlfriend for the benefit of the assembled press. There seemed to be something like a genuine rapprochement taking place.

Lynn explained, 'I was mad when Alex told me about that woman but now I have forgiven him and I know he will not let me down again. He was very honest about it and I never thought about walking out on him. Now I don't worry about other girls.' In the distance, a dog barked. The 'Hurricane' announced, 'It is all over now and we plan to get married in the near future. The temptations are there for professionals like me because we live out of a suitcase . . . Thank God there was a happy ending. This business has been hanging over me and it is a great relief to be free of it.' Lynn added, 'Basically, he's a quiet homely person who likes to stay at home watching TV.' It was a statement that carried roughly the same amount of credibility as Mrs Knievel saying that Evel was never happier than when putting up shelves in the guest bedroom. Higgins, revealing a hitherto undiscovered facility for deadpan humour, continued, 'It is a pity this all happened because I have been a good boy and pretty quiet over the last four years . . . I have learned my lesson – I have left my hellraising days behind me.'[7]

SEVEN

I'm extraordinarily patient, provided I get my own way in the end.

MARGARET THATCHER (1989)

'Miss Katherine Doyle, prosecuting, said Higgins was one of five men spotted early [at 6 a.m.] one morning behaving boisterously and apparently trying to stop passing vehicles,' reported the *Daily Telegraph*. 'When WPC Margaret Dickinson approached them the other four moved off. But Higgins remained and became abusive when told to go. He began waving his hands in the air and repeatedly prodded at WPC Dickinson. "He ordered her in a rather abusive way to get him a taxi," Miss Doyle said. At this stage the policewoman saw Higgins was unsteady on his feet and his eyes were glazed, so she arrested him.' He was fined £5 with £5 costs after being found guilty to a drunk and disorderly charge. 'He regrets the incident very much,' pleaded his defence counsel. 'Mr Higgins displayed some of the ebullience for which he is quite well known and while he would not have reached a break of three figures in this condition, clearly he would not have ripped the cloth in the attempt.' As if the counsel did not know that Mr Alexander Gordon Higgins was actually more than capable of achieving 'a break of three figures' in such a condition.

This relatively minor interlude took place while Higgins was waiting for the 'Spitfire' trial to take place, a period of seven months from the day of his arrest to his eventual acquittal. It was an unsettling time for the 'Hurricane'. As if he did not have enough to worry about there was the emergence of even more young players who wanted to take everything from him. Steve Davis and British junior champion Tony Meo were two of them. They were a cause of unforgiving and strength-sapping low-grade anxiety. Higgins had now begun to meet them on the circuit and one incident at the Middlesbrough TUC Club, just after the fight with Graham Miles but before his brief encounter with Wendy Dring in a Plymouth hotel room, revealed how much he resented the challenge to his status as the snooker wunderkind: no longer being the youngest and best on the block destroyed Higgins. Along with other disadvantages, it amounted to the withdrawal of his entitlement to clemency. Whilst conceding a two-black start to Davis, then still an amateur, Higgins went 4–1 down. He then lost two money matches, which amounted to his remuneration for appearing in the first place, and refused to finish the game with Davis until encouraged to do so by a voluble public who had wagered heavily on the outcome. For the record, he lost 6–2. *Snooker Scene* felt moved to record, 'His capacity for self-destruction is terrifying. Indeed, his behaviour is such as to virtually invite someone to attack him . . . He was lucky, many felt, to escape from the TUC Club unscathed.'

At the 1978 Canadian Open, after struggling to beat Davis, he went on to lose to Tony Meo, who only just succumbed to Cliff Thorburn in the final. Steve Davis turned professional on his return from Toronto almost as soon as he cleared customs. Meo joined him less than a year later. They would both sign to Barry Hearn's Matchroom organization. Another new player on the professional circuit, though eighteen months older than Higgins, was Terry Griffiths. As a well-behaved and dilligent professional he would join the Matchroom team in 1982 but at this stage he was effectively on his own. Griffiths had a typical working class childhood of a kind Higgins would regard as familiar. Like Higgins he also spent his formative years hanging around unemployed adults in a local snooker club, albeit Hatchers in Llanelli rather than the Jampot in Belfast, and learned the game whilst trying to gather enough money to get on a table. A prodigious ability with a cue and the will to win were the only other things he had in common with Alex 'Hurricane' Higgins.[1] Griffiths settled down early. He was married in 1969 and had a job in a colliery, a house less than two years later and, by the time Higgins had claimed his first world championship, two young children. In 1978, having left the colliery and worked as a postman and then an insurance collector, Terry Griffiths became a professional snooker player. It was a risk but he wanted to provide a secure financial future for his family. As Barry Hearn was heard to remark on occasion, '[Griffiths is] the only man in snooker who thinks a blow-job means a hairdryer and three brushes'.[2]

In a welcome development for the governing body, the fee-paying membership of the World Professional Billiards and Snooker Association was increasing exponentially. The dam had broken. The most obvious explanation was the arrival of capable outsiders such as Patrick Nally, Peter West and Mike Watterson who had persuaded major multinational brand names to become associated with the sport. Extended television coverage guaranteed that there was now serious money in snooker. The average working wage in 1978–9 was between £80 and £90 per week. The prize for a maximum break of 147 in some tournaments at this time was £5,000 – in other words, for a Higgins maximum compiled in haste, he could earn more than the average annual salary of a worker in the public sector for less than five minutes' effort. Any amateur player with anything like a century break to his name was bound to be interested. International business had been seduced by the ability and crowd-pulling potential of Higgins, more than any other player, to attract millions of television viewers and was now screaming, 'Where do we sign?' Publicity was guaranteed and the number of tournaments was multiplying so fast, they could have been in a Petri dish.

In early 1979, at around the same time Higgins was being arrested, there was the short-lived Forward Chemicals £10,000 Tournament in Manchester. It was a doomed attempt to breathe life into the Park Drive £2,000 format and was not televised. Higgins finished last in a four-player round robin. There was also the Holsten Lager International in Slough which was a landmark event for no other reason than that John Spencer made history by recording the first ever 147 in tournament play (a feat not captured by the unionized television cameramen, who were on an enforced tea-break). Later in the year there would also be the Bombay international, which Spencer won, and the £600 Tolly Cobbold Classic, which Higgins managed to snatch on the final black against Ray Reardon. The new professionals were in the ascendant as the old guard, represented by players like John Pulman, Rex Williams and Eddie Charlton were, on the table at least, being increasingly sidelined. Typically, Higgins was in his own category and, on a Venn diagram, would occupy the intersection between the first modern professionals like Spencer and Reardon who had broken through the glass ceiling in the late 1960s and the new breed of focused young men dedicated to maximizing their earnings.

Among this latter group proficiency at snooker or other 'games of skill' no longer suggested a misspent youth but, rather, the ability to make a rational career decision married to an extraordinary degree of dedication. It is why, with the honourable exception of Ronnie O'Sullivan and a couple of others, the snooker professionals performing at the Crucible in 2002 elicited the same amount of feverish excitement and hellraising, tabloid news coverage as a group of accountants on a team-building exercise in the New Forest. In 1979, however, the puritanical streak in world snooker was yet to resurface. The sport was more popular than ever before and television executives were falling over themselves to give it more coverage. It was cheap and, more importantly, it was popular with viewers of both sexes who liked nothing better than to go to bed on a Sunday after a couple of hours winding down to the narcoleptic click of snooker balls and the commentary of 'Whispering' Ted Lowe. In fact, the only thing that kept them from waking up on the sofa at three in the morning with dried spittle on their chins and a cricked neck was Alex Higgins. Nobody dared fall asleep whilst watching the 'Hurricane' in case they missed a bravura display of either spontaneous brilliance or random insanity during or after the match. He held the same fascination for the sedentary British public as John McEnroe or a motorway pile-up. And occasionally, when he was on form, a conflation of the two.

In between the Holsten Lager International and the Bombay International, Higgins was beaten by Perrie Mans in the final of the first Benson and Hedges Masters staged at the 2,700-seat Wembley Conference Centre. It was Higgins' first visit to the venue since losing the *Daily Mirror's* over-hyped 'Champion of Champions' tournament to Ray Reardon the previous year. Mans should never have won but Higgins, wearing an elaborate Chinese dress shirt under his waistcoat and indulging his fondness for licking the cue ball and cleaning it with a handkerchief (something he was subsequently banned from doing) was suffering under the pressure of his forthcoming court case. He was, however, determined to succeed. With one of his favourite tournaments, the Tolly Cobbold Classic, in the bag and the Irish title successfully defended against Patsy Fagan at the Ulster Hall in Belfast, Higgins temporarily gave up alcohol and took to drinking tea by the pint in preparation for the world championship. He felt good and disposed of David Taylor in the first round to extract a measure of revenge for his defeat in the Coral UK championship semi-finals the previous year. This time, Higgins felt that he was in with an excellent chance of claiming the £10,000 first prize. Reardon was the one to watch out for and Higgins had been drawn against the relatively inexperienced Terry Griffiths who had recently been recruited to Del Simmons' ISA stable. Griffiths, of course, had motivation beyond just having a young family to look after. He had never forgotten Higgins insulting and physically abusing a member of his family four years previously or casting him in the role of the pantomime villain to Higgins' popular underdog at the Pontins Open in Prestatyn. A man who could never open a self-inflicted wound without grinding rock salt into it, the 'Hurricane' had unwittingly given the quietly spoken man from Llanelli the taste for blood.

Griffiths was taking part in his first world championship and, had he not emerged from the qualifying rounds, was going to revert to being an amateur. That was a measure of his confidence at the time. After forty-six minutes of the first session he was holding Higgins at 2–2. By the end of the first interval he was trailing 6–2 and had been a spectator as his opponent recorded two century breaks. Higgins was flying. Griffiths gathered himself during the interval and in the evening sesssion pulled it back to 8–8. Higgins was definitely on top form but so was Griffiths. The recording no longer exists but Nick Hunter, the BBC producer then responsible for snooker, rates it as one of the greatest games he ever covered. In the final session it went to 12–11 with the outsider needing just one frame from the last three. Higgins pulled a frame back to draw level before gifting Griffiths an easy red in the final frame. He seized his opportunity and John Pulman, barely able to conceal his delight, remarked from the commentary box, 'The boy's really feeling in the pink.' Griffiths finished off Higgins with a break of 107 and, after disposing of Eddie Charlton and then Dennis Taylor in the final, became only the fourth player in history (with Joe Davis, John Spencer and, of course, Alex Higgins) to win the world title at the first attempt. He noted in his autobiography, 'There is no doubt in my mind that the victory over Alex mentally won me the championship. I then knew I could go all the way . . . Alex was top of the tree next to Reardon and I had beaten him on form. Even if I had lost that last frame, I would have been over the moon.' After the match Higgins was heard to swear, 'Fuck the tea, I'm going back to something stronger.'[3]

*

Less than a month later, on 3 May 1979, the British electorate also opted for something stronger and elected Margaret Thatcher as Prime Minister. The most seismic political shift in his lifetime did not register with Alex Higgins. As a high earner, he would subsequently enjoy tax breaks endorsed by her government but he was so self-absorbed that he was effectively beyond the political process. 'All politicians are the fucking same,' he told me when I asked him how he had voted in 2001 but it is difficult to envisage him not sympathizing with the philosophy espoused by Thatcher in October 1987: 'There is no such thing as society. There are individual men and women, there are families . . . people must look after themselves first. It's our duty to look after ourselves.' Whether he would agree with the rest of the sentence ('There is no such thing as entitlement, unless someone has first met an obligation . . .') is more debatable. Never one to waste time with long-term planning, it is the immediate restraints upon his freedom to do precisely what he wants at any given time that is his most constant source of irritation. In this respect, as in many others (including his demand for unconditional love from those with whom he deigns to form an attachment), he has a childlike quality which either attracts or repels those who have experienced it at close quarters.

Just over a week after the new Conservative Prime Minister stood outside Downing Street and confirmed that the Queen had asked her to form a government, Manchester United were due to meet Arsenal at Wembley in the FA Cup Final. Higgins, unusually for a Belfast Protestant, had adopted United as his team. Although former United manager Tommy Docherty denies today that Higgins used to hang around with his team between 1974 and 1977 and goes as far as to describe him as being 'a bit of a nightmare . . . [not my] type of company at all', there is little doubt that he had good friends in the United squad and was actually waiting in the tunnel with his friend Geoff Lomas to greet the players after they beat Liverpool in the 1977 Cup Final. Predictably enough, he was close to the Northern Ireland contingent at

Old Trafford, including Sammy McIlroy and Jimmy Nichol, but also to Lou Macari and Willie Morgan who shared his love of the high life and an occasional flutter. Two years later he could not join the team at Wembley as he was en route to a snooker exhibition he could not afford to miss. He did, however, put £800 on United to win and, four years before the introduction of the Sony Watchman, invested in a state-of-the-art portable television which weighed as much as a small child but enabled him to watch the game whilst in transit.

The game was entertaining enough but he turned the television off to save the battery at half-time and could not get it to work afterwards. It was probably for the best. With Arsenal two–nil ahead and coasting, United nicked two very late goals and gave every impression of being about to steal the game only for Alan Sunderland to slide in at the far post and take the FA Cup back to North London. As his £800 vanished Higgins listened to the second half on a stranger's radio which had to be pressed up against a train window in the frantic search for a decent signal. The chance to listen to the end of the game, although he might not have enjoyed the result, doubtless prevented the television flying through a window at the next stop and the kind of train-rage incident that would, in these less permissive times, almost guarantee him a custodial sentence.

Alex Higgins has always been a heavy gambler and once lost £13,000 in one day at Wolverhampton races (as with all gamblers, he claims he won it back the next day) but the size of the wager on something other than horses and the purchase of an expensive portable television on nothing more than a whim give some indication of the new lifestyle choices that Alex Higgins was beginning to make in the late 1970s. Perhaps the prospect of demonstrating his wealth and the power to choose who can and cannot watch the Cup Final on a boring three-and-a-half hour train journey on a hot Saturday afternoon played a part. Donegal Road and 'The Troubles' seemed a world away. He embraced golf and took holidays in Tenerife but he also had marriage on his mind. Although technically still wed to Cara, he was already living with his new fiancée in Burnage and looking for a better house somewhere else. If he settled down, he reckoned, it would help his snooker. He felt in need of sanctuary. Or, at the very least, asylum.

A series of exhibition matches in Romford organized by Barry Hearn to expose his protégé Steve Davis to the world's best players under competition conditions had convinced Higgins (and Reardon and Thorburn) that the new wave of snooker players was knocking on the front door. Terry Griffiths had already gatecrashed the party and was set to stay much longer than any of the established professionals wanted. He enjoyed a run to the final of the Canadian Open (where he lost to Thorburn, who had beaten Higgins on the way), shared the glory as Wales humiliated England 14–2 in the final of the State Express World Cup in Birmingham (the Northern Ireland team of Higgins, Dennis Taylor and Jackie Rea finished third) and then chalked up another appearance in the final of the 1979 Coral UK Championship where, after beating a frustrated Higgins in the quarter-final (and locking himself in the dressing room afterwards to avoid him), he eventually lost to John Virgo. It was all change.

The UK championship that year was notable for the fact that only one of the quarter-finalists – Ray Edmonds, a forty-three-year-old former English amateur champion from Cleethorpes – was over thirty-five. Jimmy White, Tony Meo and a twenty-four-year-old Lothario from Bolton called Tony Knowles were under the tutelage of John Virgo's manager, ex-boxer Henry West. Higgins immediately felt at home with this talented coalition of ill-educated, well-dressed, wilful young hedonists and they admired him. He was, however, struggling to get along with any players older than him. As already detailed, he had cultivated an enmity with Griffiths and, despite his invaluable help during Higgins' first months in East Lancashire, had done his best to alienate Dennis Taylor. He had already had one physical confrontation with

Cliff Thorburn and the public did not need to be told that his long-running feud with John Spencer, whatever collective nostalgic amnesia prevails today, was not for show. As for the old guard, the gentlemen with their rubicund cheeks and predilection for velvet bow ties and ruched shirts, who had dominated the game from the 1950s until Higgins' intemperate arrival in 1972, had retreated behind the scenes where they could pursue their vision of the game with more precision and the odds stacked in their favour. That is to say, behind closed doors in the WPBSA committee rooms and away from the table.

There was, in any case, a power struggle developing between the Del Simmons ISA organization, which was busy signing up as many good players as possible, and the WPBSA. It was threatening to develop into a major split. Griffiths, who had been signed to ISA in order to gain professional bookings, was worried enough by Simmons' proposed Professional Snooker Association to seek representation elsewhere. Higgins would follow two years later although his decision to move was, typically, fostered more by opportunism than anything else. In 1979 he was earning more than ever before and house-hunting with Lynn in prosperous areas of South Manchester but, before he bought anywhere, he had to orchestrate quickie divorces for both of them. He knew he was lucky still to be with Ms Robbins. He was the ultimate high maintenance boyfriend and she was a thoroughly modern young woman who had already separated from her first husband. She had once taken herself off to the South of France, met somebody and decided to leave the 'Hurricane'. He begged for another chance, she gave in and he put his mind to setting her decision in concrete. 'As usual,' she recalled, 'I was carried along by it all. Alex has a way of doing that. Before I could give the matter much thought, he took me to see his solicitor. While he sorted out his own divorce, he did mine as well. It was over very quickly.'[4] Alex Higgins divorced the mother of his first child. At the same sitting, Lynn Robbins annulled her marriage to a computer programmer who she said was 'very staid'. If she fancied a change she was about to marry the right man.

The ceremony took place at Wilmslow United Reformed Church in the Cheshire stockbroker belt five days into the new decade. It had everything one might expect at such a wedding: a vintage Rolls Royce; a blonde bride in an immaculate white designer dress; and morning dress for the gentlemen. The area was, until Neil Hamilton was defeated by 'independent' candidate Martin Bell in 1997, part of the second-safest Conservative seat in the country. It boasted a Porsche and a Ferrari dealership and the Victoria Wine in nearby Alderley Edge is still reputed to sell more champagne than anywhere else in the country. It is not difficult to imagine what the residents of this self-regarding nouveau riche ghetto[5] made of the hellraiser *du jour* walking down the steps of their local church while a phalanx of individuals held their two-piece snooker cues aloft. During the wedding photographs, the twenty-six-year-old bride, wearing the kind of perfect blonde bob you only see in the window of upmarket hairdressers that call themselves salons, appeared relieved. The groom, opting to wear a cravat, looked like the cat that got the cream. Not a man naturally given to the unforced smile, Higgins was a picture of contentment.

'Well,' says Geoff Lomas, his best man, 'That's because he was spliffed. On the morning of the wedding, all his relatives were over from Ireland and, as the time came to go to church, started leaving in taxis. Alex and myself had to wait for this old Rolls Royce they'd hired. [As soon as they had left] he pulled this joint out and I said "What the fuck do you think you're doing?"

'"Oh it'll be all right," he said. So we get in the car and he decides he wants to stop at this pub on the way to the church to have a last drink as a single man and we are running behind schedule already so we only had a half each and set off. In the centre of Wilmslow however, about half a mile from the church, the Rolls Royce got a puncture and didn't have a spare.' The bridegroom, with his unorthodox approach to convention, looked like being the party to turn up late to the wedding. Higgins and Lomas, wearing top hat and tails, began to thumb a lift to the church. 'Everybody who went past thought it was a wind-up,' continues Lomas. 'Fortunately one of the guests was late for the wedding and picked us up in his navy blue Roller.' There was more trouble ahead. 'When we got to the church there was a barrage of photographers there . . . [so] Alex started running round and putting his hands over the camera lenses and screaming "Only the *Mirror* can take pictures." Everybody was laughing but Alex didn't see the funny side, he was chasing photographers, jumping over the church wall and chasing them down the street and everything.'[6]

He started 1980 like he meant business and even an ear infection which hospitalized him on the first night of the uninspiringly named Padmore/Super Crystalate International in West Bromwich failed to prevent him from taking the £2,000 first prize. He also reached the final of the Wilsons Classic in Manchester but went down 4–3 to John Spencer after referee Jim Thorpe, who had clearly not heeded Higgins' courteous invitation to 'read the fucking rule book' six years previously, ruled another push stroke against him. Most neutral observers were of the opinion that the referee had made a mistake. In the next frame Higgins petulantly demanded that Thorpe check the black was on its spot. He refused and was castigated. Higgins was fined £200. It did nothing for his already overdeveloped persecution complex but he still felt as though 1980 might be his year. It was a suspicion confirmed by his progress in the Benson and Hedges Masters where he beat Fred Davis, Reardon and Perrie Mans to qualify for the final against Terry Griffiths in front of a record British crowd of 2,323. At the end of the afternoon session Higgins and Griffiths were tied at 4–4 but, as Griffiths was to reveal, 'Alex came up to me and asked if I wanted to do a deal on the prize money [an agreement to split it down the middle whatever the outcome of the match]. In this case, it did not really matter because we both wanted to win.' Griffiths went on to win 9–5 with a final clearance of 131. The 'deal' with Griffiths cushioned the blow but there were to be other outbursts before he reached the Crucible. Higgins was gradually working himself up.

The brand managers for Benson and Hedges were not slow to pick up on snooker's new-found popularity and decided to sponsor the Irish Masters, which was to be held at Goffs, a venue in Kildare usually associated with pedigree racehorse bloodstock auctions. Higgins was eventually beaten by Doug Mountjoy at the semi-final stage but not before being beaten by his manager. Fellow ISA director John Spencer remembers it well. 'I didn't know it at the time but Del [Simmons] had hit Alex. I can't remember why but it happened occasionally. A bit later on we were sat down at the table in the hotel with about thirty or forty other people and suddenly Del says, "Hang on, Alex has got these bastards to come and give me one." Three of the roughest guys you have ever seen walked into the bar at the other end. Del, being the bloke he was, said, "Come on, I am going to go to them before they come to me," and he went threatening them. They looked puzzled and asked what was the matter and Del replied, "What are you doing here?" They looked at each other and said, "Alex Higgins invited us in for a drink." When we looked we saw him stood behind a pillar laughing his head off.'

Spencer went on: 'People don't realize what a sense of humour [Alex] has got.' Sometimes it was hard to discern and it appeared to desert him completely in the final of the second Tolly Cobbold Classic a few weeks later. Played in between the group matches and the semi-finals of yet another new event, the British Gold Cup in Derby, the Tolly Cobbold Classic was sponsored by the famous old East Anglian brewery. It was memorable for an incident in the fifth frame of the final between Higgins and Dennis Taylor. Taylor was 3–1 ahead when Higgins was penalized seven points for hitting a red and a black simultaneously whilst trying to escape from a snooker. The decision was borderline at best. Higgins, frustrated at losing to a man he considered to be an inferior player and who he imagined owed him some snooker cues from when they were in Ireland, reacted by disputing the decision. He even asked Terry Griffiths, who until that point had been watching the contest, to adjudicate. Naturally, he refused. Taylor claimed he had not not seen it and the referee refused to reverse his decision. And then the trouble really started. The referee gave Taylor a free ball. 'This time Alex went berserk,' Taylor later recalled.[7] Higgins left his seat and appealed to the crowd, asking them if they had seen him hit the red first. It was an unseemly spectacle involving the usual drama and was captured by Anglia TV who were televising the event.

Higgins has an honourable reputation for calling fouls against himself, which is to say that if he commits a foul but the referee has missed it, he will volunteer the information. With some justification, he believes that this should protect him against the errant decisions of referees who have invariably failed to play the game at the highest level. Unfortunately, his obvious hostility to authority precludes any show of generosity from the kind of men who become referees in the first place. He has no respect for them and it shows. Consequently, they are disinclined to accede to his frequent requests to revise their latest ruling. It is a vicious circle. He irritates them, they frustrate him and then he continues to irritate them. Taylor again: 'A few minutes later, as he was walking around the table to take a shot, he muttered audibly: "Bloody cheat!" That was me gone. I couldn't hit a ball after that. I lost the match 5–4.' Although Higgins was genuinely outraged by Taylor's refusal to accept his word for the fact that he had not made a foul, he also knew that to create a disturbance would unsettle his opponent. Taylor knew it as well.

'Alex loves [aggravation],' he continued. 'It's a useful psychological weapon in his armoury when the balls are running against him . . . If I'm beaten because I can't cope with the pressure generated by the skill of my opponent's play, that's one thing. But to be beaten because my opponent cannot control his childish bad temper is something else. Professional players are entitled to some protection against that.' Taylor and the referee, Nobby Clarke, reported his behaviour to the WPBSA. He was, after other misdemeanours were taken into consideration (including a tantrum in Manchester when beaten by Jimmy White), subsequently fined another £200 for 'foul and abusive language to referees and bringing the game into disrepute'. He was driven back to Derby for the semi-finals of the British Gold Cup and, after some Olympic-standard drinking and two hours' sleep, lost only one frame in whitewashing Tony Meo. He then beat Ray Reardon to take a first prize of £4,000. Meo later commented, 'He's not human . . . nobody is entitled to play like that after what he's been through.' With £1,500 for beating Taylor in the Tolly Cobbold Classic, Higgins had made £5,300 profit, minus non-discipline related expenses, for just over a week's work. He could afford to take liberties and he knew it.

Marriage, or rather remarriage, seemed to suit Higgins. Since he had walked down the aisle at Wilmslow United Reformed Church in January 1980, he had won three major tournaments and finished runner-up in another two. He had lost the Irish title he had taken from Jackie Rea in 1972 to a presumably delighted Dennis Taylor but was still in great shape. And all without noticeably curtailing his high-rolling lifestyle. He was still a frequent visitor to Soames Casino, housed in a basement in Manchester's Chinatown, and, less than a hundred yards away, Brambles nightclub. Another regular visitor at the time was Manchester businessman Garry Kerton. 'Alex was in there a lot around then,' he says. 'He was always surrounded by people buying him drinks, usually vodka and orange, and even he couldn't possibly drink them all so he'd pass a few over to us.' Higgins, who had no snooker table in his house, was not practising as much as he should have been. He had also developed an addiction to Space

Invaders, the computer game that swept Britain in 1980. It was a game which appealed to naturally competitive people with good hand-to-eye coordination and Higgins loved it. On one occasion, having already turned up half an hour late for a challenge match in Rotherham with Steve Davis (who was also addicted to the game and demanded a machine in his hotel room for the duration of major tournaments), Higgins kept the crowd waiting for another forty minutes while he shot computer-generated aliens out of the sky. For that infraction, he was docked two world championship points, fined the usual £200 and warned about his future conduct. Again.

Subsequently, Higgins would move on to Galaxians, one of the new wave of Space Invaders-inspired imitations but enhanced with the development that the aliens now peeled off from the top of the screen to swoop down and attack the player. I know this because, as a truant schoolboy, I watched him play the same Galaxians machine for over an hour and a half in an arcade on Oxford Road in Manchester. He was chasing the high score and in a state of considerable agitation. His face twitched like the flank of an elephant bothered by flies as he licked his lips and deposited more 10p pieces. 'Fucking bitch,' he said more than once as his sciatic nerve went into spasm and he kicked the machine. Occasionally he would turn and glare at the small army of open-mouthed adolescents watching him with their blazers stuffed in carrier bags, but otherwise, he seemed totally absorbed. The instructions on the opening screen, 'The object of the game is to destroy as many Galaxians as possible without getting hit,' will have resonated with a man who was generally engaged in the business of inviting trouble while simultaneously trying to avoid 'getting hit'.

His reflexes were as sharp as ever before a world championship. As he explained in *'Hurricane' Higgins' Snooker Scrapbook*, 'I really felt 1980 might be my year – another year of the Hurricane so to speak.' But then he always thought that. This time, however, he had other considerations. Lynn was pregnant and he seemed determined to provide for his new wife and child, unlike the young family he had left behind in Australia. However, this was to be another tournament in which the new breed of young players made a mark. Kirk Stevens, in particular, started as he meant to go on with a break of 136 in a comprehensive demolition of Graham Miles before taking out both John Spencer and Eddie Charlton. Steve Davis, another player Higgins was keeping an eye on, came through the qualifying section to meet and beat both Patsy Fagan (who was beginning to experience a purely psychological difficulty in using the rest known as 'the yips') and reigning champion Terry Griffiths. At 7–1 ahead Davis boasted during a mid-session interview, 'I could see [he] was very nervous in his chair and I knew I could give him a beating.' The arrogance of youth soon was put in its place in the quarter-finals as Higgins slapped down first Davis and then a white-suited Kirk Stevens to qualify for the final against Cliff Thorburn. The 'Grinder' versus the 'Hurricane' for the world title promised a sensational clash of styles.

Several reasons have been advanced for Higgins' failure to reclaim his crown almost ten years after his remarkable performance at the Selly Park British Legion. A perennial favourite was the detrimental effects of his lifestyle but chief among them was that the two-week condensed format of the world championship gave him no time to wind down between matches. Higgins, perhaps more than any other player, needed that time and once lamented, 'It's very difficult to get yourself in the right frame of mind for two particular weeks of the year. Ideally, you need a month off to prepare.' Obviously, that was impossible. There were too many lucrative exhibitions and ranking tournaments to attend. For the final with Thorburn, however, it seemed as though he had managed to get himself in the 'right frame of mind'. He had taken to wearing a purple fedora for the championships, a piece of typical showmanship that the crowd loved and seemed to be a direct challenge to Cliff Thorburn's image as the 'Rhett Butler of the green baize'. The Canadian was frequently thus referred to and undeniably possessed the distinguished air of a paddle-steamer dandy from the ante-bellum South. Consequently, he generated a sizeable female fan club who called themselves the 'Super Grinders' and advertised the fact by wearing tight-fitting white T-shirts with their allegiance printed across their chests. In fact, Higgins and Thorburn were probably the two most popular players with the female viewing public: Higgins, the vulnerable little boy lost, and Thorburn, the precise opposite. The final had all the makings of a classic. It did not disappoint.

Higgins was utterly irresistible and took five of the first six frames. He was still four ahead at 6–2 and 9–5 before Thorburn started, as his nickname suggests, to 'grind out' results and level at 9–9. The press became increasingly excited before the resumption of hostilities the next day. The television audience, after seventy hours of snooker coverage, grew to over 14.5 million. The traditional interpretation of what happened next, and one which is supported by Higgins, is that he lost his self-discipline and began to 'play to the gallery' – yet another theory that has been advanced to explain the relatively meagre haul of titles when set against his sublime ability. 'That is how I lost the [1980 World Championship]. Playing to the crowds, trying to do it the flash way,' he noted a year later in his *Snooker Scrapbook*. The question remains, why did he lose his self-discipline? The pressure was intense but he had triumphed over it before and would do so again. Thorburn's style was also a factor, frustrating Higgins at every turn and confining him to his seat – the definition of purgatory for a hyperactive crowd-pleaser. But the former world champion had been 50 points ahead in four frames and yet lost them all. The answer lies in the way Higgins prepared when he had convinced himself defeat was inevitable. This is by no means exclusive to snooker players. It is a self-defence mechanism: to lose while you yourself and your opponent are on top form is unqualified defeat but to throw everything away by showboating is not quite a full defeat and means that the next time you meet the same opponent, you can believe most easily that you have the beating of him. In these situations, the eventual loser is the first to accept that he is going to be beaten.

To everybody (except perhaps one of the protagonists) it was by no means certain that at 9–9 Higgins was going to lose. Thorburn went two ahead, Higgins levelled, Thorburn pulled away again and Higgins caught him. At 12–12 it looked too tight to call but, as Thorburn began to pull ahead, Higgins, his tie long-since discarded, began to take on longer pots for less tangible reward. Sometimes he pulled them off, sometimes he failed. The Crucible was enthralled but the viewing public were not. In London, 140 miles away, terrorists from Khuzistan province in Iran had seized the Iranian Embassy on Prince's Gate and had already killed two hostages. As the SAS went in at 7.30 p.m., the BBC suspended coverage of the snooker to bring live footage of the breaking news outside the embassy. There was uproar and the Corporation received a record number of complaints demanding that they put the snooker back on at once. The fourteen million licence-payers watching the game had a point and, after ten minutes' coverage, the BBC switched back to Sheffield. At 16–15 and with Thorburn needing only two frames for victory he missed an easy brown into the middle pocket from less than a foot away. 'I almost died,' he confessed a year later. 'I was thinking, "If I pot this I might win the world championship."'[8] Thorburn tended to internalize his emotions and 'sat like Patience on a monument/ Smiling at grief.'[9] He watched Higgins, his shirt unbuttoned and at his reckless best, pull the game back to 16–16 and was able to summon reserves of strength to fight back. Higgins was condemned to sit out the final two frames as Thorburn compiled a break of 119 in one and then went on to win the clincher. Higgins could not hide his feelings, which was why the public loved him. They watched as the chance to become world champion slipped through Higgins' fingers and were glad, at that moment, to be mercifully exempt from the stress and pressure. But their hearts went out to him.

He drank too frequently, occasionally dropped ice into a glass as his opponent was about to take a pressure shot and lit up the sponsor's product for want of something better to do with his hands. When he fancied neither a drink nor a cigarette he flicked his hair and shifted about in his seat like a guilty schoolboy outside the headmaster's office. On this occasion his immediate destiny was in the hands of Cliff Thorburn who, after claiming the title 18–16, became the first man from outside the United Kingdom to win the world championship. He deserved it. When both players retired backstage they discovered Lynn Higgins waiting with a cake topped with the icing sugar conceit, 'Alex Higgins, 1980 World Champion.' Higgins did not throw it at her or anybody else and was sufficiently well-behaved for Thorburn to tell the *Sun* the next day, 'Marriage has calmed him down a lot.' Even Higgins was something approximate to sanguine. 'One defeat isn't the end of my life. I've got talent and ability,' he said. 'I'll bounce back.'

EIGHT

She left me when my drinking
Became a proper stinging
The devil came and took me
From bar to street to bookie

SQUEEZE, 'UP THE JUNCTION' (1979)

'You've caught me at a rather tense moment,' he slurred into the camera. It certainly looked like it. He was wearing a ripped dress shirt, a cravat, an old cream waistcoat and something that resembled a gun holster. He crashed down on a stool next to an old piano, still holding his cue. 'Tonight,' announced Oliver Reed, holding up a glass-blown ornament, 'I am playing for this trophy and you know how important these things are to us.' The audience laughed. Reed had his dark hair slicked down like Ray Reardon and was hamming it up, imitating Higgins by lighting two cigarettes at once, twitching and pouring half a bottle of Smirnoff into a pint pot. 'I understand, Hurricane, that you have calmed down a bit,' he continued with an arched eyebrow, putting pauses in exactly the same places a policeman might whilst interviewing a recidivist house burglar without an alibi. 'Tonight, Hurricane,' he said, moving right along, 'I am going to use that famous shot that you taught me that night on this table at Broome Hall, where I must admit you took quite a lot of money off me . . . but didn't I win at the bar?' Reed plays as if to break the reds and then, by way of simple trick photography, appears immediately at the other end of the table as the cue ball crashes into a garish toy clown which rocks to and fro. It was not the best gag in the world but the studio audience assembled for *This is Your Life* loved it. Higgins produced a wan smile.

In late 1980, however, Eamonn Andrews and the famous red book were a couple of months away and the Hurricane had already taken steps to secure his own image for posterity by agreeing to cooperate on an autobiography to be ghost-written by Angela Patmore. In between losing to Cliff Thorburn in the final of the 1980 World Championship and meeting Patmore for the first time, Higgins had travelled to Toronto. He loved the CNE Open. Making sure the fly on your trousers was buttoned was almost considered by the organizers to be an excessive attention to detail and he was allowed to play in a T-shirt. It was like being at the Jampot again but without the frequent beatings, coins for the light meter and having to score for the older players. He was not on top form, however, and went out to Griffiths in the semi-final before Thorburn won for the third consecutive time. His gruelling schedule took him from Canada to the Champion of Champions event at the New London Theatre in Drury Lane. The theatre had been the home of the Benson and Hedges Masters until 1978 but this event no longer received television coverage (and therefore sponsorship) and made an estimated loss of £30,000. Higgins went out early to Doug Mountjoy, the eventual winner, but was left to play a dead frame for the benefit of the paying public. 'He was in a foul mood,' shudders Patmore at the recollection of it all.

'It was about 1 a.m. and Alex had been watching *Quatermass* which had been serialized on television and he thought I was Maxine [a middle-aged woman on the programme who gets killed in a van]. I said "No, Alex, my name is Angela Patmore, I'm a writer and we are going to do a book together called '*Hurricane' Higgins' Snooker Scrapbook*." I had to explain to him that he was going to have to do some work and he told me to come to his hotel tomorrow. I waited for him in the foyer but he was three hours late and, when he eventually came down, gave me a bollocking for not coming up to his room in the first place.' The familiar attempt to see what he could get away with. 'I soon found out this was going to be par for the course,' she recalls, 'and then realized why the other players had reacted like they did when I had been backstage and announced that I was doing a book with Alex Higgins.' Some of his fellow professionals had laughed at the sheer audacity of the idea (one ghost-writer had already left the project with a stress-related mental illness) while those with an ounce of humanity just winced. The rest made their excuses and left. 'I wasn't looking forward to our first inter-view,' she remembers with academic matter-of-factness. It lasted about ten minutes and yielded nothing.

'I had to tell Del Simmons [his manager] that he had been paid for his time but I could not get him to cooperate. Del told me not to worry, he would set something up. And he did. I was invited to watch Alex play golf at Wentworth with Del, Cliff Thorburn and the footballer Danny Blanchflower. It was freezing but Alex was totally absorbed in the game. I tried to interview him between strokes. At the ninth hole everybody was telling stories and Alex was no longer the centre of atten-tion. He seemed to shrink. I noticed that this was the thing with Alex. If people weren't worshipping him he got very small. I thought "This guy has been misjudged, he is actually very shy and insecure." The best way to deal with him is to win his confidence and treat him like a shy person who appears to be very conceited.' The book took 'twelve weeks of hell' to finish and was rushed out in time for the 1981 World Championship. At the same time Higgins was collabo-rating on the book, he was not eating properly and was drink-ing to excess and played in eight major tournaments and exhibition matches all over the country. Also, his wife was expecting a baby. He was mentally and physically exhausted and it was beginning to show.

In the State Express World Cup, Ireland (featuring Higgins, Taylor and Dublin-born Patsy Fagan) won only one tie, against Australia, and were sent out at the semi-final stage by Wales after Ray Reardon took the final frame against Higgins. Chasing the high score on Space Invaders or perfecting his swing on the golf course were both taking up more of his time than practising but he still possessed enough talent to make it to the final of the Coral UK Championship. He arrived at the venue having had no sleep. On this occasion it was after a night spent with Lynn who doctors believed was about to go into labour. It was a false alarm and a clearly fatigued Higgins beat Willie Thorne by two frames to set up a meeting with sixty-six-year-old Fred Davis in the quarter-finals. He established an 8–3 lead whilst on automatic pilot before his venerable opponent staged a fight-back by way of a delicate snooker on the pink with only the last two colours and the cue ball on the table. As the white ball rolled behind the black Higgins was heard to remark, 'Why don't you just lay down and die.' Davis, who was either deaf or reluctant to take the advice on offer, pulled it back to 8–6 before Higgins finally qualified for the semi-finals. After the game he was, by his own standards, contrite and held hands with Davis throughout a post-match television interview. He explained: 'Fred knows I don't mean a thing by it.' This blithe assumption of tolerance coupled with wilful amnesia masquerading as a half-hearted apology is the hallmark of what should be known as the 'Higgins Defence'.

Reardon played his best snooker in years and came back from one behind to lead 4–1. Higgins, playing on pure adrenaline and relishing the challenge, eventually pulled level before winning 9–7. In the other semi-final Steve Davis annihilated former world champion Terry Griffiths 9–0. If there was ever a result which made people sit up and take notice of Davis, this was it. With his arrogant but casual 16–6 dispatch of Higgins in the final Davis claimed his first major professional title with something to spare. It was the heaviest defeat ever suffered by Higgins in a major tournament. Davis knew he had the ability to beat the 'Hurricane' because Barry Hearn, in his unceasing quest to provide the best available opposition for Davis, had contracted Higgins to play 'his boy' at the Grosvenor House Hotel a few weeks before. For Higgins it was just another time-consuming but well-paid assignment in front of a celebrity crowd. Even Eric Morecambe was there. Davis, putting the finishing touches to his remarkable work ethic, treated it like the deciding frame of a final session at the Crucible. Higgins had already worked out what Hearn was trying to do but could not resist the money on offer or the chance to put Davis in his place. He lost 5–2.

And Davis was not the only new professional trying to deprive Higgins of his livelihood. Jimmy White and Higgins were from similar backgrounds and played the game in the same way: if a game was worth winning it was worth winning with fluidity and panache. There was no other way to play. It was how the better players in the pool halls of Belfast and London began to recognize you. It was how you got people talking. It was how you got people excited enough to bet a percentage of their hard-earned wages on your ability to beat somebody else. Consequently, both players shared similar strengths and weaknesses. Alex Higgins understood Jimmy White but Steve Davis was different. Davis terrified him. He did not know how his mind worked. This young man had not misspent his youth (he even had O levels – at that time, in snooker as in football, a reasonable cause for suspicion) yet could play with methodical and calculated brilliance and was now starting to beat him. He was a machine and, to make matters worse, he had Barry Hearn looking after him. You did not just take on Steve Davis, you took on both of them.

The irony was that, without the 'Hurricane' coursing through snooker in the early 1970s like a barium enema, Hearn might have missed the financial possibilities accruing from the game and Davis, at best, would probably be nothing more than a very good club snooker coach charging £5 to £7 per half-hour for tuition and an extra £5.94 per hour for the lights over the table. But Davis had Hearn and Higgins was on his own. Of course, he had a manager. He had the same relationship with managers as Imelda Marcos had with kitten heels but he never had a Barry Hearn – a single-minded, success-obsessed, money-driven monomaniac with a long-term plan and the best interests of his most important client at heart. To all intents and purposes, a father figure who could protect him and nurture his talent. Hearn describes his relationship with Davis at this time as that of a 'big brother'. Higgins never had that. His relative autonomy, unchecked by wiser counsel, manifested itself in a hatred of Davis which was both genuine and apparent and exactly what the game needed. Some people called it jealousy. Higgins liked to think of it as righteous indignation.

The game had seen nothing like it since the fastidious Tom Reece and the reckless Melbourne Inman had given billiards a rivalry to savour during the first forty years of the twentieth century. On one occasion, after an Inman fluke, Reece enquired, 'How do you do that?' Inman, without looking up, simply replied, 'I believe you know my terms for tuition, Mr Reece.' In 1919, as the Right Honourable Lord Alverstone, the President of the Billiards Association and the judge who had informed Dr Crippen that he was to be 'hanged by the neck until he was dead' nine years previously, presented Inman with a trophy there was another incident. A recently defeated and clearly aggrieved Reece declared, 'Excuse me, my lord. But if you knew as much about Inman as I do, you would have given Crippen the cup and sentenced Inman to death.' Higgins and Davis, however, amounted to something more than a music hall double act. Higgins hated Davis like cats hate dogs and told anybody who would listen. Davis, for his part, has recently said, 'Unfortunately my overriding memory is one of not wanting to be in the same room with him . . . I never hated Alex Higgins but I never liked him . . . it was just that he was part of my snooker life so I had to collide with him.'[1] He took out his measure of revenge in the relatively safe environment of the televised snooker tournament.

While Alex Higgins was chasing around the country in every mode of transport available to fulfil diary commitments arranged by his management, Steve Davis was relaxing in Blackpool and focusing on the Coral UK Championship. Hearn knew that his ginger-haired money-making machine had to be divorced from the daily grind of the modern snooker professional. And he was absolutely right. At the end of his first autobiography, Higgins reflects, 'I'd like to get into the position where I could just play a few exhibitions and concentrate on tournaments but I'm not financially sound enough to do that. Hopefully, in the near future, I shall be able to afford a schedule like that, to give myself a chance.' Barry Hearn was busy providing Davis with just such a schedule. He had already worked out that the income that Higgins was chasing in exhibition matches all over the world was more easily available through lucrative endorsements with cue and table manufacturers and other commercial concerns (some of which, after Davis became world champion, even Edward de Bono might have struggled to connect with professional snooker). If the rest of the sport needed evidence that the Hearn–Davis method was working (which it didn't) the half of the partnership with a cue provided it by winning £5,000 at the Wilsons Classic less than a week after the Coral UK.

Davis fared less well at the Benson and Hedges Masters shortly afterwards but by then the other top players had already registered his arrival. The most consistent, in-form and dangerous established players in the world at this time were Thorburn, Griffiths and Higgins. However, the new world champion was already regretting his decision to settle in Britain,[2] Griffiths was struggling to come to terms with losing his title and Higgins was beginning to wonder if he would ever win it again. It was not exactly a collective crisis of confidence but opportunity was knocking and Davis and his manager walked straight in. Thorburn, in particular, discovered that winning the world championship was not the key to unbridled wealth and success he might have imagined. Del Simmons was looking after his bookings and told him to prepare for a busy year but Thorburn did not want to work excessively hard and he also thought that, as world champion, he should be able to charge more for personal appearances and exhibition matches than anybody else on Simmons' books – specifically including Alex Higgins who was then charging £600 per night for an ordinary club exhibition. 'You can't,' Simmons told him. 'Why not?' he asked. 'You just can't.' Even without his title, the 'Hurricane' was still the biggest draw in the game and Simmons knew it. So did Higgins.

He tossed a crushed packet into the bin and took the cellophane off another before it had even hit the bottom. With practised ease, he pulled out a No. 6 and lit it in one deft movement. 'Please put that out, Mr Higgins,' instructed a nurse as he turned his back and walked away towards the door. By the time he got there he had already smoked the first cigarette and lit up another without even thinking. It was a bitterly cold December day and he needed a drink. Although his semi-permanent state of general agitation could be compared to the nerves experienced by an expectant father, on this occasion it was the real thing. His wife was giving birth at St Mary's Hospital in Manchester. There had already been the scare just before the UK Coral Championship and, given the necessary participation of Higgins in at least one stage of the process, the situation was predictably fraught with danger and difficulty. The baby was born ten weeks prematurely and delivered by Caesarean section. Higgins was there to witness the birth of his second child. It was a little girl and the young couple decided to call her Lauren. He would later confess, 'Being of a nervous disposition, I don't suppose I should really have been there in the first place. Looking back, I wouldn't have missed it for the world.'[3]

Lauren was to make her first, but by no means most memorable, television appearance a few weeks later on *This is Your Life*. The producer, Jack Crawshaw, remembers it as being, 'A lovely way to end the programme.' The organization required to surprise Higgins and then arrange for nearly thirty of his close family and friends to be waiting for him in a television studio without arousing his paranoia was impressive enough but other factors served to make it remarkable. In the first instance, Higgins had instructed his wife that if she was ever approached to collaborate on *This is Your Life* for him, she should refuse. This made things problematic but was nothing compared to the mutual hostility felt between Lynn and his family in Belfast, particularly his mother Elizabeth. Following an argument five days after the birth of Lauren the two women were not even talking, which made liaising over what to include in the show extremely difficult. There were heated disagreements. Another factor causing a headache was the timing of the broadcast, as Higgins had engagements nearly every day of the week. The production team got round this by booking Higgins to appear with 'comedian' and 'pop star' Joe Brown in the Pot Black Club in London ten days after he had beaten Terry Griffiths in the Benson and Hedges Masters (when he had become the first player to qualify for four consecutive finals). It was his second Benson and Hedges Masters title and was won in front of a British record crowd of 2,422 for the final session.

Davis' early exit to South African champion Perrie Mans made the victory sweeter but Higgins was in devastating form. After oversleeping and nearly missing his quarter-final with Doug Mountjoy – an inevitable by-product of a life on the road and a newborn baby at home – Higgins went on to win 5–1. He was in no better state for his semi-final against Cliff Thorburn. The man who had beaten him in the 1980 World Championship final went into a 4–1 lead as Higgins struggled with an upset stomach which he ascribed, with characteristic eccentricity, to 'some West Country mustard'. During the thirty-minute mid-session interval he fell asleep and then lost the next frame to leave Thorburn, like a man waiting to step off the end of an escalator, needing only one more for victory. As Higgins pulled it back to 5–3 the pressure began to affect his opponent who then lost the next two and the decider after a Higgins fluke while 35–6 behind in the final frame. *Snooker Scene* felt moved to report, 'Three factors – a reprieve, a big crowd getting right behind him and . . . the kind of fluke which seems to convince him that the gods are on his side – combined to unlock Higgins' ability and produce his magnificent charge.' Unlike the vast majority of his contemporaries, in early 1981 Higgins had never lost from a commanding position in the final session of a major tournament. He always managed to step off the escalator first. He beat Griffiths 9–6 in the final[4] to claim the £6,000 first prize and complete, as Eamonn Andrews put it to an alarmed and bewildered Higgins in the Pot Black Club, 'a sensational win'. He went on, 'You have taken the big money snooker world by storm and you are known internationally as the "Hurricane" for the express action that you bring to the game . . . tonight, this is *your* life.'

It is hard to overstate the popularity of *This is Your Life* in the early 1980s. With just three channels available to the public, to appear on the primetime show was an accolade which meant that you were a national celebrity. It meant that you had arrived. This would normally appeal to Higgins' sense of his own self-worth and the reluctance to appear on it he previously expressed to Lynn can be interpreted as shyness or a desire to preserve his family's privacy. 'It is fair to say that we were a bit more than usually nervous,' explains Crawshaw. 'We didn't know how he was going to react, he was so unpredictable. We'd been led to believe that he would enjoy it once he got back to the studio but it was getting him there really. We recorded the pickup [when Andrews appears] and then went live in the studio. It was a little bit fraught.' There was also a concern that Higgins might be, in the words of a former defence counsel, '[displaying] some of the ebullience for which he is quite well known'. In the event he was fine but genuinely shocked. As Andrews appeared, he actually took a couple of steps back and lost the ability to speak. 'The thing I remember most about him is that he was like a little boy,' says Crawshaw. 'When we left the club he put on this huge sheepskin coat with his little pixie face staring out of the collar and he was very nervous. In the car on the way back to the studio he was asking myself and Eamonn who was going to be there but we couldn't tell him as it would ruin the surprise.' He had nothing to worry about. There were no embarrassing surprises.

The guest list was nothing if not eclectic. Amongst members of his family and snooker players such as Jackie Rea, John Virgo, Steve Davis and John Spencer, it included 'Radio One DJ' Dave Lee Travis; 'straight from pantomime' Dickie Henderson; 'top comedian' Dougie Brown; 'former England football captain' Emlyn Hughes and Suzi Quatro, who claimed to have lost £400 to Higgins in a game. 'And I want my money back,' she joked. 'That's Mickey Mouse money,' Higgins can be heard to say as the host talks over him. They were all, it transpired, the celebrity halves of a recent ITV Pro-Celebrity snooker tournament (Joe Brown had been Higgins' partner). Oliver Reed appeared in the pre-recorded segment which began this chapter and several Manchester United players also made the journey down to London but the show was light on appearances from genuine friends. Lynn Higgins considered the entire experience to be embarrassing and also claimed that, 'At the party afterwards . . . one of the family had a few drinks and slapped me across the face.'[5] Jack Crawshaw does not seek to contradict her but remarks, 'I would have heard about that. To my mind it was a very happy show.' The arrival of Lauren in the arms of her maternal grandparents certainly seemed to herald the arrival of more responsibility and a further stabilizing influence in the life of Alex Higgins.

Typically, his appearance on *This is Your Life* and his success in the Benson and Hedges Masters increased demand tenfold for his non-tournament appearances at a time when he was seeking to reduce such commitments. He was, however, still looking for a large family home in the South Manchester area with enough space to create a snooker room (he had convinced himself that this was the only thing stopping him from regaining the world title). He needed cash and, despite the fact he could still pick up four-figure cheques in relatively low-key events like the Irish Masters and the new Lada Classic, he could not afford to say no to lucrative exhibition games. Eventually, the reward for this diligent application of the Protestant work ethic was a four-bedroom house on Bridge Drive in Cheadle, a prosperous suburb in South Manchester. The property, to borrow from the lexicon of the estate agents who, at the time of writing, have it on the market for £475,000, 'encapsulates 1960s classic design' and is also 'A property of undoubted quality and individual style . . . [a] magnificent, architect-designed detached bungalow' which boasts a 'sweeping driveway' and a twenty-nine by nineteen foot en-suite snooker room. It resembles George Best's former house less than five miles away in Handforth, Cheshire. The journey from East Belfast to Cheshire was not impossible, it seemed. Higgins bought the house and set about creating a snooker room. Eventually he would buy the Westbury table upon which he won the 1982 world title and install it in a room which is now being sold, with some irony, as an ideal 'teenager suite or granny/au pair accommodation with separate access'. (The table is still there and available for purchase by separate negotiation. The asking price is 'between £4,000 and £6,000'.)

He was making an effort to settle down. His ghost-writer Angela Patmore noted that he even cooked for Lynn on occasion: 'When she came out of the maternity hospital, Alex didn't just knock up the odd TV dinner, he'd make food like pork with a really elaborate sauce. He prided himself on his ability to cook . . . I never met the undisciplined, selfish hoodlum, the room-wrecker, the nose-breaker, the uncooperative rude little Irish oik I was expecting to meet from reading large quantities of newspaper cuttings.' Jackie Rea, the former Irish Professional champion who had first advised Higgins to come over to the mainland, was also familiar with the other side of Higgins at this time. 'I used to live about five minutes away from him when he lived in Cheadle,' he smiles through rheumy eighty-two-year-old eyes. 'I suppose I was a bit of a father figure for him. I used to drive him about and look after him and make sure he got to events on time but Lynn was very good for him. She wouldn't stand for any of his nonsense and it meant he had a stable influence in his life although he would still get into trouble when he was with his hangers-on. They would tell him how great he was and buy him drinks and I don't think he could really handle it.' Of course, this relative domestication did not mark the beginning of a new puritan phase in his life but it did mean that, for the time being, he had a place of refuge from the storm. There were still wild nights out and binges back at the house with friends and 'hangers-on' but Higgins was also mixing with another crowd altogether and had found a kindred spirit in the man who had wanted to put him on the West End stage with Keith Moon.

Oliver Reed had taken an interest in the career of Alex 'Hurricane' Higgins from the very early 1970s. According to Stephen Ford, an urbane bon vivant and friend of Reed, 'He was fascinated by this little Irishman who had the same healthy disrespect for conventional morality as himself. He was also impressed by what he had read in the papers about him'. Reed engineered a meeting at his sixty-five-acre Broome Hall estate and Higgins, naturally flattered, agreed to attend. The film star sent his friend and unofficial chauffeur Dezzie Cavanagh to collect Higgins from Dorking railway station. When they pulled up on the gravel drive he greeted him with the words, 'So you're the "Hurricane". I shall call you Hig the Pig.' Reed was using Higgins' own method of introduction, albeit infused with a certain theatricality, to see what he could get away with. The answer was nothing and until Reed died in 1999 the two competed at and for anything. 'A typical night, or rather a typical couple of nights, would begin with a few drinks in a converted bar that Ollie had built at his house,' recalls Ford. 'Then there were a few games of snooker for money and then arm-wrestling or one-armed push-ups or whatever else they could think of but it was always for money or a forfeit. They were both incredibly competitive but also loved a gamble and a drink. They were made for each other.' On one occasion after Reed had left Broome Hall and moved to Guernsey, Higgins flew down to stay with him. The pair immediately set off on a two-week binge which, after drinking the house dry, culminated in Reed pouring a bottle of his wife's £200 Giorgio perfume into a half-pint glass and daring 'Hig the Pig' to drink it. Naturally, Higgins obliged. He was violently ill for two days. When he had made something of a recovery he mixed Reed a cocktail of crème de menthe and Fairy Liquid and watched as the international film star drank it. 'He was burping bubbles for a week,' laughs Ford. 'But Higgins had the last laugh. He was farting perfume. They must have thought he was the messiah.'

Stephen Ford eventually invited Higgins and Reed to one of his legendary dinner parties at his house in London. He had been a professional ice-skater but had met Reed as a successful businessman in the South of France. They had insulted each other in a bar and got on straight away. As a wealthy expat in Saint-Jean Cap Ferrat on the Côte d'Azure, Ford was friends with a number of glamorous and influential people including David Niven, Gregory Peck and the writer Harold Robbins. Whenever they were in London they attended one of his house parties. These events were characterized by life-threatening drinking and signing the ceiling. 'People just stopped when they passed out,' he explains, ordering another bottle of wine. 'It was a fabulous time but we had this little custom. At Ollie's house he always insisted that any diners inscribe their name in the top of the table with a six-inch nail. I had a new rosewood table and didn't want to ruin it so I provided marker pens. "What am I supposed to do with this, you cunt?" Ollie asked. I told him to sign the ceiling. So he did and whenever anyone came round for one of the parties I got them to do the same thing. Gregory Peck, Harold Robbins, everyone. When Higgins came he couldn't reach the ceiling to sign it so Ollie lifted him up. Unfortunately it was quite late at night and we'd all had a few and when he picked him up he stumbled and dropped him on the table. I'm not sure if he hurt himself, probably not because he was very "relaxed", but he got back up and signed it eventually. He only came round the once.'[6]

Steve Davis would have been tall enough to sign Stephen Ford's ceiling but was never invited. Not that it mattered. In early 1981 he was too busy winning titles and earning money. The Davis bandwagon was gathering momentum. After his success in the UK Championship earlier in the season he took the Yamaha Organs Trophy which replaced the British Gold Cup and was the first major tournament to receive extensive coverage on ITV. The network received such fantastic viewing figures during the four days that the first prize of £10,000 was worth less to Davis than the exposure. By the end of the year he would be able to claim victories in six major tournaments including, famously, the Embassy world championship. Before Sheffield, however, he also won the John Courage English championship after an unchallenging final against Tony Meo. He seemed unstoppable. And the favourite for the world title. 'There is no way I expect to win this year,' an unusually downbeat Higgins told the camera during a profile on the BBC *Sportsnight* programme. It was the eve of the world championship and he looked exhausted. 'I'll [soon] have my own table. I'll be able to live like a human being again and won't be hounded from pillar to post,' he said before predicting accurately that 'whoever wins out of Steve Davis, Jimmy White and myself will win the title'.

Davis beat White in the first round and Higgins in the second before outplaying Griffiths, Thorburn and eventually Mountjoy in the final. As Davis clinched the final frame against Mountjoy, Barry Hearn raced past the table to embrace his friend and business partner before clenching both fists and screaming at the television cameras. It was a vindication for his vision of how the game should be organized. As Davis would later write in his autobiographical account about his first year as champion, the predictably titled *Frame and Fortune*: 'On my second day as world champion, I attended a sales marketing luncheon. [It was] a very relaxed affair, with a few games of snooker thrown in.'

That was the Matchroom team at work but there were other new forces in snooker and Del Simmons, by now the £13,000-a-year commercial manager for the WPBSA, had been busy building a rival entity. The International Snooker Agency was signing up players like Higgins, Reardon and Thorburn while Simmons was also trying to attract, or rather accommodate, potential sponsors for new events. There had been five major professional tournaments in 1977, five years later there were twelve. He also arranged a number of endorsements for his players by virtue of his work as a consultant to a snooker equipment supplier who looked after Adam Custom Cues and Aramith Balls. According to his advertisement, Higgins found the new 'Aramith Pro' ball 'very pleasing to play with', although the choice of words might not have been his. Simmons had also arranged for some modelling work for Higgins with the high street retailer John Collier Menswear. Meanwhile, Davis had earned £3,000 from computer game manufacturer Atari for a fifteen-minute photo session and agreed a fee of £25,000 to provide a column for the *Daily Star*. He also put his appearance money up to £1,500. This was a source of great irritation for Higgins but there was nothing he could do about it on the table. He was still not practising enough. To compound matters an exhausted Steve Davis, who had flown to Jersey in between the quarter- and semi-finals of the inaugural Jameson International to fulfil an exhibition engagement, would beat Higgins again on the way to the final. The new event at the Derby Assembly Rooms provided his fourth major tournament victory in succession and took his winnings to well over £50,000 since the start of the year. Higgins had won less than £15,000 in the same period.

The situation then took a turn for the worse. Yet another new event, the Langs Supreme Scottish Masters, was organized (or rather, disorganized) for the Kelvin Hall in Glasgow. It was to receive limited television coverage from BBC Scotland but was played in a half-full oversized venue that lacked atmosphere. The organizers even failed to employ a recorder to keep an official note of the score and, of course, Higgins was the player to suffer for this oversight. Having beaten Vic Harris, he met Cliff Thorburn in the semi-final. In the fifth frame Higgins was given only 8 points when he should have been awarded 12. The error was not spotted immediately but when somebody at the BBC alerted Higgins to this injustice he took out his frustration on everybody in the vicinity including, naturally, the referee. Davis noted, 'Like so many people I find it increasingly odd that when a controversial incident occurs in snooker, Higgins is usually the man in the middle.' He was being sarcastic. Thorburn went on to win 6–2 before losing to Jimmy White who, at nineteen, became the youngest ever winner of a major professional tournament. It confirmed to Higgins that the boy he had first seen play five years previously also had a big match temperament. It was extra pressure for the 'Hurricane'. And it showed.

Davis was also under pressure. His new lifestyle was more demanding than anything he had experienced before. But he did not help himself. Shortly after beating Higgins in front of an extremely partisan crowd in Manchester, he was scheduled to accompany him on a ten-day tour of the North East and Scotland. Hearn knew it was the biggest box office draw in the game and would also be a difficult few days for Davis. But business was business and, accordingly, he had secured the exclusive rights for the sale of all merchandise at every venue. Part of that merchandising arrangement included posters of Alex Higgins. On the first night, as he walked past the stand and saw his image being sold to the public Higgins snapped and scattered the offending items all over the floor. He also declared that he would only autograph posters that were bought from him and threatened the promoter with a walkout if he was not allowed a cut of the action. The promoter called Hearn. Hearn explained the precise meaning of the words 'legally', 'binding' and 'contract' and threatened to pull Davis out of the event. To the immense relief of the frantic promoter, an uneasy truce was finally agreed when Hearn permitted Higgins to sell his own posters but retained the right to sell them also. Davis shudders at the memory: 'As expected, Higgins blew his top and continued to be obnoxious right through the ten days. He gave everyone hell. We stayed at the same hotel, but I made certain we kept well apart.'[7] In fact, he made so certain that he opted to make his own way from town to town rather than be chauffeured in the same car.

A glutton for punishment then, Davis agreed to appear in a *Daily Mail* golf competition at Wentworth a few days later with Higgins and several other players including John Spencer and Cliff Thorburn. Barry Hearn also agreed to play. Spencer had played golf with Higgins before and found the experience unusual. 'He would hit the ball,' he laughs, 'And then take off after it before you had taken your shot . . . I was playing with Del [Simmons] and Alex once in Canada. He'd already gone marching off after his ball and as Del and I came round the corner all we could see was Alex up to his neck in water getting golf balls out of the pond . . . I still don't know what he was doing or why he was doing it but we couldn't stop laughing.' On this occasion Higgins was playing with Barry Hearn who had set himself up as the course bookie and made Thorburn favourite. Higgins and Hearn also had a side bet of £100 and at the last hole, the Matchroom boss was winning by one. Higgins asked the caddie for advice on a shot. This in itself was a surprising development as not only had he completely ignored him up until this point but, when playing in a Pro-Celebrity tournament with Terry Wogan and Australian golfer Greg Norman at Turnberry, he had threatened to 'knock the block off' the six-foot two-time British Open winner if he offered one more piece of advice on how to play a bunker shot.[8] Back at Wentworth, Hearn had dropped on to the green but Higgins hit the ball much too far and, to the astonishment of none of the assembled, had a heated argument with his caddie. This was Higgins preparing his defence for the defeat he felt sure he was about to experience. Losing in such a manner conveyed the impression that he had only been beaten by events beyond his control or which had conspired against him.

Jackie Rea is adamant that had Alex Higgins not been from such a poor background he would have been a better golfer than he was a snooker player. 'Golf is a very expensive game,' he says. 'Alex was from a working-class ghetto in Belfast and there were no facilities. If he had started early enough, there is no doubt in my mind that he would have gone on to be a top professional golfer. He loved the sport and he had the will to win.' Rea would occasionally join Higgins for a game of pitch and putt at Bruntwood Park, a popular eighteen-hole municipal course less than five minutes' walk from Bridge Drive. It was perfect for Higgins. Phil Brennan was twenty-two when he first met the 'Hurricane'. He had been in the queue for over half an hour and was now second in line when Higgins and a friend asked if they could push to the front.

'You are joking aren't you?' asked Brennan, rhetorically, before telling them to get to the back.

'This is Alex Higgins,' replied the man with the former world snooker champion. 'We've got to be at a match later on and so we would appreciate it if you would let us play in front of you.'

'I don't care who it is,' said Brennan, 'He will have to get in the queue like everyone else.'

'Look, here's my autograph,' offered Higgins, testily scribbling on a packet of No. 6 cigarettes. 'Just let us play the fucking course will you.' The charm offensive was unsuccessful and Brennan dug his heels in.

'Sorry mate,' he explained, 'I don't want your autograph, just get to the back of the queue.'

He takes up the story: 'Just as I'm about to gloat and take the congratulations of everyone for standing up to the queue jumpers, the bastard in front of me says, "I would like your autograph, Mr Higgins, you can play before me if you like." Giving me the biggest smiles they could muster, he and his pal handed over the fag packet he had just signed and strolled onto the course. Following his successful "tee off" from the first, he then turned to the bloke in front of me and shouted, "Keep hold of that packet, son, it will be worth a fortune when I become world champion."'[9]

NINE

He could control a crowd but he did not want to control himself . . . Yes he was an alcoholic, yes he was wild and unpredictable and yes he could be an incredible asshole at times, but people put up with that because he was a genius.

DANNY SUGARMAN, BIOGRAPHER OF THE DOORS, ON JIM MORRISON

The confidence was all on the surface. He was looking gaunt, drinking too much vodka and there were problems at home. His tournament earnings had dwindled as his snooker suffered from a lack of practice and perhaps even a diminution of his hitherto impregnable self-belief. He was also seeking new representation. In Higgins' opinion, Bristol-based ISA boss Del Simmons was guilty of not devoting his undivided attention to him and working him too hard. He was undeniably guilty of the first charge (he was working for the WPBSA and as a consultant for other business interests) but as regards the latter, it was his job to provide work for his client. That is, generally speaking, what agents do. Given Higgins' inability to take responsibility for his own actions, Simmons was an easy target. The fact that he had negotiated an increase in appearance fees for the 'Hurricane' from £50 per night in 1976 to £1,500 less than five years later seemed not to matter. Higgins was bitterly unhappy. He drank to alleviate the depression arising from his circumstances but in so doing simply exacerbated the problem. He could not even find sanctuary at the table. The Northern Ireland team did not really perform at the State Express World Cup and were beaten by Wales in the semi-final (Steve Davis winning a single frame tie-breaker for England against Ray Reardon, representing Wales, in the final) but that was as nothing compared to his first-round exit to Davis in the inaugural Northern Ireland Classic. He capitulated in front of his home crowd in the Ulster Hall, Belfast. He was devastated. Another concern was the continued progression of Jimmy White who overcame Davis in the final, although this was tempered by his genuine affection for a player he had encouraged since he had first seen him play at the United Services Club in Balham.

Appropriately enough, Alex Higgins first met Geoff Lomas at the Club and Pub Exhibition in Manchester in 1973. Lomas was selling vibrating armchairs for arthritis sufferers while Higgins was demonstrating pool tables for a local firm called Hazel Grove Music. He wanted to try out one of the chairs and agreed to have his picture taken whilst enjoying its remedial properties as long as his mother could have a free one. Lomas politely rebuffed his request but when they bumped into each other a few months later Higgins recognized him and called out, 'It's Mr Arthritic Therapy.' He can remember faces in the same way he can intuitively read a snooker table – that is, with unnerving facility. Lomas was already interested in snooker and would go on to open Potters in Manchester in 1976, but at this point their friendship was bound together by the pursuit of a hedonistic lifestyle. They went out drinking, gambling and, as it was popularly known at the time, 'pulling birds' and when the club eventually opened Higgins treated it as a home from home. If he grew weary through either drinking or practising or, more often than not, both, he simply went to sleep on the benches inside the club. Potters was in the right place at the right time and was soon a successful enterprise making Lomas a familiar figure on the professional circuit. He also had contacts outside the game including Harvey Lisberg, a

Manchester-based entrepreneur with a music business background and an impressive curriculum vitae. Lisberg had managed 10CC through his company Kennedy Street Enterprises but, impressed by the increasing television coverage and viewing figures for snooker, was keen get involved in the game. Lisberg and Lomas set up Sportsworld to manage Jimmy White.

The Coral UK Championship did not have preferred tournament status for Alex Higgins. He had never won it and had been comprehensively beaten in the final the previous year by Steve Davis. Given his fragile mental state, the 1981 event did not promise him much but managed to deliver even less. It was, according to *Snooker Scene*, '[His] most indifferent performance in a decade of championship snooker.' After struggling to beat the relatively unknown Dave Martin[1] in the second round and then pushing past David Taylor in the third, he went 4–0 down against Tony Meo before the interval in the first session of the quarter-finals. Geoff Lomas was backstage. 'I went into his dressing room and he said, "I don't know what's wrong, I can't pot a ball." I said "Come on, it's not that bad, Alex. You can beat Tony fucking Meo can't you?" Don't get me wrong, Tony Meo was a good player but Alex was on a different planet.' He certainly was. Meo won 9–4. It was a cruel winter night outside the Preston Guild Hall and as Higgins pulled up the collar on his sheepskin coat to keep out the driving sleet, his world seemed in more danger of imminent collapse than it had ever done before. Del Simmons was to blame. Steve Davis was to blame.[2] Lynn was to blame. His father was to blame. The weather was to blame. The Preston Guild Hall was to blame. The fan who asked for his autograph was to blame. Everybody was to blame. Everybody that is apart from Alex Higgins. That went without saying. He asked Geoff Lomas to manage him that night.

'I told him I didn't want to cross Del Simmons but explained that if he cleared it with him we might have a deal,' smiles Lomas, ruefully. Based on this assumption, and more aware than anybody of what exactly he was taking on, he called a meeting with Lisberg. Sportsworld were about to take on Tony Knowles but agreed to also deal with Higgins and he signed a contract agreeing to a standard 25 per cent management cut. 'He told me he had sorted everything but he hadn't even mentioned it. Luckily Del was OK about it.' When the change in management was announced to the press, Simmons confessed in an elegant use of understatement that it was 'in many ways a relief'. He went on, 'I got involved in management because I was friendly with certain players. Financially, I don't need it but I have stayed in it to carry out my responsibilities to them. I wish Alex all the luck in the world. Naturally, I shall expect to be paid for any engagements or contracts I have negotiated on his behalf but I would never attempt to retain a player who wanted to go elsewhere. That kind of relationship never works.' As Kirk Stevens and Cliff Thorburn announced their intention to return to Canada, Simmons' International Snooker Agency got out of player management. Sportsworld, in an attempt to move the sport closer to the world of showbusiness, demanded £1,000 appearance money for their players to play in major tournaments. The WPBSA held an emergency meeting and, quite rightly, refused to sanction such a move.

The change in representation was definitely a positive for Higgins but it had no effect on the way he lived his life. He was spending less than four or five days a month at home by this stage and his absence was a source of such domestic disharmony that Lynn went on holiday to Majorca without him. She took her mother with the intention of having a 'bit of a think' about the marriage. Her husband, however, was caught in a catch-22 situation. Due to his fundamental unhappiness and the loneliness of life on the road, when he did eventually return to Bridge Drive the last thing he wanted to do was practise. Inevitably, that meant he could not get back to a standard which would enable him to win enough tournaments to spend less time on the road. It was an intolerable burden for a man who most close acquaintances considered to be on the verge of a nervous breakdown. The duties of a father and husband and the banal demands of everyday life also took their toll, although he avoided them whenever possible. To the perpetual chagrin of his wife, a typical day between tournaments or exhibitions would almost inevitably involve a couple of pints of Guinness before noon and then half a dozen vodka-oranges in the back of the Kenilworth public house whilst studying the form in the racing press with the unwavering application of a tax lawyer looking for a new loophole.

Eventually satisfied, and probably armed with a 'cert' provided by one of his friends in the racing game, he would either walk or be driven to place his bet. 'He usually had a minder or driver with him,' remembers Clive Davenport, the former manager of the bookmakers nearest the pub. 'He was always hard work,' he volunteers with an audible sigh. 'In those days we would have a board man who would write up the odds with a marker pen and, if a horse came down from 5/1 to 4/1, Alex would insist he had backed it at the higher price when he knew full well that he hadn't. Then he would say, "Do you know who I am?" and I would ask the rest of the shop, "We've got a fella here who doesn't know who he is, anybody else got a clue?" That used to drive him mad. But then he deserved it, he treated the shop like he owned the place.' On one occasion, frustrated at being unable to buy a racing paper, he began taking down the pages that had been pinned up in the shop and tried to reassemble it for his personal benefit before being asked to leave the premises. He was barred at least twice. If he then wanted to play snooker he would catch a taxi or be driven to Paul Medati's Masters Club in the centre of Stockport, ten minutes away. 'He used to love the table in the matchroom because we kept it to a really high standard,' remembers Medati, also a professional snooker player. 'Sometimes he would be waiting outside when we opened up and would stay until 3 a.m. the next morning. All the students and everyone used to come in to watch him and the room was packed and he'd play all night for them. He loved it.' Lynn was less keen.

*

'DAVIS DOESN'T SCARE ME NOW.' The headline said it all and 'now' was the operative word. It was September 1981, in between the Jameson International and the Langs Supreme Scottish Masters, and Higgins felt compelled to declare: 'I don't fear Steve any more. I've got my game together again and I feel I'm the only person capable of beating him.' White proved him wrong in the next tournament but Higgins was trying to convince himself. It was an anguished howl from a wounded animal. It became apparent just how badly wounded when, less than three months later and a matter of days after the defeat to Tony Meo in the Coral UK championship, he checked himself into the Highfield Nursing Home in Rochdale. 'Alex "Hurricane" Higgins is in a hospital bed crying his heart out. A tray of food remains in front of him, untouched. Alex can't eat. He keeps throwing up,' wrote Noreen Taylor in the *Daily Mirror*. 'A tray of lager sits nearby. Alex can keep that down . . . And therein lies the problem. But Alex is loath to admit it. All he can admit between sobs is that he is frightened and confused.'[3] The huge number of female fans he had managed to attract by this stage ran the gamut from young girls entranced by his bad-boy image and looks to the old ladies who sent him letters of encouragement and lucky mascots. They were attuned to his vulnerability. It was very attractive. The male fans who bothered to read between the lines discovered a new side to the 'Hurricane'. Most assumed he was just 'drying out'. Those who bothered to read the piece learned, 'When I finish [playing] I'm so lonely. I've cried myself to sleep many nights in hotel rooms . . . a bottle of brandy seemed to make the loneliness and the depression easier to bear.' It made him very human. The 'People's Champion' even more so. And, of course, they loved him for it.

During this cathartic exercise he took time out to respond to the mention of his nemesis with Pavlovian helplessness. '"Davis", he snorts, "I'll tell you what I'd like to do to Davis . . . I'd like to stick his cue . . ."' He then told Taylor where he would like to stick the cue and although she did not feel able to share the precise destination with her readers, it is fair to conclude that it was not a cue rack. He then continued with pathetic inaccuracy, '[He] will be haunted by me until I'm carried out in a little brown box.' He was fragile. He was, according to the woman sent to interview him, 'the big deal snooker king who is now just like a small, bewildered boy in pyjamas wondering what has gone wrong with his world'. Alex Higgins was prescribed complete rest and medical supervision but, with characteristic disregard for his health, checked himself out after a series of 'tests' had served to convince him he was not having a breakdown. Within a week he was in York to play Steve Davis. This is what people mean when they refer to him as 'self-destructive'. The label follows him round like a scent. Davis remembers 'slaughtering' him. After the match had ended Higgins took the microphone from the MC and got up on the stage to thank his supporters for their loyalty. 'In the words of Muhammad Ali, my greatest hero,' he began, 'I want to say that I can return! I shall return! I will return!' The audience started applauding and even Davis joined in. He could afford to be generous, he was in superlative form and, after a nine-day round-the-world trip, began the new year with a 147 in the Lada Classic. He eventually lost to Terry Griffiths in the final but he had still become the first professional to record a maximum break in a tournament and on a table that conformed to Billiards and Snooker Control Council standards.

The world championship was only a few months away and Griffiths was starting to play with a real sense of purpose. He followed up his victory in the Lada Classic with another trip to the final in the Benson and Hedges Masters. Higgins looked frail and had two chances to level the game when 5–4 down but failed to take them and was beaten in the semi-final. Griffiths was eventually overcome by Davis who had his name engraved on the trophy and placed it on his mantelpiece next to the UK, World and English titles. He was soon to win the Tolly Cobbold Classic in Ipswich but Higgins was not there. The event had doubled in size and now boasted eight invited players but an incident the previous year had ensured that Higgins was not one of them. 'The Peachey family used to run the event and on one occasion Mike Peachey invited some of the players to his house,' remembers Steve Davis, trying to suppress a smile.

'There was a parrot in a cage and it had no feathers whatsoever. It was bald and looked very strange. We were being shown around the house and somebody said "What's with the parrot?" and the guy just erupted. He said, "Alex Higgins will never set foot in this house again." And so, obviously, we asked why and he said, "He got his jacket, slung it over the cage, opened it, grabbed the parrot and scared the living daylights out of it. The next day all its feathers fell off and he's never ever coming back.'[4] In the absence of Higgins and Griffiths, Davis easily overcame Dennis Taylor to claim the £2,000 first prize. It took his earnings from first prizes in major tournaments alone to £85,000 in fourteen months. He took another £10,000 in the Yamaha Organs Trophy a few weeks later. Once again, his victim was Terry Griffiths. Higgins failed to make the last eight.

After losing to David Taylor at the group stage and issuing the obligatory declaration of injustice (referee Len Ganley adjudged that Taylor had not deliberately missed the reds whilst attempting to escape from a snooker, Higgins thought differently) the 'Hurricane' told his quietly spoken opponent, 'Don't ever speak to me again. Don't speak to my wife or my daughter. Don't even speak to my cat.' It was a relatively mild outburst by his standards but suggested that he was not in the right frame of mind to mount a sustained challenge for the game's major honours. His wife had told the *Daily Mirror* before Christmas, 'I can make him a cup of tea and he'll complain. He takes a few sips, says it tastes sour, and then he'll go and throw up. I tell him not to be so silly but it's very worrying. He's that temperamental.' The marriage was clearly in deep trouble. She went on,

Recently he's been telling me that he's been going to bed around one when he's been away on tour. But I know from various friends of ours that he's been up until four playing Space Invaders . . . I never worry about other women. When Alex is away he rings me at least three times a day. He's not going to be doing that if he's got some woman tucked away is he? . . . I think he knows that if I got to hear of anything I'd be gone when he came back.[5]

'Playing Space Invaders' can be taken to be something of a euphemism in this instance.

He was in a truculent mood and had already announced that he had no intention of playing in the Irish Professional Championship. After losing the title to Dennis Taylor in 1980 he had been irritated by the title holder's decision not to play him in his first defence and was also unhappy about the decision to take the tournament outside Belfast. Until 1982 the Irish Championship was played at the Ulster Hall on a challenge basis. The previous year Taylor had opted to play Patsy Fagan but the new tournament format precluded taking such decisions. Higgins still refused to play, claiming with a straight face, 'I have a commitment to play in Jimmy Tarbuck's golf tournament in Spain.' The promoter offered the public their money back but Higgins had a change of heart at the last minute and turned in Coleraine only to be beaten 16–13 in the final. He took £2,200 for finishing runner-up but only by winning one match and then losing to Taylor. Higgins performed better in the Benson and Hedges Irish Masters at Goffs, the bloodstock auction house, and fought back from 4–0 down against Cliff Thorburn to win 5–4. He was drawn against Steve Davis in the semi-final and confidently predicted that he would 'destroy' him.

Given Davis' recent run of form, it carried little conviction and the man he called the 'Ginger Magician' raced into a 3–1 lead. Higgins received tremendous backing from the vociferous supporters who had inspired his comeback in the previous round. However, frustrated at his performance on the table and conscious of the ease with which Davis was winning, he turned on them. Choosing an unusual time to make his point, the 'People's Champion' waited until the crowd were virtually silent before instructing his own fans to 'keep their traps shut'. The referee, John Smyth, advised Higgins to 'behave like a professional' and threatened him with disqualification. Davis won 6–2 and then lost to Griffiths in the final. It was the fifth major final both players had contested that season and, naturally, they were installed as favourites for the forthcoming Embassy world championship. Higgins was fined a then-record £1,000 for his outburst and went into the Highland Masters in Inverness, a recent addition to the burgeoning list of tournaments, in desperate need of a good performance to boost his confidence. He was whitewashed 6–0 in the semi-final by John Spencer and paid £200 for a taxi to take him back to Manchester to play golf.

Once again, he needed to do something. He decided to leave Sportsworld. Jimmy White shared the same management company. 'In [Sportsworld boss] Harvey Lisberg's opinion,' he wrote in his autobiography, *Behind the White Ball*,

Alex had been the greatest draw of all time but it had been ten years since he had last won the world title and the wide press coverage of the drama of his private life had frightened off all the sponsorship deals. 'If we'd had Alex when he was twenty-five or so, maybe we could have done it,' was [his] opinion. In their eyes, that left me to carry the flame . . . In a tide of alcohol and acrimony, Alex walked out, much to Harvey's secret relief.

Geoff Lomas was distraught. 'It was all right for Harvey,' he says twenty years later, stubbing out a half-smoked cigarette in an ashtray in a TGI Fridays in North Manchester. 'He didn't have all the day-to-day aggravation with Alex but he still let him go a couple of weeks before the world championship.' He lights up another Marlboro Light, shakes his head and exhales as he sighs, 'I still can't fucking believe it. Two weeks before the world championship . . .'

Terry Griffiths had prepared for Sheffield by locking himself away. He subsequently announced that he was 'feeling pretty good' before carrying on in the same inspirational vein. 'I have been practising very hard and am looking forward to my first match,' he said. Davis had been on the road and could claim to have earned almost £600,000 in the previous twelve months. However, the exhibitions and public appearances he had undertaken to maximize his earning potential as world champion had put him under the kind of pressure Higgins had been experiencing since 1972. He was whitewashed by Ray Reardon at the Highland Masters as Higgins was experiencing the same discourtesy at the hands of John Spencer. The difference was that Davis was young and inexperienced enough to still feel confident. Too confident. 'I decided my first tough match [in the world championship] would be in the semi-finals against John Virgo or Reardon,' he went on the record as saying. 'I prepared myself mentally for a struggle at that stage, and no earlier.' Higgins also pronounced himself confident. It was a default setting, but, as Shirley Fisher, an unlikely blend of friend, fan and physiotherapist, told the documentary team behind *Like a Hurricane: the Alex Higgins Story*: 'He always said he was going to win but no, I don't think he was confident.' He had just been rejected after approaching Barry Hearn to manage him. As he confessed later, 'I decided it would be best for me to join the Hearn camp.' Higgins realised he would have to lose some of his freedoms but he also appreciated how Hearn looked after his players. It was said that he even kept their cheque books in a drawer in his office. 'I was prepared to swallow the indignity of that for a slice of the action. Hearn had different ideas. He turned me down point blank, saying I was impossible to manage.'[6]

'These grey hairs have come from other activities [but] Alex Higgins would have reduced these grey hairs to baldness I'm sure,' explains Hearn. 'He would have been a nightmare to manage because of his mood swings and because of the type of person he was. I had the pleasure of managing

Jimmy White on two separate occasions in my life . . . and that was a pleasure, if different. Alex Higgins would have been a nightmare. I was very happy to book him, very happy to use him and he never let me down once in all the years . . . I certainly had plenty of aggravation with him but he never let me down once. But beyond that, no thank you.' Higgins maintains that having Hearn as a manager could have changed his career but the man behind the Matchroom team was adamant. '[He] would mention it on occasion but Alex would have mentioned it to a hundred other people on different occasions . . . it was a full-time job. You know with someone like Alex you have to live with them . . . he needed an arm round him, he needed to be told how good he was, he needed to be built up all the time . . . he needed friends and funnily enough he never really had a lot of friends.'[7] Besides, Higgins was a 25/1 outsider for the world title. He had no chance and that was where the serious money was to be made. Higgins approached Del Simmons who agreed to take care of his interests once more.

Simmons held a genuine affection for Higgins and knew how to deal with him. Paul Medati witnessed his technique at first hand a couple of years later. The Masters Club in Stockport was staging qualifiers for a major ranking event and, consequently, had a number of the top referees invigilating. Higgins at this stage did not have to play in the qualifiers but, despite having a snooker table at home, wanted to use the matchroom to practise. Unfortunately, such an arrangement was not possible as the WPBSA had hired the main table. The situation was patiently explained to him. 'He's called me over and I've had to say, "Alex, I can't do anything about it,"' explains Medati. 'So he's phoned Del Simmons up and he's going absolutely off his head . . . I didn't mind him playing on there because the crowd would have stayed all night and we would have sold a lot more beer but it was up to the WPBSA and Del Simmons was the main fella.' At the time Simmons was Higgins' manager, contracts negotiator for the WPBSA and therefore de facto Chief

Executive Officer. A conflict of interests which would lead to problems later. 'Eventually, Higgins said, "Here, Paul, you're wanted on the phone." Del just said, "Look, I know you can't do anything about it so just keep talking to me, after we've been talking for a bit just go back and tell Alex there is nothing you can do." So we had a chat for about five minutes and then I gave Alex the phone back and Del told him there was nothing anyone could do and he bought it.' Face saved, point made.

Hearn had no time for mind games. He wanted to devote his time to Steve Davis. And his devotion never wavered. Even in late spring 1982 when Davis, the hottest favourite in the history of the game, lost his title. 'It never crossed my mind that Tony [Knowles] could beat me,' Davis shrugged afterwards. 'On paper, it looked a pushover.' It was. Knowles beat him 10–1.

'Right until [the score reached] 6–1, I just laughed at my luck,' he reflected with hubristic resignation in *Frame and Fortune*.

I kept waiting for the bad run to stop so that I could work my way into the game. Then I sensed that it wasn't exactly going to stop, and I knew I was on my way out . . . When I left The Crucible that Friday night, I was trailing 8–1. I refused to be despondent and went straight to my hotel and ate a huge steak [and] washed it down with a glass of champagne . . . Barry summed up the situation when he ordered the champagne and announced to our entourage, 'We normally drink this at the end of a successful tournament, so rather than wait, we'll drink it now.'

Tony Knowles went to a nightclub. Steve Davis went in-off on the first break of the opening session the following morning. And then Dennis Taylor lost to Silvino Francisco while former world champions Fred Davis and Cliff Thorburn were also knocked out. And then Terry Griffiths was beaten by Willie Thorne. Higgins, who had eased past Jim Meadowcroft (his former practice partner and occasional chauffeur from

East Lancashire), wondered if this might be the year he reclaimed the title. He had already backed himself at 25/1 but was now made 4/1 favourite.

He told anybody who would listen that this was his year. After six seeds went out in the first round people started to believe him. He even started to believe it himself. He kept saying he was doing it for Lauren and, along with a bizarre variety of other pendants and keepsakes from fans all over the world, kept her dummy with him as a talisman. He also took to reading the Bible and sucking a crucifix. He was staying in one of the few hotels near the Crucible that would actually take his business (he would later have a manager book him in under an assumed name) and Lynn and Lauren were regulars in the players' room. The other professionals welcomed them as he seemed to be calmer in their presence. Regrettably perhaps, they were not there the day after the Meadowcroft game when he had a physical altercation with an electrician. Higgins had been practising (and probably gambling) with Kirk Stevens late into the night and the electrician, not unreasonably, wanted to turn out the lights and go home. Higgins, reprising his favourite master and servant role-playing game, objected. When the electrician refused to back down he ripped off his identity badge, tearing his jumper in the process, and swore at him. The former world champion was also reported by a member of the security personnel for urinating into an ornamental flowerpot. He apologized to the electrician but was booked to appear before the WPBSA on 17 May. Traditionally, the appointment with Mr Higgins came just before 'any other business'. In the meantime, he had Doug Mountjoy to beat.

Despite the fact that Mountjoy was seeded six and Higgins eleven,[8] the clever money went on Higgins. There was momentum building. He turned up for the opening session in a fedora, and greeted the crowd by doffing it and sticking out his tongue. As usual, they loved it. He knew they would. Even the usually undemonstrative Mountjoy registered the flicker of a smile. The private thoughts of Ted Lowe are unrecorded. With the crowd on his side, Higgins got straight down to business: tie off, cuffs rolled up, a cigarette on the go and a shirt of dubious sartorial merit. Mountjoy was snookered on the blue in the opening frame but escaped by judicious use of the rest. The blue was on for Higgins but the pink, lying next to the cushion, seemed unpottable. 'One consolation there, Rex,' expostulated Lowe, 'the pink has gone safe.' 'Yes,' replied Williams, 'You beat me to it . . . I was just going to say the same thing myself, that could be the saving grace for Doug.' Higgins, chewing gum, paced around the table like a jaguar. And then pounced. He shot the blue into the side pocket with left-hand side, coming off the bottom cushion and knocking the pink over the same pocket which had just consented to accept the blue. 'What a great shot that is from Higgins,' whispered Lowe, choking on his words. It was not just great, it was sensational and utterly defined the man. The audience actually gasped at the audacity and arrogance of it all. It was breathtaking. Higgins twitched. But only because he could not help it.

He went 8–7 ahead in the next session and, in keeping with the tone he adopted when addressing the media ('I would kill to win the world title again') he wore a blood red shirt. Mountjoy wore maroon. It was almost as if the sponsors had dictated the livery. Higgins had a medallion around his neck which ticked like a metronome as he hung over the table. He was wearing a double-breasted waistcoat and, when he was not playing, made use of his time by scratching his head and drinking a pint of blackcurrant. Meanwhile, Mountjoy puffed away on the sponsor's product. The table between them was crowded with ashtrays, glasses, both half-empty and half-full – the usual detritus from a good night out. As Higgins took the sixteenth frame, Mountjoy leaned back in his chair, poker-faced. When he subsequently missed the pink and Higgins doubled it into the pocket it must have crossed his mind that the game was up but he fought on until 13–12. 'The gods answered my prayers,' announced Higgins dramatically after the final ball dropped in. At the end of every session adolescent young men asked Higgins to sign their programmes. He refused. He was focused on the next challenge although he still found time to deliver a sideswipe at Steve Davis. 'He needs perhaps six months away from the showbiz side of the game to get back to where he was,' Higgins announced, without even bothering to conceal his glee. 'He has lost all his freshness.' He could afford to 'glory in slaughter', a phrase that was temporarily in vogue after Denis Healey accused Prime Minister Margaret Thatcher of doing precisely the same thing whilst prosecuting the Falklands War.

The next challenge was to beat Willie Thorne, the man who had beaten both Terry Griffiths and John Spencer. Higgins was honest enough to admit, 'I am not hitting the balls all that well at the moment but the further I go in this tournament the better I'll get.' He knew it was going to be tough and he was not wrong. Thorne had a reputation for achieving more 147s in non-tournament situations than any other player on the circuit and could make the compiling of large breaks look effortless. As he racked up 143 at the start of the second session, the highest break of the championship, an out-of-focus Alex Higgins can be seen, pale and drawn, looking round the referee like an old woman craning her neck round the side of a bus shelter. He has the cue resting in the crook of his arm and is clicking the flint on his lighter as though he might be on a sponsored smoke. The *Belfast Telegraph* led with the optimistic headline, 'HIGGINS STAYS IN CHARGE'. He was never behind and, although it was fraught, he eventually prevailed 13–10. His bizarre regime, involving the substitution of vitamin pills for food and going to bed at 7 p.m. before waking nine hours later and travelling to the Crucible to practise, seemed to be working. The semi-final was next.

'Jimmy's at the bottom of the list, he's young and I'm thirty-three,' replied Higgins with a rattlesnake smile when asked by TV presenter David Vine to assess the chances of the four semi-finalists. '[Eddie] Charlton', he added, before pausing and then delivering with perfect comic timing, 'is whatever he is.' Ray Reardon had the honour of receiving the only backhanded compliment. 'As for Count Dracula [Reardon's quasi-affectionate nickname], if he's got a full moon he can do anything.' Higgins had no immediate business with Steady Eddie or the undead, it was his unseeded protégé he had to beat. As he put it himself, 'the "Whirlwind" against the "Hurricane" – it would be more at home in the Florida Keys.' Jimmy White had enjoyed a relatively pain-free journey to the semi-final. He had come through the qualifiers and dispatched a dispirited Cliff Thorburn and then both Perrie Mans and Kirk Stevens with little obvious difficulty. 'The other semi-final', an appellation that on this occasion fitted it like a bespoke suit, affected an air of nonchalance in front of a number of empty seats. Reardon won 16–11 but the footage can be watched only on fast forward. Everybody was waiting for Higgins and White. The young pretender was expected to win and emerged as the favourite at 7/4 with Higgins and Reardon at 9/4. 'I have only had about half a dozen wild shots in the championship this year,' said Higgins, declaring his new cautious approach. 'I am certainly not going to take any chances against Jimmy. [He] is a dangerous man but then so am I. It should be a marvellous match.'

Before walking out to begin the contest Higgins waited until his name was announced. Using a trick he had learned from Geoff Lomas, he then waited thirty seconds longer. Just long enough for the audience to wonder whether he would turn up at all and begin to speculate what kind of mayhem had taken place backstage. The expectation served to excite the crowd. White, looking even younger than his nineteen years and like an extra from *Grange Hill*, was in traditional 'black tie', Higgins was wearing a black satin shirt with lavender collar and cuffs. Tie off. The former world champion shot into a 4–1 lead before twice complaining about various technical irrelevancies to John Williams, the *Pot Black* referee who had been in charge during the farcical 'rain stopped play' championship game between Higgins and Fred Davis in Manchester in 1973. White had nothing to lose and therefore nothing to fear. He pulled the sixth frame back with a clearance of 69 in less than three minutes. One ball every ten seconds. He then carried on to build a lead like he was playing Top Trumps. If he lost this one, he would almost certainly win the next. He did not seem to care and went 8–6 up. He was in control but, ultimately, Higgins wanted and needed it more.

Higgins was 40 points behind in the next frame. There were 59 points on the table. It was the final frame of the penultimate session and, in a white dress shirt with black collar and cuffs, he approached the table with his familiar arrogance, as if he might be smearing insects into the carpet with every step. White missed a difficult red but Higgins was at the table before the cue ball had come to a rest. He sank a long one into the bottom pocket on his way to a break of 8. White responded with a faster and even more dramatic long pot into the other bottom pocket. The audience, getting carried away, were reprimanded by the referee. White missed a sitter that would have taken him to 9 points. Higgins snookered him. The tension was causing unforced errors. White swerved out of the snooker but left his opponent with half a chance on a long red. Higgins disposed of it with the cold-hearted efficiency of a truant picking off rats with an air rifle. After an extended bout of safety play Higgins took the frame on the final black. He shook hands with his opponent and, his hair raffishly askew, walked back to the table, stroking his chin and sticking out his tongue. He acknowledged the crowd and sank into his seat like a boxer collapsing into the corner after a heavy round. He drained whatever was in his glass. The whole process took less than seven seconds. Even with his back to the crowd, all eyes were upon him. He won the last three frames of the third session in thirty-four minutes to take the game to 11–11.

The entire nation was gripped. In a flat that once belonged to Sid Vicious in Maida Vale, North London, a founder member of the New York Dolls and the future guru behind mid-1980s pop experiment Sigue Sigue Sputnik had the television on. Johnny Thunders was spaced out on heroin. Tony James, who had also been in Generation X with Billy Idol, was trying to explain the intricacies involved in the game of snooker to him. 'At first he wasn't interested,' remembers James. 'But as he watched Higgins he became more animated. He loved it. He was, shall we say, in his typical state of being but he was transfixed. I remember it like yesterday. It was the all-time classic game . . . Higgins was my hero. I only met him once. We were at a party to celebrate the opening of the Hippodrome. I caught him out of the corner of my eye and then suddenly the crowd parted and he walked up to me. He wanted to know if I could get him any charlie.' And? 'I couldn't help him. Obviously . . . Thunders loved him though. It was the best game of snooker I have ever seen and Thunders was right there with me. It was an incredible thing to watch.'

For the final session, Higgins turned up in a cobalt blue shirt. White went ahead but in the next frame Higgins potted the brown after hitting five cushions. *Snooker Scene* claimed it touched six but they were one out. It hardly diminished the feat. 'What a lucky fella Alex is,' despaired the commentator. There did not seem to be much luck about it. The protagonist regarded the table with a shake of the head, like a builder preparing a quote for a loft conversion and, job done, offered no gesture of surprise. Both players were smoking and drinking. In the next frame White made a break of 46 in the time it takes to make two rounds of toast. It was to no avail. A defiant and by now perfectionist Higgins went ahead for the first time since White had tied the match at 4–4. He was a mass of nervous tension, picking his nails, drinking too fast, walking back to his seat with his hand on his hip and the cue held like an épée. It was cut and thrust indeed. White led 15–14. In frame 30, needing one more to win, he struck first with a break of 41. As the camera zoomed in on a sedentary and depressed Alex Higgins, his thoughts were captured perfectly by commentator Jack Kareham as he observed, 'Alex [is] finding it hard to bear I think at the moment.' Almost immediately Jimmy White missed a black.

Higgins addressed the table with unusual consideration. He needed to win this frame for the match. He had made the decision to play safe, still an alien doctrine but one which he felt able to embrace when absolutely necessary. And it was, at this point, absolutely necessary. White remained standing. The shot was not safe enough and the teenager started potting balls like he was involved in practising rather than contesting a world championship semi-final. 'You get the feeling that this could be the winning break,' added the disembodied voice on the television. And then White missed. 'So Alex breathes again,' it gasped. There were enough points on the table for Higgins to win and the following ten minutes are generally regarded to be the greatest display of tournament snooker ever witnessed. He claimed to have been inspired by Ali against George Foreman in 1974 when he found it necessary to rebuild his game but this was putting it into full effect. A wildly popular comeback against all the odds.

Angela Patmore, an authority on the mindset of the professional sportsman,[9] was not surprised. 'In order to get the best out of himself in a dangerous situation [Higgins] had to go very near the wire to be able to play to the height of his game. His optimum performances came when he was about to lose . . . he would deliberately place himself in a position of being about to lose in order to bring out the best of his genius. And then you'd see the reaction of the crowd. When he was losing they'd sink down but when he started to build up they would literally roar, it was as if their lives depended on it. They were identifying with Alex because he was the "People's Champion". He represented them in some way.'[10] In the 1982 World Championship semi-final, it was a study of grace under pressure – only momentarily disturbed when Higgins stuck Lauren's dummy in his mouth and cleaned one of the balls with a cloth (a fly reference to the fact that

'Bring my baby, bring me my baby . . .'
(*Trevor Smith*)

The 1982 world champion with his baby, his trophy and his cheque. In that order.
(*Mirrorpix*)

The happy family: Alex, Lauren and Lynn. 'This is where my problems really begin,' Lynn told the wife of another professional later that night. (*Trevor Smith*)

The sorcerer and his apprentice. Higgins and White during their epic 1982 world championship semi-final. (*Trevor Smith*)

His mother and father celebrate their son's second world title with the neighbours and the nearest trophy to hand. Higgins was otherwise detained and could not get back to Belfast the next day. (*Pacemaker Press*)

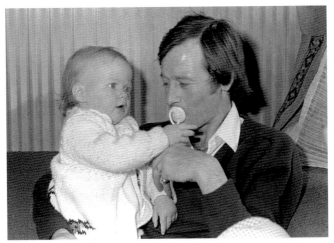

Father and, for a while, the most famous daughter in the country. (*Trevor Smith*)

Packet of fags, can of lager and a pile of fan mail. Life had been worse and would be again. (*Mirrorpix*)

Steve Davis (*left*) with orange juice. Alex Higgins (*right*) with cigarette. (*Trevor Smith*)

Right: Higgins with Eddie Charlton. It is fair to say that they did not care for each other. (*Trevor Smith*)

Left: Higgins demonstrates his feelings about the WPBSA mandatory tie rule. (*Trevor Smith*)

Below: 'Nobody can read a table like me, nobody.' (*Trevor Smith*)

Higgins in tears after the 1984 world championship final. He had been in the audience. Steve Davis had just beaten Jimmy White. (*Trevor Smith*)

Higgins and Dennis Taylor pictured four years before the infamous clash between them. (*Trevor Smith*)

Left: One of the publicity photographs for the release of 'The Wanderer.' (Back row) Jimmy White, Alex Higgins, Tony Knowles, Kirk Stevens. (Front row) Rick Parfitt, Francis Rossi. Parfitt and Rossi were not on the record. (*Trevor Smith*)

Right: At a Miss American Football pageant in 1986. (*News Group Newspapers*)

Left: Alex Higgins about to experience a champagne supernova on a yacht in the South of France in 1989.
(*Jim Duxbery/Rex Features*)

Below left: The young man on the left is a pre-pubescent Ronnie O'Sullivan.
(*News Group Newspapers*)

Below right: The pride of East Belfast.
(*Getty Images UK*)

the WPBSA had banned him from cleaning the balls by licking them). He was motivating the crowd to motivate himself.

He potted a long green and an equally difficult red. The cue ball disappeared behind the yellow and then he potted an exquisite black ('That's a tremendous shot under pressure,' announced one of the commentary team before adding with just a soupçon of syntactic inversion, 'a lot of courage Alex has got.') The two sides of his face twitched independently. He knew he could not afford to make a mistake and let White in. That was his concern. He sank a blue into the top pocket with just enough side to get onto a vulnerable red ('Another beautiful shot'), an easy black, a red and, to reduce the difference to 25, another easy black. The six-year-old Ronnie O'Sullivan was watching him in front of a Redifusion television set in Essex. 'He had a lot of bottle,' says the 2001 World Champion. He is a man who is acutely aware of what it takes to win the world title. 'He pulled shots out of the bag and [managed] clearances that, to this day, you will never see again. Unless another Alex Higgins comes along.' He smiles and then raises his eyebrows and smiles, as if to say 'like there could be another Alex Higgins'. 'He just cleared up from impossible positions. I still watch the video [of the 1982 semifinal] and I think that it's the most stupid clearance I have ever seen in my life. I don't know how Jimmy must have felt afterwards but he must look back and think it must have been his destiny not to win the world title . . . you watch it now and you just think how did he clear up from there?'

With furtive glances towards the scoreboard, his brain working out the kind of mathematics Alan Turing had to invent a computer to undertake, Higgins dropped a red into the centre pocket. All the important balls were on their spots. He took an easy black and then tore into the colours. He needed all of them and, as he said later, 'I was in no mood for snookers.' He compiled a break of 69 and it meant everything. As he journeyed back to his seat he raised a finger. In a non-offensive way for once. At 15–15 it might have meant 'one more to go' or 'I'm number one' or he might have meant something else altogether. But, whatever he meant, there was certainly a spring in his step. He sat down, had a drink and lit a cigarette. He knew qualifying for the final was a matter of minutes away and so did his opponent. White took the first six points of the deciding frame before letting Higgins have a look-in. When he got the chance he took it. Confined to his seat, White was demoralized and looked it.

'Alex [is] rising to the occasion here,' explained the BBC unnecessarily. 'This really is something.' It was more than something. It was the 1968 Elvis Comeback special with an open-necked shirt and a waistcoat instead of a black leather one-piece suit and a cue instead of a guitar.

With a break of 52 on the go, Higgins split the reds. The balls did not run for him but he still managed to pot one. Jimmy White looked as though he had just received his CSE results. After Higgins' break of 59 he needed all the reds. He managed a red and a blue and then missed another simple pot. Game over. Higgins knew he had won. Another difficult red also disappeared down the centre pocket like a mouse with a piece of cheese in its mouth. White needed snookers. At 63 behind with 51 on the table, he was merely putting off the inevitable. As Higgins smirked at a difficult cut which went into the middle pocket, White resigned himself to losing. He was a young man and there would be many other opportunities to win the world title. As Higgins snookered himself and fouled on the yellow White conceded and proffered his hand. Higgins took it, pulled him close and gave him a kiss. They were both emotional. The audience stood up to acclaim the winner. He picked up one of his lucky charms, pressed it to his lips and then slipped it into his pocket like he was dropping a cube of chalk in there. 'I'm doing this for Lauren,' he would tell the press after phoning his mother in Belfast. 'I've got the ten-year itch. There's nothing wrong with my marriage but I've got a ten-year itch for the world title.' Everyone had heard it all before. Ray Reardon was installed as the favourite.

TEN

The moment when Higgins – the ultimate symbol of rebellion and threat – reached out for Lynn and their daughter – these two angels – to join him – was, and is, one of the most dramatic and emotional moments of sports television ever shown. It just had everything: punk rock meets *The Waltons*.

JIM SHELLEY, TV CRITIC OF THE *DAILY MIRROR*

Lana Turner called it 'The Paragraph'. It was a moment of such pivotal importance in the life of the glamorous 1940s film star that whenever somebody wrote about her, they had to include at least a paragraph about her relationship with gangster Johnny Stompanato and, in particular, the way it ended. Her daughter stabbed him to death as he embarked upon one violent disagreement with her mother too many. Although the Alex Higgins 'paragraph' also places the daughter of an occasionally notorious celebrity centre-stage, it has altogether happier connotations. In early May 1982, however, it was a couple of weeks away. Margaret Thatcher had just dispatched a task force to the South Atlantic to persuade an Argentinian military junta to relinquish their grasp on Las Islas Malvinas. Even snooker was temporarily reduced to a walk-on role. But, just as he had persuaded the general public to disregard the SAS raid on the Iranian Embassy two years previously, Alex Higgins would change all that. The national television audience would not tolerate the vulgar intrusion of matters of international geopolitical import as a major snooker tournament was taking place.

Ray Reardon entered the Crucible in a pink shirt with white collar and cuffs and bowed to each section of the crowd, smiling broadly. He looked like a well-presented travelling sales representative from a Dennis Potter drama set in the 1950s. Higgins turned up in a dark satin shirt with a purple waistcoat and a striped tie. As he got to his chair he ripped off the constriction around his neck with the look of a man who had just bitten into a lemon when he was expecting an orange. His hair was washed but unruly. He looked angry. This was the fourth time he had qualified for the final of the world championship. He had won it only once. Ray Reardon had appeared in six finals and won every one. He soon went into a 2–1 lead. In the fourth frame Higgins approached the table like a bantamweight John Wayne, dragging his cue along the floor behind him. He produced a pulsating display of controlled snooker and racked up a break of 118. By the end of the first day he was leading 10–7. On Sunday morning Reardon was dressed exactly the same. Higgins was wearing a navy blue satin shirt with a gold star motif. Reardon took the first frame of the day after Higgins fouled on the black. For the next twenty minutes the 'People's Champion' was a picture of contrition, picking his nails, smoking and offering an art-class perfect representation of the studied frown. Reardon made a break of 95.

The world championship did not need promotion but Higgins was busy talking it up all the same. He was interviewed for BBC Television during the interval by David Vine. 'I would love to do it for my little girl because I don't think I've changed over the years,' he smiled. It was a non sequitur but then Higgins had always regarded the guiding principles of linguistics in the same fluid manner as any other restraint upon his personal freedom. 'I get into all kinds of controversial scrapes and what have you but deep down I do like to please people, I do appreciate other people playing good snooker against me and I love to actually see the furtherance of snooker no matter what anybody else says. It would be nice to be the "People's Champion" again.' It was typical Higgins, a blend of the vulnerable artist and the contumacious rabble-rouser. He was a big enough attraction on his own but Reardon also had a huge following, although drawn from a more conservative sector of society. On recent form alone, both men were lucky to be in the final and the contrast between the two most famous names in the sport made for a fascinating final. Their wholly distinct styles of play underlined the differences. Reardon adopted the casual insouciance of an off-duty gendarme walking his dog along a Parisian boulevard whilst Higgins skirted around the table like a man trying to finish one last game in the pub before his wife arrived to take him home. Despite the variance in approach, however, they were almost always neck-and-neck. After all, the first man to win eighteen frames would be the new world champion. At 9 p.m. on Sunday, it was 15–14 to Alex Higgins. Reardon was wearing a light blue dress shirt and black bow tie. Higgins was less formally attired in a green shirt with red cuffs and collar. It is the shirt people often remember him wearing because of what would happen before the night was over.

In the next frame, and 12 points ahead, Reardon inadvertently potted the white. He reacted with the bloodless smile of a government spokesman. Though he tried to hide any fragment of disappointment from his opponent, he looked at the table as if he had been the victim of a grievous sleight of hand. Higgins would never have a better chance. Before taking a shot he removed fluff from the table with exaggerated care, walked around it checking the angles, placed the cue ball in the 'D', removed it and started again. In ten years as a professional he had learned something about gamesmanship. He looked above the camera to check the score and bit the inside of his cheek. This was a crucial pressure shot. He nailed a red into the centre pocket. The white stopped exactly where he wanted it like he was back in the Jampot and betting that he could roll the cue ball up the table and leave it on top of a sixpence. He went next for an audacious pink and got it. He was on a break of 36 but missed the red and then let Reardon in for a break of 7. Fortunately for Higgins the remaining red was on the cushion and Reardon had to go for it. He missed it and left it on for Higgins who took a break of 8 to lead by 29 points. Reardon needed snookers and, after a nervous safety game from both players, forced an error on the brown before taking full advantage with a long pot that knocked the blue off the cushion. Higgins bowed his head and retired to his seat to bite his nails. At one point he saw the camera on him, flinched and took a mouthful of the large vodka and coke he had in a pint pot next to him. Reardon cleaned up to level the scores at 15–15. Higgins shot him a filthy stare.

Reardon returned to his 'corner' just before the last interval and lit a cigarette. Embassy, of course. He seemed relaxed, pulling faces for the benefit of the crowd and, perhaps, even himself. '[Sometimes] when you are sitting there . . . you feel like screaming or shouting for help,' he confessed in a television documentary in 2001. 'That's why I didn't show too many nerves really and yet I was a nervous wreck. Alex was also a nervous wreck. He was more likely to show his [nerves] than I would be but I was as nervous as him.'[1] Reardon was performing at the table, unconsciously taking his lead from method acting guru Constantin Stanislavsky who wrote in *An Actor's Handbook*, 'True acting can absorb an audience, making it not only understand but participate emotionally in all that is transpiring on the stage.' Reardon knew that Higgins fed off the energy of the crowd and was trying to vie for their attentions to cut off his supply. His efforts were largely in vain. Higgins did not have to try and compete, he was a man under pressure and could not hide it. At a time when men were not encouraged to display their emotions publicly, it made him compelling to watch. Steve Davis admitted as much last year. 'We were once playing an exhibition match,' he smiled. 'I am at the table and he is smoking and drinking away but the audience aren't watching me, they are looking at him because he was more entertaining in his chair than

I was knocking in the balls. I know this because I was watching him myself.'

After Eddie Charlton had been beaten by Reardon in the 'other semi-final' he predicted, 'Ray is too good for Alex. [He] won't be able to cope with his style. Ray will win the championship.' With a maximum of five frames left, it didn't appear to be that clear-cut but, having won the last three frames in succession, Reardon was beginning to feel the same: '[When] I got it back to 15-all I thought that I was going to win. I was on top of the situation, I'd ridden the storm and I was back in charge of the operation . . . the interval came along at a very inopportune time, I would have liked to have gone on for another one frame and got my nose in front but I didn't. When he came out he was steaming. [Higgins] was sizzling when he got back out on that table.'[2] He certainly was. In the next two frames Reardon potted just two reds and a green as Higgins, twitching, chalking the cue and perhaps sensing some kind of resurrection, went 17–15 ahead. One frame to go for the 1982 World Championship. At the start of a potentially title-clinching frame, Reardon potted the cue ball without a point on the board. Higgins was soon at the table. He potted a red and stunned the white to get on a black. The reds, like one of Senator Joe McCarthy's recurring nightmares, were everywhere but Higgins' positional play let him down. He managed to extricate himself with the use of the rest but he was still in trouble. A difficult black into the bottom pocket prompted the capacity crowd of 900 to erupt and Ted Lowe to intone with typically sombre purpose: 'Everything starting to flow now for Alex Higgins.' Listen carefully, and you can still hear him say it.

At 30 points ahead he rotated the rest three times on the table. It glinted under the television lights like the flash of a silverfish caught in the sunlight. Reardon struggled to maintain the deception of a man at ease. Whatever the look upon his face, his mournful dark eyes gave him away. At 63 Higgins potted a blue into the centre pocket and managed to disturb the reds. It was a shot of exquisite artistry. The commentators, sensing the direction of the game, began to cautiously wind up the proceedings, describing Reardon as 'frustrated but helpless'. At 72 the crowd started to get restless. At 78, Reardon lit up a cigarette and, feigning composure for all he was worth, held it in his right hand at an acute angle to his wrist as if indulging in a moment of post-coital reflection rather than seeking the solace permitted a condemned man. He would later claim: 'You can only win when you are at the table and he was at the table . . . so [when] he'd gone past a winning break of 80 [I wanted him] to pot them all because I didn't want to go to the table, I didn't want to go and concede.'[3] Ted Lowe announced, '[Higgins is] going out in a complete blaze of glory here . . . controversial, temperamental but a terrific talent for the game of snooker.' At 92, with the frame and the world title in his hands, he allowed his concentration to be broken in order to joke with the crowd. At 100, the Crucible exploded. He could not lose and everybody present knew it. He played to the gallery with all the inhibition of a £20-a-trick hooker and hit a break of 135. He had saved the best until last, putting himself in imminent danger of losing and then responding in the most dramatic style imaginable, as indeed he had in previous rounds against Doug Mountjoy and Jimmy White. There was a standing ovation. Even Reardon was on his feet with a fixed grin held firmly in place. He turned to shake hands with Higgins who walked up to him, embraced him and buried his head into his shoulder. The new world champion had been holding it together for almost three weeks and was physically and emotionally shattered.

All about is bloody chaos. Sponsors, fans, people in suits with no specific purpose, the jockey Peter Madden (a close friend of Higgins), officials, newspaper photographers, television people and security guards all swamp the playing area. David Vine is in there somewhere ('There was no way I was going to stick my oar in, it was wonderful television') while Higgins tries to suck in air and look for his family like a small child lost on the beach. The protocol is for the winner to be presented with the world championship trophy by some corporate executive or other from Embassy cigarettes while smiling for the camera. His crestfallen victim puts on a brave face. But protocol and Alex Higgins go together like suckling pig and the Vegetarian Society. The suit with the trophy proffers his hand but Higgins does not even look at him. It remains outstretched for an eternity in front of over fourteen million television viewers. When he eventually shakes it there is no eye contact until the man holding the trophy pushes him on the shoulder to attract his attention for the benefit of the serried ranks of photographers assembled in front of them both. Higgins tucks his hand inside his waistcoat and hugs himself. He uses his other hand to beckon Lynn and Lauren forward. He is crying but not uncontrollably. He is given a cheque for £25,000 which he does not even look at and accepts like he has just been handed a receipt at the supermarket. Through the sobs, he mouths, 'Bring my baby, bring me my baby.'

Lynn was in the audience with seventeen-month-old Lauren. The people behind urged her to take Lauren to her father but she was reluctant to intrude on his moment of triumph. Eventually she conceded. 'Alex was pleading and the crowd nudged us forward,' she revealed later.[4] As they push their way through the crowd, Higgins gives away his trophy to hold Lauren and kiss his wife. God knows where the cheque is. The flashes, like a bank of strobe lights, light up the tears on his sallow cheeks. He is oblivious. He needs his family. This is his 'paragraph'.

What happened during the next twenty-four hours is difficult to ascertain. He certainly gave the obligatory press interviews, telling Ronnie Harper of the *Belfast Telegraph*, 'Look what winning the title did for Steve Davis. He will be a millionaire soon but I'm the player the people want to see. I'm the "People's Champion" . . . the pressure will be off me now and I've promised to be very good in the future.' In the press conference he definitely predicted, with a similar degree of inaccuracy: 'Now this will give me financial security for life. I should be able to do a lot of things that I haven't been able to do in the past, like getting my golf handicap down and having a better family life.' It was his 'I have a dream' speech. There are witnesses to a celebration party at the Grosvenor House Hotel in Sheffield later that evening and, somewhere in the archives, there will be documentary evidence of his appearance before the disciplinary committee of the WPBSA the following morning.[5] The rest is up for grabs. In 1986, a drug dealer called 'Smokey Joe' Thickett revealed that he had supplied Higgins with cocaine at the victory party in Sheffield. 'We went into a cubicle and Alex told me that he wanted all the cocaine I had on me. He had been on at me all week to send him some from Manchester, even by taxi, but I'd told him it was too risky. Now I had three grams on me. I gave him half which he lined up on the cistern. As we left the cubicle Eddie Charlton . . . came through the toilet door. "Eddie darling, I've just won £70,000 [Higgins had also backed himself at 25/1]," bubbled Alex. "Don't let it go to your head," replied Eddie.'[6] With a certain irony. It should be noted that Higgins denies this version of events but, whether chemically enhanced or not, he was certainly in a state of euphoria. It was estimated that he could realize a minimum of £300,000 in his year as champion.

As Higgins allegedly put a rolled-up £10 note up his nose, Julian Barnes, the *Observer* television critic, also sniffed. 'Higgins's enormous popularity,' he wrote, 'springs less from the authenticity of his origins than from his embodiment of an important and consoling myth. That of the Hero as Mess.' In Lynn's opinion he certainly was a mess. She left the celebration party early in the morning after accusing him of being drunk. The next day she would return to Manchester and leave for Portugal with Lauren. They would be on their own. 'When [Higgins] got to his Cheadle home after the party,' continued Thickett, '[He] phoned me for three grams. I took them myself and when I got there he had

another woman with him. Lynn had already left.' Before
'Smokey Joe' and the mystery woman arrived at Bridge Drive,
Higgins had to appear in front of the WPBSA charged by ref-
eree John Smyth with telling the crowd to 'keep their traps
shut' at the Irish Masters and urinating in an ornamental
flowerpot at the Crucible (the electrician had dropped the
charges of assault after an extremely rare apology from
the transgressor). In keeping with the amateur nature of the
World Professional Billiards and Snooker Association, Ray
Reardon, the man who had just lost £12,500 by failing to beat
Higgins the previous evening, was on the disciplinary panel.
He remembers: 'The meeting was due to be called at 10 a.m.
prompt. The board are sitting there and at one minute to ten
the intervening doors open and in walks the maître d' of the
hotel, pushing a great trolley with a dozen bottles of champagne and orange juice. "With the compliments of Mr
Higgins, gentlemen," he said. You see, the boy's got style.'[7]
Higgins escaped with a £1,000 fine.[8] It would have been £500
but Higgins, impatient as ever, burst into the room and
demanded to know, 'Have you arrived at a fucking decision
yet?' The fine was over twice as much as he had received for
winning the title in 1972 but only 4 per cent of his prize
money ten years later. 'If my fellow professionals feel I have
to be fined £1,000 for conduct I thought was acceptable in
the particular circumstances existing at the time I shall pay
the fine. In principle, perhaps I was wrong,' he said.

Higgins arrived home from Sheffield to his 'luxury bungalow' and a bed sheet with the words 'WELCOME HOME
WORLD CHAMPION' written upon it and draped over the
window next to the front door. The new world champion
made straight for his local, the Kenilworth. Alan Hart, a regular, heard the story first-hand.

'The publican was called Declan Masterson, he was a good
mate of mine and he told me what happened. He said he had
been asleep and then all of a sudden he heard a tap on the
window. He was on the first floor so he ignored it at first but
when it happened again and again it woke him up. He pulled

back the curtains and there was Alex Higgins, the world snooker champion, with the trophy under his arm, throwing stones up at the window and demanding to be let in. Normally he would have told him to piss off but, to be fair, he had just won the world title. And so Declan opened up just for him. I think that whole scenario must have been approximate to heaven for Alex Higgins.'

It might have been but the country's fascination with snooker was approximate to hell for Auberon Waugh. He opined in the *Daily Mail*, 'Karl Marx thought that religion was the opium of the masses, but he never had the opportunity to watch other people playing snooker from the comfort of his own armchair.' Incredibly, Waugh appears later in the Alex Higgins story.

'After leaving Sheffield I stopped at a motorway café,' recalled Steve Davis, the new world champion, in 1981. 'A few kids came up and asked for my autograph and wanted to know "Is that really the World Cup?" It was lying on the seat. I said "Yeah! Great, isn't it?" I was as excited as they were.' One year later Higgins was not talking to children or eating an all-day breakfast in a Little Chef, he was draining glasses of vodka and orange and wondering what time it was. Some deluded fools hoped winning the world championship would serve to satiate him. Others feared the worst. His wife belonged to the latter camp. 'I remember standing [at the Crucible] thinking: "Well, he's done it" and feeling absolutely nothing,' she revealed in *Alex Through the Looking Glass*. 'I was pleased for [him], but, at the same time, apprehensive about what lay ahead. I said to one of the players' wives backstage: "Here we go. This is where my problems really begin." And I was right.' She was. Within eighteen months she had left him. In the immediate future he had the whole summer to gather his thoughts before the Langs Supreme Scottish Masters in September and the start of the next season. Naturally, he spent the summer avoiding his responsibilities, playing golf and drinking in the Kenilworth. Tony Brough is now a teacher in North Manchester but in the early 1980s he used to be employed as a paper boy by Butler's newsagents in Cheadle. 'I used to deliver papers to Alex Higgins on a Sunday but never really came across him until I turned up one morning and found him sitting on the wall at the bottom of the drive. I think he had been thrown out of the house by his wife. I just handed him the paper and he said, "Thanks babes." I got a £5 tip off him that year.'

Whatever the demands of his marriage, he still had a diary full of engagements. One of the first was a series of games against Steve Davis which, of course, were a sell-out. Davis, stung by his humiliating exit to Tony Knowles at the Crucible, was on top form and won every game. The new world champion was not unduly concerned. As a result of the peculiar way the WPBSA decided the rankings on the basis of results in the three previous world championships Higgins, despite being docked two points for misconduct at an exhibition match at a leisure centre in the Midlands, was ranked second, behind Ray Reardon, while Davis was fourth. The rest of the summer was spent touring the country, basking in the glory of his reclaimed status. When he was not beating Jimmy White 19–7 in front of 2,000 spectators in a challenge match at the National Stadium, Dublin, he was in the local. In fact, he was anywhere but home. Unless he brought somebody back with him. The late Boyd Milligan, a staff photographer with the *News of the World*, was an excellent darts player but refused to take Higgins on for £100.[9] Eventually they agreed to play for £1. Milligan won. Double or quits took it to £2 and then £4 until he was owed £64. They had also been drinking while playing and Milligan consented to return to Bridge Drive after last orders at the Kenilworth. He had the intention of drinking some more but when they arrived at the house of the world snooker champion he was persuaded to go for another double or quits on the green baize. Milligan, whose best break was 8, lost. Lynn was in bed with Lauren pressed up next to her as the two men played into the early hours of the morning. She was also pregnant with her second child.

Higgins tuned up for the new season with a series of exhibition matches against John Spencer in the South of England. Next came the Scottish Masters, the Jameson International and the low rent Professional Players Tournament, which were all due to take place in the space of a month. Normal service was temporarily resumed as Davis won the Langs (beating Higgins in the final) but then Tony Knowles claimed his first major title at the Jameson International by beating David Taylor. Higgins, driven to the event by his wife and penalized one frame in the first round for turning up late, lost to Griffiths. It was the first non-world-championship event in which world ranking points were awarded. The new Professional Players Tournament, essentially a non-sponsored, unseeded and untelevised tax avoidance scheme dreamed up by the WPBSA, also carried ranking points but, with a first prize of just £5,000, Davis pulled out to concentrate on more lucrative projects and in so doing denied the tournament a certain legitimacy. Hearn claimed, 'This year Steve will earn £350,000 before he takes his cue out of its case . . . if he is fully rested I don't think he can be beaten.' Reardon eventually won the event, overcoming Higgins in the second round, to claim his first major trophy since 1978. The new world champion, however, had a full diary which included recording a single called 'Bazooka Snooker' with The Hot Shots (himself, Jimmy White and Tony Knowles). It was the obvious next step. He had already been immortalized on vinyl by Georgie Fame in a track released on My Records and dedicated to him called 'The Hurricane'. Unfortunately, The Hot Shots represented only one incarnation of his musical career. He had also recorded a single as Alex 'Hurricane' Higgins called 'One Four Seven'. Recorded in the country and western idiom, it is, potentially, the worst song ever commited to vinyl:

One Four Seven, that's my idea of heaven/ Got to keep trying, keep them all flying . . . somehow. It'd take a team of eleven to stop me taking it, making or breaking it now. [10]

The image of Alex Higgins stood in front of a microphone taller than himself and believing he was about to be bigger than John Lennon is one to treasure. He bought a large number of copies himself. He would still be trying to get rid of them years later.

Naturally, he went on tour. Not to promote the single but to take full advantage of his time as world snooker champion. His chosen support act was Jimmy White. They travelled around Northern Ireland in a motor-home with the promoter George Armstrong and a driver until Higgins tired of the conditions and demanded they stop at a country pub in Derry. They did and, in the early hours of the morning, Armstrong absconded with the takings. All their belongings, including the world championship trophy in a presentation case, were inside the van with the driver who had not been paid. Higgins asked and then demanded to be reunited with the trophy but was refused access. Frustrated and irritated, he retreated to the bar and called the police. A constable on a bike arrived and enjoyed as much success as Higgins in his efforts to cajole the driver to open up. '"I'll shoot him," Alex snarled. "No, I'm a guest here. I'll have him shot!"' White remembered him declaring.[11] Reinforcements were called, two television camera crews, a couple of radio journalists, the local priest and his congregation turned up. This being Northern Ireland before the Good Friday Agreement, so, eventually, did an armoured personnel carrier. As White noted, 'It occurred to us that the driver had got food, a tankful of water that had been filled only the night before and a chemical toilet. He could hold us off for a month . . . "I know I'm stupid, but he's won," Alex said and got out his cheque book. Waving it like a flag of truce, he banged on the van door. "Okay," he shouted, "I'll pay up. How much are you owed?"'[12] It cost Higgins £250 to be reunited with the trophy he considered to be his personal possession.

Having Higgins as world champion made the WPBSA slightly anxious. The sponsors and the public, or at least those who had not met him, would not stand for Higgins' suspension. He was the world champion. He had had his papers stamped again. Consequently, they contented themselves with petty gestures like the reinforcement of the policy on the players' dress. The medical dispensation which released Higgins from wearing a tie now had to be approved by the governing body's medical officer. Failure to comply would result in a minimum fine of £250 and the risk of suspension. The ruling came into force for the Coral UK championship in late November and, for once, Higgins followed the party line. He was relatively content, particularly so after beating Steve Davis the month before in the State Express World Cup (in a generally dismal showing from Northern Ireland). His propensity to argue and cause trouble with the authorities was usually in inverse proportion to his performance at the table and he was in superlative form, what he called 'cruising' – 'the moment when suddenly everything goes silky-smooth without trying. It's golden.' In the second round of the Coral UK he trailed Dean Reynolds 1–5 but he was playing with an unfamiliar cue after the one which had helped him clinch his second world championship was broken in transit. Higgins is known for his ability to adapt a cue to his particular requirements and he worked into the early hours of the morning to try and transform the replacement. He sanded it down and shifted the weights but to no avail.

In the interval between the afternoon and the evening session he attempted to repair the cue he had used in Sheffield six months previously. He cut it open, inserted a rod of bamboo to lighten it and shortened it by almost an inch. He then came back to win 9–8 and beat Spencer and Reardon before meeting Terry Griffiths in the final on 4 December. Griffiths had been stung by criticism suggesting that his world title was a freak result and, newly signed to Barry Hearn's Matchroom team, resolved to prove otherwise. He succeeded, although the match went to a deciding frame. Higgins banked a runners-up cheque for £6,000 plus another £1,000 for a break of 137 – the highest of the tournament.

Griffiths continued his mini-renaissance with a journey to the final of the Hofmeister World Doubles, the first professional doubles championship. He was paired with Doug Mountjoy and eventually lost to Steve Davis and Tony Meo 13–2 in the final. Higgins partnered Eddie Charlton, a pairing they agreed in spite of their mutual dislike and diametrically opposed views on life, the game of snooker and just about everything else. 'I don't have to speak to him,' said Higgins about one of the most ill-conceived partnerships in sporting history. Christmas brought a temporary respite from tournament snooker of almost a month but relaxation was not on the agenda. Lynn was heavily pregnant and the relationship was suffering from Higgins' drinking and extended absences from the family home. 'Alex got carried away with himself,' she explained subsequently . . . 'I was used to lonely nights with him out of town but it . . . got to the stage where I'd have to find out from friends what he was up to. He never told me anything . . . I knew there were other women. I could sense it when he came home.'[13]

The state of his marriage was beginning to affect his performance at the table. He lost to Bill Werbeniuk for the first time in tournament play in January 1983 at the Lada Classic (Davis won again) and then, for the second time, a fortnight later at the Benson and Hedges Masters, which was eventually won by Cliff Thorburn, the Canadian's first major title since beating Higgins in the final of the 1980 World Championship.

He had a dull thud in his kidneys. At least he thought it was his kidneys. It could have been his liver. It was familiar enough anyway. Lynn was on his case and the next baby was imminent. The situation was something that did not really bother him as he tended to avoid spending much time at home. In late February he was readmitted to the Tolly Cobbold Classic after his own idiosyncratic take on Monty Python's dead parrot sketch was forgiven. He immediately incurred a fine for ripping his tie off and playing in an open shirt after Dennis Taylor, his first-round opponent, reported him to the WPBSA for infringing their new, all-important dress code. Higgins also referred to the tournament as 'Mickey Mouse' which was not held by its organizers to be a constructive comment. In the Yamaha International Masters tournament in Derby, yet another addition to the burgeoning professional snooker circuit, Higgins did not even make it out of the group stage. He was, however, determined to beat Taylor a week later and reclaim the Irish Championship. The competition had been moved back to Belfast (although not the Ulster Hall) and, after beating Jackie Rea and Eugene Hughes, he made the most of polishing off Taylor who was wearing his coaster-style spectacles for the first time. The victory seemed to mean as much to Higgins as the capture of the world title the previous year. In the interval between the first and second sessions he promised to 'get stronger and stronger to win back the title that rightly belongs to me anyway'. He was as good as his word and took home another £6,000 (plus £300 for the highest break). He also made the penultimate stage of the Benson and Hedges Irish Masters at Goffs, despite a playing surface he judged to be unacceptable.

He was drinking vodka and milk between visits to the table but explained on RTE, the state television channel in Ireland, 'I played well, but, I mean, when you had to sort of gee yourself up to take the table into account as well as your opponent, then it is just not on. I was pleased I played well because I am very deeply into these vitamin pills . . . I have been taking something like twenty-three a day.'

'My goodness me,' replied presenter Jim Sherwin.

'Ah no, I did this last year at Sheffield . . . can I mention the name?'

'No, certainly not because I want to talk to you about your . . .'

'Well, it's Shackley . . . Shackley Vitamin Pills.'

'Thanks very much.'

'I have been taking them religiously because . . .'

'I'm glad I stopped you from mentioning all that, Alex, because you know it does me good.'

Higgins went on to predict his retirement in four months' time before, in another live interview with Sherwin, confessing, 'There is no shame in being beaten by Ray Reardon because he is one of the old professionals that you can look up to . . .'

'Do you like that "old" before it, Ray?' asked Sherwin of his fellow studio guest.

'No.'

'He has only got twenty years to live,' added Higgins thoughtfully before imploring his old adversary, 'Just for me, do it for me . . . let's hope Davis gets through and you can do him as well.' He finished the interview with an unexpected flourish, 'I am going to watch a movie tonight . . . Peter Sellers in *A Shot in the Dark*.'

'That sounds a bit like the way you were playing today,' added Sherwin, desperate to make some kind of point.

Higgins was the only absentee from the subsequent presentation ceremony and this occasion marks the first recorded airing of the line which would inevitably accompany Dennis Taylor's popular trick shot routine for the next twenty years. 'Alex would have loved to have been here,' he explained. 'Unfortunately, he went back to Belfast to help launch a ship but wouldn't let go of the bottle.'

Jordan Higgins was born in March. It was a less problematic birth than Lynn had experienced with Lauren. The complications were all at home. The world championships were less than a month away and Higgins was attempting to fit his extended duties as a father around his need to practise, drink heavily and party. Lynn warned 'Smokey Joe' Thickett that she would report him to the police if she caught him selling or giving cocaine to Higgins but, as Thickett revealed to the press, 'What Lynn didn't know was that Alex was also getting regular supplies off a guy who took his missus to Alex's home. They did it sneakily with his missus chatting to Lynn in the living room while they did the deal in the snooker room.' According to the *News of the World*, Higgins hid his cocaine in one of the many trophies that decorated the house. Jackie Rea, the Northern Irish professional who lived five minutes away from Higgins in South Manchester and was a surrogate father figure, still blames several foreign players. 'They brought it over,' he explains, leaning forward and opening a tin of brown powder. 'It's snuff,' he says, answering my stillborn question, before taking a pinch between his thumb and forefinger and shovelling it up his nose with practised dexterity. 'The hard stuff, the white stuff . . . certain players took to it and unfortunately Alex was one of them. Fame came too early for him. I was a man when people started to pay me any attention, I'd already fought a war and had been in the navy for seven years. I'd been around and I knew what was what but Alex had no idea how to deal with it all. I had to look after him plenty of times when he was out of his head.'

For the 1983 World Championships in Sheffield, Higgins had enhanced his dietary regime. The vitamins were still there but were now supplemented by honey, which he spooned into whatever alcoholic concoction he was drinking at the time. As defending champion, he had a particular responsibility to perform and started as he meant to go on by comprehensively beating Dean Reynolds, Willie Thorne and Bill Werbeniuk to earn a semi-final match against Steve Davis. He was also the subject of a largely positive documentary shown on the eve of the championships. It glossed over some of his more notorious misdemeanours and, as the *Daily Mail* put it, 'told you everything about Alex Higgins that was fit to print'. Higgins was the biggest draw at the Crucible and he traded on it, sometimes literally. 'At one point, the year after he won the title, he was selling posters of himself but had worked out a scam,' smiles Steve Davis, looking at his shoes and shaking his head. 'He was signing one set with a gold pen and the others with a silver one. It was £1.50 for one signed with the gold pen and £1 for the others. Now bear in mind it was the same colour ink. Well, he had a queue of people waiting for his signature with the gold pen. They all fell for it. It was marvellous to behold.'[14] Davis bursts out laughing, not at the expense of the paying public but at the audacity of his most intractable opponent. Darren Hill was hanging around outside the Crucible. He also wanted an autograph, regardless of the colour of pen the world champion was holding. 'My friends and I couldn't get into the venue but we were in a queue to get the "Hurricane's" signature,' he remembers. 'He was absolutely drunk and hanging out of his dressing room window which overlooked the road to the NCP underground entrance on Norfolk Street. People were tying their programmes to some rope and he was lifting them up and signing them. The group of people who were gathered there loved every minute of it. Somebody was telling him to come away from the window but not before he spotted a female punk rocker walking below and minding her own business. He poured a pint of beer on to her head. It was a great shot and her pink hair was stuck to her head. After a few obscenities from both parties Alex was pulled back from the window with great applause from us below.'

Higgins surrendered tamely to Davis in the semi-final, even admitting that he had been 'stuffed' (he had no choice, Davis won 16–5 with a session to spare), and did so again in the semi-final of the Langs three months later. By that time he had already appeared on the front of the *Daily Star* after apparently giving referee John Williams the 'V sign'[15] and travelled to Australia to compete in the Winfield Masters. While there, and despite a warning from Eddie Charlton that he would 'biff him' if he misbehaved, Higgins insulted Michael Cleary, the Minister of Sport for New South Wales, asking him what exactly he had done for the game of snooker. Cleary is reported to have told the events manager, 'Get this little fella out of here before I dong him'. Higgins also failed to make a press conference because, still recovering from the night before, he could not be woken. He then left to stay with his sister Isobel in Sydney. If his performance in Australia was to influence the decision not to invite him the following year, then his general irresponsibility was to influence Lynn to take the children and leave him. She moved back in with her parents just over a mile away from the family home. His behaviour and drinking were out of control and she took steps to prevent him from seeing his children.

'Oh, not that, anything, anything but that,' sobbed Higgins when he returned from an exhibition match in Belfast to be told the news. 'I'm devastated,' he continued, 'I didn't know how bad it was until I read about Lynn's divorce application in the papers.' This seems probable. The editor of *Snooker Scene* and BBC commentator, Clive Everton, has known Higgins since the early 1970s. 'He is only interested in himself,' he offers. 'I think he is self-obsessed. All sports people are self-obsessed but with him I think it is taken to a special degree.' Higgins' solicitor commented, 'He wants to be reconciled with his wife and reunited with his kids . . . He is shattered. It will be fatal if he sits in the house just brooding and grieving about what has happened.' This comment almost turned out to be terrifyingly prescient.

'If he sneezed, they'd say he spat on the floor,' said Bill Werbeniuk of the treatment Higgins received at the hands of the press in the early 1980s. The Canadian also refused to attend a press conference as a gesture of support for the beleaguered former world champion. Higgins went out to Dave Martin in the qualifying rounds of the Jameson International and to Mike Watterson in the Professional Players Tournament. Watterson was the former promoter of the world championships but would later be stripped of his responsibility for the most successful event in the sport's history by WPBSA Promotions Ltd.[16] Higgins lost to Spencer at the Yamaha event and went on to lose in the early stages of the Tolly Cobbold in Ipswich. He was not focused. In the meantime Davis had won six major tournaments since the start of the year, including the world championship, and had been invited to speak at the Conservative Party Conference. He was being patronized by the establishment in every sense of the word but it threw into greater relief Higgins' anti-hero status. Davis was the working class Tory who had 'improved himself' by dint of hard work, Higgins was the outsider who did not court the acceptance of those who sought to hold him back. That is not to say he was a socialist (he certainly lacked any shred of class conscious-ness); rather he was an individualist with a Protestant upbringing and a strong libertarian streak. This could have made him a classic Thatcherite, but he did not trust anybody or think about politics enough to care. In the State Express World Cup he lost to low-ranking Ian Black and Eddie Sinclair. Davis and England (Tony Knowles and Tony Meo) won the competition for the second time in three years. Higgins told the press conference, 'My mind is just not on snooker these days.' He would try and kill himself before the season was over.

ELEVEN

Higgins apparently threw a television set from an upstairs window . . .
Three windows in the front door were broken and a window in the back
door as well. Items in the house were smashed and clothing strewn about.

CAROLE MUNDY, PROSECUTING (1985)

The top of the bottle came off easily enough. The tablets fell into his hand like Tic-Tacs. He looked at them. And then, like a child, he swallowed them all, counting them as he did so and declaring his love for his wife. Lynn, holding Lauren close to her, watched him as he finished off the bottle and washed it down with champagne and then took their child back into the bedroom. They were on a make-or-break holiday in Majorca. 'There I've done it,' he triumphed like an irritating adolescent at a house party before announcing his intention to go to a bar down the road and adding a final flourish, 'If you want to go and get a doctor, do so. If you don't that's up to you – I don't care!' Lynn thought he was faking the suicide and would make himself sick the moment her back was turned but when she could not find him she began to panic. He was eventually found slumped unconscious against a bar.[1]

His suicide attempt did not emerge until *Alex Through the Looking Glass* was published in 1986. If his suicide attempt was genuine it was not the characteristic behaviour of the self-obsessed and, confirming Lynn's initial suspicion, certainly not the kind of thing a natural-born survivor would even contemplate. That is why the first reaction of the woman who shared his life was to assume he was 'shamming'. As a difficult child might determine to hold its breath for a potentially life-threatening length of time, so Higgins is entirely capable of staging a self-pitying suicide attempt. In the event, he nearly died. The medical staff in Majorca told his wife to prepare for the worst. Uncannily, he pulled through after being in a coma for forty-eight hours. 'He must have the constitution of an ox,' Lynn recalled. 'The doctors said he came within ten minutes of death.'[2] He discharged himself the next day and flew back to Manchester without telling anybody. If it had all been an attempt to play on the sympathies of his wife, it worked. She agreed to take him back if he would check into Cheadle Royle, a private hospital ten minutes' walk away from their house which specialized in helping patients with a variety of mental illnesses. 'I was surrounded by a bunch of headcases,' observed Higgins. It was less than a revelation. 'I gave it two days. On the second day, I walked into the session and they were all doing anagrams. I took one look and said to the doctors, "I've had enough of this. I'm going home – ta-ta." On the way out I added: "By the way, the answer to the anagram is operation."'

In November, less than one month later, he was in the final of the Coral UK championship in Preston. As the first session came to a close he was yet again on the wrong end of a 7–0 scoreline to Steve Davis. Lauren was celebrating her third birthday in Cheadle. She waved at her father on the television screen in the corner of the room. The game was shaping up to be a humiliation rather than a contest and, after the party, Lynn went to be with her husband. She was really trying to make a fresh start and had even taken up golf so that she could accompany him on the course. It was a Saturday afternoon when she arrived at the Guild Hall and news of her arrival filtered into the bar where, naturally, most of the press had congregated. Phone calls were made to the Manchester newsrooms of all the daily papers and within minutes vehicles full of news reporters and photographers were breaking the speed limit up the M6. Higgins issued a curt 'no comment' when asked about his relationship and although he and Lynn were smuggled out of the Guild Hall by the back entrance, it was not a wasted journey for the press corps. The former world champion was gaunt and haggard. He had a lost a stone in weight during the last month. But Higgins was staging a fightback and had come back to win after losing the first four frames to Murdo McLeod in the first round, beaten Paul Medati 9–1 and then Tony Knowles in front of a full house, before disposing of Terry Griffiths in the semi-final. Even at 7–0 down Higgins was convinced he would beat Davis and win the title that had eluded him for so long. He loved to play in front of enthusiastic audiences and the capacity crowd at the Guild Hall lifted him.

Reunited with his wife, he was confident and in no mood to capitulate. He took the first three frames of the next session and eventually pulled back to 8–7 behind. After the third session it was 11–11. Davis cracked and by the end of the match Higgins had recorded one of the 'most astonishing recoveries'[3] in snooker history to win 16–15. 'I'm very happy to be home,' he announced of his recent reconciliation with Lynn. He could equally have been talking about his return to a position of pre-eminence in the snooker hierarchy. 'It's made a great difference to me,' he continued. The £12,000 cheque for winning the title meant little compared with being granted access to his children once more. During his separation from Lynn he had won just one game in three tournaments. *Snooker Scene* reflected, 'Higgins was alight with the flame of self-belief as Davis unaccustomedly struggled with self-doubt . . . if Higgins, holding only his domestic Irish championship, needed a major title at this stage of his career, snooker perhaps needed even more an interruption to the seemingly endless flow of Davis successes.' Higgins, who had been selling his posters in the lobby for 80p to undercut the £1 price charged by Davis, was as delighted as punter W. A. Martin was distraught. The latter had travelled from East

London to watch the snooker for a week and put his life savings (£7,000) on Steve Davis to win at 4/6. Barry Hearn and the rest of the Romford Mafia had also lost money. Higgins had been drinking cream stout for the duration of the championships ('for the sugar . . . I'm a very poor eater when I'm away from home') but behaved himself impeccably. He was back in the spotlight but, on this rare occasion, for all the right reasons.

Three days after his victory he appeared on *Harty*, a midweek chat show hosted by the eponymous Russell Harty, and a couple of months after that *A Question of Sport*. Both programmes were memorable. The late Russell Harty was a camp, former school teacher from Blackburn noted for the kind of straight-talking interview technique that has all but disappeared from current television schedules. He introduced Higgins to the audience as an 'orphan collie' who, presumably in a reference to his behaviour at the Crucible in 1982, had sprayed the plants backstage after mistaking them for lamp posts. Higgins did not rise to it. He had cracked lips but looked relatively healthy and was wearing a dinner jacket and bow tie. Although Harty seemed nervous, he still baited Higgins at length.

Harty: Why is it that so many people you play with say such rude things about you? Steve Davis said he liked playing you because you were obnoxious.

Higgins [slurring his words slightly]: Well, they could be a little bit jealous and perhaps because I get the people on my side [turns to audience, which laughs] and perhaps they can't do that.

Harty: Now, you've also got a bit of a reputation for alcohol. Do you have to use that for fuel?

Higgins: No, I've always enjoyed a pint when I play and if you have got 500 people in a crowd and they see you with a glass word travels . . . It doesn't mean I drink fifteen pints like Werbeniuk and I don't start at seven o'clock in the morning.

Harty: You start at 7.30 a.m. do you?

Higgins: No, no. I have a drink at midday . . .

Harty [interrupting but seeming suddenly less confident]: Have you had one tonight?

Higgins: No, no.

After a series of trick shots, Harty introduced Lynn and Lauren.

Harty [addressing Lynn]: His form has been dodgy recently and so has your marriage? What happened to make [your marriage] dodgy?

Higgins [also addressing Lynn]: I'll leave that up to you, I didn't leave the camp.

[The audience titters nervously]

Lynn: No . . . erm . . . I was a little bit tired of him and also he wasn't practising very much, he wasn't spending much time at home . . . our lives seemed to drift apart and I went home. Since then we've sorted ourselves out haven't we? [she flashes a glance at Higgins] . . . And that's all I am saying.

His appearance on *A Question of Sport* was less emotionally fraught but he still managed to contest a decision with perennially-happy host David Coleman during the one-minute round. Higgins was insistent that his team had claimed (correctly) that Eleoncio Mercedes was a flyweight, and not a bantamweight, boxer.

Coleman: No, he's a flyweight.

Higgins: We said flyweight.

Coleman: No you didn't.

Higgins: Yes we did.

Coleman [with a strained smile]: No you didn't.

Higgins: We said flyweight first and then we said bantamweight.

Coleman: No you didn't.

Bill Beaumont [interceding as team captain]: We said it for the wrong guy.

Coleman moves the game on.

Higgins [under his breath]: Flyweight.

The arc of the last few months was almost impossible to comprehend. From the worst form in his career, a separation from his wife, a suicide attempt, time in a mental institution and a reconciliation with his family to the capture of the Coral UK championship after a remarkable comeback against the best player in the world, incessant press coverage and appearances on the most popular mainstream television shows in the country. And all in less than a financial quarter. This was the breakneck speed at which Alex Higgins was living his life.

'He is rude, arrogant, ignorant and a real troublemaker,' explained Eddie Charlton when asked why his former World Doubles partner (the incomprehensible arrangement had been dissolved for the 1983 event) was not invited to the Winfield New Zealand Masters and Australian Masters in the summer. When pressed, no specific accusations were made and Higgins was not given an opportunity to clear his name but it seems probable that his bust-up with the Minister for Sport for New South Wales had not advanced his cause. Rex Williams, the WPBSA chairman, commented, 'We did not take this decision lightly or on hearsay. The incidents were substantiated by another player. Alex will have to learn how to behave himself when he is abroad.' It was the kind of patronizing admonishment the parent of an errant pupil might receive after an eventful school trip. The decision was supposedly taken at the behest of the sponsors. Higgins launched an ultimately successful appeal (even a *Sunday Telegraph* editorial was sympathetic to him)[4] but he was not about to take any lectures from Charlton and Williams. They did not understand the intolerable provocation he frequently found himself unable to ignore. Trouble found Alex Higgins like lucrative endorsements found Steve Davis. The opening night of a snooker club in Waterford in the Republic of Ireland illustrates the point.

Higgins was asked to play an exhibition in front of about 240 people. It was a small club and space was at a premium.

The condensation was running down the windows and there was no air conditioning. As he prepared to take his second shot after the break he returned to the seats that had been put on one side for the players. There were two women sitting in them. 'Look,' he explained patiently, 'You can't sit there. I can't [be standing around the table] when it is not my shot.' The women refused to move. Higgins was being paid to play snooker so, uncharacteristically, he let the issue rest for the duration of the exhibition. He then returned to the Tower Hotel three hours later. He was with his friend Tommy McCarthy. As they entered the hotel bar they noticed the same two women. The women had been drinking and were now accompanied by two men. There was an altercation, or as Higgins put it,

I had already told the husbands twice. I said, 'Now look boys, for fuck's sake, I was doing an exhibition and they were sat in my seats. Let's not have a wind up.' The women were fucking attention seeking and whatever. I must admit I had all my hair then. Well, I'm on the dancefloor and it kicks off as one of the men tries to throw one at me and I duck but then the other [man] steps in. I am still with the one I've just hit but his wife's on my back and so I'm doing this [drunk, he stands up and showcases his wild fighting style]. Suddenly, it's gone from one man, one woman and another man who hadn't got my type of footwork to four of them, two women and two fucking men. With no referee. Out of the blue, Tommy says 'I have had enough of this' and wades in. But what you don't know is that he only had one arm, he lost the other one when he was 20-odd and anyway, when he throws a punch his fucking arm comes off.[5]

This is one of Higgins' favourite stories. What happened next is not recorded but the idea of Higgins belabouring his startled assailants with the flesh-coloured prosthetic limb is irresistible.

Eddie Charlton paired up with Bill Werbeniuk for the Hofmeister World Doubles in December 1983 while Higgins decided to forge a partnership with the altogether more suitable Kirk Stevens. They met in the quarter-finals. Charlton and Werbeniuk won 5–1. Higgins took a holiday. It was the last event of the year but also the beginning of another run of poor form. The Lada Classic in Warrington and the Benson and Hedges Masters brought scant reward. He lost 5–1 in both, to John Parrott in the second round and Tony Knowles in the quarter-finals respectively. In the latter, *Snooker Scene* reported, '[Higgins] was strangely lacking in form and sparkle.' His marriage was under pressure again and he felt neglected by Del Simmons, who had a new £60,000 salary to justify and was spending an increasing amount of time on his work for the WPBSA. And Davis was still getting under his skin. He seemed unstoppable and won the Lada Classic, the Tolly Cobbold Classic, the Yamaha International Masters and the Benson and Hedges Irish Masters (where he scraped past Higgins in the semi-final) before the world championships. He was also the top prize-money earner with £103,216 while Higgins was only sixth with £28,500. These figures do not take into account endorsements or other activities or the difference would have been even more marked.

Meanwhile, Barry Hearn was putting in deeply anti-social hours to establish a tournament circuit in South East Asia. He realized that the sport was approaching saturation point in Britain and was seeking additional revenue streams and other opportunities for the players he was looking after. When he agreed to organize the Camus Hong Kong Masters he tied the deal in with advertising contracts for Davis, Terry Griffiths and Tony Meo. There was also a plan for a Camus Bangkok Masters and events in Singapore and Kuala Lumpur. It was all kept in-house. The Matchroom House. Higgins wanted in but Hearn was adamant. No chance.

The world championships, frequently a barometer of Higgins' mental state, yielded a first-round exit to a twenty-year-old former insurance clerk, Neal Foulds. It was a tight game (10–9) but Higgins, perhaps missing the challenge or the status of underdog to inspire him, went out. A year later

Foulds was ranked number three in the world. He was one of the best young players in the country and – unlike Knowles beating Davis 10–1 at the same stage in 1982 – it was no disgrace to lose such a close game. However, he seemed distracted again. Rather than take advantage of his early elimination to return to the family home in Cheadle, he opted to reappear at the Crucible to lend Jimmy White some support. His young protégé had already disposed of Eddie Charlton and Cliff Thorburn, neither of whom Higgins exactly considered close personal friends, and had qualified for a semi-final against Kirk Stevens. It was to be an absorbing match with Higgins providing succour when White was 10–12 down going into the final session. He eventually prevailed. As did Davis in the other semi-final. It was the 1983 Coral UK final all over again, with White assuming the role of Higgins, the impetuous underdog with a prodigious natural talent, and Steve Davis playing himself. Higgins took temporary ownership of a monitor in the press room. It was an enthralling contest which Davis just edged but the depth of feeling between Higgins and White was demonstrated by the fact that White played in a suit which Higgins had lent him.

The relationship had been cemented on many occasions since White had turned professional but there was always a tacit understanding that Alex Higgins was the senior partner. And, like the older professionals before him, he did not appreciate any challenge to the status quo. When the twenty-one-year-old White called him from the Elizabeth Taylor suite at the Gresham Hotel in Dublin, a high-rolling hotel room of the highest order, to ask him if he was able to play a couple of exhibition matches at short notice he agreed. After all, the Elizabeth Taylor suite has its own cocktail bar. The promoter booked Higgins into another suite on the floor below. 'He took one look at his own suite and, with that pained expression that I was getting to know so well, said, "This can't be right. I always stay in the Elizabeth Taylor suite when I come to Dublin,"' remembers White in *Behind the White Ball.* Higgins assumed White would instantly swap suites but, as he had several friends staying with him in the room (including sundry members of UB40), he refused. 'When I wouldn't give way,' he wrote,

Alex took himself and his valise up to my suite and, dressed like Noel Coward in a marvellous white suit, ensconced himself at the bar. That night, he moved into the bathroom . . . where he spent all night sleeping in the capacious bathtub, still wearing his white suit. I got him though. A couple of nights of discomfort was enough – the day after, he was back in the suite below, although he never stopped sniping, trying to make me feel guilty.

The commitment to play two exhibition matches was honoured ('Maybe we weren't sober but, as someone said seriously back then, "How can you tell?"') but this was the life that Higgins was beginning to miss in the summer of 1984. The freedom to just take off with no consideration other than the fulfilment of his personal hedonistic agenda. But he also loved and needed his family and the security that offered. It was a tension he could not resolve.

Lynn resolved it for him by moving back in with her parents again in August. She took four-year-old Lauren and sixteen-month-old Jordan. 'This time it's for good,' she told the press. 'I've had enough of him. I'm really not going back again. I'm seeing my lawyer about a divorce this week . . . I can't go into details because I have to put my children first. I gave it a second go but now I realize it's hopeless. I want some peace and quiet so I can start thinking about my future with the children.' She also took time out to stress that the threatening phone calls from an anonymous caller had nothing to do with her decision. In *Alex Through the Looking Glass* she expanded upon her motivation. 'The doting father we saw when Lauren was born had vanished. Jordan never got the same attention. Now kids were a drudgery, something he couldn't be bothered with.' Higgins had certainly tried to adapt to family life when Lauren arrived. Mike Dolman was an ex-miner who became a lifeguard at Pontins in Prestatyn in 1982. Higgins was there to play in the Pontins Open, the event he had won with some style after turning up uninvited in 1977. 'Alex came up to me and said he couldn't swim,' remembers Dolman. 'He had just had the baby girl, he was going on holiday and he wanted to be able to take his baby into the water. He asked if I could give him a few basic swimming lessons so he would be safe in the water with her. I said of course, come about nine and it will be between me and you . . . that night he got knocked out of the competition, got blasted out of his head on drink and couldn't be arsed turning up.' Another good intention sacrificed at the altar of vodka and orange.

'I feel I must write to you in order to express my abhorrence at the loutish behaviour of Alex Higgins at the close of the Jameson tournament in which he was well and truly beaten by Steve Davis,' complained Peter M. Rooke (Cheltenham) in the letters page of *Snooker Scene*. Higgins, having already been beaten by Davis in the semi-final of the Langs Scottish Masters, the first tournament of the 1984–5 season, reacted to another humiliating 5–1 defeat at his hands by smacking the cue ball off the table with ferocious intent. It was tame stuff by his standards but to lose control at the table indicated a certain frustration not just with his private life but also with his performance. He was now ranked ninth in the world. The Jameson International and the Rothmans Grand Prix (which superseded the previously unsponsored Professional Players Tournament) were both ranking events in the new scheme of things. The new professionals who had joined the association as the sport expanded to fit the space permitted by the television schedules and the generosity of the sponsors had forced the change after finding themselves frozen out of the top sixteen as they had not appeared in the last three world championships. This was not good news for Higgins as he went out of the Rothmans in the second round to former shipping clerk Mike Hallett (then ranked just inside the top thirty). It was not like the early days when there were only twelve professionals. Hallett was a competent professional who eventually climbed into the top ten although Higgins maintained that he was 'possibly too nice' to become a world-class player. There were plenty of others on the circuit who were not and who wanted a share of the money that the top professionals were dividing amongst themselves. In the 1984–5 season the top eight prize-money earners won more than the rest of top fifty put together. Davis was number one with £182,501. Higgins came after Dennis Taylor and Cliff Thorburn with £101,133.

Even Higgins' previously undisputed crown as the bad boy of snooker was under threat. Tony Knowles received £25,000 from the *Sun* during the Embassy world championship for a three-part story concerning his manifold sexual exploits. Rex Williams for the WPBSA once again: 'We are very concerned to maintain the first-class image of professional snooker. It is those high standards which have brought professional snooker its present level of public support and popularity.' He did not go on to explain why Alex 'Hurricane' Higgins was the biggest draw in the game. Knowles, in receiving an unprecedented £5,000 fine, smashed Higgins' previous record fine by a multiple of five. Barry Hearn, by now a board member at the WPBSA, noted a year later, 'For [Knowles] it was a disaster. I mean, we fined him five thousand quid for bringing the game into disrepute and a lot of people on the board were in favour of slinging him out. There was a high feeling. It definitely would've cost him quarter-of-a-million in lost earnings.'[6] It would take more than that to overtake the money Higgins had sacrificed for his lifestyle. He would soon have the dubious honour of having paid the record fine in his possession once again. Meantime, everywhere he looked there were players trying to overtake him in one field or another. Steve Davis, quite correctly recognizing himself as 'the start of the new era' and admitting that he was subse-quently supplanted himself, now has a philosophical take on it. 'I had some amazing battles with Alex Higgins . . . he was a fighter. As any era changes, the best of an old brigade go down fighting.' And, much to the chagrin of the 'new era', Higgins was anything but finished.

His first priority was to defend his Coral UK title in Preston. He was always a big event player and the size of the crowd, the money on offer and the pressure turned him on. He rose to the challenge and progressed until he reached the semi-final where he found Cliff Thorburn in his way. It was, as ever, a tight game with no quarter given but with Thorburn leading 6–5, Higgins (as he did with his petulant outburst at the Jameson International) violated even his own peculiar code of ethics. As Thorburn recalls it, 'In the 12th frame, I snookered myself (after potting a red). I nominated green but John Smyth, who was the referee, didn't hear me and called a foul. Naturally, I said that I had nominated so the referee then asked Higgins. He said that he watched my mouth all the time when I played and that I definitely hadn't said anything. So then I asked the referee to ask the crowd and about ten people said that I had nominated, but Higgins still said that he hadn't heard.'[7] By common consent, Thorburn had been heard nominating the green. Higgins was quoted in *'Hurricane' Higgins' Snooker Scrapbook*: 'Opponents who are willing to stand by and see me fouled by the referee unfairly and yet say nothing must be pretty desperate to beat me by any means they can.' Dennis Taylor, the player to whom Higgins was referring, reflected, 'It struck me as peculiarly ironic, in the light of all that fuss, to see Alex sit silent in his chair . . . when Cliff was penalised.'[8]

Higgins needed to win. Thorburn, thoroughly aggrieved, denied his opponent the use of the cue extension he had previously agreed to share with him. '[His refusal to back me up] completely threw me,' continued Thorburn. 'I was angry and I also felt saddened for Alex and his stupid attitude.' The Canadian could not concentrate and Higgins went on to win 9–7 to set up a rerun of the 1983 final against Davis. Higgins immediately went 5–0 down the next day and was suffering at

8–2 before winning six out of the next seven frames to pull the score back to 9–8. If Davis had a weakness at this time it was, as Higgins had exposed twelve months previously, an uncertainty when a large lead began to be eroded. In the event, he managed to win the next frame and then never looked back.

Higgins was not finished with 1984 yet. In the final tournament of the year, the Hofmeister World Doubles, he finally found the perfect partner – Jimmy White. Davis and Meo were going for a hat-trick of titles but the 'Hurricane' and the 'Whirlwind', an unprecedented combination of destructive weather systems, blew them away 9–6 in the semi-final. Cliff Thorburn and Willie Thorne were beaten with ease in the final and Higgins picked up a half share of £34,500. There are worse ways to prepare for Christmas but Higgins was living on his own and wanted to be back with Lynn and the children. Although they had maintained contact and he was determined to facilitate a reconciliation, he was still physically separated from them. He was low, keeping his spirits artificially high in the traditional fashion. It was in this frame of mind that he entered the Mercantile Credit Classic (a ranking event which had replaced the Lada Classic) in Warrington in early January. He took a beating from Steve Davis in the second round. They could not seem to get away from each other and were drawn together again in the Benson and Hedges Masters later that month. Wembley was never a favourite venue for Davis. 'The crowd was always pretty boisterous at Wembley,' he remembers. 'And they rooted for Jimmy [White] or Alex. Even though I was born in South East London I was never considered to be a London player. When you are of the ilk of myself and Stephen Hendry you have to understand that people are not going to warm to you. You will get respect but you may not get the warmth enjoyed by the players who wear their hearts on their sleeves, the ones seen as more human.' On this occassion, however, Davis was not on his own – the Romford Mafia turned up mob-handed. Higgins made the most of his usual vociferous support.

The match was tight. Davis took the first, Higgins the next two. Davis tied. Twice Davis needed the black to win the frame and twice he delivered. Higgins, feeding off the tension between certain sections of the crowd, pulled back to 3–3. Davis went ahead again only for Higgins to catch him. Davis led 53–0 in the decider but let Higgins in and never scored again. Wembley shook as the final ball went down and the Irishman turned to the crowd and exclaimed, 'We're fucking back.' A BBC microphone picked up the seven-letter adverb and opted to broadcast it. The indiscretion received just three complaints but Higgins was not finished yet. As Davis later said, 'The best of an old brigade go down fighting.' On a pastel-coloured sofa at TV-AM the next morning, when asked about his feelings towards Steve Davis, an exhausted Alex Higgins said, simply, 'I hate him.' Although he went on to say how much he respected his ability and, despite the fact that Davis, when asked later in the day to respond, reciprocated directly, Higgins was fined a punitive £1,500 by the WPBSA. He lost to Terry Griffiths in the next round but he had made his point. He could beat Davis. He was back and he also had a plan to get Lynn and the children back. 'With the help of friends,' he confessed, 'I managed to undermine Lynn's resistance . . . I figured that a house move and a fresh start could tilt the balance and bring us back together.' He engineered a meal out with another couple in Prestbury, part of the South Manchester stockbroker belt. Higgins and his wife were still on good enough terms to go out together with another couple but food, as usual, was not on his mind. He had seen a place he liked called Delveron House.

It was a peculiar-looking, sprawling arrangement of buildings born of several disparate types of architectural inspiration, including the executive-standard mock-Tudor Barratt House and the Kentish oast house whilst referring obliquely to a motte and bailey castle. In other words, it was a six-bedroomed house in Cheshire available for £235,000. Lynn had turned up her nose at the details in the estate agent's window but closer inspection, after Higgins suggested they pull into the drive of the empty property on their evening out, revealed a magnificent oak-panelled snooker room. 'He just swept me off my feet again . . . he turned to me in the car and said: "Shall we buy it?" I reminded him that we'd split up. He said: "Oh go on, Lynn" . . . From there I fell into his trap.'[9] Higgins' charm, when employed in the pursuit of self-interest, is never to be underestimated. His form benefited immediately. He went into the Dulux British Open (formerly the non-ranking Yamaha International Masters) in a better frame of mind but, for once, was not the story. Kirk Stevens, by this stage a cocaine addict who had taken to mixing the drug with soda water in order to ingest it more quickly, had his most successful tournament to date. In the final he met Silvino Francisco, who had beaten a rejuvenated Higgins 9–6 in the semi-final. It was the first major final with two non-British participants but does not linger in the mind for that reason. It is chiefly remembered for the fact that Francisco, at one stage 8–3 ahead and then dragged back to 9–8, followed Stevens to the toilet during an interval and, after a 'physical and verbal' assault upon his person, accused him of being high on drugs. Stevens denied it.

Francisco eventually won 12–9 but, having told a grateful reporter from the *Daily Star* that Stevens was 'out of his mind on dope', effectively lifted the lid on some of the backstage activities at major snooker events. It is impossible to know whether the WPBSA's decision to introduce mandatory drug testing for the world championships in Sheffield a couple of months later, at the behest of board member Barry Hearn, was the result of prior knowledge that the tabloids had the story or some other impetus, but Francisco was still hauled before the disciplinary committee, fined a record £6,000 and docked two ranking points for the 'assault' on Stevens. Subsequently, Stevens would deliver the *Daily Star* with another heaven-sent exclusive. The headline said it all: 'I AM

A DRUG ADDICT'. 'I am helplessly addicted to cocaine,' he confessed. The story appeared on the opening day of the World Championships in March 1985 and, on appeal, Francisco had his fine reduced to £2,000 and his points returned. It was the beginning of the end for both of their careers. Francisco, ironically, was arrested in 1997 for trying to smuggle cannabis with a street value of £155,000 into Dover. Before Kirk Stevens hit the front pages, however, Higgins was able to reach three more finals, winning one and losing two. In the Guinness World Cup, an All-Ireland side comprising Higgins, Dennis Taylor and Eugene Hughes pipped England A (Steve Davis, Tony Knowles, Tony Meo) to the title as Higgins won five of his six frames. In the Benson and Hedges Irish Masters semi-final stage, Higgins recorded his fourth win over Davis in their seventeenth meeting in a major tournament but eventually lost to Jimmy White for the first time in a competition. He later surrendered his Irish title to Dennis Taylor at the Ulster Hall. He may not have been at the top of his form going into the world championships but he was nearer to it than he had been for a while.

Despite the media overreaction to Kirk Stevens' drug revelations in the *Daily Star* and the heavy presence of news reporters, the 1985 World Championships will for ever belong to Dennis Taylor who, after coming so close for so many years, beat Steve Davis on the final black for the title. Higgins went out to Terry Griffiths in the second round and told the snooker press that he believed the introduction of drug tests was an imposition. Amongst the players there was talk of set-ups and honey traps. 'I'm looking over my shoulder all the time,' Higgins said. 'There's pressmen everywhere. This has taken some of the gloss off Sheffield and some of the gloss away from snooker.' But nobody was really listening. That was not the story. The largest ever post-midnight television audience in British history, 18.5 million people on a Sunday night/Monday morning, watched Dennis Taylor sink to his knees as the enormity of his achievement dawned on him. As he noted wryly, 'It has taken me thirteen long years to become an overnight success.' He had been 8–0 down and upstaged even Higgins' Coral UK comeback of two years previously. Davis had surrendered a seemingly impregnable lead once again and was understandably distraught. The rest of the population were delighted. The *Irish Independent* noted, 'Unlike many sporting celebrations in this country, this one had no political barriers, no religious bias and no counter-demonstrations.' The lack of any sectarian edge underlined Taylor's popularity. Within a week of winning the title he had received a rapturous reception as he played an exhibition in the Shankill Leisure Centre. Quite something for a Catholic in the heart of the hardline Protestant community in East Belfast. Higgins' thoughts are largely unrecorded. Davis may have been his *bête noire* but Taylor, a fellow Ulsterman, was now rivalling him for popularity. Perhaps the genial Irishman with the trademark spectacles was the new 'People's Champion'.

Life at Delveron House was not wildly different from life at 2 Bridge Drive, apart from the arrival of an au pair to help Lynn with the children. It had quickly settled into the familiar pattern. Lynn looked after the children while Higgins was away from home, playing golf or exhibitions and tournaments. There was a great deal of playing. When he was not at home he could be found in the De Trafford Arms in Alderley Edge. Steve Marshall used to shoot pool with him there until they removed the tables. 'When they did that we used to go out to the Robin Hood in Rainow [about twenty minutes away by car] to take on the locals and Alex used to tag along with us sometimes. On one occasion, he had had his usual "150 pints" of Greenalls bitter and had lost a bit of cash to some of the locals. He was getting a bit aggressive on the way home and annoying some of the girls in the car so much that we kicked him out in the middle of nowhere at around midnight. I never did find out how he got home.' A week later Marshall went to Yesterdays nightclub, a venue popular in the mid-1980s with attractive blonde women in little black dresses from Cheshire and the many professional footballers who lived in the area. 'I was not looking forward to seeing him again,' continues Marshall. 'I thought he might kick off but when he arrived he was wearing that enigmatic Irish grin and promptly shook my hand and climbed onto the piano in the bar. He gave a rendition of "If I knew you were coming I'd have baked a cake". Lauren had just been in her first school play and she had sung that particular song. He was on top form.'

He may have been when he was on top of a piano at Yesterdays nightclub but on the table, where it mattered, he was way below par. His ban had been rescinded and he travelled to Australia to enter the Winfield Masters but had to play twenty-five miles away from the main competition as he was barred from the venue for previous misdemeanours.[10] He lost anyway (to John Campbell 4–1). He seemed to be sleep-walking as Jimmy White beat him 5–0 in sixty-two minutes in the Langs Scottish Masters, the traditional curtain-raiser for the season. It was the first whitewash of his professional career in a ranking event and it was not a surprise. Despite the acquisition of an oak-panelled snooker room, he was not practising. Steve Marshall adds: 'He once came round to my dad's house when he was on holiday and fell asleep under the dining room table for two days.' It was not the kind of regimen likely to deliver a return to form or representative of the 'wholesome family values' the Conservative-voting denizens of the Prestbury area like to project. This might be a good thing. Throwing a television through the window while your young family hide under the sheets in a locked room, however, is almost always a bad thing. As Keith Moon could have told him, had he been alive, wrecking a hotel room is one thing, wrecking your own house is something altogether more stupid. As Higgins also took a golf club to several windows he would have done well to think about that.

Lynn had suspected that her husband was showing the au pair something more than trick shots in the snooker room in the early hours of the morning. On the night the television set ended up on the lawn, she hid on the landing to listen to the conversation between her husband and the young Spanish woman she had hired to help out with the domestic duties, and was sufficiently alarmed to venture downstairs. Higgins found her eavesdropping. She accused him of following the au pair to the pub and trying to seduce her. Higgins snapped. Lynn screamed. Higgins claims he then phoned her parents to bring some kind of sanity to the proceedings. After talking to her daughter, Alex Higgins' mother-in-law called the police. A breach of the peace is a very serious offence in the kind of area into which the Higginses had moved. As a general rule, multimillionaires do not appreciate having to put up with the kind of neighbours who throw perfectly good audio-visual equipment out of an upstairs window or require the intervention of the police to restore order in the middle of the night. 'It seems there had been a heated argument between the couple,' argued Carole Mundy for the prosecution. 'It was to such an extent that Higgins apparently threw a television set from an upstairs window . . . Three windows in the front door were broken and a window in the back door as well. Items in the house were smashed and clothing strewn about.' Mr Howard Bradshaw, for the defence, offered weakly, 'I am asked to emphasize specifically that at no stage during the evening was Mr Higgins in any way intoxicated. And at no stage in the course of the arrest was he physically aggressive towards the arresting officers.'

Three policemen arrived at Delveron House. '[They] had it in for me,' Higgins explained with a certain inevitability. 'They roughed me up good and proper,' he said as if auditioning for a part in *The Sweeney*. 'It was completely unnecessary – my nine and a half stone against three burly coppers. They shouldn't have been there in the first place. I may have had a few drinks but . . . [a statement which may or may not fit like a dovetail joint with the declaration delivered to the court by his counsel].' Higgins made for the knife drawer during the struggle and said, 'That's it. There is only one way for Alex Higgins to end it.' Fortunately, it was to not to be: 'He went berserk as they put the handcuffs on,' claimed the prosecution. He was questioned in Macclesfield police station, just three miles from his new home. He was put in a cell 'with just a packet of fags for company'. Lynn put the children in the car and left him once again. He was released after two hours. He had to be in Stoke that afternoon to play Dennis Taylor in the Goya Matchroom Trophy.[11] The papers had already got hold of the story. 'MY LOVE BUST UP' screamed the front page of the *Mirror*. Taylor won 5–1 with Higgins conceding the last frame despite only needing one snooker with all the colours left.

TWELVE

JOE CABOT: . . . Okay, quickly [pointing at the men as he gives them a
name]. Mr. Brown, Mr. White, Mr. Blonde, Mr. Blue, Mr. Orange, and
Mr. Pink . . .
MR. PINK: Why can't we pick out our own colours?
JOE: I tried that once, it don't work. You get four guys fighting over who's
gonna be Mr. Black . . . So forget it, I pick. Be thankful you're not Mr.
Yellow . . .

QUENTIN TARANTINO, *RESERVOIR DOGS* (1992)

The season had not started well. He had been to Australia
for the Winfield Masters and entered two other tournaments, won a total of two frames and been arrested. His wife
and children had left him again. A week after the row, there
was talk of divorce, with Higgins telling the *Mirror*, 'There's
no hope of us getting back together,' and then, the next day,
informing the *News of the World*, 'I don't know whether our
marriage can be saved but the most important bond is our
love for our kids.' Lynn added, 'We're determined not to
squabble over them.' It was, in any case, unlikely she would
lose a custody battle. The news that Higgins had received a
bullet in the post with the message 'You won't see the next
one coming' was casually dropped into the conversation as
though it might have been an oversight. More details of his
private life were about to be brought into the open as the
wife of his friend and ex-manager Geoff Lomas sold the story
of a decade spent socializing with Alex and Lynn to the

tabloids. The Coral UK championship at the Preston Guild Hall in November 1985 was a welcome distraction and he claimed he was dedicating himself to practising for eight to ten hours a day. Such application helped him get through to the fifth round, where he met Jimmy White. Higgins went 3–1 ahead but White was not labouring in a low gear and eventually beat him with ease.

On the domestic front, he bought Lynn a £65,000 house near her parents in Heald Green. Although Higgins had started dating again, he still hoped to orchestrate a reunion with his wife. His luxury six-bedroomed house in Cheshire was a lonely place. Dudley Doust, who interviewed him for the *Sunday Times*, just before the game with Jimmy White, wrote: 'The house was empty . . . [it] had an odd dishevelled Higginsian feel about it: a galleon lamp, all sails down, lay floundering on the floor and, for some inexplicable reason, dozens of new light bulbs were scattered in their packets across the front hallway.'[1]

Tony Francis was working on *Alex Through the Looking Glass* at the same time and produced a similarly bleak vignette: 'In the corner of the cavernous still unfurnished lounge stood a wilting Christmas tree, encircled by fallen pine needles.' Higgins had planted himself in the middle of the room. 'Around him his essential belongings: television set, settee, electric fire dragged from its customary position in the hearth, ashtrays, cans of lager, and, literally at the end of its tether, a telephone.' Higgins was, and still is, incapable of dealing with the minutiae of everyday existence. To call and hire a housekeeper would have taken less than half an hour with the *Yellow Pages* but he cannot or will not apply himself to such mundane tasks. He is therefore absolutely dependent upon others. This is what drives his well-honed feral cunning. It is absolutely necessary for his survival. There is usually someone who can bail him out. Take the court case for example.

After he received the summons he asked his new girlfriend to write to the court and explain that he would not be able to attend as he would be defending his Hofmeister World

Doubles title with Jimmy White in Birmingham (they crashed out in the first round). Unfortunately, it was later claimed, she put the address of her flat in Manchester at the top of the letter and the second summons was delivered to the wrong address. After Higgins failed to turn up for the hearing, a warrant was issued for his arrest. He was competing in the semi-finals of the Kit Kat Champion of Champions tournament in Nottingham – only the eight professionals who had won the world championship were eligible (plus the recently retired John Pulman). Higgins beat Thorburn on the final black in the first round but, on the morning the warrant was issued, went down 6–1 to Steve Davis in the semi-final. Higgins did some fast talking to the clerk of the court from a telephone at the venue, asserting that since the police had arrested him at his house they should really have known where to send the summons. This, surprisingly, won a temporary reprieve – much to the dismay of the assembled reporters (or 'reptiles' as the players habitually referred to them). The hearing was set for 27 December 1985. Higgins turned up at Macclesfield Magistrates Court looking like a prototype Reservoir Dog with his hair slicked back, and wearing a dark topcoat and a white shirt and black tie. The undisputed Mr Black was fined £200 and bound over to keep the peace for twelve months. He would manage less than thirty days.

'I was kicked while out riding a horse called Dreadnought at five o'clock this morning,' he told the press pack assembled for the Mercantile Credit Classic in early January. His fecund imagination had not let him down. It was, he felt, a satisfactory explanation for the cuts and bruises to his chin and cheeks and swollen eye, which was a riot of colour from aubergine and yellow through to dark blue. He still qualified for his first ranking quarter-final of the season by coming back from behind to edge past Dennis Taylor 5–4 before, remarkably, losing to WPBSA chairman Rex Williams in the quarter-final. But the press did not want to know about that.

Something did not ring true. There was too much unsolicited circumstantial detail about his fall from a horse: the name, the time of the accident. It smelt like a cover-up. And, besides, since when did Alex Higgins go riding at five o'clock in the morning? 'YOU LIAR!' announced the *Sun* with a simple but effective front-page splash. The truth was far more prosaic and, once caught out, he issued a hastily worded statement. 'I had a disagreement that was settled privately behind closed doors and I regret that it happened. I did go horse riding but that is not how I got the black eye. I made up that story to take the pressure off me before such an important game.' It was not one of his more successful strategies. The story had already leaked and Higgins was later forced to confirm that he had been involved in a fight with Paul Medati, a forty-one-year-old fellow professional and owner of the Masters Club in Stockport.

'He was on it all day,' recalls Medati fifteen years later. 'Drinking, all sorts, you know what I mean? He was absolutely out of his head and it was a Saturday night and he was hassling me to play him. I'm like, "Alex, I've got a club full." So he said, "I am playing Dennis Taylor in the morning."' The implication was that he needed to practise and the Masters Club had some of the best tables in the North West of England. The WPBSA even sanctioned the club as a venue for the qualifiers for the UK championship, the Hofmeister world doubles and the world championship before moving the whole circus to Blackpool. 'I played him the best of five in the matchroom [a separate room away from the main part of the club],' Medati sighs, 'I beat him three-nil. We played for £100 and then it was double or quits, best of seven. And I stung him again but he was [trying to deal with his domestic problems] and all that shit and I just said, "I'm going now, keep the money, I don't want the fucking money." So he says, "You don't fucking like me." I said, "What's up with you?" He said, "You don't like me," and some other stuff. I told him I had a club to run. He says, "Come in, Paul, and shut the door." I went back in, shut the door and we were arguing like hell. Well, it's kicked off between us hasn't it?'

Higgins was calling Lynn on the phone between frames and maintained that Medati told him that his marriage was over and flew into a rage. 'He threw the first punch,' avers Medati with some credibility. 'I was trying to calm him down because he had loads of problems.' Higgins boasted later of comprehensively winning the fight before adding, by way of an unoriginal postscript, 'You should have seen the other guy.' As was widely reported later, Medati lost his toupee in the scuffle but, predictably, the two men differ wildly about what happened. What is certain is that Higgins subsequently asked a friend to drive him to the house he had just bought for Lynn in Heald Green about fifteen minutes away. She would not let him in.

Medati called him at Delveron House later and they agreed to say nothing about the fight. It is a measure of the celebrity status 'enjoyed' by snooker and the top players at the time that such a precaution was considered necessary. A black eye allegedly received in a nightclub altercation by Matthew Stevens (the runner-up in the 2000 World Championship) just before a major promotional photoshoot endorsed by the governing body was, on the advice of former CEO Jim McKenzie, enhanced rather than covered up. With a certain irony, the sport has today become so lacklustre that it now actively requires the dramatic input of players who have a life outside the practice room. Stevens is widely considered to be one of the brightest young prospects in snooker, but most people would struggle to pick him out in an identity parade. In the mid-1980s he would have been as famous as Bob Geldof.

In 1986, snooker had no need for such self-conscious media manipulation. Even Ray Reardon merited a tabloid front page when his wife accused him of being unfaithful. A fight between 'Hurricane' Higgins and anybody, never mind a fellow professional, was always going to be a story. It eventually made the *News at Ten*. When the truth emerged, Medati found himself under siege. 'The *News of the World* wanted to see me,' he recalls, with something less than misty-eyed nostalgia. 'They offered me £40,000 to talk about drugs [and their prevalence in the game] and I said no. I phoned the WPBSA to ask their opinion and they said, "You can say whatever you want so long as you don't say anything about drugs." So I didn't . . . Anyway, I sold my story elsewhere and got a few grand. Higgins got twice as much as me and then we had a good drink over it.' Medati still runs the Masters Club in Stockport and Higgins is still welcome. It was, improbably, Medati who gave him a lift into the centre of Manchester in the first chapter of this book when I had to call in a favour from a friend to babysit him. 'I couldn't get rid of him out of the club,' says Medati. 'I kept saying, "Alex, I am not staying here all night, I am going." So, at the end of the night he said, "Well, will you drop me off in Manchester?" I said, "Right." As I'd promised my girlfriend a meal we dropped him off in Chinatown and then, within about five minutes, I got a speeding ticket which cost me over £60. I also lent him £30 so it cost me £100 to give him a lift to Manchester. I should have given him the money for a fucking taxi.'

As far as Higgins was concerned, the handling of the 'black eye incident' during the Mercantile Credit Classic in Warrington and the fact that he had been required to face a press conference when he should have really gone to ground signalled the end of his relationship with Del Simmons. Paul Hatherell, the WPBSA tournament director, was, in his opinion, also responsible for throwing him to the dogs. This enmity would manifest itself shortly. Higgins went on to demand his prize money (£6,750) while still at the venue but the organizers would not accede to his request and he became verbally abusive. Frustrated and hounded, he then threatened to 'blow the lid off the game'. His price was £300,000. The tabloid press were already operating under the assumption that they were currently engaged in some kind of lid-blowing exercise anyway and he had no takers.

But his outburst did suggest that he might know or be part of something. So the popular press went to work on him. It was Alex Higgins season again. He travelled to Ostend for the BCE Belgian Classic and reached the semi-final. When he returned it was to headlines such as 'HURRICANE IN COCAINE SENSATION' ('£1,000-a-week habit of snooker star Alex' – an allegation that Higgins quite reasonably rejected as ludicrous) and 'SUICIDE BID BY ALEX' ('Alex doped, drunk and near to death' – also patently untrue). The *Daily Star* ran a Higgins story every day for a week. The *News of the World* EXCLUSIVE with drug dealer 'Smokey Joe' Thickett and the casual betrayal of one of his most high-profile clients came out on the first day of the Benson and Hedges Masters at Wembley. Higgins subsequently denied it. A capacity crowd gave Higgins a standing ovation when he walked out for his first-round game with Terry Griffiths (he lost 5–4).

His form had been fitful since Lynn had left Delveron House. He played well enough to beat Neal Foulds in the Rothmans Grand Prix at the Hexagon in Reading but, having declared that he was going to 'channel everything into snooker from now on', ran into Steve Davis who inflicted upon him a second career whitewash in a ranking event. It was also the second that season. Davis has admitted to feeling 'humiliated' after his defeat to Taylor at the Crucible the previous year and was building up to reclaim his world championship. He was mining a rich seam of form that he carried into the Dulux British Open. The Dulux, still trying to shrug off the bad publicity of the Kirk Stevens–Silvino Francisco controversy in 1985, was a pivotal event for many reasons. Gordon Burn, who followed the snooker circuit in 1985–6 researching his book *Pocket Money*, noted that certain figures within the game were beginning to appreciate that it had reached saturation point and was now in real danger of lapsing into a long, painful decline. Burn quotes Barrie Gill, the chairman of CSS, the biggest sports promotion company in the country who had introduced the game to both

Mercantile Credit and Dulux. '[The WPBSA] came to us,' he told Burn.

We found them two new sponsors but then . . . [it was like] we invited you in, we needed your help, now please piss off. This is a private club, almost, making its own rules, keeping its own purse, doing its own PR, issuing its own judgements and participating in its own tournaments . . . You can't be everything in one package. It isn't possible. You can't run what is potentially a world sport in the TV age, in-house. Because it's inevitable that the vested interests will prevent its expansion . . . the next step is critical. The whole game needs a rethink and a restructure.[2]

It was a prophetic statement that failed to find a receptive audience. Other financial predators, however, were beginning to circle. They had sensed that the sport was sending out distress signals. Though it was not, yet, thrashing around in the water, there was the faint and distinct smell of blood.

Howard Kruger preferred to be known as 'H'. He grew up in the South East of England and looked every inch the successful young 1980s entrepreneur: Bentley Corniche; ostentatious watch; tiepin; blow-dried hair; and a wardrobe full of shiny business suits which he fondly imagined might make him look like Richard Gere in *American Gigolo* but actually made him look like an overweight timeshare salesman from Luton. He fancied moving into big-time snooker management, Barry Hearn's turf, but the differences between Kruger and Hearn were crucial. Hearn had made his own money and looked after his players, particularly Steve Davis, with paternalistic consideration. He had also expended substantial amounts of time and money attempting to take the game into the Far East (he ran summer tours for his Matchroom players into Hong Kong and Singapore), South America, North America and anywhere else there might be a dollar to chase. Kruger's father, Jeffrey, by way of an incidental aside, ran the Kruger

Organisation which promoted concerts featuring the Eurythmics, Wham and the Jacksons (amongst others). It had offices in Belgravia, New York and Los Angeles and 'H' had already had some dealings with sports personalities when he ran a sports agency that worked with clients such as Sharron Davies and Torvill and Dean.

It was preparation for managing Alex Higgins in the same way that a pantomime season with the Crankies in West Bromwich might provide valuable experience for a coast-to-coast tour with Motley Crüe. The first contact Howard 'H' Kruger had with snooker was Tony Knowles. They met whilst on holiday in Spain in 1986 and Knowles asked him to become his business manager. They shared an interest in water sports. At that time, Knowles had failed to deliver after beating Steve Davis 10–1 in the first round of the world championship in 1982 but by playing consistently in ranking events was still ranked fourth in the world. Barry Hearn's evaluation of his cash-in with the *Sun* as 'professional suicide' was proved right when a follow-up story from his ex-girlfriend Suzy Harrison was sold to the same paper. She claimed that he liked to make love while dressed in stockings, suspenders and panties. Kruger recommended that Knowles claim to have worn women's underwear only once at a fancy dress party and detailed his PR man Greg Millard to limit the damage. The Mackenzie-era *Sun* attended the press conference and responded in typical fashion. 'KNICKERS!' was all the headline said. It was all it needed to say. Today such a revelation would probably secure Knowles sympathetic coverage in the style press and an endorsement from Rimmel, but in the mid-1980s the adverse publicity served to affect both his game and his health. He was in hospital for the Dulux event, discharged himself, played, was beaten and went back to convalesce. The stress had caused his body to break out in boils. Kruger, presumably entranced by the coverage one man's alleged predilection for female undergarments could deliver, agreed to become Knowles' manager and aimed to establish a stable of talent to rival Hearn, who had just recruited Willie

Thorne and Neal Foulds to his organization. Kruger decided to call his outfit Framework.

Hearn professed no interest in Jimmy White (who had just won the Mercantile Credit and finished runner-up in the Benson and Hedges to take his winnings to almost £80,000 in the four weeks since Christmas) despite the fact that statistical evidence revealed that he was becoming a bigger crowd-puller than the 'Hurricane'. 'H' was already working as an agent for Jimmy White (usually a 10 per cent commission for organizing bookings, rather than the 20–25 per cent earned by managers) and would soon become his manager. But his next acquisition had to be Alex Higgins. The deal was announced at a press conference before the semi-final at the Dulux British Open in Derby. 'How much did Del [Simmons] pay you?' asked one of the 'reptiles' with comic intent. Kruger must have already sensed that something was awry when Higgins had been forced to register in a hotel fifteen miles away in Nottingham. His client was not welcome across vast swathes of Derbyshire and, in fact, much of the rest of Britain but 'H' put on a brave face. 'After dealing with pop groups Alex is a saint . . . we can get round his tarnished image.' Kruger smiled uneasily as the press pack wrote down his words and shook their heads in unison.

Higgins had, in fact, bought out the final year of his contract with Del Simmons before receiving a signing-on fee from his new manager. Simmons, who was often in an impossible position of his own making with mutually incompatible commitments to Higgins and the WPBSA, signalled his relief when he said: 'I can forget all the times I would happily have strangled him because deep down, I'm very fond of Alex.'[3] Three weeks later 'H' was still optimistic. 'I was very, very tough,' he said, 'the first time I met with Alex. I wasn't sure whether I wanted an involvement with him or not. But what can I tell you? I'm used to dealing with artistic-stroke-temperamental people. And that's what he cried out to me. That he wanted to be treated correctly, which he never has been in the past . . . "Everything I do," I told him, "is

professional. Everything you do is now a reflection of me."
With me now it's all yes-sir no-sir. He calls me boss.'[4] The last
part of that bold declaration can be treated with the same
respect with which most juveniles regard the 'No Bombing'
entreaty at the local baths. Alex Higgins calls nobody boss.
Least of all a rich kid ten years his junior.

A few days before signing with Kruger, Higgins had said,
'I'm not going to be at the top for much longer – three or
four years and that will be it. I don't like the hassle any more.
I'd like to have a good, hard four years at snooker and then
quit the game and get on with life.' A sceptical and sage Clive
Everton noted, 'Even if he should accrue, in the next four
years, enough money to last him the rest of his life, a doubt-
ful eventuality, where could he find, other than in snooker,
the sense of purpose which holds him together, albeit
sometimes by the most fragile of threads?'[5] After the press
conference, despite a pre-tournament working holiday
in Dubai where he rattled in a 147 break and just missed
another on the final black, Higgins lost a one-sided semi-final
to Steve Davis ('I'm disappointed, not dissipated,' he
announced, bizarrely). It would prove to be a portent. The
Irish Benson and Hedges Masters provided nothing more
than an insignificant defeat at the hands of Tony Meo in the
first round. The glamorous-sounding Car Care Plan World
Cup was more rewarding.[6] The red tops were still gunning
for Higgins but he was in high spirits as he led the Ireland
team (featuring Dennis Taylor and Eugene Hughes) to a successful defence of their title, beating Canada 9–7 in the final.
As *Snooker Scene* reported: 'At the after match press conference Alex Higgins is not only over the moon but out of his
brains and under the table. Well almost. And why not?' He
had endured a difficult few months.

The next stage in Barry Hearn's master plan was for the
Matchroom organization to go multimedia. The term was
not yet common currency but, in this dreadful instance, it
entailed releasing a 45rpm single to coincide with the 1986
World Championships. You might know it as 'Snooker

Loopy'. The verse is as follows:

> *Snooker loopy nuts are we/ Me and him and them and me,*
> *We'll show you what we can do/ With a load of balls and a snooker cue.*
> *Pot the reds, then screw back/ For the yellow, green, brown, blue, pink*
>   *and black,*
> *Snooker loopy nuts are we/ We're all snooker loopy.*[7]

'Snooker Loopy' by the Matchroom Mob (featuring Chas 'n' Dave) reached No. 6. In purely statistical terms, that makes it more successful than 'Emotional Rescue' by the Rolling Stones (No. 9, June 1980), 'How Soon is Now' by The Smiths (No. 24, November 1985) and 'Sub-Culture' by New Order (No. 7, November 1985). On a unit-shifting basis it is almost on a par in the UK with 'Holiday' by Madonna (No. 6, November 1983). Framework, who had just signed Kirk Stevens, had their own plan. Higgins suggested a reworking of 'The Wanderer' by Dion. The assembled Framework 'supergroup' assumed the name Four Away and featured Tony Knowles, Jimmy White, Higgins and Kirk Stevens. Unfortunately, Stevens treated the title of the single as a suggestion and went missing before the photoshoot for the front cover, which featured the three remaining members of the group playing air guitar with their snooker cues. Higgins went for an animated and slightly unsettling look. Tony Knowles and Jimmy White seem uncomfortable, as though they have been suddenly press-ganged into being hapless onlookers during the reconstruction of a murder on *Crimewatch*. In one of those glorious moments when peculiar celebrities from unorthodox corners of the entertainment industry are forced to acknowledge and deal with each other as functioning human beings, 'H' arranged for Rick Parfitt and Francis Rossi of Status Quo to be present in the car park for another photoshoot. The tenuous connection was that Status Quo had also recorded a version of 'The Wanderer' and were just about to embark upon yet another comeback tour.

Harvey Lisberg, the manager of 10CC and partner of Geoff Lomas in the Sportsworld venture, will have been relieved he had nothing to do with it. Howard Kruger, by contrast, fuelled by the over-confidence that comes as standard with relative youth and inherited wealth, assumed that snooker was merely a stepping stone and that Barry Hearn was his next step. The Matchroom Mob made it onto *Top of the Pops* as Four Away's atrocious cover of the 'The Wanderer' failed to trouble the compilers of the Top 50. Kruger complained about the free coverage the BBC gave 'Snooker Loopy' during almost every edited highlights feature but, essentially, there was no glory to be had. As somebody once said about the Falklands War, it amounted to nothing more than two bald men fighting over a comb. But Hearn was worried about Kruger and, subconsciously perhaps, even seemed to be starting to dress like him. Which was a mistake.

Kruger kept Greg Millard on a retainer to look after Higgins, Knowles and Kirk Stevens. The Framework organization seemed to be applying radically different criteria to Matchroom when it came to recruiting players. Hearn was established. Kruger, with his background in rock music, seemed to fancy being Lee Marvin in *The Dirty Dozen*, rescuing lost souls from the stockade and presenting them with one last chance for redemption: Knowles (crippled by sexual revelations in the tabloids); Stevens (self-confessed cocaine addict) and Higgins. Jimmy White had potential enough to represent an attractive target for any ambitious manager but, after a trip to China and the Far East at the invitation of Barry Hearn and the Matchroom team, was persuaded to swap allegiances. His ghosted biography did not evade the issue.

Howard and I finally parted over an exhibition that he had set up in Brighton between me and Alex for a fee of £2,000 a piece. I forgot about it and, while I should have been down there having my picture taken by the press, getting into my dinner jacket, doing all the publicity, I disappeared. Howard went potty. He careered around London in his Roller, looking in all my regular hiding places, eventually tracking me down in some really scruffy dive where I had fallen asleep on a filthy floor under the table. He dragged me out, stuffed me in the front seat of the car and off we roared down to Brighton. The car was beautiful, carmine red with an all-white interior, from the thick wool carpet to the leather upholstery and even the facia, which was made of some kind of bleached wood. And there I was in all this splendour, fast asleep, and filthy as a chimney-sweep. When I scuffed my grimy sneakers over the white facia Howard went mad, but there wasn't much he could do. By the time we got to Brighton I was awake enough to play, though I can't remember a thing about it. When it was time to settle up, Howard insisted, 'I owe you nothing. Your filthy shoes have ruined the inside of my Rolls.'[8]

Lynn and Lauren arrived at Sheffield for the world championship but there was no possibility of re-creating the emotional scenes of 1982. Lynn claimed she was merely bringing their daughter to watch her daddy play snooker. Daddy was beaten 13–12 by Terry Griffiths in the second round. In many respects his early exit was a relief. His ranking had risen from ninth to sixth but his personal life was as chaotic as ever. Joe Johnson, a 150/1 outsider from Bradford and someone who got on tolerably well with Higgins, won the title that year. Higgins was genuinely pleased for him as it also meant that Davis had not reclaimed the biggest prize in the sport. Other pressing issues included the progress of a teenage prodigy called Stephen Hendry, who had become the youngest ever Scottish Professional Champion at the age of seventeen. Higgins had already played him in a series of exhibition matches and considered him to possess immense talent. Steve Davis had also taken note. Ian Doyle, the man entrusted with nurturing the talent of the boy, had stepped in to keep Higgins at a healthy distance ('It's a big, bad world out there,' he remarked once, pointedly) but had also taken note of the Hearn Method. '[He] brought big names down to Romford before Steve [Davis] turned professional,' he explained in *Pocket Money*.

We've done it the other way about. We've sent Stephen out to the public halls to play players on their own tables. The home guy is always the one the folks in the hall are supporting, so you go in and find the atmosphere faintly hostile . . . after two or three frames, though, the hostility seems to disappear. They're right behind you as you go out the door because they know they've seen a player. Steve Davis at the same age had maybe forty percent of the ability Stephen does. There's nobody outside Higgins and White who reads the game as instinctively.

Even Higgins, when prompted, conceded that Hendry was, at the same age, a better player than himself. Davis and Higgins had both seen the writing on the wall and although Higgins possessed the self-deluding confidence that comes with natural ability, in truth, they both knew the next generation was demanding recognition. Higgins had seen it before, but now Davis knew what it felt like.

If Higgins was feeling sorry for himself even his self-absorption must have buckled to accommodate the news that Kirk Stevens had collapsed outside a club in the West End of London. The *Sun* provided a shorthand diagnosis: 'KIRK STEVENS IN COCAINE COMA'. He pulled through. Higgins felt for Stevens. He could relate to the situation of the young man who had sought him out in a club in Canada almost ten years previously. Stevens was far away from home; lonely; living on his wits; struggling with an addictive personality; surrounded by hangers-on; possessed of negligible self-discipline but a breathtaking talent with a cue; he was a gambler, drinker and someone not predisposed to reject a chemical fix to pick himself up. He was also a womanizer. The image guaranteed him a substantial postbag from teenage girls and dissatisfied housewives but precluded the lucrative commercial contracts that would have provided a degree of stability in his life. Even cue endorsements at that time could yield up to £100,000. Unfortunately, having confessed to cocaine addiction he had transformed himself in the popular imagination from the best-looking young player on the circuit into a desperate, drug-addled degenerate. In short, he was corporate poison. By comparison, Alex Higgins was, to those who had never met him, hard to distinguish from the Archbishop of Canterbury.

Back on the circuit, Dennis Taylor retained his Strongbow Irish title with Higgins as a less than gracious runner-up (despite a cheque for £5,000 and £400 for the highest break of 96). The dominance of Taylor, now with the Matchroom team, did not please Higgins. It was as though by winning the world championship and acquiring his own popular following, the bespectacled Ulsterman had forgotten his place in the scheme of things. *Snooker Scene* reported with the faux solemnity of a headmaster addressing morning assembly, while keeping an eye on a couple of likely suspects: 'Somebody has gone mad and wrecked the residents' lounge in the Lansdowne Court Hotel and we all have a good idea who. The upshot is that the hotel [have told] the Strongbow people that their post-final party will not, after all, be hosted there.' There was always somebody who had to ruin it for everybody else. It was usually Alex Higgins.

The season, however, had been a comparative success: he had a new manager in whom he had some confidence and had risen up the rankings. His prize money for the 1985–6 season was a respectable £77,317, a bit down on previous years but satisfactory after a year of domestic turbulence. The summer brought occasional periods of ascetic dedication to practice but he had fallen out of love with the game and bouts of excessive misbehaviour were occurring with increasing frequency. Failing to attend a disciplinary hearing after his actions at the Mercantile Credit Classic eight months previously (it was difficult to charge the governing body of acting with undue alacrity) resulted in a deferment of the hearing. The WPBSA would soon have much more to concern them anyway. Higgins was drinking heavily but he was only building up. The next season would produce more fallout than the explosion that had ripped through Reactor 4 at Chernobyl earlier in the year, an event that momentarily even knocked snooker off the front page.

The Langs Scottish Masters was the traditional season opener and Higgins started well, making it to the final. There he met Cliff Thorburn, the holder. There was no love lost between the two men and they both wanted to win more than they wanted the £13,000 cheque. The game was no classic. Thorburn edged ahead but then Higgins won four frames in succession to lead 7–5. The thirteenth frame was the most contentious and Higgins, adjudged to have missed the blue, created a ten-minute disturbance by challenging the decision of the referee and demanding to be shown the shot on a BBC Scotland monitor. It did not unsettle the Canadian, if indeed it was meant to, and Thorburn went on to win 9–8 after taking the last two frames. In his victory speech Thorburn, who had agreed with the referee and thought that his opponent had indeed missed the blue, acknowledged that his opponent was a 'great player'. He did this because, as he was to reveal later,

[I wanted] to make things a bit easier because I just knew that I was going to have problems with him. Up in the sponsor's room, I'm having a drink with Ted Lowe, who had been doing the commentary, and Bill Malcolm [a BBC Scotland producer] and there were a couple of members of the press stuck round the corner. Alex is fuming because he's lost and he brings up the incident about the blue ball. He said he'd hit it and I said he didn't. I mentioned the incident in Preston the previous November when the referee hadn't heard me nominate the green and Alex said that this was completely different.

Then he said, 'You're lucky' and I said 'Why's that?' He mentioned something about drugs and I said, 'What do you mean?' He started to walk around the room and he said, 'You know, the bags of white powder.' He never actually mentioned cocaine but this was obviously what he meant. I said, 'Listen, you'd better shut up. You're way out of line here. If you don't want me to do the same thing that I've done to you twice before, then don't say anything.' [9]

Thorburn was not so much hinting at the proximity of immediate and substantial physical violence as threatening him
with it. He was referring to two incidents: one in 1973 and
another nine years later. Higgins understood. On the first
occasion he had borrowed £50 from Thorburn for a poker
game and given him his wedding ring as surety. Later that
night Cara, Higgins' first wife, demanded the return of the
ring but Thorburn refused. Higgins was with her and pretended to faint. As Thorburn remembers the event, 'I went
to pick him up but I turned my back on him and the guy
grabbed a bottle. I grabbed him and threw the bottle down.
I got my left arm round him and just pounded his head until
my hand got sore.'[10] The night he beat Thorburn in the 1982
Benson and Hedges Masters, Higgins had not been drinking
in moderation. He was again playing cards but not, on this
occasion, with the Canadian former world champion.
Thorburn just happened to be sitting next to a female companion of Higgins. Aggrieved about something or other and
drunk, Higgins confronted him. As Max Beerbohm, an
admirer (and occasional detractor) of Oscar Wilde, once put
it, 'Vulgarity has its uses. [It] often cuts ice which refinement
scrapes at vainly.'[11] Higgins took Beerbohm's advice. 'You're
a Canadian cunt,' he declared, 'and you can't fucking play
either.' Thorburn punched him to the floor. The fight was
broken up but, after Higgins repeated the insult two or three
times more, when he made to shake hands with his tormen-
tor Thorburn kicked him, to use his expression, 'right in the
nuts'.[12]

The 'little bags of white powder' story made all the papers.
It also made Thorburn's life a misery. He received death
threats, presumably from the militant wing of the anti-drugs
lobby, and had his house daubed in paint while two companies who had him on contract, BCE (manufacturers of
snooker tables) and Scottish Provident called emergency
board meetings to decide if they still wanted his endorsement. Meanwhile, Higgins was knocked out of the BCE
International at Derby in the early stages (it had replaced the

Goya event in the snooker calendar) and travelled to Reading for the Rothmans Grand Prix where he progressed to the fifth round before being beaten by Rex Williams for the second time in consecutive games. Williams, as chairman of the WPBSA, had already approved disciplinary measures against Higgins and would do so again. The fact that Higgins was also his opponent in certain tournaments was an amateurish arrangement which few other sports would contemplate. 'I've no sour grapes but I was on a hiding to nothing after the last time I played him,' said Higgins afterwards.

The relationship between board members and the other professionals was untenable. The Association had already sent every professional a letter in May which informed the membership in the traditional legalese that they, effectively, had to do exactly what they were told. Clause five stated that any player who wanted his case to be heard by the board rather than an independent counsel (appointed by the board) would have to sign a declaration, '[agreeing to] waive any breach or potential breach of the rules of natural justice arising from the composition of the council [board] and/or any alleged benefit to any member or members of the council [board] arising from the penalty imposed'. In other words, the players were being asked to waive their right to declare that the board members who sat in judgement at disciplinary tribunals, their competitors on the table, had a vested interest in either fining or suspending them. The barely discernible noise in the background was the sound of Joseph Stalin spinning in his grave while trying to kick himself for not thinking of it first. A lawyer consulted by *Snooker Scene* for their September 1986 issue commented, 'This looks like an attempt by the WPBSA to circumvent the rules of natural justice. It would give the WPBSA powers which no other tribunal in this country claims.'

On this occasion Rex Williams had recently imposed a £2,000 fine on Higgins after his various misdemeanours at the Mercantile Credit Classic in Warrington (demanding his money and becoming abusive when told that was not possible and threatening to 'blow the lid' off the game of snooker). One of the complainants was Paul Hatherell. Howard Kruger complained about the length of time it had taken to resolve the issue while Higgins added, 'I'm disappointed. Over the last nine months I've been a shadow of my former self for one reason or another.' It was, remarkably, only the seventh time in his career that he had been fined by the governing body. An occasionally solitary Christmas came and went. But he had a semi-final appearance against Steve Davis in the BCE Canadian Masters upon which to reflect. In the new year he was beaten by twenty-seven-year-old Belfast-born Northern Ireland Amateur Champion Jack McLaughlin in the Dulux British Open, who reflected, touchingly: 'It's hard beating your hero.' There was the obligatory argument with a referee (Higgins denied he had sworn at former London Underground employee John Smyth, the man who had offi-ciated during his 1982 World Championship success, and shrugged, 'All I said was that I would feel safer on a tube train if he wasn't driving').

With the Warrington disciplinary problems finally sorted out (and yet another fine paid) there were some signs that his form had returned. He approached the UK Open, now sponsored by Tennents, in something approaching high spir-its. It was a confidence which seemed entirely justified as he beat Stephen Hendry 9–8. Higgins was fulsome in his praise for the teenage prodigy and smiled, 'I had to try to slow him down.' Hendry had gone 3–0 ahead and subsequently needed only one frame to win before Higgins staged a grand-stand finish (*Snooker Scene* noted: '[He] has always had a gunfighter's nerve when he has only one bullet left'). 'He is a better player than I was at his age,' offered Higgins with one hand before adding (and taking away with the other), 'But having said that, it's a different game now. It's a potting game. The pockets are easier.' Uncharacteristically, he con-fessed, 'I felt so daunted by him because he's so fearless. I couldn't keep him away.' He seemed unusually humble but then beat Dave Martin to set up a match with Mike Hallett which he won 9–7. He then called his estranged wife. The press conference afterwards was notable for an outburst directed at the governing body and complaints about the table. 'The pockets are closing the gap between the best players and the others,' he said. 'The game has been devalued and has lost its magic. It's all down to the WPBSA and I'm disgusted.' He had been drinking.

When he left the press conference at the Guild Hall he went downstairs to the players' room and had another drink. He was required to take a routine drugs test which had been introduced for the 1985 World Championships after the Stevens–Francisco furore and then applied to all ranking events. Ann Yates, working for Paul Hatherell at that time and soon to become WPBSA tournament director in her own right, witnessed what happened next. '[All the players] used to get a bit upset about the drug tests . . . [Higgins] used to say, "I was tested the last time," and, no matter how you tried to explain it, he used to go off the wall when you'd say the words "drug test". Paul Hatherell was the one who had to ask him, it was the formality. So Paul went up and . . . I knew there was going to be murder straight away, you know. And right enough [Higgins] called him all the names under the sun so I just took Paul aside and said, "Get out of here because we've got no chance if you stay about." There was another guy called David Harrison who was the master of ceremonies but also worked on the tournaments as assistant tournament director to Paul. And he had a better chance with Higgins than Paul so I just [told Hatherell] to leave us and go. I sent him upstairs to the hospitality room to stay out of the way.' It was a fraught situation and the security staff were all briefed to ignore Higgins, no matter what the provocation. Yates believed it was a ploy for him to take a punch, pretend to fall down dead and get out of whatever trouble he was in. Which was, by this stage, becoming more serious by the minute.

'I saw him come through the players' room door,' shudders Ann Yates at the memory of it all. 'There was a young security man on the door [and Higgins] pretended to trip and threw a pint over him. Naturally the kid jumped up and he was a big bloke. I said, "Just walk away." And he did. Then [Higgins] came over to me and started all the shouting and roaring about the WPBSA. They were always wrong and . . . persecuting him and all this kind of stuff. Then he said he wanted to see David Harrison.' Yates was concerned that an already difficult situation was beginning to gather momentum. Like a hurricane perhaps. She consented to Higgins' request. Harrison could look after himself and agreed to talk to him. Higgins turned to Yates and said, 'I want you to go out of the room because I don't swear in front of ladies.'

'I'll give him credit for that one,' she says, 'He never actually swore in front of me or at me. He said lots of other things but he didn't swear. So I went outside the door . . . I knew he had the glass in his hand but I didn't know what he was going to do with it, you know. And I heard him talking to David and [then] I heard a thump which was my cupboard being hit. The next thing I know the partition [in the middle of the room] has come out at an angle with Higgins on the back of it, still holding his pint. David had actually had enough and pushed him across the room. It was a comical scene but very frightening at the time. You know, horrific really. The partition went back up and the two of them stumbled out into the corridor. At that point Paul [Hatherell] had decided to come back down to see what was happening and walked right into it. Higgins just charged at Paul, caught him by the throat and headbutted him.'[13] Blood was pouring from the cut just above the WPBSA tournament director's eye as Higgins set about the business of trying to choke him with his own tie.

THIRTEEN

A woman rang to say she heard there was a hurricane on the way. Well, don't worry there isn't.

MICHAEL FISH, BBC WEATHERMAN, BEFORE THE WORST STORM TO HIT BRITAIN SINCE 1709 (1987)

The press were on the floor above and oblivious to the scene unfolding beneath them. David Harrison, the assistant tournament director who had agreed to talk to Alex Higgins and had subsequently become embroiled in a physical confrontation with him, now had to take further decisive action to prevent his boss, Paul Hatherell, from being strangled. He grabbed hold of the scrawny hand that was pulling the knot on the tie even tighter and explained to Higgins that if he wanted to play snooker ever again he would be best advised to release his grip immediately. It was an ambiguous threat that implied both disciplinary measures and broken fingers. Higgins, however, seemed able to appreciate the dangers of both options and let go. As Ann Yates recalls, 'Then he went into the players' room and started ranting and raving in there. We sent upstairs for Del Simmons.' Simmons was not, technically, his manager at this point but was the contracts negotiator for the WPBSA and known to hold some influence over him. John Virgo and John Spencer were with Simmons and, having known Higgins for years, also decided to come down. The doors were closed to keep the press out. 'I decided that I would try and calm him,' continues

Yates. 'I went in and I said, "Alex, for God's sake just stop it. Look what you've done already, you're in major trouble. Unless you stop now you're really going to be [in even more trouble] and he actually caught me by the shoulders, and it was the only time he ever physically handled me but it wasn't truculence, it was desperation.

'"It's like I am destroyed," he said. "My wife and children have left me."

'And now he's crying and I'm just getting him down when Del Simmons and the rest of them open the door and walk in. Well, he just went through the roof.' It was at this point when he also, literally, went through the door and the wall. The door was the type that traditionally accompanies a temporary partition. Higgins punched three holes in it. As the marketing department at the Preston Guild Hall is able to confirm, it has been kept as an unusual souvenir of the winter night sixteen years ago when Alex Higgins lost the plot. Unfortunately, the plasterboard in which he also punched a hole has not been preserved. He had not finished. Yates again: 'They all spilled over into my office which was across the way. He came out into the corridor where the caterers had stacked plates from the players' room, he started to pick them up and . . .' Yates makes a noise which indicates he was using them as frisbees. 'There were missiles flying. I mean I can laugh now but I promise you I was horrified at the time . . . our security man put his arms around him to [prevent him from throwing the plates] but he was putting cigarettes out on his hand, you know. It was an unbelievable scene. He was ranting and raving . . . he had a ball of foam in his mouth and I had never seen anything like it.'[1] At that point John Virgo advised someone to call the police. Higgins had not just crossed the line, he had taken a run-up and gone for the Commonwealth long-jump record. A police car was at the front of the building in short order.

Despite the best efforts of the WPBSA to keep a lid on the situation, the news reached the press room when somebody rushed in and shouted, 'Higgins has just nutted Hatherell.'

Chaos was now in full effect on two floors of the Preston Guild Hall. Newsrooms were alerted and phones were left hanging in mid-air as journalists rushed for the door. The story was given greater impetus by the recent publication of his ghosted autobiography *Alex Through the Looking Glass*, in which he confessed to using cannabis and cocaine and *Pocket Money* which depicted the high-rolling lifestyles of several people involved with the sport. His timing was less than perfect although his reappearance on the front pages probably did little to harm sales of both books. The *Sun* hinted at a correlation between his drug-related confessions and his response to the request that he take a drug test, but these were to prove erroneous as his urine sample was eventually found to be negative. The paper also quoted an eyewitness as saying, 'I saw two police officers dragging Higgins out of the players' room. He was screaming, "Leave me alone. I've got my own car."' It was a dramatic misreading of the situation. They were not offering him a lift. He was taken to Preston police station and detained until he had calmed down. He was then released. It was generally reported that he had been involved in a 'backstage scuffle' but board member John Spencer was quoted in the press describing the events as 'serious'.

The immediate aftermath of the 'backstage scuffle' necessitated an emergency board meeting of the WPBSA. Nine board members (Barry Hearn was in Japan) had originally been scheduled to meet at the weekend to discuss, along with other matters, Higgins' outburst at the Langs Scottish Masters when he implied strongly that Cliff Thorburn indulged in the recreational use of cocaine and complaints from three separate referees that he had been either physically or verbally abusive during the pre-televised stages of the Dulux British Open.[2] 'The board of the WPBSA will meet tomorrow morning to receive a report about the [headbutting] incident and will then take such action as the board considers necessary within the rules of the WPBSA,' droned a clumsily written statement. One of those 'rules' included a seven-day 'cooling-off period' before any action could be taken. The loophole permitted Higgins to continue his progress in the Tennents UK Open. Paul Hatherell, to his eternal credit, decided not to press charges but Chief Superintendent Keith Mackay of the Lancashire Constabulary was adamant. 'The police can still take action whether or not there has been any complaint,' he said. 'We are making inquiries to establish exactly what happened last night. It will be necessary to speak to both men involved.' A day later he revealed, 'We are preparing a file for the Crown Prosecution Service.' Higgins was still subject to a twelve-month order to keep the peace.

The wheels of justice were beginning to turn but, before that, some crisis management was required from Howard Kruger, who was possibly reassessing his blithe declaration ('Alex is a saint . . . we can get round his tarnished image') at the press conference called to announce that he had agreed to manage him. Another press conference was called. This time the venue was the doorstep at Delveron House. The invitation was extended to at least thirty print, television and radio journalists. As usual, having placed himself in very real danger and with a ready-made audience, Higgins did not disappoint. He waited just long enough to torment the broadcast media who needed time to prepare items concerning the hottest news story of the moment or 'go live' and then opened the front door. Never one to let down his public, he wore a fur-lined trapper's hat with his fringe poking out from beneath, an ankle-length sheepskin coat and a crooked grin. Kruger was standing next to him, still looking like a fat timeshare salesman. Higgins seemed in remarkably good spirits. He even staged a stunt when, in mid-flow, his mobile phone rang. In late November 1986 a mobile phone was a status symbol on a par with dating Heather Locklear. It suggested rock 'n' roll millionaire status, an impression which a six-bedroom Cheshire mansion did little to dispel. From the perspective of the twenty-first century, however, the phone resembled the kind of black rubber brick school children are compelled to fish from the bottom of the local swimming pool. 'Business is fine,' he said into the rubber brick, 'Send more money.' It was Higgins telling the press that they were there for his benefit and not vice versa.

'The most important thing at the moment for me to do is to actually turn round and do well at Preston tomorrow,' he said. 'Do you think you will be in the right frame of mind for tomorrow's match?' a female BBC accent asked from the front of the press scrum. There was a pause interrupted only by the staggered whir and click of camera shutters. 'I think I will be in the right frame of mind, [but] there's one thing I'd like to say, I hope my public comes and supports me . . . I've no doubt they will.' Kruger, in a double-breasted topcoat and mullet, looked nervous and uncomfortable, constantly shifting from foot to foot. The fact that his client turned up for a crucial press conference dressed like an extra from a Second World War drama set on a North Atlantic frigate was probably not his idea. So much for the 'He calls me boss' conceit. As Higgins turned to re-enter his house, the ground floor curtains already drawn against any further intrusion, another voice asked, 'Could you face life without snooker, Alex?' Kruger can be heard to whisper, 'No more questions,' but the words seem to get stuck in his throat. Higgins, in the most inspired and least stage-managed moment of his whole career, cut his manager short, looked into the television lights to his right, squinted, and replied with a rhetorical question, 'Could snooker face life without me?' And with that, he turned and went back into dark and lonely Delveron House. Kruger followed him and shut the door.

The next day, Higgins returned to Preston to play young Welshman Wayne Jones in the Tennents UK Open quarter-final. In London, by happy coincidence, on the day of the events at the Guild Hall, the listings magazine *Time Out* hit the streets. It featured an interview with Higgins that Howard Kruger had designed as part of an image change for his client and an attempt to publicize *Alex Through the Looking*

Glass. Higgins was immaculately attired and, for the picture, was shot in an expensive hotel with a well-read copy of *Deadeye Dick* by Kurt Vonnegut[3] at his side and a picture of Lord Mountbatten in the background. This was an image change indeed. Kruger had also sent his PR man Greg Millard to sit in on the interview. It was pretty tame stuff with Higgins breaking ranks only once to complain that his son Jordan was learning the rudiments of the game on a Steve Davis-endorsed miniature table and adding that watching Davis play was like 'watching your stools float'. Other than that he explained that he was interested only in getting on with his snooker and that 'the press have left me alone for a while. I suppose it's not the hunting season yet.' The three-hour WPBSA emergency meeting at the Crest Hotel in Preston ruled that the extensive list of charges, including the 'alleged' headbutting of Hatherell, would be put to the player and then to an independent tribunal. It then issued another statement confirming the board 'would not tolerate this type of behaviour'. The Hatherell incident, or one like it, had been coming and is synonymous with the kind of behaviour attributed by Theodore Millon to people suffering from Borderline Personality Disorder. He wrote: 'Borderline individuals go through "transient periods" in which irrational impulses are exhibited and fears and urges that derive from an obscure inner source take over and engulf them in an ocean of primitive anxieties and behaviours . . . these episodes of emotional discharge . . . afford relief from mounting internal pressures.'[4]

Higgins' internal pressures notwithstanding, 'his public' turned up to support him in huge numbers and cheered as he entered the arena with his hair unwashed, wearing a creased white shirt. Perhaps Barry Hearn had been right when he told Gordon Burn a few months earlier, 'I've been waiting for Higgins to be destroyed for years. He's looking worse and worse. There's nothing on him. Sores all over his face . . . but, the fact is, people like watching the process. This is what I think is one of the biggest things in our game.'[5] He was, it had to be said, still huge box-office. Wayne Jones was number fifty-six in the world and having reached the quarter-final of a ranking event for the first time, was not sure what to expect. He soon had a fair idea as Higgins won the first six frames of the day. The twenty-seven-year-old mounted a valiant fightback but Higgins eventually prevailed 9–5. As he had predicted the previous evening, he was in the right frame of mind. The semi-final almost inevitably involved a meeting with Steve Davis. The Guild Hall had become their chosen theatre of combat. It began in 1980 when Davis brought the 'Hurricane' to his knees 18–6 to win his first major title but also embraced the 1983 final when Higgins came back from 7–0 down to beat Davis, then world champion, in the final frame. The match three years later failed to live up to the billing and Davis won without any drama. Higgins, however, had taken himself to the place he went whenever he needed to come out fighting. He was relieved to discover that he still knew where to find it. Davis went on to beat Neal Foulds in the final to claim £60,000 and become the first snooker player in history to win more than £1,000,000 in prize money.

Higgins was aware that, after headbutting a WPBSA official, he could be either stripped of ranking points, suspended or, most likely, suffer a combination of the two. He would certainly receive a record fine. He could also, feasibly, be banned from the game for life. The need to earn some money was pressing. He was behind in his alimony and the Inland Revenue were keen to collect a six-figure sum in back taxes but, having delegated responsibility for his financial affairs to Howard Kruger, this news still awaited him. Although he harboured hopes of a reconciliation with his wife and children, he was also involved in an almost regular relationship with a psychology graduate called Siobhan Kidd. As he said himself, 'I know people will say that as a psychologist Siobhan will have a perfect case study in me.' The tabloids tended to refer to her as a former cocktail waitress (and almost always as a 'stunning blonde') but she was actually a professional art restorer. As a former friend of Higgins who insisted upon anonymity remarked, 'She was intelligent, kind, sensitive and gorgeous. Just what she was doing with him is anybody's guess.' Although Siobhan was hopelessly in love, the romance was at this time switched to an 'off' setting. Higgins was concentrating on his snooker and needed to accumulate ranking points and prize money as quickly as possible.

The Hofmeister World Doubles was the next tournament on the calendar and, although not a ranking event, had provided a measure of success in the past. The previous year he and White had thrown away their title after a night of heavy drinking and an argument about money but this time they were more focused. In fact, it helped that they were able to focus. It was the ultimate crowd-pleasing ticket. For the two simultaneous matches taking place either side of a screen bisecting the auditorium, 679 spectators watched White and Higgins while just four took in the other game. 'When Alex and I are alight, we're alight,' noted White, philosophically. 'When we're not, we're not. There's nothing either of us can do about it really.' Referring to a horse he had backed but that had lost on an objection, Higgins told a press conference after his fourth-round success against Rex Williams and Graham Miles that 'You mustn't weaken, sometimes adversity can be a friend.' Or, in his case, a persistent stalker. White and Higgins went out in the next round.

The court case took place in mid-January. He was charged with assault causing actual bodily harm and criminal damage. He admitted the charges and was fined £250 (£200 for the assault and £50 for the door). His solicitor, Anthony Burton, presented Preston Magistrates Court with a report by Professor David Goldberg, a psychiatrist, which recorded that Higgins, 'suffered mentally and physically when preparing himself psychologically for a game, when playing a game and in particular when recovering from a game'. It also noted that, because of factors such as the break-up of his marriage, he had become 'to a certain extent a recluse'. The court had been lenient but Higgins had been before a magistrate on several occasions and was not unduly concerned about another slap on the wrists. He was worried, however, that the governing body might expel him from the association and thus effectively end his career as a professional snooker player. He would have to wait until April to find out. It was on his mind at the Mercantile Credit Classic just before Christmas when he was dumped out in the fourth round. The Benson and Hedges Masters at Wembley was traditionally the first event of the new year and had a reputation for attracting spectators who did not behave with the quiet appreciation of snooker crowds at other venues. Jimmy White, as an unreconstructed and fully paid-up member of the London working class, was a huge favourite with the more disruptive elements of the crowd. And so was Alex Higgins. There was an enormous roar when he turned up to play Terry Griffiths in the first round. He had 'stuck the nut' on his boss and that made him something more than an anti-hero. It made him a bona fide, regular kind of hero to some of those present. That ticket touts could charge up to three times face value for any match involving Alex Higgins confirmed his status as the 'People's Champion'.

Griffiths was booed during the game but went into a 4–2 lead. As Higgins fought back he asked his supporters for some quiet and won the last three frames. After beating Joe Johnson and Tony Meo he qualified for the final against Dennis Taylor. Higgins was determined to win and adapted his game accordingly. He embraced a cautious, tactical approach and resisted the temptation to take on the kind of breathtaking long shots and improbable cuts with which he had made his reputation and which other players left on to tempt his arrogance. He was playing a percentage game. At 8–5 ahead and leading by 40 points in what should have been the deciding frame he made an unforced error and let Taylor in. It cost him the game. Taylor won that frame and the next three to secure his first major title since the Canadian Masters in 1985. Higgins needed the win much more. He took home a cheque for £28,000 (rather than the £51,000 which Taylor received) but the money was not the point. One error cost him another title and the opportunity to advance his case that the WPBSA could not ban him for life. 'I haven't seen him play better for some time,' said Taylor. It was true. He was on the ropes and fighting back, a quality which always served to endear him to the public. The fact that he had usually put himself on the ropes in the first place was overlooked. The ranking points he was trying to accrue before the tribunal were welcome and the provisional list (before the world championships) saw him comfortably placed at eighth. The forthcoming Tuborg World Cup, which the Northern Ireland team had won the previous two years, offered an opportunity to earn a sizeable proportion of the money the WPBSA were about to take from him. The same team (Higgins, Dennis Taylor and Eugene Hughes) won again without Higgins losing a frame and he made over £10,000. He picked up a much smaller cheque for going out in the first round of the Benson and Hedges Irish Masters to Terry Griffiths from which he was subsequently docked another £500 for being abusive to Kevin Norton, another tournament director. He was soon going to need all the money he could get his hands on.

The independent disciplinary tribunal met in London on 4 April 1987 with Gavin Lightman QC sitting in judgement. He had conducted the appeal tribunal following the Silvino Francisco–Kirk Stevens affair in 1985. Higgins, having already pleaded guilty to the offences at Preston Magistrates Court, also faced charges relating to several other offences, including 'the little bags of white powder' accusation levelled at Cliff Thorburn. He was fined a record £12,000 and banned from five tournaments: the European billiards championship (he had decided to try his hand at the sport); the Matchroom Irish championship; the Fidelity Unit Trusts International; the Rothmans Grand Prix; and the Canadian Masters. Lightman had the power to reprimand, impose an unlimited fine, suspend a player from one or more tournaments, deduct ranking points or expel the miscreant. It was a

generous ruling, one that did not disqualify him from entering the world championships which were due to start in a
fortnight. Ray Reardon, a board member who was unable to
sit in judgement on Higgins at the tribunal (as with all the
playing members who, it was argued, had a vested interest in
keeping him out of the way – hence the involvement of
Lightman) appeared on TV-AM to declare that he thought
Higgins had got off lightly while Barry Hearn, another board
member, told anybody who would listen that he should have
been banned for at least a year and that snooker had been
made a 'laughing stock'. Unsurprisingly, Alex Higgins was
not of the same opinion and went on *Wogan*, the most popular mainstream television chat show on British television, the
next day to give his reaction.

Higgins appeared on stage with Kruger behind him. They
were both dressed in matching pale-grey, double-breasted
suits and looked like a couple of 1980s estate agents on their
way to a wine bar. Terry Wogan introduced his celebrity guest
as someone who has had a 'stormy life'. Higgins sat down and
unbuttoned his jacket before crossing his arms. His body language was defensive.

Wogan: The bad boy of snooker gets dragged up before his peers,
  what have they done to him?
Kruger: Well, they have fined him £12,000 and suspended from the
  next five tournaments.
Wogan [to Higgins]: Are you sorry?
Higgins: I'm sorry, yes of course I'm sorry because I don't think the
  incident was defused when it could have been.

It is fair to conclude that Wogan was asking if he regretted his
behaviour but it was absolutely typical of Higgins to interpret
the question in a purely self-centred fashion, as if Wogan had
asked: 'Are you sorry about what has happened to you?'

Wogan: What did you do?
Higgins: I was being intimidated. When you play snooker for large

stakes I treat the game with that importance. We are dealing in cash situations now . . .

Wogan: But it was the headbutting.

Higgins: Yeah, it was that but I've had run-ins with that particular person for five or six years . . . ideally it is not very nice to head-butt someone [audience laughter].

Wogan: Can I add a personal note? When we met for the first time you were the epitome of kindness, very nice to my children, a very quiet and gentle man. I find it hard to reconcile that with the reports that one sees in the paper about your behaviour. Do you have a dual personality?

Higgins: I have got a short fuse but, equally, behind the scenes of snooker there's a lot goes on that never meets the eye . . . [there are] lots of cliques and bitchiness . . . and sometimes, if your face doesn't fit, that's just the way it is . . . for twelve or fourteen years I have been used and exploited.

Wogan persisted with his gentle line of questioning . . .

Wogan: So when you come back from your six months we'll see Hurricane in a bow tie?

Higgins: I'll come back playing to win. I'm quite heartened by a new resolve that I'd like to do it again because, after all, to go ten years from one world championship to another shows you can sustain your interest through thick and thin and I'm sure I can win again.

The next tournament would be the last one before the six-month ban kicked in. It was the world championships in Sheffield. A 'close associate' told one of the tabloids, 'This is a special time. He would get more of a buzz out of winning this title now than from any other championship. He wants to win it in "Hurricane" style and then lie low for a short while before a series of different projects in the next six months.' Kruger reflected, wishfully, 'Alex is well prepared for the world championship. His playing is still electric . . . we have helped him to prepare and now all he has to do is take it.' He went out in his second-round match to Terry Griffiths. Davis took the title for the fourth time. Higgins' ban did not extend to invitation events or exhibition matches and he used his free time to make as much money as possible. He also suggested that he was going to learn how to drive and to swim. In the event he achieved neither ambition, dated Siobhan, spoke to Lynn about getting back together, went to Australia for the Winfield Masters (and reached the semi-finals), tested positive for the use of beta blockers having been legitimately prescribed them for hypertension[6] and was arrested twice. Once for creating a scene outside the house of his in-laws in Heald Green which Kruger said his client 'regretted', and then again, less than a week after receiving an official caution for his previous misdemeanour, at Manchester Airport during a heated exchange with Lynn. He was detained and then released with no charge on this occasion. The season had started without him and he was also making the most of his relationship with the bottle. Barry Hearn reckoned: 'This season is his last chance to roll his sleeves up and show what he can do but it'll be very difficult for him to come back. He's nearly forty, not a little boy any more.'

Lynn Higgins was determined to get a divorce. She wanted to bring some closure to the situation. If she had been in two minds (which she did not seem to be) the incidents at the airport and outside the house belonging to her parents would have helped her to decide. Higgins put Delveron House on the market after he had been arrested in Heald Green and moved in with Siobhan Kidd in a flat in Fallowfield, the student district of Manchester and less than ten minutes from the centre of the city. He asked her to marry him. She said she would think about it. It was while living at her flat that he encountered student Kevan Cooke. 'We caught the 192 bus back to Levenshulme but stopped off at [the restaurant] Farooqs for a bite to eat,' remembers Cooke. 'There was a short drunk slumped over the counter giving the staff a torrent of abuse. For no apparent reason he turned around, looked at myself and my friends and said "You're all clever cunts." Then he turned his attentions back to the staff again. It was the former world snooker champion himself. The next thing he did was hail a taxi by staggering out of the takeaway and into the middle of the road where he stopped and swayed from side to side. When a taxi eventually pulled up he came back into Farooqs to collect his food and then asked us if we wanted to share the taxi with him. We declined his kind offer and he disappeared into the night.'

The headline screamed: 'HIGGINS BRIDE IN SUICIDE BID'. He had, it transpired, returned to the flat they shared and found Siobhan lying semi-conscious on the floor next to an empty bottle of tablets and called for an ambulance. She needed to have her stomach pumped. Higgins had decided to leave her and try one last reconciliation with Lynn. The suicide attempt, as he was perfectly placed to realize after his near-fatal overdose in Majorca, was Siobhan's last desperate throw of the dice to keep him. It seemed to work. Two days later they were hand in hand as Higgins turned up at the Norbreck Castle Hotel in Blackpool for the first phase of the the Mercantile Credit Classic, his first tournament since the ban. Higgins told the press, '[The reason for the suicide attempt] was a misunderstanding,' but Pat Hammond, who lived in the flat below, knew it was another episode in what she characterized as 'a very stormy relationship.' Hammond is now in a nursing home in Essex but still remembers the rows. 'I said to her on two occasions, "Why do you stay with him?" She said, "because I care for him, I love him and there's some money in it too you know."' It is impossible to gauge the context in which this comment was made. It could easily have been ironic or humorous, but it is symptomatic of the complexity of any relationship involving Alex Higgins. 'Sometimes,' continues Hammond, 'When he was left in the flat alone, after he'd had a bad time, he used to call his ex-wife's name out. He just referred to her, you know. Come and help me. He didn't seem to have anybody that he could turn to very much.'[7]

*

The provisional world rankings placed him at seventeenth, just below the crucial top sixteen who receive automatic entry to every WPBSA tournament and can count upon minimum earnings of £35,000. Higgins, without really trying, disposed of former English Amateur champion Tony Jones 5–0 to qualify for the televised rounds of the event. Less than a week later he returned to the Preston Guild Hall for the UK Championship. He was back on the treadmill and, despite his protestations to the contrary, happier than he had been on the outside looking in. The significance of the venue and his return to big-time snooker provoked a predictable chorus of approval from his fans ('It is well known that I am the people's champion and they can't take that away from me,' he said after beating Steve Duggan). He made swift and efficient progress to the fifth round where, as though the rules of the competition insisted upon it, Steve Davis was waiting for him. 'It will be like cat and mouse,' predicted Higgins enigmatically, 'but I'll be the cat this time because I like hot tin roofs.' Nobody was quite sure what he meant but Davis won 9–2 anyway. They would meet again in the last sixteen of the Mercantile Credit Classic in January but Davis was not troubled on his way to a 5–0 whitewash and his twentieth victory in twenty-four meetings with Higgins. The Irishman was short of matchplay and it showed. Against his stablemate Tony Knowles and in front of a capacity crowd at the Benson and Hedges Masters, some familiar complaints resurfaced. He accused Knowles of being in his eyeline when he was taking a shot. Higgins often adopted these tactics in a tight match. It served the dual purpose of providing an excuse should he lose while also denying his victor the satisfaction of having won a fair contest. He beat Knowles on that occasion but was knocked out in the next round by Mike Hallett.

His return, which had been greatly anticipated by the media and the snooker public, was something of a disappointment. 'I shall return' he had boasted, 'like Muhammad Ali.' Ali won the world championship three times but Higgins seemed to be all punched out. He failed to make a mark in the World Doubles (with new partner Eugene Hughes), the Irish Championship, the British Open and even the World Team Cup which Northern Ireland had won for the past three years. They were all competitions in which he had thrived. Now even these were denied to him. There was a brief resurgence in the spring when he made his largest competitive break of the season (an unremarkable 71) in beating Dennis Taylor during the Benson and Hedges Irish Masters before disposing of Cliff Thorburn. Davis finished him off in the semi-finals. It was hardly the Rumble in the Jungle. Higgins played the tournament with a bruised and swollen hand after, it was half-explained, he had punched a wall in frustration the previous week. He had also lost over a stone in weight and delivered a rambling monologue during the press conference after the game with Taylor in which he compared himself to the fourteenth-century kings of Ireland. The violence, weight loss and stream of consciousness oratory for the benefit of the press all indicated that Higgins was unravelling fast.

He would not find solace in the world championships. His performance in the final tournament of the season was another reliable indicator of the parlous state of his mind. He was humiliated 10–2 in the first round by twenty-two-year-old Maltese professional Tony Drago. Instinct told him he was in trouble after the first frame and he tried to intimidate Drago by telling him to 'be professional and sit down' after callow enthusiasm had drawn Drago to the table before his opponent had reached his seat. The man from Malta reflected later, 'I said nothing. I knew what a great player he had been and I tried to forget that in case it put me off and just [tried to] think about how he was playing this season. But I didn't expect it to be that easy.' The key is in the tense: 'I knew what a great player he had been.' It was clear that the younger players now regarded Higgins in the same way he had started to think about Ray Reardon in 1982. His six-month sabbatical had not left the game as bereft as he had hoped it might and now yet another new wave of players, twenty years his junior, wanted what he had left behind. Or rather, forgotten to take with him. As far as Higgins was concerned, the defeat to Drago was the worst moment of his professional career. It also confirmed his place outside the top sixteen in the world rankings for the first time in seventeen years. 'He hit me like a ton of bricks,' he shrugged before dusting off one of his statements of bald defiance and pulling it off the shelf. 'Maybe it will do me good,' he said. 'It could take me back to the grassroots . . . I think I have another world championship inside me.' He was trying to convince himself. *Snooker Scene* intoned gravely: 'His game is a mere husk of what it was. To halt the downward slide he needs to pay heed to some of the game's boring basics like keeping still on the shot, deficiencies for which his then uneroded co-ordination enabled him to compensate when he was a younger man.'

His private life, forever engaged in a symbiotic relationship with his snooker, was also in freefall again. He had granted Lynn a divorce but she chose the *Daily Star* as a vehicle to rebuff stories that she had spent all his money and had even charged him £40 for sex. She was hurt and striking out. His relationship with Siobhan had also collapsed after he had wrecked the flat they shared. She started a relationship with somebody else. Steve Davis received an MBE. It was a summer of discontent for Higgins although it is possible that the ban had given him a taste for the freedom of life without tournament snooker. It could, however, just have given him an insight into the emptiness of life without it. He was out of control. A fight in a fish and chip shop and the unnecessary publicity it attracted finally convinced Howard Kruger to place Higgins in the financial equivalent of an isolation ward. 'This is not a parting of the ways,' said Kruger as he established a separate company called Alex Higgins Promotions to market and manage his most high-profile client. 'We could have had some major bust-ups but he has been pretty well behaved. It is simply that I don't want him tarnishing anything that we're trying to do with the other players. Certain sponsors have not been keen to be associated with Alex and I don't want his reputation rubbing off on the team as a whole.' Four days later Higgins headbutted the assistant manager of the upmarket Manchester nightclub Applejacks. 'There was blood everywhere,' said a witness. 'I think the man had a broken nose.' Kruger might have had a point but his move came just before an entirely foreseeable tax demand of £100,000 arrived for Alexander Gordon Higgins in October. Kruger had also, due to the five-tournament ban, been denied his percentage of some serious money on the circuit. Higgins was 'assigned' a new manager called Robin Driscoll.

The distrust between Higgins and Howard Kruger was mutual. The lifestyle of the latter was also the stuff of legend in the snooker world. At an event in Preston, a rival manager had been paged on the public address system to contact his driver. Within minutes, Kruger was paged to contact his pilot. As Jimmy White revealed subsequently, 'Howard's style was very flamboyant . . . but Alex, who doesn't drive, blew the lid off the set-up when he discovered that, while he was travelling everywhere by train like a peasant, he was paying for Howard to descend like a demi-god from his chopper at the various venues.'[8] This particular manager–client arrangement seemed in danger of imminent collapse but Higgins found temporary sanctuary in his rekindled relationship with Siobhan Kidd. 'I love him very much,' she said, 'and he is not the madman he is made out to be.' He would spend a night in the cells and be in court before the end of the year charged with throwing an ashtray at her and smashing a drinks trolley at her flat after a row about his second wife. For the time being, however, the relationship was an oasis of relative calm as he struggled to recover his form and a place in the top sixteen. This would, of course, require practice and with no snooker room he had to travel into Manchester or to the Masters Club in Stockport. This was fraught with dangers and temptations which he was not always best equipped to resist but he enjoyed walking into snooker clubs and hustling. He would never grow tired of that.

The new season opened as the previous one had ended, with Higgins losing to unfancied opposition keen for a major scalp. On this occasion it was to Murdo McLeod, a former baker ranked number forty-eight in the world, in the Fidelity Unit Trusts. The next indignity involved a journey to Glasgow for a tournament available only to players outside the top sixteen. It was like Frank Sinatra singing 'New York, New York' in a karaoke bar or Elvis entering an Elvis impersonators contest and finishing second. Whenever his pride was dented there was always a chance of trouble and this occasion was no different. He turned up with a black eye for his first match, claiming that he had received it after an altercation with a revolving door, and then, the next day, arrived for a game with his other eye blacked. He looked as though he was wearing an extremely cheap pair of sunglasses. His subsequent range of complaints included the venue, the tables and the host city. He also refused to take a drugs test after losing in the final. He was reported to the WPBSA and, as day follows night, was fined £500 with £1,500 suspended and issued with a 'severe reprimand'. Board member Ian Doyle, the manager of Stephen Hendry, reflected, 'He's still one of the world's best players but he's not doing himself justice. Unless he gets psychiatric treatment, I fear for his future.' Higgins was back in the place wherever wounded animals tend to retreat and, in the same way the great Liverpool football team of the 1970s and 1980s were always at their most dangerous just after they had conceded a goal, was ready to strike back.

The Rothmans Grand Prix at the Hexagon in Reading did not start well. He was served with a bankruptcy petition by the Inland Revenue after refusing several requests to settle the outstanding debt. He believed, erroneously, that this had been taken care of by his management. The Revenue estimated that he was earning an average of £60,000 a year in prize money and an extra £50,000 in exhibition fees. The perceived persecution was just the kind of impetus he needed. 'I'm under a bit of pressure right now,' he reflected. New Zealander Dene O'Kane was on the end of the back-lash. He was whitewashed 5–0. Neal Foulds was dispatched with clinical precision on the day Higgins learned about the intention of HM Customs and Excise to take him to the High Court, Rex Williams went the same way after daring to level at 4–4 and then Alain Robidoux was tormented in the semi-finals. Higgins went 8–1 ahead before finishing him off at 9–7. Davis, as ever, was waiting and won 10–6 but Higgins had made his point and collected £39,000 (less management deductions) towards his tax bill. The Matchroom team were not permitted to talk to the press or fraternize with the sponsors as Barry Hearn was trying to establish his own com-petition and Rothmans had pulled out as potential sponsors (Davis was fined £12,000 for this breach of WPBSA protocol and snapped, 'Perhaps I should have headbutted someone') but Higgins showed up and declared, 'It's like the *Return of the Pink Panther*.' It was, of course, nothing like it but he felt he had grounds for cautious optimism. He again asked Siobhan to marry him and she said yes.

The optimism was misplaced. He was knocked out of the Tennents UK by Tony Knowles in the fourth round and was not invited to the Everest World Matchplay Championship, because he was not in the top twelve. But they were the least of his worries. As Christmas approached he was due to appear in court three times in a week on three separate charges. This must be something of a record. At the start of the week he was warned by a lawyer working for Lynn that, as he had not paid any maintenance since June and she was behind in both mortgage payments and school fees, he had forty-eight hours to find £1,000 and then arrange how to pay the rest of the £15,000 she was owed. The lawyer also warned Higgins that he would apply for him to be sent to prison for six weeks, the maximum period possible. ('I am in a daze,' he said. 'I was stunned when the judge said he could send me to jail. No one wants to spend Christmas behind bars.') He was back again in the middle of the week but did a deal with the Inland Revenue at the London Bankruptcy Court and agreed to pay off his £100,000 arrears over six months. Two days later he was bound over for a year on another charge of breaching the peace after the ashtray–drinks trolley incident which, it transpired, had been triggered after Siobhan came home to find him drunk and asleep on the floor and poured a cup of tea over him. He was fined £300. If the judicial system had run a loyalty card scheme, he would probably have been entitled to his next trial for free.

The ceaseless bad publicity surrounding Higgins was the excuse Kruger needed to terminate their business relationship. He sold his contract to EG Promotions for £75,000 who, in turn, delegated the management of his affairs to a company called Premier Talent, a venture headed by former Celtic manager David Hay. Peter Rafferty, a co-director at Premier Talent, declared, 'After Steve Davis, Alex is the most famous name in snooker but his undoubted talents on the table have been overshadowed by his problems off.' This was not news to the gentlemen in the press room at the Mercantile Credit Classic in Blackpool. Joe Johnson crushed him 5–0. Higgins, perhaps understandably, was making mistakes he would never usually countenance. By the end of the tournament Premier Talent boss and his putative manager David Hay announced, 'When we sat down and thought about it all, we just did not want to know.' Higgins was effectively without management for the first time in his professional career. And he was a man who needed management. Siobhan Kidd knew that. She locked him in her flat to prevent him from going to the pub after a row which lasted four hours. *The Times* headline the following morning read: 'SNOOKER STAR ALEX HIGGINS PLUNGES 25 FEET TO BREAK HIS ANKLE AFTER MISTAKING A WINDOW FOR A DOOR'. Pat Hammond remembers the incident exactly. 'My sister rang me from London . . . and I said, "Just a moment, I'll have to leave the call, Alex Higgins has just gone past my window."'

*

As luck would have it, the forces of law and order were in the vicinity. 'There was a policeman there, and a sergeant,' recalls Hammond. 'And the policeman said to the sergeant, "Oh God! Do you think he's dead?" Higgins looked up and said, "No, but I bet you wish I was." It was the funniest thing.' He had broken his ankle and received extensive bruising to his head. Steve Davis thought, 'Well that's Alex out for a couple of months – good. [It was] not because I didn't want to play him but I didn't like the aggro.'[9] Davis was to be disappointed. Higgins had been invited to play in the ICI European Open a fortnight after his fall and was determined to make his way there with new manager and long-time friend Doug Perry. Perry had been a fan of Higgins for years and, as a subsequent manager put it, 'was tricked into looking after him'. He adored Higgins. The object of his affections turned up at the Casino de Deauville on crutches and, hopping round the table for three hours and drenched in sweat, beat journeyman professional Les Dodd 5–2 after 170 minutes of snooker to make the last thirty-two. Willie Thorne, who had been absent from the 1981 Jameson International because he had his broken ankle in a cast, beat Higgins in the next round and sent him home early. The invalid commented, 'I made my point and got my ranking point. I gave him a little bit of a fright and I think I was justified in coming over.' Perry added, 'You know, if anyone else lived under his pressures they wouldn't just fall out of a twenty-five-foot window, they'd fling themselves off the Severn Bridge. He's frightened himself with that fall. I think he's realized that he could have killed himself. Maybe life will really begin at forty for him.' Just to be sure, and to prevent any more door/window confusion, he moved with Kidd to a little cottage in Lancashire. Pat Hammond breathed a sigh of relief.

He was on some kind of roll. He took back his Irish championship from Jack McLaughlin in Antrim, lost to Davis in the British Open and Thorburn in the World Cup in Bournemouth but travelled to Goffs auction house on a wild card for the Irish Benson and Hedges in high spirits. His fortieth birthday was approaching. Traditionally, the arrival at such a landmark induces at least a pause for thought. 'I swear to God I haven't even thought about it,' he told the *Sunday Times* before boasting, 'It takes twenty years to become an institution.' Hearn contributed, 'He's such a Jekyll and Hyde character that I, along with many other people, never thought he'd see forty. But he's still one of the top four draws in snooker and he's made millionaires of a lot of people.' That must have provided cold comfort for a man dealing with restructured repayments to both the Inland Revenue and his ex-wife who had also been awarded half the proceeds from the sale of Delveron House and a share of his other assets. These included, bizarrely, a 1,000-acre forest in Scotland (a tax avoidance scheme from which he had hoped to fashion a bespoke cue), a quarter share in a snooker club in Oldham and a couple of units on an industrial estate in Salford. The man who had profited from Higgins' performances at the table was now keen to unburden himself of any responsibility. 'I have had three years of continual abuse both privately and professionally and have had enough,' Kruger bleated in a press release.

With a provisional ranking of thirty-seven he was given no chance of winning the Benson and Hedges Irish Masters. That was just the spur he needed. He was limping by this stage, kicking out his injured foot before him and using the pain to cut through whatever intoxicant he had ingested. Thorburn, Foulds and Parrott were swept out of the way and, suddenly, he was in the final and facing Stephen Hendry. He had noticed the rise of Hendry from a distance and had even tried him out as a practice partner during the early stages of the world championships two years previously ('You can't be too careful,' said Ian Doyle as he bundled Hendry into a car with its engine running and drove him straight back to Scotland). Now Higgins had to beat him for real. For the first time in his career he was not sure if he could do it. Hendry, if body language is any indication, was even more scared.

Higgins hobbled round the table like Richard III as the young pretender sat totally still with a nervous half-smile bolted to his face and greasy streaks in his hair. The 'Hurricane' had not won anything worth worrying about for six years, he was almost crippled and had slipped down the rankings but he was still a force to be reckoned with. He was 5–2 down but won four consecutive frames to lead 6–5. Hendry went 8–6 ahead. The audience, typically vociferous, were all for Higgins.

Hendry looked terrified but still managed to take the game to a decider. Steve Davis was taking notes. 'Everybody thought that Stephen Hendry would just wipe the floor with Alex Higgins [and] that he'd done very well to even get to the final and all of a sudden Alex showed what true grit and character he had.' Hendry made a mistake on the black but thought he was safe. Higgins went for an audacious yellow and rolled it toward the pocket but the crowd chased it in. As it dropped down they erupted into life. Higgins won and, as he did so, walked towards the camera with his arms open like some kind of messiah figure. As he sank back into his chair he was manhandled by the paying public who were hanging over the boards and just trying to touch him. A middle-aged woman who had been trying to take a picture physically barged another spectator out of the way just to get to the 'Hurricane'. Siobhan rushed from the crowd to greet him. He embraced her. It was nothing like the world champiionships in 1982 but, after his year in the spotlight, it probably meant more. Steve Davis, with the benefit of hindsight, is prepared to suggest, 'I think this goes down as his greatest ever achievement.'

FOURTEEN

(O) Higgins *Ó hUigín* (from an Old-Irish word akin to Viking)

THE SURNAMES OF IRELAND, EDWARD MACLYSAGHT (SIXTH EDITION, 1999)

Higgins was in high spirits. During the press conference after his victory over Stephen Hendry in the Benson and Hedges Irish Masters, there were no complaints about the referee, the table etiquette of his opponent or the venue. In their stead was the charming Alex Higgins, who could be generous and entertaining company when the mood took him. He had a cheque for over £27,000 in his pocket and, having switched to non-alcoholic cider for the duration of the tournament, was also sober. 'There are a few good kids out there,' he said. 'And this one's the best of them all. We'll be seeing a lot more of Stephen, but I want to make a few more people frightened.' He was as good as his word. He had been talking about intimidating his opponents whilst facing them across the table. In the event he would 'frighten' them in a more familiar fashion and it would cost him his future. The alcoholic-free cider was put on one side to celebrate his triumph against Hendry and he got to bed just before dawn. Consequently, he missed his flight back to the mainland the next morning to compete in the final qualifying round of the world championship against Brian Morgan. He eventually made it without being docked a frame. He was exhausted but still on a high and held the former world amateur champion at 8–8 before Morgan took the last two frames. Higgins' preparation, as ever, had been less than judicious. He had momentum behind him and seemed poised to launch some kind of remarkable comeback but was unable to resist the temptation to indulge himself. The 1989 World Championship would be the first since 1972 in which he did not feature during the latter stages. Steve Davis won it again.

By the end of the 1989 season Higgins was ranked twenty-fourth but number nine in the earning stakes, with calculated prize money of £100,564.11. It was a substantial sum when compared to the average annual wage of £11,325[1] but it did not take account of his alimony payments, the money he owed the Inland Revenue, and both legitimate management deductions and those which required a little more explanation. Higgins was owed money and, during the close season, successfully applied for the winding up in the High Court of Framework Management Ltd. The company had debts of £460,000, of which Higgins claimed he was owed £51,536. The application was unopposed although the company insisted that the Higgins was owed 'only' £21,000. Tony Knowles, who had been persuaded to provide Framework with a personal guarantee of £120,000 to secure its overdraft, was owed significantly more. Higgins' occasional teammate in the Northern Ireland World Cup side, Eugene Hughes, was simultaneously pursuing Kruger Holdings Ltd through the courts. It had been supposed to represent his interests but part of Hughes' claim alleged that '[The company] managed him in a thoroughly negligent, wholly unbusinesslike and incompetent manner'. The High Court found that Kruger Holdings Ltd had, failed to render the accounts required by its management agreement.

Higgins was satisfied that his application had succeeded but was frustrated that a man who acknowledged a debt to him of £21,000 still drove around in a Bentley and lived a lifestyle even Tony Knowles acknowledged to be 'too elaborate'. As if that was not enough to disturb his fragile equanimity, Kruger was still a member of the WPBSA and had been elected onto its board of directors. Higgins

demanded that his former manager face disciplinary measures from the governing body and his solicitor drew an
appropriate reference to 'an apparent conflict between
Kruger being a director of a body acting for the benefit of its
members but to the detriment of one of its members'. The
WPBSA ruled initially that it was a private matter between
Kruger and Higgins. *Snooker Scene* noted, with one eyebrow
raised, that International Travel Bureau Ltd, a wholly owned
subsidiary of Kruger Holdings Ltd, had been awarded the
contract to be the official travel agents for world ranking
tournaments in Hong Kong and Thailand.

The sense of grievance was more acute than usual. And
that always spelled trouble. He embarked upon a chaotic
world tour that in the course of six months embraced Monte
Carlo, Hong Kong (twice), Bangkok and Dubai. At the
Monaco Grand Prix event organized by Snooker Europe he
turned up late and dressed like an apprentice bricklayer, fell
out with Tony Knowles and refused to attend the prize-giving
ceremony. He took Siobhan Kidd with him to the Far East
for the £200,000 Hong Kong Open but any hopes that she
might act as a calming influence were dispelled when Paul
Hatherell penalized him for turning up late for his second-
round match with eventual finalist Dene O'Kane. He lost the
game and later that night was involved in a row with Siobhan
which, according to the members of the press who were staying in the same hotel, involved her being locked out of their
room in her underwear and screaming. He was knocked out
in the first round by Stephen Hendry. Higgins, still drunk the
following morning, left without paying his £1,000 hotel bill.
Siobhan went home as he climbed on a return flight for the
Hong Kong Cup. Whilst there he turned up late and drunk
for a television appearance. He was supposed to play a few
trick shots with Jimmy White but forgot his cue and then
walked out. He was coaxed back, eventually, and deigned to
give an approximation to an interview before making sexual
advances towards the female presenter. With the inaugural
Duty Free Classic in Dubai a matter of weeks away, he went

home for the BCE International, the Rothmans and to patch things up with Siobhan. Probably in that order.

The BCE international in Stoke, the first tournament of the season, was over after one game when he lost to Mark Johnstone-Allen. He was then reported by press officer Ann Yates for failing to attend the mandatory press conference. The Rothmans Grand Prix promised more. His form, whilst not vintage, had shown an improvement of late and he had beaten Stephen Hendry in the Benson and Hedges Irish Masters and managed to get to the final of the Hong Kong Cup before being beaten by Steve Davis. Former world champion Joe Johnson beat him in the fourth round. Steve Acteson, then working for the *Today* newspaper, was in the bar of the Ramada Hotel in Reading having a drink with a couple of WPBSA officials and some of the other journalists on the snooker circuit later that evening. '[Higgins] was sitting with his manager Doug Perry and a couple of Rothmans girls,' he told *Total Sport* magazine a few years later.

I was at another table, some ten feet away . . . [He] was in a foul mood [and] suddenly launched into Ann Yates, whose niece was staying at the hotel, demanding to know if the WPBSA were paying for the niece's room. Ms Yates politely told Higgins that, in fact, [the niece's] boyfriend was paying the bill. 'What boyfriend?' demanded Higgins. My great crime was to then say: 'Well, if you look, Alex, he's sitting beside her.' I was sitting on a low stool with my back towards Higgins.

This will have been provocation enough. Higgins had been drinking, just been beaten and was being made to look stupid by a member of the press in a crowded hotel bar. It was a combination that made lighting the blue touch paper and stepping forward seem like sage advice.

'[He] lost his rag and rushed over snarling: "Acteson, fucking Acteson,"' recalls the journalist. '[He] whipped a bony forearm around my throat and tried to yank me backwards off my chair.' Acteson, at least four stone heavier than Higgins, responded by pushing him away. Looking for another outlet for his rage he turned towards the WPBSA officials at the table, Ann Yates and Nigel Oldfield, and Dave Armitage of the *Daily Star*. Alasdair 'Ally' Ross, then of the *Sun* but also a freelance press agent for the recently wound up Framework organization, attempted to reason with him. Higgins threatened him with a large glass ashtray. When Ross moved to defend himself Higgins cried, 'Look at that! Call the police.' As Acteson concludes, 'Nobody did. It was Higgins who would have been arrested.'[2] *Today* gave the incident three pages while the *Daily Star* went with the slightly disingenuous 'CRACKPOT HIGGINS ATTACKS DAILY STAR MAN'. At that time, Janice Hale used to compile a backstage diary for *Snooker Scene* at every major event and she had seen Higgins half an hour before his game with Johnson at the Hexagon. 'He was friendly and calm enough,' she wrote, 'though with some undercurrents of edginess. Some of these may have been to do with the match; others, it seemed to me, were to do with delays in putting the WPBSA right and, in particular, having his former manager Howard Kruger removed from the board. "It's not happening quickly enough," Alex said.'[3]

The decision of Siobhan Kidd to finally kick him out of her life will not have helped. Less than a month earlier she had told the press, 'There are a dozen red roses in my living room to say there's nothing wrong between us. We are getting wed as quickly as possible and it will be a quiet affair.' Unfortunately, before that improbable scenario could take place, he beat her about the face with a hairdryer. Siobhan Kidd later told the *Sun*, 'he wrenched the hairdryer from its socket and attacked me with it. He was like a madman. His eyes were blazing and he was shouting, "You fucking bitch, I'll teach you!" He just kept going for my face and head, hitting me again and again with such force that the casing [of the hairdryer] smashed on my head. There was blood pouring down my face . . . I thought "He's going to murder me, he's out of control." X-rays later revealed she had a fractured cheekbone. On another occasion, she claimed Higgins threw her King Charles spaniel puppy, Ruby, at the wall. She finally left him for the last time.

Her brother, Philip Kidd, Higgins' solicitor, also dissolved his relationship with him. The prospect of this double abandonment (as he will he have seen it) was on his mind as he physically assaulted Steve Acteson at the Ramada Hotel. The departure of Siobhan left him emotionally bereft. The decision of her brother no longer to represent him served to frustrate his attempts to pursue his claim against Howard Kruger. Higgins was in financial administration, one step away from bankruptcy, and had to seek the permission of the Insolvency Administrator to pay the legal fees with which to defend himself. It was necessary to avoid a ban that would prevent him from earning any money with which to pay back his creditors (notably, the Inland Revenue and his most recent ex-wife). The Administrator saw fit to accept that but would not give leave for the expenditure necessary to confront Kruger in court. In his mind, there was no obvious benefit to the creditors but then he had no appreciation of the factors that affected the way the 'Hurricane' played. His mental state was as crucial as his cue action.

When Philip Kidd terminated their business relationship Higgins applied for a second postponement of the WPBSA disciplinary hearing against Kruger, arguing that his new solicitors need time to master their brief. He was refused permission. He had already been granted one postponement. Higgins, of course, was also up on a charge, for missing a press conference, verbally abusing WPBSA officals Ann Yates and Nigel Oldfield and physically attacking Steve Acteson. Kruger resigned from the association two days before the hearing by way of the fax machine in the press room at the Guild Hall in Preston, the venue for the Stormseal UK championship. He was resigning, the fax declared, to 'put an end to what can only be described as a personal vendetta by Mr

Alex Higgins turns up at Macclesfield Magistrates Court in December 1985 after throwing a television from an upstairs window at his own home. (*PA Photos*)

An impromptu press conference at Delveron House after
head-butting a tournament official at the Guild Hall in Preston.
(*Eric Whitehead*)

"And the winner, ladies and gentlemen . ."

The tabloids' view of the incident. (*Mirrorpix*)

Outside Preston Magistrates Court. Manager, Howard Kruger, can be seen behind his back. (*Peter Reed*)

Higgins claimed he had been 'kicked by a horse'. The black eye was actually the result of something else entirely. (*Eric Whitehead*)

Higgins performing during a press conference in 1994. (*Eric Whitehead*)

With girlfriend Siobhan Kidd in January 1989. Higgins' injuries are the result of mistaking a window for a door and falling out of it. He also broke 30 bones in his ankle. (*Mirrorpix*)

Right: Back at the Guild Hall three months later for a world championship qualifier and still limping. (*Peter Lomas*)

Wrapped around the table like a snake during the 1990 Pearl Assurance Championship. (*Trevor Smith*)

The Blackpool qualifiers. Like Elvis entering an Elvis impersonators competition. (*Peter Marlow/Magnum Photos*)

Left: Higgins is stabbed by prostitute and ex-girlfriend Holly Haise. The police found him hiding under a hedge.
(*Manchester Evening News*)

Right: Holly Haise.
(*Express Newspapers*)

Right: His last appearance at the Crucible. As Steve Davis said: 'The last of a dying breed go down fighting.' (*Trevor Smith*)

Left: Higgins at the Grand National in Fairyhouse, May 2001. (*News Group Newspapers*)

Below: At Oliver Reed's funeral in County Cork in 1999. The picture that brought home to the public the plight of the 'Peoples' Champion'. (*PA Photos*)

1986: In the prime of life in a hotel in London. (*London Features International*)

Higgins . . . the intentions of Mr Kruger have always been honourable and the allegations have caused him considerable anguish.' Coates and Co., Higgins' new legal representation, replied, 'We believe that Mr Kruger's resignation at this time speaks for itself . . . [Mr Higgins] believes Mr Kruger's resignation will be greatly to the advantage of the game of snooker.' His legal team refused to accept that Kruger's resignation from the WPBSA board put him beyond disciplinary action. By joining the WPBSA as a member he had agreed to give thirty days notice before resigning; also, under company law, he was still responsible for his actions as a director. 'Unless we get written reasons from Mr [Gavin] Lightman [the independent QC used by the WPBSA],' explained Higgins' solicitors, 'we shall be attending [the disciplinary hearing with relation to charges against Howard Kruger]. The incidents relate to a period of time when Kruger was a member of the WPBSA. If the hearing does not take place it will prevent allegations embarrassing to the WPBSA coming to light.'

For his part, Higgins was subsequently fined £3,000 and, through his solicitors, announced, 'Both myself and my manager, Doug Perry, felt that we had a very fair hearing and that the tribunal, in deciding on the penalties, obviously took great account of the mitigating circumstances.' The letter is probably framed somewhere. Kruger, having resigned, was only liable for a public reprimand despite being found guilty of bringing the game into disrepute on two counts – the liquidation of Framework Management Ltd owing Higgins an admitted £21,000 and telling the 'Hurricane' that the 1988 Kent Cup in Peking carried a first prize of £35,000 in order to secure his involvement (in fact, Higgins was playing for a guarantee of £5000 and the prize money on offer was so poor that losing finalist Martin Clark who was on a guarantee of £1,500, received just £120.21 after miscellaneous deductions from his management company: Kruger Holdings Ltd).[4] *Snooker Scene* volunteered, 'The following morning it became clear that if Higgins had not attended, [his] complaint and case against Kruger would have had no official existence and could not have been used as mitigating circumstances for his own case.' It took Lightman four days to hear the evidence before him and on the fifth day he gave his judgement.

That night, John Virgo, the chairman of the WPBSA, travelled to Brighton to perform an exhibition at the opening of Kruger's new club ('Harry Potters').[5] Virgo had known Higgins for over fifteen years and had even hoisted a cue aloft at his wedding to Lynn in Wilmslow. And now he was giving his imprimatur to a venture owned by a man his association had found guilty of bringing the game into disrepute only hours before. Just because Higgins was paranoid, it did not necessarily follow that they were not all out to get him. Kruger missed an initial public examination by the Official Receiver over the collapse of Framework Management Ltd by declaring that he suffered from 'nervous anxiety'. It was a condition that manifested itself in the grinding of his teeth. He had, it transpired, been prescribed a mouthguard that he needed to wear at all times. Alan Baxendale, from the Official Receiver's office, remarked that he had seen two pictures of Kruger in the local press and, 'he was wearing a beaming smile . . . I detected no trace of a mouthguard'.[6] Higgins announced, 'I will chase him to the ends of the earth. I will never give up.' He gave more vivid expression to the same sentiment when I met him in the hotel room in South Manchester eleven years later. 'I haven't forgotten that bastard,' he said. 'He'll get his.'

If the moral highground was a foreign country to Alex Higgins, he would soon return to more familiar territory. The Duty Free Classic in Dubai is chiefly remembered for two incidents and neither of them involve Doug Mountjoy putting Alex Higgins out of the competition at the quarter-final stage. The players and press were put up at the five-star International Hotel. It boasted, among other delights, a swimming pool with a bar and a disco. Higgins, drunk, but at another bar in the hotel, began dismissing the talents of young professional Danny Fowler. Tony Goulding, Fowler's manager, took it for as long as he could stand and then threw Higgins, fully clothed, into the pool. He then jumped in after him and held his head under the water before letting him breathe momentarily and demanding an apology. Higgins, a non-swimmer, refused and so went under again. This went on for some time until another player, Jim Chambers, interceded on Higgins' behalf. It was a role he was to reprise the next day when Higgins renewed his battle with the tabloid press. 'I'd been out playing golf and then clubbing it with the *Star*'s Dave Armitage, a 6'5" gentle giant,' recalled Steve Acteson, the man Higgins had attacked after the Rothmans Grand Prix. 'Well oiled, we got back to our hotel in the early hours. I headed off to bed. Dave, however, headed for the hotel disco and straight into a storm.'

Higgins had been drinking heavily. When he saw Armitage he went over to berate him but made the mistake of sticking a finger in his face. Armitage responded by knocking him over with a textbook right hook. Chambers, yet again in the wrong place at the wrong time, prevented Armitage from continuing with the beating and, in so doing, slipped and tore his ankle ligaments. Higgins made the most of the fact that he had been 'assaulted' by a journalist and agreed not to press charges if he was allowed to host a press conference in the bar. He recited the usual catalogue of iniquities perpetrated upon him by the fourth estate. It was as dull as it was predictable but the chance to lecture a captive audience was too much temptation to resist.

The British leg of the Higgins world tour took in low-key performances at the Stormseal UK championship (out in the fourth round to Willie Thorne), the Mercantile Classic in Warrington (beaten by John Parrott at the same stage) and then the Benson and Hedges as a wild card (lost to Steve James 5–2) before a bravura performance in the Pearl Assurance British Open in Derby. He reached the final but then capitulated to French-Canadian Bob Chaperon after a strangely lacklustre first session which saw him go 4–1 down. He fought back but eventually lost 10–8 to the immeasurable relief of the bookmaking fraternity. He was disappointed but picked up £45,000 for finishing second (the biggest pay cheque of his career) and enough ranking points to guarantee him a place in the top sixteen for the 1990–91 season.

A brief sojourn in France followed (Steve James beat him in the first round of the European Open in Lyons) before a performance in Bournemouth in the British Car Rental World Cup that is remembered by all who saw it and millions who subsequently heard about it on the national news.

The Northern Ireland team, captained by Dennis Taylor, qualified for the final against Canada. Higgins, who had captained the national side before, was not happy with a position subordinate to a man he regarded as an inferior player but he could not do much about it. Taylor, for the sake of a quiet life, allowed him the limelight. Higgins wanted to go on first and did, drawing with Alain Robidoux. Taylor should have been on next but Higgins would not hear of it. He stayed on the table and left the Irish 6–2 down at the interval. Higgins then demanded a team meeting in the ladies' toilets on the grounds that they might be overheard in the gents'. Taylor announced that, as he was currently in line for the £6,000 first prize for the highest break of the competition (71 against Paddy Brown in the semi-final), he would not be sharing any of the individual prize money. Higgins, emotionally vulnerable and highly agitated, switched to his despicable alter ego, and is said to have insulted Taylor's dead mother before threatening him.[7]

It was unforgivable behaviour but even then he would have got away with it had he not delivered such a swaggering post-match press conference after Northern Ireland had eventually lost to the Canadians 9–5. 'In my estimation,' he said, 'Dennis Taylor is not a snooker person. He is a money person. The more he gets, the more he wants. He will never be sated. He puts money before country. He belongs back in Coalisland. He is not fit to wear this badge, the red hand of

Ulster.' It was a curiously sectarian and uncharacteristically patriotic deliberation from an avowedly apolitical creature. Somehow he had fallen into that alien groove. It could have expressed a need to crawl back into the protestant womb in which he grew up or, more likely, be a childish attempt to hit out with whatever weapons might be to hand. When news of his comments reached Taylor, he shook with rage and gave a press conference of his own. He claimed that Higgins had delivered a motivational speech to the third member of the team, Tommy Murphy, that amounted to the single sentence 'You played like a cunt', before detailing what Higgins had said to Taylor himself. 'He said, "I come from the Shankill and you come from Coalisland,"' disclosed Taylor. '"The next time you're in Northern Ireland I'll have you shot."' This was before the first IRA Christmas ceasefire for fifteen years. Higgins, typically, issued a denial: 'I never mentioned the Shankill. What I said was, "I'd blow his brains out if I had a gun."' A spokesman for the Ulster Defence Association (UDA) went on the record to declare that Dennis Taylor was welcome in Protestant Belfast any time. Higgins realized he had gone too far and was even prepared to confess to wanting to shoot a fellow professional snooker player rather than admit to dredging up sectarianism. The media lapped it up.

Higgins issued a pro-forma apology through his manager Doug Perry: 'I now publicly retract [the remarks made to Taylor]. I very much regret my outburst. In this tournament, I was not playing for Alex Higgins or for financial gain. My heart was in doing my very best for my country. My final apology is to the people of all the thirty-two counties of Ireland for any hurt or embarrassment caused to them.' It is, if nothing else, a historic declaration embracing both Ulster pride and a political appreciation of those who sought a united Ireland. It was, as American President Lyndon Baines Johnson said of the resolution that allowed American ground troops into Vietnam without declaring war, 'Like grandmother's nightshirt. It covers everything.' Taylor was not so sure and replied, 'I've read his apology but I'll still be sending in a complaint. Some of the things he said are unprintable.' It was not the beginning of the end of Alex Higgins – that was already some years past – but it was this moment when the currents took hold of him and began to drag him under. He would try and fight back to the surface (and on rare occasions make it) but he could not gulp enough oxygen into his lungs during those brief communions to sustain himself. As Clive Everton put it at the time, 'The underlying trouble is that Higgins has reached the age of 41 with a set of emotional needs scarcely modified since infancy: an insatiable lust for the limelight, an imperious wish to have his own way and a yearning for unconditional love expressed as an assumption that he will be forgiven no matter what he does.'[8]

Higgins was able to turn the furore about his behaviour into a force which would drive him forward. Having missed the previous year's world championship, he was able to gather himself together to beat James Wattana in the final qualifier at Preston. He also had time to turn up at the house he had bought for Lynn in Heald Green and, denied entry, throw the skateboard he had bought for Jordan through a window. News of this latest incident, coming so soon after the publicity accorded the 'death threat' to Dennis Taylor, went round the surrounding area even before it appeared in the *Manchester Evening News*. It was assumed he was on the rampage again and people in the immediate vicinity drew their curtains. Vanessa Fitton lived on the same estate: 'They used to live at the back of us. I heard a commotion and then just thought, "Here we go again." He was round quite a lot at that time, causing trouble and what have you. If we ever heard police sirens late at night we used to look at one another and go, "Higgins is here again."' The police were called and he was subsequently fined £50. Once again, everything was building up, slowly, inevitably, to a destructive crescendo. He drew Dennis Taylor in the Benson and Hedges Irish Masters quarter-final. Taylor was tainted as the player who would always 'choke' on the big occasions; a reputation he shed after his 1985 world championship victory over the 'Hurricane', the instinctive genius who usually played best when his back was against the wall. This was the first game between the two since Higgins had allegedly insulted Taylor's mother and threatened to have him shot. Steve Davis called it 'the grudge match of all time,' but in retrospect this was merely the sound of the orchestra tuning up.

The arena at Goffs was packed. Future world champion Ken Doherty told the documentary-makers behind *When Snooker Ruled the World*, 'There was no way in the world I was going to miss that, no way. I thought there was going to be a fight before they started.'[9] Higgins swept his hair into place with a comb, checked himself in the mirror, straightened his emerald green bow tie and declared himself 'dapper'. In the other dressing room, Taylor was talking to himself. 'I was determined I wasn't going to lose that match,' he told the camera. '[I was] standing in the dressing room just looking in the mirror and . . . shouting to myself, "You can't lose, you can't lose" . . . it's the only time I've ever done it. I had something to prove because of what had gone on before.' Higgins received his usual noisy welcome. Taylor followed him out and bowed to the crowd before walking to his corner. His opponent looked unflustered as he dealt with the national newspaper photographers who had been sent to capture the moment. The two players shook hands but Taylor refused to look Higgins in the eyes. The game was of secondary importance to the televised drama being played out in the round. Higgins also wanted to win but he wanted to win with style. He ripped off his tie and got down to business.

'He played some really flamboyant shots,' remembers Taylor. 'When he played to the crowd it was a little bit like he wanted to really rub your nose in it, he wanted to humiliate you.' After one audacious frame-winning pot came off three cushions and dropped into the corner pocket, Higgins lifted his cue above his head. If it was an attempt to mock or mimic Taylor's famous world championship victory celebration in 1985 it was premature. Taylor never looked like losing and eventually won 5–2. The post-match formalities were observed but as Higgins went to shake hands he met Taylor's outstretched palm and pulled him forwards. It was as if to say, you might have beaten me but I'm still Alex 'Hurricane' Higgins and you come to me. Remember your place. It unbalanced Taylor and forced him to make eye contact. Higgins is a picture of genuine menace at this moment. Resentment and bitterness are etched upon his face. He had been drinking. To the people who knew him well, it was a face that promised trouble. It was a face that could clear a hotel bar faster than a bomb scare. Taylor turned away instantly and raised an arm above his head. In the event Higgins delivered nothing more than a rambling monologue to the press and was escorted to his dressing room muttering imprecations. At least qualification for the 1990 World Championship might offer some form of redemption for the worst season he had ever endured.

Steve James was 4–1 ahead and cruising in the first round but the score flattered him. Higgins found a rhythm and pulled it back to 5–4 before the interval. He then won the first frame of the next session to tie the game at 5–5 before James recorded a 16 red clearance (after a free ball) and a break of 135 in the eleventh frame. Higgins was then confined to his seat for most of the evening. James won the next four frames and Higgins was out. He pulled the cue ball to the cushion and conceded. James shook his hand and returned to his dressing room. Higgins sank into his chair and nursed a triple vodka and orange with his cue nestled in the crook of his arm. He took a gulp and then decided, before the glass had reached the table, that he wanted another one and then he repeated the action until he got tired of the pretence and sank the lot. The balls had been cleared away and a cover placed over the table but still he sat there. An enterprising producer at the BBC kept the camera running. Two dozen spectators opted to stay in their seats just to confirm Barry Hearn's brutal but accurate observation five years previously that people 'like watching the process' of Alex Higgins falling apart. They could watch an inebriated and lonely middle-aged man sat in the corner of a pub for free but they would pay to watch Alex Higgins. It was almost as though they were drinking with him. The bolder members of the audience asked him if he wanted a drink just so they could tell their friends that they had bought the 'Hurricane' a drink. He let them. He was in the mood. The camera stayed on him until the lights went out and then he went to his dressing room, put on a bow tie and made his way to the press conference. It was estimated that he had dispatched twenty-seven shots of vodka during the game.

As he walked along the corridors backstage at the Crucible rage overtook him. He was too drunk to stop it. He thought that he had probably played his last world championship game at the venue although he was unable to come to terms with the unpalatable truth. He had paid £100 to enter the world championship in 1972 and won £480. The winner of the 1990 tournament would be presented with a cheque for £120,000. He was not oblivious to the fact that he had almost single-handedly dragged the sport into the modern age. But, as he considered the enormity of that achievement, he had also to reckon that he was almost bankrupt, in arrears with the Inland Revenue, single again, virtually homeless and facing yet more disciplinary action from the WPBSA. These thoughts may or may not have been at the forefront of his mind. They may just have been somewhere in a consciousness fogged by 40 per cent proof vodka. Wherever they were, he was almost certainly not daydreaming about running through a field of wheat with the sun on his face and a dog at his heels as he approached the door to the cramped press room back-stage at the Crucible. 'Thanks for coming down, Alex,' smiled WPBSA press officer Colin Randle. He held open the door for him. Higgins said nothing but punched him in the stomach and then made his way to the front of the room as though nothing had happened. His speech to the assembled media merits repeating in full. It was delivered without notes:

Well chaps, the current events over the last few weeks have not been very good, this way or the other. So I would like to announce my retirement from professional snooker. I don't want to be part of a cartel. I don't want to be part of a game where there are slush funds for everybody, where players are mucked about. I do not want ever again in my lifetime to get less than job satisfaction.

If Derek Jameson, for instance, can leave the News of the World and go to Sky TV there has to be a place for me in this life. I would like to congratulate Steve James. He's a nice lad, he means well but I am not playing snooker any more because this is the most corrupt game in the world. It needs to be brought to the attention of [the Department of] Trade and Industry.

There are an awful lot of people running about this world who put their kids through certain schools, feeder schools, grammar schools and you get absolute tossers doing jobs for exorbitant money. Well, I don't really want to be part of it. You can shove your snooker up your jacksie, I'm not playing no more and it's not sour grapes, nothing, it's the truth.

I wish Cecil Parkinson and Maggie Thatcher would do a probe into snooker, then we would actually find out the real truth. The 'Hurricane' doesn't want to be part of this tripe, no disrespect to Northern people because I like tripe. There's a thing called job satisfaction. I don't want to be part of a cartel, corruption, whatever. That is the end of the story. I hate it. I abhor it. I'm not going to break the cue because I like the cue but it is a corrupt game.

A journalist attempted to ask a question, but Higgins interrupted . . .

Excuse me, I've not finished. I've not finished. Rock on Tommy. The people who work within the game appal me. I won't be using a cue again. I've had all sorts of shit thrown at me by the media in the past six or seven years. I was supposed to be a stalwart of the game, the guy who took all the brunt. The kid who took all the brunt is absolutely sick up to here [he points to his chin]. I am not prepared to take it any longer. It has interrupted my private life, my children's lives and . . . a few relationships. Let's see how you do without me because I ain't playing no more.

I might do overseas trips and teach kids from Amsterdam. I don't like the WPBSA – the way they do things. They can throw me out, shove me out . . . I couldn't give a damn. I don't believe you [looking at one journalist in particular] judging me. I cannot handle some of the untruths. I am going to the Law Courts. I am going to fight the newspapers. I have got plenty on my plate. One of the first papers I go for is the [*Daily*] *Star*, the *Sun* and what's that other one? Apart from all the newspapers the ideal thing is the WPBSA is near *sine die* corrupt.

With that he stepped off the stage and made for the exit. On his way out he was asked: 'Will you reconsider?' He replied: 'No, no, no, none whatsoever. There is no way. I don't want to be part of this. I don't want to be part of corruption. No more snooker from the "Hurricane".' As the press corps exchanged glances and wondered how the hell they were going to report a resignation speech that embraced Cecil Parkinson, the stomach lining of a cow, the iniquities of a two-tier education system, children from Amsterdam and a catchphrase associated with popular comedy double act Cannon and Ball, Randle revealed what had happened before Higgins had got to the microphone. There was the story.

The next day, Higgins issued a statement through his manager Doug Perry: 'This was not a spur-of-the-moment action. It was the build-up of five or more years of total frustration and anger on his part about the way snooker has been run. He feels frustrated that there appears to be one set of rules for some and one set of rules for others. Last night was not just a protest by Alex Higgins for Alex Higgins. His concern is for the game and for the new young players coming into it.' Nonsense of course. It was nothing more than a protest by Alex Higgins for Alex Higgins but it served to reveal the fundamental truth that Higgins equated himself with the game. In his mind, he was snooker. Even if Stephen Hendry was just about to steal his thunder and become the youngest ever winner of the world championship.

As the white Mercedes stretch limousine edged its way through the photographers and camera crews outside the disciplinary tribunal on 1 July 1990 he knew what to expect. And it was not going to be good news. He had already admitted punching Colin Randle, bringing the game and the governing body into disrepute, abusing WPBSA chairman John Spencer and threatening to have Dennis Taylor shot. Gavin Lightman QC considered expelling Higgins from the association but after hearing various mitigating factors and submissions with regard to his future conduct, opted to ban him for the duration of the 1990–91 season, dock him twenty-five ranking points and demand that he pay £5,000 costs. Looking smart, if uncomfortable in a tie that was obviously too tight, Higgins told the press from the doorway of the WPBSA offices in Bristol: 'I've a great love for snooker and I shall continue to play one way or another. I'm disappointed but I'll just have to take it like a man.' He looked chastened. Subsequently he would thank the board 'for their fair consideration'. He was engaged in the business of bridge building but the currents were now too strong for him. Beyond the legalese, the stark facts were that Higgins, for a year at least, had no means of earning a living beyond the exhibition circuit. He was invited to appear in the non-WPBSA sanctioned £1 million Sky World Masters promoted by Barry Hearn, but when it became clear that seven of the top sixteen players, Stephen Hendry prominent amongst them, would boycott the event if Higgins turned up, he declined the invitation.

An evocative piece in the *Today* newspaper captured him during his period in exile, playing an exhibition match on an industrial estate in Whitham as the rest of the snooker world gathered in Preston for the Stormseal UK championship:

While [sixteen-year-old] James Vicarey compiled his crisp breaks, Higgins just sat with that attitude of affected disinterest which players employ when they are off the table. He swallowed his lager and drew so powerfully on his cigarette that it shone like red neon through the blue smoke . . . after his defeat by Vicarey, Higgins took a short break. 'Gone off to the practice table I suppose,' said one [spectator]. 'Come on, get Alex out of the bar,' shouted another.

When he's winning, Higgins likes to make fun of his opponents. One beaten youngster potted the final pink and lined up the black. 'Come on now, concentrate,' sneered Higgins. 'This could be a break of 13. Take your time.' And when he played a woman later: 'I think you must be used to playing on a table with no pockets.' . . . [the night before he had] complained about the noise and then asked for some lights to be turned off.

'I wish he was married to my wife,' said someone. 'I hate her' . . . I wanted to ask Higgins about [the difference in his approach to the game when playing novices] but his agent Doug Perry wanted £1,000 just to talk to him. 'And he won't say nothing then because I can go to one of the grubby papers and get 20 grand.'

When he was not playing on industrial estates, he was hustling, drinking all day and gambling. He should have been practising. After all, he knew that with no ranking points he would soon have to suffer the indignity of playing through the qualifying rounds for the major tournaments against hungry young professionals and experienced club players determined to make a name for themselves. He found the humiliation intolerable.

He used the time of his enforced absence to record a video called 'I'm No Angel'. It was an attempt at an autobiography but also, presumably, an exercise in reputation rebuilding. As *Snooker Scene* reflected in a scathing review, '[it] attempts the impossible: a whitewash job on Alex Higgins'. It came out in time for the Christmas market and Higgins made another appearance on *Wogan* to promote it in November 1991. His fellow guest was the writer Auberon Waugh who was there to sell his printed autobiography, *Will This Do?* The vast majority of the viewers had heard of either one or the other, with the snooker player by far the more famous. Higgins turned up in a Gio Goi jacket (the Manchester fashion house had previously supplied him with clothes from their successful 'F*cked Up' range)[10] and a baseball cap. Waugh was wearing a Look-At-Me-I'm-An-Eccentric pinstripe suit with his tie tucked into his trousers. They were introduced simultaneously as 'a couple of hell-raisers . . . one striking fear into all and sundry with a cue and the other often doing the same with a pen'. It was, the producers must have assumed, a master-stroke. There was bound to be some kind of friction with Higgins as the unpredictable and occasionally violent working-class hero and Waugh as the opinionated blue-blood class warrior.

Higgins was cute enough to realize what was going on and bought a copy of Waugh's book before the show. He was on his best behaviour and defended the man sitting next to him on the sofa after one mean-spirited recollection from Waugh about his childhood. 'I've read the book,' said Higgins, 'and it's only because the working class were picking on him.' 'Thank you Alex,' said Waugh after a couple of beats. He seemed utterly confused by the unilateral disarming of his fellow guest. This was Higgins at his cunning best. Continuing with the charm offensive, he went on to draw a parallel between himself and Waugh with reference to a quotation from *Will This Do?* 'I have to refer to the book Terry,' he told the host, 'this is what might bring myself and this man together: "Looking back over my career to date and all the people I have insulted, I am mildly surprised that I am still allowed to exist".' And with that he turned to shake hands with the editor of the *Literary Review*. 'I've never really thought of myself as Alex's blood brother but having met him this evening I can see that we are,' exclaimed Waugh. They were both skilled at the vituperative arts and a measure of mutual respect was evident. Wogan despaired, 'Here I am trying to create abrasion and you are flinging yourself at each other.'

Lynn Higgins featured in the video ('He has a lovely side to him') but his current girlfriend, Laura Jane Croucher, whom he had met in a Manchester coffee bar in 1990, was conspicuous by her absence. She was attractive, vivacious, 'sort of recognized him' when she first saw him and thought he might be a jockey. His relationship with Siobhan Kidd was in its final death throes. Croucher was working as a call girl under the pseudonym Holly Haise. Higgins started talking to her and, as she put it, 'It went on from there.' It certainly did. 'At the time I was doing well. I had a new car every three months, an £80,000 apartment, lots of beautiful clothes and I went to all sorts of upmarket events. Even so, there was something about Alex I fell for,' she told the *People*. Higgins was to have some form of relationship with her for the next seven years. Until just after she stabbed him in August 1997, in fact. 'He was a buzz to start with. We were both champagne mad – and I always paid. Over the years I'd say I spent £50,000 on Alex. Once we spent £25,000 on a trip to America. Then when we came back we stayed in the Ritz Hotel in London and he trashed the room. That cost me even more.'[11] Haise has gone public about her relationship with Higgins several times. She told *Woman's Own* in 1998, 'Alex was [my] first proper love, I was infatuated with him.' She was financially independent and claimed to have a regular client who was a multimillionaire. She would subsequently boast that she had received over £1,000,000 from him before he died but her circumstances certainly did not support such an assertion. She was living in a council house in Swinton, a nondescript suburb of Manchester near Old Trafford football ground. Higgins would subsequently move in with Haise and her young daughter Sam.

The thoughts of the two-time world champion as he turned up at Trentham Gardens in Stoke on 1 August 1991 to register for the qualifiers for all the major tournaments are unrecorded. He was now ranked 120th in the world. The whisper that Alex 'Hurricane' Higgins had entered the building went round the 400 other entrants like an uncharitable murmur at a funeral. For his first game he arrived in purple suede shoes and was whitewashed by twenty-year-old Adrian Rosa, a young man who had lost all his previous pre-qualifying events, and was therefore out of the Rothmans Grand Prix before he had had time to unpack his suitcase. He was determined to reclaim his position in the top sixteen but over the next eight weeks also failed to qualify for the Asian Open, the Mercantile Credit Classic, the Regal Welsh Open, the Pearl Assurance British Open and the European Open. He did, however, secure a place in the Dubai Duty Free Classic and the televised stages of the UK Open whilst also managing to get arrested at Uttoxeter racecourse after arguing with champion trainer Sir Gordon Richards in the owners and trainers enclosure. After a night in a police cell, he was released without charge. He had qualified for two out of ten tournaments and recited the usual litany of complaints (referee, opponent and table) when he was dumped out of the others. By the end of the month he had earned just £1,150. Upon his return to the professional game, he reached the quarter-final in Dubai before losing to Steve James and then faced Stephen Hendry in the UK Open on 16 November 1991. His progress in Dubai was rewarded with two ranking points but he needed to beat Hendry to gain enough points to avoid the debilitating business of competing in the qualifiers at the start of the following season. There was a lot at stake.

Hendry brushed him aside like a beggar at a cashpoint and led 6–2 at the interval. Higgins appeared in the players' room and began a foul-mouthed tirade before making eye contact with Hendry just before the start of the next session. 'Hello,' he announced, 'I'm the devil.' Hendry, resolutely unshocked, went on to win 9–4. The conversation between the two of them as they shook hands after the game remains subject to interpretation: Higgins claims he said, 'Well done Stephen, you were a bit lucky,' while Hendry claims he said, 'Up your arse, you cunt.' Higgins was put on another charge. Ian Doyle, Hendry's manager, commented afterwards, 'Higgins must be removed from the game . . . he is a demented, raving lunatic.' Higgins lodged an official complaint. The hearing into the accusations and counter-accusations was postponed four times. The prevarication granted Higgins enough time to enter the world championship qualifiers (he was eventually beaten by Alan McManus) and, in April, the Irish Benson and Hedges where he went down 5–3 to Ken Doherty in front of a capacity crowd at Goffs. It was the final tournament of the season and Higgins celebrated after the match by demanding that a patron of the Lillie's Bordello nightclub in Dublin swap clothes with him and stripped down to his boxer shorts to facilitate the change.

It was not the only time he found himself unexpectedly semi-naked in Dublin in 1992. Marianne Faithfull was playing Pirate Jenny in a wildly successful adaptation of Bertolt Brecht's *Threepenny Opera* at the Gate Theatre. She had spent a drunken, wild night with Higgins in the 1980s when she was still drinking too much and although she could not remember much about it, he had clearly not forgotten and rang her up. 'He was,' she recalled in her autobiography two years later, 'Small and weedy but charismatic, and very, very cool in a mad way.' She met him in a public house after rehearsals. 'He has a well-deserved reputation as a lunatic, so I consulted a few friends about what I should do. [One of them said]: "If you're hell-bent on sleeping with Alex Higgins, don't do it in your own home – go to a hotel."' It was good advice and Faithfull resolved to follow it. She also provided Higgins with a list of preconditions. He was to pick her up at the theatre at 11.30pm and take her to a hotel. He would then have the benefit of her company for two hours, no more. The two wilful hedonists were soul mates with something beyond a shared (and in Marianne Faithfull's case, alleged) predilection for Mars bars. A healthy disrespect for the Establishment was not the least of it.

'On the way to the hotel,' she continued, 'I began to think I was absolutely insane! He's a well-known madman . . . so I gave [him] a big lecture in the taxi: "Look, Alex, I want you to be really cool. I know you're going to find this difficult, but control yourself when we get to the hotel. And, whatever you do, for God's sake do not mention my name. Have you got that?"' He confirmed his understanding of the arrangement and then walked into the hotel bar and ordered himself a vodka and tonic and a sparkling mineral water for his companion. Most of the clientele knew who he was but failed to recognise the 'Girl in a Fur Rug' from the infamous Rolling Stones trial of winter 1967. It was an oversight which was corrected as soon as Higgins went to check in. "Don't worry, Faithfull,' he shouted, 'when I check in at the desk I'll call you Vicki, not Marianne."' She added, casually, 'I guess I'll never learn.'[12] It was yet another shared characteristic.

Higgins engaged Robin Falvey, a highly-respected London solicitor, to defend his interests at the disciplinary tribunal called to deal with the accusations levelled by Hendry and Doyle. After several postponements it finally met at London's Law Courts in August 1992, nine months after the events were alleged to have taken place. Falvey tore into the WPBSA like a starving dog in a butcher's dustbin. His first task was to prevent Gavin Lightman presiding over the case. Lightman had remarked at the tribunal which handed Higgins the one-year ban, 'This is the last time you have a chance to prove to the board and myself that you can do credit to the profession.' Falvey successfully argued that such a statement was prejudicial. When the disciplinary committee, comprising four of Ian Doyle's fellow board members, eventually met in August, five of the seven charges were dropped including the claim that Higgins had used 'gratuitously foul and abusive language' about Hendry and then congratulated him in a robust fashion after his victory. It had taken eight months to get to this stage and neither Doyle nor Hendry was in attendance. Falvey had intended to cross-examine Doyle. Higgins was eventually fined £500 for verbal abuse directed at former press officer (and now tournament director) Ann Yates and the same amount again for failing to show match referee John Street 'appropriate dignity and respect'. The two new fines brought Higgins' total to £23,200 in twenty-one years as a professional.

There is something about Blackpool that is very Alex Higgins. It might be the faded glamour, it might be its brazen honesty or it might just be its remarkable and enduring popularity. Whatever it is, Blackpool is the British working-class take on Las Vegas and Alex Higgins is still a hero to the people who pack out its hotels and boarding houses every summer. He is one of them and has never pretended to be anything else. The decision to locate the qualifying school for the ranking events in Blackpool made sense beyond even logistical considerations: snooker still mattered in Lancashire and it brought together the people who watched the sport with those who played it. Which is not to say that the Norbreck Castle Hotel was anything like a sporting citadel. It was then a functional, peeling and soulless building, as far from the relative televised luxury of the Crucible or the auction ring at Goffs as it was possible to get. Players and members of the public looking to kill a few hours before the pubs opened drifted around like delegates at a conference for the badly dressed. The snooker tables were partitioned off behind grey panels. It was like being inside a battleship. Higgins considered it an affront to his dignity and behaved accordingly. Ann Yates, as tournament director, did not relish having to deal with him. Nor did anybody engaged in an official capacity. 'Every one of [the referees] was scared stiff of him,' remembers Yates. 'We had a rota comprising the top eight referees [and] one of them would have to referee him – they wouldn't sleep the night before. But all our staff were like that the minute he'd arrive to play. The alert would go out. "The eagle has landed" was the call over the radio. And you know you had to watch where he went and what he did because you didn't know where there was going to be a confrontation. All my staff dreaded the day he would come to play.'[13] Out of the nine ranking tournaments, Higgins won eight of his opening matches and looked determined to climb the rankings at the end of the 1992–3 season. It was a much better start than the previous year. He had not really practised, other than hustling in snooker clubs, but went back to the safety game he had developed when his natural flair and potting ability had first begun to wane. It carried him a certain distance until, one by one, he was eliminated from the majority of the ranking tournaments and was left with a competitive interest in the European Open, UK Championship, British Open and the Embassy World Championship. He reached the last sixty-four of the Embassy by beating Kirk Stevens. 'I felt sorry for Kirk because he isn't anywhere near the player he was,' said Higgins before adding, 'then again I suppose you could say the same about me.' It was a candid admission from a man not given to lucid self-appraisal.

He was back in a more familiar state of mind after being knocked out of the world championship by Brian Morgan in the next qualifier. He was humiliated 10–1 and insisted: 'I would like both [of us] drug tested. On this form Davis, Hendry and Jimmy White wouldn't have stood a chance against him. It was surreal snooker . . . never in ten years will I believe that result.' Morgan, understandably, bridled at the accusation and demanded a drug test. As a teetotal non-smoker he was quite confident of the outcome. Higgins later apologized. Inquisitive holidaymakers who ventured inside the Norbreck Castle would have seen Higgins, Stevens and Cliff Thorburn at close quarters but, had they tired of indulging a nostalgia for the 1980s, they might have also noticed the progress of sixteen-year-old Ronnie O'Sullivan, who became the youngest player ever to qualify for the Crucible by beating Mark Johnstone-Allen. It was his seventy-fourth victory in seventy-six professional matches. After a month at the Norbreck Castle, a hotel from which he was (of course) banned from staying, Higgins was left in just two ranking events, the Royal Liver Assurance UK Championship and the British Open. He went out of both competitions early and with customary bad grace. After his 5–0 whitewash by John Parrott in the British Open he singled out referee John Williams for the usual treatment after he refused to allow him to clean the cue ball during the first frame.

'Am I here as a stopgap for one of the top thirty-two players to knock out?' he asked. The silence was deafening. 'I'm not sure I'll go through that Blackpool rigmarole again,' he said to nobody in particular. He would, of course. He had left it a bit late for a career change.

FIFTEEN

Wild men who caught and sang the sun in flight,
And learn, too late, they grieved it on its way,
Do not go gentle into that good night . . .
Rage, rage against the dying of the light.

DYLAN THOMAS, 'DO NOT GO GENTLE INTO THAT GOOD NIGHT' (1951)

At the moment Alex Higgins sank a punch into Colin Randle's solar plexus backstage at the Crucible in 1990, Belfast-born artist Rodney Dickson had just made the decision that the former world snooker champion was a subject worthy of immortalization. 'I was watching him on the television after the game with Steve James, he was just sitting there drinking and I thought that was kind of the end and so I resolved to paint him. I started working on the picture at that time and phoned his manager Doug Perry but got no response from him for a long time. I kind of gave up but two years later had another go. This time I got a better response. Doug said, "Why don't you come and meet him?" So I drove up and met Alex that day and asked him if he was up for the idea and he said "Yes."' Higgins did not 'sit' for Dickson (as the artist puts it, 'Can you imagine Higgins sitting for anyone or even keeping still for any length of time?'), but did meet with him on several occasions. The portrait still hangs in Art Gallery 5 at the Ulster Museum. It pictures Higgins emerging from the dark and dominates the room with its brooding and tragic presence.[1] 'I am not any kind of sports fan,' explains Dickson.

My interest in Alex as a snooker player or sportsman is not really the thing for me. I was interested in the way he led his life. You can liken him to Jimi Hendrix. Or, as an artist, to someone like Van Gogh or Jackson Pollock. People who did exactly what they wanted in their life as young people and could get away with it because they had this incredible talent.

The reason the painting is quite dark is to make it atmospheric. The idea that he was emerging from the shadows behind the snooker table and coming into the limelight to do his stuff is still quite powerful. In my mind I was thinking about the time he played Steve Davis and came back from 7–0 down to win [in the 1983 Coral UK Championship]. I remember talking to Alex about that and him saying that it was his greatest victory. The picture is supposed to be him emerging through the doorway, after the interval. He told me he knew he was going to win the match even though he was 7–0 down. That is why it is dark. The haunted look is because whenever he was playing he always looked like he was being tortured but it was also to reflect his traumatic life. On the one hand, he was a great snooker entertainer but on the other he had such a fucked-up private life. I tried to capture the trauma of it all.

Dickson succeeded. There are no postcards of the painting at the Ulster Museum because Higgins wanted money to turn up at the opening of the refurbished gallery and claimed, erroneously, that they did not have copyright permission to show the painting. Dickson sighs, 'I think they were worried Alex would come in and do something terrible to the museum.' Artist and subject have met each other on a few occasions since the painting was completed, most recently when Dickson flew back from his base in New York in 2001 to visit friends in his home town of Newtownards, eight miles away from Belfast. 'It was unbelievable,' he recalls with astonishment. 'I was just walking up the street and this taxi stopped and a guy asked me for directions to some street and then Alex opened the door of the taxi and said, "Hello Rodney." I was completely shocked. I didn't recognize him at first because he looked so thin but then I just said, "Hello Alex." And with that the taxi driver drove him off into the night.'

The 1993 World Championship was a lacklustre affair. Stephen Hendry seemed invincible and the 'Hurricane' was not there, although Higgins' fellow professionals did not share the sense of loss felt by the paying public and the television audience. A month after winning the title Hendry was awarded an MBE. In a brave move, the apparatchiks working for the Crown (and not, for once, in a judicial capacity) had invited Higgins to Buckingham Palace the previous summer for a celebration of forty years of sporting achievement during the reign of Queen Elizabeth II. It was a rare acknowledgement of his status by the establishment. In his pocket he carried a monochrome picture of himself wearing a paper crown. It had been taken on the occasion of the Queen's coronation and showed him surrounded by other children in the terraced streets of Protestant Belfast. He was in the limelight at the age of three. Exactly four decades later, he was at a garden party in the grounds of Buckingham Palace. He behaved impeccably and drank nothing stronger than tea. But he was never likely to become a Member of the Order of the British Empire or receive any other honour 'bestowed for meritorious service to the government'.[2] There had been too many headlines. There would soon be many more.

He had ten-year-old Jordan with him for an afternoon during the Blackpool qualifiers in October. Despite claiming that he had caught a chill after taking his son on the log flume at the Pleasurebeach, the brief reacquaintance with his family proved sufficient inspiration to yield a first-round appearance against Tony Knowles in the £325,000 Skoda Grand Prix and an appointment with Dennis Taylor in the Royal Liver Assurance UK Championship. Knowles beat him 5–1 and prompted the outburst: 'Prize money levels have fallen while the salaries of officials have gone up. The public don't know the truth.' The *Guardian* announced 'HIGGINS

LOSES IN A WHIRL OF ANGER'. The grudge match with Taylor less than a month later was more eagerly anticipated. The 1985 World Champion had not spoken to Higgins since he had been threatened by him during the World Team Cup Final in Bournemouth three and a half years previously. It was the first time they had met across a table since Taylor had beaten him in the Benson and Hedges Irish Masters at Goffs three weeks after the notorious 'I'll have you shot' declaration.

Higgins was ranked at number fifty-six. Taylor was out of form, had lost his last five games and was in danger of losing his place in the top sixteen for the first time since the ranking system was introduced in 1976. He was, however, determined to prevail and won 9–3. *The Times*' subeditors went with 'HIGGINS CONTINUES DESCENT' as a headline. 'I've lost quite easily,' he said after the match. 'I'm disappointed but there are plenty of other tournaments.' The default checklist of complaints was eerily absent. It was unsettling. Reporters who had already written their first paragraph had to lose all references to the referee and the table. It could have been that he was as tired of reciting the usual excuses as the press were of listening to them. A more likely explanation, perhaps, is that an innate suspicion that the 'scum' from the 'fish and chip papers' were waiting to pounce upon any uncharitable comment he might make about Taylor persuaded him to keep his mouth shut. His reticence did not presage a new relationship with authority – it was just prudent. He dropped five places in the provisional rankings after the defeat but took home £1,850.

He would spend Christmas away from his family, living in a room in a hotel in Mansfield owned by the uncle of an aspiring young professional and busied himself playing exhibitions all over the country. The new year promised a return trip to an out-of-season and rain-lashed Blackpool for the 1994 World Championship qualifiers. He had not made the final stages of the tournament since he punched Colin Randle. Any seaside resort is bleak in January, the self-styled 'Vegas of the

North' particularly so. The trams rattled by on rusted rails, local children stuffed their pocket money into video machines in empty amusement arcades as pensioners in grey and beige made their weary way up and down the Golden Mile. With nothing better to do, they often ended up sheltering from the wind and spray whipped off the Irish Sea at the Norbreck Castle, on the North promenade. There they could check the list of names posted in the lobby, until they saw a name they recognized: T. Knowles; E. Charlton; C. Thorburn; A. Higgins. Everyone who bothered to turn up to the qualifiers – the old ladies, the other young professionals and the few assembled journalists – liked watching Alex Higgins. There was always a capacity crowd of twenty-five watching the 'Hurricane' including, on this occasion, a young woman from Brazil.

Laura Alves had seen Higgins play a couple of times when she lived in England and had written to him on several occasions. Back in England in January 1994, she made the pilgrimage to Blackpool to see him play again. Spectators needed tickets to see Alex Higgins and Ronnie O'Sullivan. '[An offical said] "I'm sorry, madam, you can't sit there." "But I want to watch this match," I replied. "I'm sorry. You'll need a special ticket for games involving Mr Higgins. Either you go outside with the crowd and be among the first twenty in the queue, or you might ask him and come in as his special guest.' The queue was already too long and so she decided to ask Higgins as he arrived. '"Hello Alex," I said, "I need a ticket to watch your match. I'm from Brazil, do you remember me?" "Oh! The little girl! Your name's Laura."' Higgins then found an official and demanded, 'Give her a ticket. She'll have one for every match of mine.' He also gave her a badge that enabled her to walk in and out of the players' area. It was an act of genuine kindness. Laura Alves now runs an Alex Higgins fan club on the internet.

His first match was against Colm Kelly, a man ranked 241 in the world. He had to win this and the next two to make it to the Crucible. It took him eight hours, sucking on

Marlboro cigarettes and ordering halves of Guinness to be brought to the table, before he scraped through 10–9. He had been behind at the interval but improved dramatically, as always, during the evening session. His next opponent would be Andrew Cairns, a well-regarded young player who had seen off Eddie Charlton in the previous round. Higgins carried his form from the latter half of the previous game into this one and won 10–5. 'He smashed me round the table,' said Cairns. 'I couldn't believe what he was doing.' He had one more round to go. The draw was not kind and had paired him with Tony Knowles, who was ranked twenty-third and had almost whitewashed him in the Skoda Grand Prix less than three months previously. Knowles settled in well and was leading 6–3 at the interval.

Higgins, in search of inspiration, left the Norbreck Castle and made for a pub thirty yards away. He had already drunk a few pints while playing and, as he went to step over a small perimeter wall, tripped and fell. His cue case broke most of his fall but he grazed his stomach and cut open his arm. He picked himself up and, rather than go to the A&E department at the Blackpool Victoria for the stitches he certainly needed, carried on to the pub. He had no option. He could not afford to miss the evening session. When he returned he had his arm wrapped in a bandage fashioned out of a bit of cloth and pulled the score back to 6–4 inside ten minutes. Blood, however, was beginning to seep through his shirt and onto the cloth. The pain was visible, particularly when he needed to use the rest, but he played on and dominated the final two frames to win 10–9. He was delighted and revealed his wound for the photographers before declaring, 'Those people who say I've got no heart should see this.' He went on, 'I'm just thrilled to be back at the Lord Mayor's Show and I'm looking forward to Sheffield again. All these ranking points are the thing for me. I want to get back up the rankings.' It was the first time he had reached the last thirty-two of a ranking tournament since the Dubai Duty Free Classic in October 1991.

*

Ken Doherty awaited him in the first round at the Crucible although his new friend, Penny Thornton, could probably have told him that. She was the astrologer for the *Today* newspaper and had previously provided advice to Diana, Princess of Wales. The *News of the World* quoted her saying, 'There's nothing like the love of a good woman. We're happy together and Alex is putting his past behind him – he's a changed man. He's not a tearaway now and I wouldn't be with him if he were.'[3] It is unclear whether his relationship with Holly Haise was in the 'on' or the 'off' setting when Higgins met the astrologer but Thornton, presumably after prolonged reference to several astrological charts, seemed keen to tell the press the following day, 'We are friends, but it is a friendship born out of astrological interest and rumours of a romance are grossly exaggerated. I have given Alex in-depth astrological advice. How much of this has contributed to him turning the corner and how much has to do with his own determination is impossible to evaluate.'[4] It was certainly made more difficult by his decision to walk out of the BBC Belfast TV studio seconds before a live broadcast and then register another ban, this time from Tramp nightclub in London, for smashing two ashtrays.

Dublin-born Doherty was a highly rated young player who idolized Higgins. As world champion three years later he would say, 'Snooker owes [Higgins] a great debt. He was its first innovator, first real superstar and he did much to make the game what it is today.' But in 1994 he could not afford to be so generous. Higgins had prepared for his grand return with a series of exhibition matches in Britain and Ireland with Jimmy White and others. That he had not had time to practise showed, as he went 4–0 down and looked to be on the verge of losing the fifth. Doherty was 63–0 ahead before Higgins got a chance. He forced his young opponent into giving away 16 points in penalties and then won the game on the pink. The audience roared their approval and he went on to win another two before Doherty finished the first session 6–3 ahead. Higgins was elated – he was back at the

Crucible and back in the limelight. He had felt his game loosen up, although that may have been a result of his unrepentant consumption of Guinness.

He felt good and entered the arena in formal dinner wear accessorized with highly polished shoes and a maroon fedora. He smiled to the crowd. As Clive Everton noted, 'He was singularly adept at raising the emotional temperature of any audience.' Higgins, in turn, fed off their enthusiasm. But not on this occasion. Doherty won the first two frames of the evening session, Higgins pulled it back to 8–4 and then, in the thirteenth frame, asked referee John Williams to move as he was standing in his peripheral vision. It was an old tactic of Higgins but Williams was an experienced official and refused to move. The crowd sided with Higgins, naturally, and he sustained the argument for several minutes until Williams promised to award the frame to Doherty if he did not play on. Doherty won it anyway. Higgins won the next two frames but defeat came at 10–6 when he conceded on the brown. After the game, Doherty noted, 'He can be very intimidating. His aura and the crowd sometimes put you out of your stride.'

The press knew what to expect from Higgins: 'The people who referee our games have given themselves a professional tag but they're not players. Some of them don't know how to walk backwards. I know how to do that with six glasses of Guinness inside me . . . I'll be back next year.' In fact, he had just made his last appearance at the Crucible. During the course of his oration he held up a packet of Marlboro cigarettes, a gesture that infuriated the sponsors. He was not going out quietly. Williams, presumably satisfied that he had successfully held his ground, declined to report Higgins for his behaviour. Higgins was still the talk of the press room thirty-six hours after he had left the building. A rumour surfaced that he had refused to take a post-match drug test. Nigel Oldfield, the WPBSA's events manager, neither confirmed nor denied the story as he declared, 'Any matters relating to drug testing are confidential and strictly between us and the players.' The rumour of some kind of angry scene was given substance when it emerged that Higgins had returned to room 337 in the Sheffield Novotel and a window had been broken. A spokeswoman said, 'I don't think he'll be staying here again.' Eventually, it emerged that Higgins had objected to being subject to a drug test and the manner in which he had been asked to submit to it.

If one episode demonstrates the way in which WPBSA treated Alex Higgins, it is this one. After the match with Ken Doherty, Higgins was asked to provide a urine sample by Dr David Forster, a respected Sheffield-based neurosurgeon who also operated as the governing body's medical officer and chairman of its drug committee. There was no 'drug-testing station' backstage at the Crucible Theatre. Higgins, who had just been beaten and seemed to be in a state of such acute agitation during the interval that his manager Doug Perry doubted whether he would be able to finish the match, was asked to provide a sample after a random selection process. He thought he was being victimized, having been 'randomly selected' on a recent occasion, but followed Dr Forster to the gents' toilets. These were occupied and so they tried to make use of the ladies'. That proved impossible and Higgins was led from one backstage toilet to another. He considered the process degrading and said so. Words were exchanged. The witness statement of the medical officer included the allegation that, '[Higgins] finally picked the 'A' packet [containing the urine sample] squeezed it and threw it to the floor. The bottle inside clearly broke because urine began to seep out of the zip.' Higgins refuted the allegation but, however the bottle came to be broken, a drug test was still possible as the doctor had already decanted some of the sample into another, unbroken packet. Dr Forster told Higgins that if he refused to provide another sample he would be contravening WPBSA regulations and his stance would be taken to be indicative of supplying a 'positive' sample. Ann Yates supported Forster and the drug committee. She told Higgins it was in 'the rules'. That was in April.

On 22 July the WPBSA issued a press release. It said: 'Alex Higgins has been requested to attend a disciplinary enquiry in connection with a possible breach of the rules of discipline at the Embassy World Championship. A date for the enquiry has still to be set.' It was eventually arranged for 20 December. *Snooker Scene* noted, '[Higgins was not] charged under the Drug Control Regulations which appear in the WPBSA's Articles of Association – which provide that all cases in alleged breach of these rules must be heard by an independent legally qualified chairman appointed by the board – but under the much vaguer rules of discipline which do not require this.' Robin Falvey, at this point owed something like £40,000 by Higgins but not anticipating imminent remuneration, destroyed the case put up by the board with brutal professionalism. 'It was quite obvious that the doctor and Ann [Yates] had simply not bothered to look at the rules and I asked them questions in cross-examination . . . the answers were so unbelievable, I asked [them] if they could point out the rule to me. They looked and said, "Well, it's not there." And I said, "Why did you say that then?" "Oh well," one of them responded, "we just say that to everybody."' The failure to provide an additional sample could not be taken to be equivalent to a 'positive' test and Higgins was acquitted. But that was not enough for the WPBSA.

The tribunal (comprising John Spencer (chairman), Geoff Foulds (vice-chairman), Ray Edmonds, Bill Oliver and Mike Watterson) announced through Matthew McCloy (the WPBSA solicitor) that they were 'worried' about two other matters: namely, the destruction of the sample bottle (subsequently discarded and therefore not available as evidence) and the fact that Higgins had held up a packet of Marlboro cigarettes at the press conference following the Embassy World Championship. Falvey reflects, 'They suddenly came up with two new offences which he had never been charged with. They hadn't even given anybody the opportunity to deal with them. I think it is quite abominable . . . just appalling.' Ann Yates had left the premises and Higgins' legal representation was unable to cross-examine her about the new charges that had taken eight months to surface. Falvey had no time to prepare a defence. He protested but was ignored. Spencer announced that Higgins had been found guilty under rule 1A which states that, 'Members must conduct themselves at all times in a manner consistent with their status as professional sportsmen.' Higgins was fighting for his livelihood.

It was the kind of inelegant catch-all clause favoured by autocratic regimes as disparate as the government in Pyongyang and the House UnAmerican Activities Committee. Falvey demanded to know the 'rule 1A' accusations against his client. He was quoted in *Snooker Scene* thus: 'What happened next was something of a disgrace. Mr Spencer glanced at Mr McCloy who simply shook his head. Mr Spencer then indicated that he was not prepared to tell me the reasons which constituted the breach.'[5] The WPBSA rules did not allow for an appeal. Falvey went after every board member involved in the 1994 farce, those who had played a part in the 1992 fiasco *and* Yates, Forster and McCloy and levelled charges against all of them. He did not make himself popular. 'I can't describe how I feel about the way they conducted proceedings,' he says, 'but it's not positive. The truth of it was that I was a thorn in their side and they didn't like me because I fought.' And won? 'Yeah, I suppose I did in a sense.'

Once the guest in 337 had been asked to leave the Sheffield Novotel, his brief renaissance on the table seemed to be over. It was the end of the season in any case. He awoke to an exclusive with Holly Haise in the *Daily Star* that, amongst other things, alleged: '[Higgins] told people he was living out of a suitcase and earning peanuts, when all the time I was financing him.' He was also thrown out of his temporary home in the hotel in Mansfield after neglecting to give it a namecheck at the press conference. Once again, he had nowhere to live and the news that Delveron House had recently been on the market for £590,000 did not escape his attention. It looked like being a long close season. He spent it travelling the country to fulfil exhibitions and trying to find somewhere to sleep for the night. Although Higgins was known to be unhappy at Haise's suggestion that he was living on her earnings, he nonetheless attempted a reconciliation with her but she was not keen to take him back. She eventually relented but then threw him out again. If he can be said to have been living anywhere, he was occasionally domiciled in Manchester. He knew a vast number of people in the city and it helped to keep loneliness at bay. It also offered a bed for the night. He patronized the Masters Club in Stockport and several pubs near his old home in Cheadle. The George and Dragon was a favourite.

'He came in one afternoon,' remembers former *News of the World* reporter Alan Hart, who was having a quiet drink at the bar with landlord Peter Morrell. Hart knew him from the Kenilworth, another old Higgins haunt, and had first encountered him in 1973 while on the Isle of Man to cover the Summerland disaster ('He was being ejected by a bouncer having been refused credit'). 'When he came into the George and Dragon,' he continues, 'he was wearing a large purple fedora and a cape. He walked in, shook Pete's hand and ordered a drink. He said he'd been on holiday so I asked him where he'd been. He snarled, "I came here for a fucking drink, not to be interrogated by the press."' He was clearly on edge. He had another major WPBSA disciplinary hearing hanging over his head, nowhere to live and, having failed to make the top sixteen, faced the snooker equivalent of community service once again. He entered the qualifiers for six events but left Blackpool with nothing more than an entry into the Royal Liver Assurance UK Championship in Preston. His form seemed to have deserted him as a new generation of unremarkable young professionals like Troy Shaw and Nick Fruin proved irresistible. The Skoda Grand Prix qualifier against Mark Flowerdew was a case in point. It was a tight game and Higgins had a number of opportunities to win but failed to take them and went down 5–4. As his potting game deteriorated further, he took refuge in his defensive game. Higgins, almost the patron saint of preposterous excuses by this stage of his career, claimed he had been hampered by an injury to the thumb on his bridge hand that had resulted from a game of football with his son.

The UK Championship was his only window of opportunity. He needed some stability to prepare for the tournament and called Holly Haise. He asked her to take him back. '[I need] feeding, loving and building up,' he told her. Haise demanded to know about the details of his relationship with Penny Thornton. He assured her it was just a platonic relationship, she believed him and he moved some of his belongings into her house. With a base he could prepare for his first-round match with Nigel Bond, ranked number eleven in the world. It was a daunting task. He had not overcome a player ranked in the top sixteen for over three years but he knew the Guild Hall well. The staff there were equally familiar with him. Things seemed to happen when he was there. This was to be no different. Jeremy Wilson was in the crowd: 'I used to travel to quite a few of the tournaments as a Higgins fan in the late 1980s and early 1990s. His match against Nigel Bond is a favourite memory even though he was obviously well past it at this stage. There were eight tables in play, including Ronnie O'Sullivan [the defending UK champion, and the youngest player ever to win a ranking tournament] and world number two John Parrott, but Higgins must have had more than 1,000 unapologetically noisy fans around his table, compared to a handful for the others. It seemed to upset Parrott quite severely.

'[Higgins'] fans were disgracefully behaved,' he continues. 'The referees from other tables were constantly telling them to be quiet. Higgins loved it and told [referee] Len Ganley "You won't shut this lot up."' Higgins thrived on the atmosphere and, feeling at home, instructed Bond to sit down and move out of the way whenever he felt like it. He won 9–5 after five tense black-ball games. 'It was,' says Wilson, 'undoubtedly his best post-ban performance . . . a last reminder of the old days.' Drew Henry was beaten 9–7 in the next round as Higgins rediscovered his form. A match with Steve Davis loomed. Unfortunately, the prospect of a final rematch in the familiar theatre of their rivalry was ruined by Dave Harold who first defeated Davis and then went on to deprive Higgins of a place in the final eight by beating him 9–4. Higgins had been playing in front of the television cameras at Preston for the first time since 1987 and reacted to his loss in the usual way:

'I would rather have had a man off the street to referee the match than John Street [Higgins had been fined £500 three years previously for allegedly attempting to intimidate Street at the same venue]. If you have a gut feeling that a referee wants you to get beaten, it's soul destroying. As soon as I walked through the curtains and saw he was the ref, I knew I had no chance. I think they should send him for an eye test.'

Unusually, rather than declaring his intention to retire, he went on to say, 'I am going to continue. I cannot walk away from snooker.' The governing body, having listened to a tape recording of the press conference, subsequently declined to take any action. The 'drug test' incident was already in the pipeline at that time. Another charge could begin to resemble persecution.

There were no other tournaments pencilled into his diary before the end of the year but the entry 'Find somewhere to live' might have been apposite. When Holly Haise readmitted Higgins into her house in South Manchester he moved in with a black suit bag. While he was out playing, Haise found several letters from Penny Thornton which Higgins had kept. She read them and discovered evidence that suggested their relationship had been more involved than she had been led to believe. Haise called the press and told them of the contents of the letters. She claimed that one contained the line, 'Before we went to bed together, you said you wanted "feeling sex, not just sex". And you certainly picked the right woman. But that all seems to be very different now. It's all very one-sided and I think I'm worth a lot better treatment . . . as far as I am concerned, this is it.' Haise, demonstrating her capacity for explosive rage, took his belongings into the back garden. 'He knows that I can be a very volatile person,' she said. 'On the spur of the moment I decided to burn his beloved black bag and all that was inside it . . . I put it in a tin dustbin and set it alight. There were papers in there, a suit, shoes and shirts, even his passport.'[6] Higgins did not come back to the house that night but rang the next morning. 'I told him all I could see was one shoe and a sock smouldering, nothing else was left . . . he went berserk and said he hoped I burn in hell.' He had no belongings, was without a home again, and had the disciplinary tribunal pertaining to events at the UK Championship to look forward to five days before Christmas. The qualifiers were also on the horizon. It was another winter of his discontent.

The pressure was building. Back at the Norbreck Castle, Higgins qualified for the final stages of the British Open with a 5–4 victory over Darren Clarke and went into the sixth qualifying round of the Embassy World Championship with a reasonable hope of beating Tai Pitchit, a Thai who had spent some time as a novice monk in a Buddhist monastery. Higgins went 7–3 down but was fighting back and in a commanding position in the eleventh frame with a break of 102 under way. He potted a red with perfect position on the black but then, as he had done in Preston during the UK Championship the previous April, asked referee John Williams to move. He knew Williams would refuse but it was a kick against authority and it would also unsettle his relatively inexperienced opponent. Williams stood firm once again. An argument ensued which Higgins must have known he could not win. As he went back to take his shot he bowed his head over the cue and it rapidly became clear that he was sobbing. He continued to cry as he potted the black and completed a total clearance of 137, tears falling onto the cloth as he went through the colours. It was his highest break in the twenty-three years he had competed in the world championship. He took one more frame as Pitchit eventually won 10–5. The young Buddhist commented afterwards: 'I couldn't believe what was going on. I've never seen anything like it before. Why did he cry? He was on a century break.'

Higgins did not discuss the reasons behind his lachrymose performance beyond declaring, 'It is the first time a referee has brought me to tears . . . the man is incompetent, negligent and didn't know the rules laid down by the Referees Association. I'll be talking to my solicitor about suing Mr Williams or the WPBSA or whoever's responsible.' He might as well have added that he was suing the bar staff at the hotel for not serving his Guinness at the right temperature. It was, after all, his standard operative procedure. In April he travelled to Plymouth for the 1995 British Open. He didn't stay long: Steve James beat him 5–3 in the first round. It was James' first win for seven months. Higgins made his excuses (referee, table and television lights) and left. Before he went back to Manchester however, he left a gift of a pair of trousers, a waistcoat and a note to John Higgins, a young Scotsman whose only connection to him was a shared surname. The note read, 'To John, from the Hurricane. Hope they fit.' The younger Higgins eventually won the tournament and commented afterwards, 'I think he likes the idea of me using them because, if I am doing well, his name will be remembered too.' It was an uncharitable, but probably accurate, observation.

Cedric Ulett did not accompany Higgins to Plymouth but he was with him the following month, when they were both arrested. Ulett, now a successful financial adviser with his own company, had seen Higgins around but first met him in the Circus pub in Ardwick in 1981. 'I was certainly the best pool player in the area and everyone wanted to match us up on the table,' says Ulett. 'We were both up for it and I beat him. Higgins has a good memory and he never forgot me after that.' When Ulett graduated to Paul Medati's Masters

Club in Stockport in 1990 he encountered Higgins again. They got on. 'It was a good time,' he says now. 'There were a lot of professionals playing out of there, people like Kirk Stevens and Warren King, we would play them with a four-black start.' It was never dull when Alex Higgins was around. 'You had to know how to deal with him and not let him get away with anything,' he smiles. 'He's like a child.'

It was a curious relationship with the younger man taking on the role of counsellor to the older of the two. 'I helped him with some of his emotional issues,' explains Ulett. He also employed his knowledge of the commercial world to help sort out some of Higgins' complicated financial matters ('He had a pension but thought it was worth millions just because he was Alex Higgins, he didn't appreciate the fact that it was only worth what you put in'). He also socialized with him. As Higgins could not drive and did not possess a car, when a promised lift from Oliver Reed to a Pro-Celebrity golf tournament failed to materialize, Ulett agreed to be the designated driver. It was an enjoyable afternoon. Higgins even won a television for his prowess on the golf course. 'Everybody was well oiled,' Ulett says. 'Apart from me. Over the course of about eight hours I had two beers, a brandy and a glass of wine. At one point I caught a young lad aged about fifteen or sixteen trying to nick the TV and told him to put it back and he did. I think it might have been him who tipped off the police.' Shortly after leaving the golf club at 2.30 a.m., Ulett, with Higgins in the passenger seat and Jim Lewis, a friend from the Masters Club and Higgins' future manager, in the back, was pulled over by four police cars. By any measure, it was an excessive response to a possible case of drink-driving. There were blue flashing lights everywhere. 'Let me handle this,' said Higgins.

Inspector Peter Hulse told the court that Higgins was staggering around the second lane of the A556 shouting abuse. He also noted that his speech was slurred and his eyes glazed. PC Phillip Sale claimed Higgins had waved his mobile phone under his nose and then told yet another member of the

Cheshire constabulary, 'You are not having the fucking keys. Look at all you fuckers in uniform.' It was claimed that it took three officers to handcuff him. Higgins, who gave his address as that of his manager Doug Perry in Hertfordshire, denied all the accusations and both Ulett and Lewis supported him. Ulett failed a breath test and all three were taken into custody. Higgins was spitting fury in the cell. Lewis, having done nothing more than sit in the back seat with his seat belt on, was released with a caution. Robin Falvey, representing Higgins, suggested there was, 'Something distasteful [about the case] . . . I have never in my experience heard of four or five police cars with up to nine officers going to deal with a drunk driver.' The magistrates in Northwich fined Higgins £150 for being drunk and disorderly. 'It is only right and proper that the parents of those young people [who attempted to emulate his skills] expect a far higher standard of behaviour than you exhibited on that night,' intoned magistrate Malcolm Whalley gravely.

It was an eventful summer. Three weeks after his adventure in Cheshire he was mugged in Didsbury, Manchester after taking £175 out of a cashpoint (he flagged down a passing police car to report the crime but it took several minutes to extract the relevant information from the complainant – 'He was absolutely legless,' said one officer. 'Apparently he'd been on an all-day bender'). He had also agreed to play a series of exhibition matches against John Higgins in June. On the eve of the world championship, he told the *News of the World*: 'I still think I'm good enough to be ranked number eight.' He was forty places wide of the mark. Before another trip to Blackpool he went to Spain with Cedric Ulett in order to appear on a television show for expats called *Boland Live*. They were put up in the El Paradiso hotel in Malaga. It had a golf course, as stipulated by the star guest. 'We only had one round,' laughs Ulett. 'There were too many arguments. It's like when you're in the car and, even though he can't drive, he still tells you what to do or where to go. Even so, we had a good time in Spain. Freddie Starr bumped into us in Puerto

Banus, took one look at Alex and couldn't get away fast enough.'[7] Higgins, in exuberant mood, got on stage during the filming of *Boland Live* and, clearly enjoying himself, danced to 'Mustang Sally'. It was Higgins in his element: fêted and unrestrained. When allowed to do whatever he wanted, he was, by common consent, great company. Yet as he stepped back on to the plane, he changed. The flight back to Manchester experienced some minor turbulence and Higgins ended up having an argument with the pilot and accusing him of not being able to fly a plane. It was another manifestation of his inability to deal with anybody in a uniform without wanting to take them to task.

Blackpool in September promised nothing more than the illuminations and an end-of-the-pier show featuring Keith Harris and Orville. And the qualifiers of course. The 'Hurricane' swept in at the beginning of September. Four days later he was out of the Thailand Classic, Skoda Grand Prix, German Open, Royal Liver Assurance UK Championship and the Regal Welsh Open. His form was wretched and during his 5–0 defeat in the UK Championship qualifier to Karl Broughton he managed only three double-figure breaks. 'I don't think disillusionment is a strong enough word to describe the way I feel at the moment,' said Higgins. 'These things [referring to the dilatory manner in which the WPBSA were dealing with the sixteen counter-complaints levelled by his solicitor] stretch on for months on end and I always seem to come to the qualifiers under a cloud from one charge or another. I just want a fair crack of the whip.' Broughton delivered a far more telling sound bite. 'After the first couple of frames I just speeded up my game and attacked because I knew if I gave him a chance he would mess it up.' The disrespect was as shocking as it was unapologetic. Nobody had said anything like that about Alex Higgins before. He no longer mattered to the new generation of snooker players. As Higgins was whitewashed by Broughton, Paul Hunter and Matthew Stevens, two teenage players who shared something of the 'Hurricane's' rebellious spirit and approach to the game, made it through to the final stages.

Hunter, who came back from behind to win the 2001 Benson and Hedges Masters tournament after a bout of well-publicized extra-curricular activity with his girlfriend during the interval, is a charming young man with just a touch of the rapscallion about him. When asked about Alex Higgins in a pub in Yorkshire six months after his success at Wembley, he just shrugged and took a sip of lager. 'Yeah, of course I know about [Higgins],' he said. 'But Jimmy White was the one I always remember. He was my idol. I always used to watch him because I liked the way he played and that was the way I play.' Hunter is two years older than Lauren Higgins.

After the disappointment of the qualifiers Higgins wound down at a nightclub in the town. Nigel Jones found him to be in a mood which could even be described as upbeat: 'There were loads of celebrities [in the nightclub]. Keith Harris was there, the twins from *Neighbours,* Joe Pasquale, Les Dennis, Su Pollard and quite a few others. Alex Higgins literally bumped into me and we chatted for a long time. He was a great character and even let us take photos.'[8] His career was in freefall. If confirmation was required it was provided by his subsequent agreement to represent Europe in the Mosconi Cup, a televised pool equivalent of the Ryder Cup promoted by Barry Hearn in Basildon, Essex. It was reminiscent of Randolph Turpin and Joe Louis, two of the most talented boxers ever to grace the ring, turning to the grubby business of professional wrestling in order to make a living. A crowd of seventy-three witnessed Higgins being put to sleep by more competent opponents in a nine-ball doubles match. And so it was back to Blackpool.

If these return trips to the Golden Mile seem repetitive, imagine how it felt for Alex Higgins. The second he either pulled up outside the only hotel which would take him or shambled off the train at the end-of-the-line station and heard the seagulls, countenanced the overweight mothers in ill-advised jogging bottoms with their unruly children, and grabbed his cue case, his new status had already been confirmed. The 1996 qualifiers were even less rewarding than usual. He failed to make the final stages of any ranking competition for the first time in his career. He wore a beret for the last two frames against Chris Scanlon in the seventh qualifying round of the European Open (it didn't help – he was beaten 5–4) and found fault with a refereeing decision on his way to a 5–1 defeat by Marcus Campbell in the International Open. Provisionally rated at number seventy-seven in the world, he made the final stages of nothing more than the Regal Welsh Open. If there was any consolation to be found it was in the propinquity of Cliff Thorburn's decline. The 1980 World Champion lost his eighth successive match as Higgins was put out of the Castella Classic British Open by twenty-nine-year-old Indian professional Yasin Merchant. Higgins was left with nothing but the world championship qualifiers in order to save his season. He was beaten by part-time market trader Surinder Gill 10–7. 'My livelihood has been taken by the [World Professional Billiards and Snooker] Association,' he explained afterwards. 'I hope to disgrace the people who run this game. I fear the worst for this rotten gathering of old men and young boys who call themselves snooker professionals.' It would have had more impact if he had not reeked of alcohol as he delivered his latest rant. In the Sweater Shop International Open qualifying round, after a protracted argument with the referee, he sent the cue ball flying off the table.

The list of nineteen complaints filed by his solicitor against the WPBSA was all he had to hang on to. It was less than a thread and the governing body were intending to discipline him further for abusing two senior referees at the qualifiers. He took advice from Robin Falvey and issued an apology: 'I wish to unequivocally apologize to Lawrie Annandale and Alan Chamberlain [the two referees concerned] about remarks made to them and to the WPBSA for remarks which I made about the Board, which are at this stage inappropriate . . . I have been under a great deal of strain recently, not

only because of the strain imposed by my impending proceedings against the WPBSA and its Board members.' He
was still serving the suspended one-year ban and if the tribunal found against him it would be activated and deprive him
of another year of his career. The tribunal was called for
5 August and looked like preventing him from playing the
autumn qualifiers, but an adjournment enabled him to compete. It made no difference: he failed to qualify for any ranking competition, suffered three whitewashes and won only
four frames in six matches before refusing to play in the
Thailand Open qualifier because Annandale was officiating.
He also walked out of his British Open match because John
Williams was the referee and then withdrew from the
German Open claiming that he was ill. He had not felt well
for a few months but had opted to do nothing about it. When
he eventually went to see a doctor, nodules were discovered
in his throat and he underwent an operation to have them
removed. Analysis subsequently proved that they were
malignant. He knew he was ill, but he was very stoic. He was
determined to live.

As usual, his performance on the table and his behaviour
away from it were engaged in a mutually destructive but symbiotic relationship. In late February 1996 he went to visit
Oliver Reed in his farmhouse near Cork. 'I come here to
rest,' he explained. 'I'm used to smoky snooker halls in big
cities. Oliver invites me for weekends to relax, breathe the air
and walk the dogs. I think he likes it when I'm here. I sleep
all day then get up at night and wash all the dishes for him.'[9]
There was more than plate-washing going on and the usual
drinking and bravado bets took up most of the time. During
a previous visit Reed had pulled a lance off the wall and
chased Higgins round the house with it. A few days after
returning from Ireland, Higgins spent a night behind bars
for kicking a fourteen-year-old friend of his son. The boy had
walked in on Higgins and Lynn as they were discussing
Jordan, had been 'truculent and impertinent' and Higgins

had reacted in his usual fashion. Perhaps unnecessarily, charges had been brought. The recovery from the operation to remove nodules from his throat necessitated a trip to the Costa del Sol, and the adjournment of the court appearance in Stockport. Two days before his court case, he was escorted from Epsom during the Derby meeting by three stewards after becoming drunk and aggressive. At the Crucible, Ronnie O'Sullivan physically assaulted WPBSA official Mike Ganley. He was fined £20,000 and given a two year suspended ban but allowed to continue in the championships. Higgins regarded this as evidence that the WPBSA was not even-handed.

In front of magistrates to answer the charges resulting from the incident with the fourteen-year-old boy, Higgins pleaded guilty. Robin Falvey argued in mitigation, 'Mr Higgins is at the crossroads of his life. The illness is a very difficult thing for anybody to have to face and it must be worrying. He's not the man he was in terms of snooker. His ranking is going down [ninety-nine at that time] and his ability to earn is virtually negligible.' As indeed Falvey could attest. In a dramatic break with legal practice, Higgins' solicitor was working for him with no realistic expectation of payment. 'I just felt that sometimes you have to make the decision to try and help as best you can and that is why I continued [to work for him],' he says now. 'I was promised money but there came a stage where he couldn't pay me. I carried on helping him as best I could because otherwise he was going to be treated just abominably [by the WPBSA].' Higgins was given a twelve month conditional discharge and ordered to pay £115 costs. Two months later he helped comfort an eleven-year-old girl who had just been involved in a road accident. He called an ambulance and stayed with her until it arrived. The child's father, Mr Breckwoldt, announced, 'He took charge of the situation and was really superb . . . Alex always seems to get a very bad press but this incident shows there is a good side to him.'[10]

The pressures continued to build up. He required treatment for his illness, endured his worst season in professional snooker and, in terms of prize money, had earned just £9,025. He had also used up most of his credit with friends and admirers and was forced to apply to the WPBSA benevolent fund (to help players who had fallen into 'genuine hardship') in order to secure somewhere to live. He had to fill in application forms for everything. It was a benevolent fund that would not exist if he had not made the Belfast to Liverpool ferry in the late 1960s. The former world snooker champion was officially 'of no fixed address' and living on handouts from people who were prepared to give him 'loans'. The player Neal Foulds was to receive interest-free loans totalling £30,000 from the benevolent fund to help settle a tax bill. His father, Geoff Foulds, was a key figure on the WPBSA board and eventually became chairman. In October, the WPBSA agreed to put Higgins up in the Pymgate Lodge Hotel in Stockport at a negotiated rate of £30 per night. At around the same time, Ann Yates felt compelled to report him for his decision to walk out of the Thailand Open qualifier in Blackpool. She had no choice. His manager Doug Perry stood by him. 'Alex is a one-off,' he said, in a statement that nobody could take issue with. 'I'm interested in him as a person as well as a snooker player. Despite what people say, he's still a terrific human being. I will battle on in pursuit of justice for my player. He deserves that and does not always get it.' Higgins has always inspired remarkable degrees of loyalty and loathing, sometimes within the same person at the same time.

Perry collapsed and died, aged fifty-one, in December 1996. Higgins was bereft. He was now more alone than at any previous time in his life. Crushing blows were arriving with the regularity of midsummer charter flights into Alicante: he was fighting cancer; had not been invited to compete in a doomed attempt to breathe life into the *Pot Black* format; was knocked out of the qualifiers for the world championship by Darren Limberg (the world number 205) having been 5–1 ahead and then refused to fulfil his post-match press conference responsibilities. He was also certain to be ranked outside the top sixty-four in the world (he was actually 136th) and would therefore have to enter the newly instituted qualifying school in Plymouth if he wanted to join the 1997–8 professional circuit. When his sorrows came, they came not as single spies but in battalions[11] although it is unlikely Shakespeare was in his mind when he jumped on a bed at the Pymgate Lodge Hotel in January 1997 and told four members of the local constabulary, 'I am a British spy, you can't do this.' They had been called to the hotel after he had attempted to throw one of the other long-term guests through a plate glass window. He was arrested for a breach of the peace, but not before he had threatened to have two policewomen shot and declared, 'I am not leaving. You are all English bastards. This is an invasion of my privacy.' He spent a night in the cells and then delayed his hearing the next morning. As his duty solicitor explained, '[He will be brought from the cells] as soon as he stops shouting at me.' When he turned up to court two months later in a waxed jacket, grey sweatshirt and a baseball cap, he alleged police harassment. He gave his address as the Dickens Inn, near Middlesbrough, where he was staying with a friend.

The case was one embarrassment too far for the WPBSA and a memo leaked to the *Mirror* revealed that, once an outstanding storage bill for £70.50 was settled, '[The board] will not grant any further assistance.' The governing body had met his hotel costs and private medical care and paid for the storage of some furniture. The figure totalled £3,500. Secretary and fund trustee, Mike Veal, did not confirm or deny the story, saying instead that he 'was not prepared to comment on any individual beneficiaries'. It might have proved problematic in any case as, at one point, the accounts for the benevolent fund had not been audited for three years. In the world championship two months later Ronnie O'Sullivan would make a maximum break of sublime brilliance in five minutes and twenty seconds. He received

£165,000 for this achievement – £515 per second. On that basis, Alex Higgins received just less than seven seconds' worth of financial remuneration from a sport he had done so much to popularize since 1972. Jim McKenzie was the WPBSA Chief Executive when I met him in November 2001. He had recently been reinstated after a prolonged bout of internecine warfare. He was about to be ousted again a month later in another spasm of infighting. McKenzie was coy at first and did not want to further antagonize elements within the association, but he did admit that if Higgins was just starting in the game now, he would be handled very differently.

'We would market him in the same way we are trying to market Ronnie O'Sullivan,' he explained. 'We would get him alongside an exceptional personal management agent, someone who could protect him from his own worst vices and could help to manage his public profile without taking away from his personality, leaving his sort of laddish edge alone.' When asked if Alex Higgins had been treated fairly by the WPBSA, he went on: 'I don't really know how to answer that. I understood some of the issues that Alex was involved in with this association and in my previous time in the organization [July to December 1997] we tried to create a situation where we were able to look after Alex's interests better than we had done previously. And I was involved in trying to help him readjust to the changing circumstances outside of the disciplinary committee . . . the answer in all honesty is that I wouldn't really know enough about the workings of this or that disciplinary committee but I will say that Alex's situation could have been handled considerably better from a patriarchal point of view and also from a PR and commercial point of view. I think Alex's demise hasn't served snooker well . . . My view is that the disciplinary processes that we have in place now are more equitable. I wouldn't say that what proceeded was a kangaroo court [but] there was potential for that [to happen].'

Robin Falvey is less circumspect. 'In some of the hearings

he was treated grossly unfairly, particularly the one involving the drugs . . . he was just badly treated in judicial proceedings. The only person who treated him fairly was Gavin Lightman [used by the WPBSA as an independent counsel], who is a High Court judge now. At least I was appearing in front of a lawyer [when representing Higgins] and I got proper treatment . . . Alex was dealt with very badly and, although I wouldn't say that he didn't bring a lot of it upon himself, from a lawyer's point of view that doesn't mean to say that you treat him any less well in a judicial process then anyone else. He has to be treated equally whether it be the WPBSA or anything else.' Falvey no longer represents Higgins but adds, 'I always liked him and I still do. I remember when he came down and he did a charity thing for a friend of mine, so I can't say anything bad about him.' In March 1997 Falvey had still not received any response to the nineteen charges he had levelled against board members and officials with regard to Higgins' treatment in two previous disciplinary hearings – one dealing with complaints levelled by Hendry and Doyle in 1992 and the business with the sample bottle in 1994. Higgins had a High Court writ outstanding to force the board to respond to the charges. Another change of board at the AGM in 1997 did not alter that but it did remove some of his long-standing disciplinary tribunal adversaries. When Bill Oliver was voted off a joyous Higgins shouted, 'Don't cry for me Argentina,' to which Oliver responded, 'No problem. At least I won't have to deal with arseholes like you any more.'

He was outside the top 100, he had to qualify for every ranking event, the exhibition matches had dried up, his game was in terminal decline and he still had to answer disciplinary charges relating to comments he had made to two referees in Blackpool fourteen months previously. If found guilty a £5,000 fine and a one-year ban would be activated. Compared to his private life, however, his career provided reasons to be cheerful. He found swallowing difficult, his voice had become hoarse and there was a persistent feeling of something in his throat. He was convinced the cancer in his mouth had spread to his throat and had stopped smoking. He was also homeless and had moved back in with Holly Haise. He was separated from his children because, as he admitted, 'there was always trouble' when he went round to the house. His mother had died in January ('She did everything for me,' he sobbed when we first met. 'She was the greatest woman who ever lived, I wish she was still here'), soon to be followed by his friend and manager Doug Perry, and he had no money. He could not drive and was reliant upon friends for handouts and assistance. Jim Lewis and Cedric Ulett tried to help him out. 'Basically, his name was still worth something and is to this day and he just needed some help to sort out some exhibition work. We'd always got on and we just sort drifted into becoming his co-managers,' explains Ulett. 'It was a question of knowing how to deal with him but it wasn't like with Doug Perry, it was much more informal, just helping a mate out really . . . I remember he once asked me if he could borrow £500 to get back to Ireland and I agreed to lend it him if he could give me an assurance I would get it back. He just said, "Jimmy White will give it you back." I phoned Jimmy and asked him. He said "yeah" and sent me a cheque to cover it.'

The relationship between Alex Higgins and Holly Haise was frequently violent and the volatile personalities of both people did not make for a blissful coexistence. The crossfire was certainly no place for a third party such as *Daily Star* photographer Peter Wilcock to be. Higgins had been banished to the caravan parked on the drive having returned to the house drunk the previous night. As he slept, Haise called the news desk at the *Star* and they sent Wilcock round to get a picture. 'Holly let me into the house,' he remembers. 'It was a tip to be honest, full of pentangles and all kinds of satanic stuff. It was a weirdo's palace really. She was polite enough, pleasant and well-dressed but the house was weird. She said, "He's in there . . . I want you to take a picture of him."' The photographer approached the caravan and peered through the window. It was dark inside because Higgins had stuck newspaper over the windows. Wilcock continues: 'I gingerly opened the door, put one foot in and this blanketed figure sort of lurched up. He looked bloody awful, so I took a picture and just shot out of the door. The next thing I know Higgins comes out with a silver luggage trolley and starts wielding it round his head . . . and then he set about me.'

Higgins assaulted Wilcock and left him winded on the floor. Holly Haise started screaming, 'I'm going to call the police, you bastard.' Higgins knew she was not bluffing and ran. 'My last image of Alex Higgins,' Wilcock laughs four years later, 'is of this wild, unkempt figure hurdling the garden fence.' The police dissuaded the photographer from pressing charges. 'They said, "It's up to you but he may well get sent down and you'll get nothing out of it . . . he hasn't got any money." Well, I have always had a soft spot for Higgins and I decided just to put it down to experience. I've still got the scar on my back.' The 1997 Embassy World Championship approached and, even though he was not going to be taking part, Higgins' body clock had been attuned to the tension and stress at that time of year since the mid-1970s. It was as though he was primed to go off in late April and early January (when the qualifiers began), although he could, of course, go off at any time.

He had his hair cut almost down to the scalp and travelled to Sheffield. It was the last tournament of the season and just because he was not involved did not mean that the event should be denied his presence. He chose the occasion to give a frank interview with the *Daily Record* during the course of which he compared his treatment at the hands of the WPBSA to that meted out to Ronnie O'Sullivan. Higgins observed that while he had urinated in a potted plant at the Crucible and away from the public and been fined £1,000, O'Sullivan had done the same in the foyer at an event in

Plymouth and had been fined only £500. He also drew attention to the money Neal Foulds had received from the benevolent fund and said, '[If the money could be used to pay off tax bills] £100,000 would have saved me about a million quid in assets and my lovely house in Cheshire.'[12] The contrast with his life in a caravan in the front garden of a council house in Swinton could not be more stark. *Snooker Scene* described the arguments he raised as 'eminently fair' although it noted that his suspension and the docking of his ranking points for punching Colin Randle in 1990 and O'Sullivan's purely financial punishment for biting an official in 1996 may have had something to do with the length of their respective 'records'.

Ken Doherty won the world title by beating Stephen Hendry 18–12 in the final. It was a popular victory and the laid-back Irishman became the first player to win both the amateur and professional world titles. Two days after he claimed the £160,000 first prize the twenty-seven-year-old new world champion announced his intention to play in a benefit match for the man who had inspired him to take up the game. He already owned a part share of a racehorse with Republic of Ireland international footballer Niall Quinn called Hopping Higgins – it had been named in celebration of Higgins' performance at the 1988 Benson and Hedges Irish Masters when he limped round the table after falling from a window. Doherty now wanted to give something back. 'It's so sad to hear he is on his knees,' he said. 'It's important we lift him up again . . . he is the man who made a fortune for the rest of us.' Lewis and Ulett helped to organize the event with sponsorship from the *Sunday World* newspaper. The 2,300 capacity Waterfront Hall was booked in Belfast for 19 June. There were tentative plans to use the event as a springboard for some kind of career renaissance but the priority was to raise some money for the 'Hurricane'. Doherty appeared for free while Higgins received £10,000 up front (and not £50,000, as reported in the press). 'It was the best exhibition he ever did,' says Lewis today. 'The hairs go up on the back of my neck just thinking about it.' The event was a sell-out. There was an unspoken idea that this might be the last opportunity to see the 'Hurricane'. It was the biggest crowd in front of which Doherty had ever performed. He was accorded a huge welcome but nothing compared to the noise and emotion as the MC announced: 'It's all been said about this man. Twice world champion, one of Belfast's finest . . . Alex "Hurricane" Higgins.' He was twenty minutes late but looked immaculate in a cobalt blue shirt and dark blue trousers and waistcoat. There was a standing ovation. He soaked it up as he looked around the Waterfront Hall. It was like a cathedral and everybody was there to worship Alex Higgins.

The game, whilst not exactly scripted, went to 4–4 before Doherty won the final frame. Unlike most other sports in which there is a constant atmosphere generated by the spectators, snooker requires silence for the players to perform at the highest level and the difference between the artificial silence during the game and the eruptions during the breaks between frames and at the end of the match can, in the right circumstances, create a wall of sound. This was one such occasion. As it ended, the crowd advanced, determined to have a piece of the 'Hurricane' – an autograph, a chance to slap him on the back, anything. 'Can you imagine what it is like to be faced with 2,300 people wanting to talk to you' asks Victor in the pub I visited on my second trip to Belfast. He is an old friend of the Higgins family and was at the Waterfront Hall that night. 'It could be terrifying and I wasn't even the one they wanted to talk to. The pattern would always be the same, fans would come up and ask him if he was alright and then ask him if he was still playing. The first cut is the deepest but can you imagine that another few hundred times in a couple of hours? Even the Pope would tell you to "fuck off."'

Higgins has always had a peculiar relationship with his fans. Dennis Taylor once claimed, 'Alex's worst fault, in my view, is not the way he treats other players, but the way he treats his fans . . . he even threatens them with physical violence just because they've asked for his autograph at a moment he found inconvenient.'[13] Steve Davis remembers a child in tears at an exhibition because Higgins had ripped his autograph book in half when asked to sign it. ('His mother came up to me and said, "Look what your friend has done to my boy's book." I was like, "It's nothing to do with me."') In the 1980s he had a stamp bearing his signature made up in the Far East. He used it to expedite the signing of autographs until it became apparent that his fans demanded something more. Against this image of the uncaring celebrity are the legion of stories of Higgins taking time to visit his fans in hospital, without a journalist or a television crew in attendance. The only autograph he signed at the Waterfront Hall was for a disabled child. Doherty stayed for an hour signing pieces of paper and programmes while the audience were told that, 'Mr Higgins has had to leave for family reasons.' In truth, he just wanted to get out. Had the sponsors thought about it properly there could have been an autograph table selling pre-signed posters, but that did not happen and Higgins, faced with the deluge, retreated to his dressing room with members of his family, old friends and whoever else could talk their way in. He left by a back door. The money, whilst not a fortune, would help him find somewhere to live. In five weeks he would be at the qualifying school in Plymouth for the new season. Perhaps a new start was on the cards.

He had not won a tournament for eight years and turned up at Plymouth Pavilions rated number 156 in the world. He needed to win four games to qualify for one of the thirty-two places on the main snooker circuit. He lost his first game 5–1 to the Neil Mosley (world number 182) in the first qualifying school event. He pulled out of the other qualifier. Ann Yates knew what to expect. Her last involvement with him at Blackpool had resulted in her telling him, 'Right, you're [in my office] again, what have you got to say? You've got two minutes to tell me what you have to say because I've had enough of listening to you, is it any different to what you've been saying to me every other day?' He told her, as he had done many times before, that (as she worked for the WPBSA) she was, technically, his employee. 'I said, "Well OK, we've had all that before . . . have you anything new to say?"' Yates was standing in the middle of the room and angry. 'I said, "Get out because I'm not having you [complaining] any more in this office."' The next time she met him was in Plymouth. 'He was a pathetic creature,' she reveals. 'We had a ruling that players couldn't wear baseball caps or shorts in the players' room or the hospitality room. That was a ruling brought in by the board . . . and the rule was there and I had to enforce it. And so did my staff. He came in the night before to practise . . . one of the players came running into my office and said, "You've got to get down to the players' room quickly, Higgins has got the security man by the throat."' The unnamed player was not exaggerating. 'I just ploughed up,' remembers Yates. I said, "What are you doing?" As I walked up I listened to what he was saying to the security man . . . [It was] I know you . . . I know where you live. And this is the sort of thing he used to do. Now that's horrendous, you know, the guy's doing his job . . . and he had him by the throat. So I just asked what was going on.' He had been asked to take off his baseball cap.

'[He] went berserk,' Yates recalls. 'It's a semi-public area and the public are starting to gather out there . . . and I'm standing there looking at this guy who is screaming at me [about] the human rights courts and all the rest [of it] is coming out again . . . he is so angry now he's spitting, and my blouse is soaked from his spittle. And I just looked at him and said . . . "You either behave now and stop this or I'll have you put out." He said, "Your fellas dare not touch me." He knew it. So I said, "This time, Alex, I'll call the police. I'll have you thrown out. One way or another you are not going to disrupt all the other players here who are fighting for their lives. I've had enough."

'He said, "I bet you won't." I said, "Watch me."'[14] The house manager Dave Cottrell also asked him to leave. He refused and police eventually escorted him from the premises at about 4 p.m. Twelve hours later bouncer Steve Graham found him lying on the floor outside Images nightclub in the western Approach area of the city. He claimed he had been 'done by three bastards' and said one of them had an iron bar. The number of assailants had been reduced to one by the time he was taken to Derriford Hospital with injuries to his face, a bruised right hand and a sprained ankle. A source in A&E told the *Sunday Mirror*, 'He wasn't very co-operative.' He discharged himself at 8.30 a.m. and a detective subsequently announced, 'We don't know whether he was attacked or fell over.' Higgins was unable to give any description of his assailant but the police treated it as assault. He did not return to the Pavilions. Instead, he made his way back to Manchester. 'I loved him . . . I still do but I don't want to be with him any more,' Holly Haise revealed to the *People*. 'He's too frightening. We were together for six years but now we don't speak. It's irretrievable . . . he beat me up for the first two years of our relationship. I eventually paid a boxer £1,000 to walk into a club and publicly humiliate him. He walked in, hit Alex twice on the nose and said: "Don't ever hit Holly again." He never did. Maybe I should have left him when the beatings started but I didn't because I was in love with him.'[15]

Higgins frightened Lynn to the extent that she locked herself in the bedroom as he wrecked the house with a golf club and threw a television through the window. He also attacked Siobhan Kidd with a hairdryer and tore a chandelier from the ceiling. The news that he had beaten Holly Haise was not a surprise. The definitive work on the psychology of the men who are violent in intimate relationships, *The Abusive Personality*, notes that the personality traits common to men who beat their partners are a tendency to externalize blame and undergo cyclical build-ups of tension and explosion. With regard to celebrity batterers the book continues, '[Most are] arrogant, calculating people who are self-assured at best and coldhearted. [They have] anti-social personalities [and are] narcissistic, self-absorbed people who feel they are "special" and the rest of the world is beneath them.'[16]

The country woke up on 15 August 1997 to the news that Holly Haise had stabbed Alex 'Hurricane' Higgins three times. There had been an altercation at her house. Her version of the account involves Higgins, drunk and aggressive, turning up on her doorstep. She alleged that she had prepared some chicken fajitas for his supper but then he started to physically abuse her and threaten her father. When he left the room she dialled 999 and left the phone off the hook. That was at 5.30 a.m. The police turned up at the house and, unable to gain entry, broke down the door to find Haise seeking refuge under a table. Higgins was persuaded to leave but returned three hours later and walked into the house past the unhinged front door. She then alleges that he kicked her in the stomach and hit her over the head with the telephone receiver. That she picked up an eight-inch boning knife and stuck it into him three times is not disputed, however. Twice into his right shoulder and once in his stomach. He was wearing a white T-shirt and the blood began to saturate the cotton immediately. A neighbour heard them rowing and pulled back the curtains in time to see the former world snooker champion covered in blood outside the front of the house. The police were called again. His thirty-four-year-old ex-girlfriend was sobbing uncontrollably, repeating, 'I've stabbed him, I've stabbed him.' The police found a knife with blood smeared the length of the blade and, then, Higgins in a front garden hiding behind a bush, slowly bleeding to death. He turned on the police, claiming some kind of conspiracy, but was eventually convinced to go to hospital. He discharged himself, against medical advice, and climbed into a taxi just as the pubs opened. His assailant was taken to Eccles police station in the back of a police van and remanded on bail. Higgins did not press charges and Holly Haise was later cleared of wounding him with intent to cause grievous bodily harm after the prosecution admitted that it faced 'evidential difficulties'. As she left court she said, 'Of course I stabbed him. I have admitted it from day one. But I still love him deeply. I want to marry him and put his life back on the rails.'

It was too late for that. His daughter Lauren went to the papers to plead with him to give up drinking. 'Despite all the things he's done, he's still my dad and I do love him. I don't want any harm to come to him,' she said. 'He needs treatment [for his drinking]. When he gets drunk his personality changes and he gets very aggressive but he doesn't think he's got a problem.' She also revealed that they had not spoken for six months. 'I was talking to him about going to college but all he did was talk about himself. I said, "Dad, don't you want to listen to what I've got to say?" and he started getting aggressive. He told me to go and rot in effing hell so I just put the phone down. But he was drunk. If he was sober, he wouldn't say that to me.'[17] From 'Bring me my baby' to 'rot in hell' in fifteen years, it was an indication of how far he had fallen.

He did not show up for the Embassy World Championship qualifiers at the Norbreck Castle. He was now ranked 177. His nominal opponent, Justin Buckingham, a twenty-four-year-old roofer from Oxford, was awarded a 10–0 whitewash and shrugged, 'Alex should seriously think about giving the game up because he's got no chance of getting back up anywhere near the top players any more . . . he used to be a quality player but he's lost it. When I knew I was down to play him, I said it was a good draw . . . none of the young players are worried about playing him nowadays. You don't fear Alex Higgins, that's long gone.'[18]

The reason for his non-appearance was said to be ill-health. The press reported it with due scepticism but it was the truth. The cancer had spread to his throat and after seeing three separate specialists, hoping that one might contradict the previous diagnosis, he resigned himself to the struggle. Clive Everton has referred to snooker as the 'glue which held Alex Higgins together'. For the first time since the early 1970s the 'Hurricane' was not on the circuit and, with all his attendant dilemmas, was now fighting throat cancer. It is one of the most difficult forms of the disease to combat and he was given a fifty-fifty chance of surviving. He told people he had eight months to live but put off the surgery necessary for as long as possible. An invitation from Benson and Hedges to attend a gala dinner at the K Club followed by a parade of champions at Goffs to celebrate their twenty-first year of snooker sponsorship served as a welcome distraction. Within a year, he would become a prominent litigant in a class action to sue the industry whose hospitality he was now accepting, claiming that the sponsor's propensity to give out free cigarettes had been a cause of his illness. As if to make a point, he poured a glass of wine into the pocket of Jim Elkins, the Benson and Hedges director of special events, but missed the parade of champions. Higgins later received a black eye in the tournament hotel from a man with a Jewish wife who objected to his observation that Hitler had 'not done a very good job'. The police were called. Alex Higgins was not invited to the Twenty-fifth Anniversary of the Benson and Hedges Masters at Wembley the following February.

In May 1998 Holly Haise appeared on the daytime TV show *The Time, The Place* talking about domestic violence. The researchers had ambitiously tried to secure Higgins' involvement in the programme. According to the researcher, Jim Lewis, by then acting as his manager, declined on his behalf. When presenter John Stapleton asked what attracted her to him, she answered, 'Well, it certainly wasn't his overcoats.' Details of his illness became public knowledge a month later and he moved back to Northern Ireland. It was, as his East Belfast contemporary Van Morrison had hinted whilst namechecking him alongside James Joyce, Samuel Beckett, Oscar Wilde and George Best on his 1993 track 'Too Long in Exile', time to go home. After an exhibition match with Jimmy White in Larne he announced, 'I'm dying.' At the exhortation of his few remaining friends he finally underwent nine weeks of intensive radiation therapy at the Ear, Nose and Throat Department of Belfast's Royal Victoria Hospital. Two months later, in September, he underwent major surgery for the removal of a lymph gland to prevent the cancer from spreading further. The hospital described him as 'comfortable'. The *Daily Mail* described him as 'Fighting for his life'.

The ordeal left Higgins enfeebled. He went to live near his sister Ann in Lisburn and took to eating different varieties of cake before washing them down with gallons of tea. It was all he could swallow. As he was recovering from the surgery, Holly Haise went to the press again. He threatened her with a civil prosecution over the stabbing and demanded that she call him Mr Higgins. By the end of the year he was convinced he was not going to die. He had never stopped drinking but was now smoking again and, on a visit to Manchester, stopped in at the Masters Club. Paul Medati, the owner who had given him the famous 'I-was-kicked-by-a-horse' black eye in 1987, was playing cards with some friends. 'Nobody wanted to play him,' he sighs. 'He was in the matchroom on his own and then came out and declared, "I've barred myself." Then he climbed into a taxi and left. I didn't think anything about it until the barmaid said, "Come and have a look at the state of this" . . . he'd taken the pictures down off the wall, removed the photographs and jumped on all the frames. He's still got [the photos].'

'All he seems to live for these days is his day in the High Court with the WPBSA defending the action he has brought,' reflected *Snooker Scene*.[19] With his professional career seemingly at an end, he was, for once, beyond the jurisdiction of the governing body. And all was not well with the WPBSA. In summer 1998, the organization employed a company secretary, Martyn Blake, a man who had drunkenly gatecrashed the dinner table of unfortunate sponsor Jim Elkins and guests at the Irish Benson and Hedges Masters. The WPBSA also retained a solicitor, Matthew McCloy, who had been handcuffed to his seat on an American Airlines flight in October 1995 after the flight crew became alarmed about his behaviour. McCloy pleaded guilty to a charge of disorderly conduct in a New York courtroom and received a conditional discharge. In July, Higgins discovered that he had been awarded legal aid in his High Court action against the WPBSA. At the time of writing, and because the governing body have refused to deal with the charges levelled against them, the case is still outstanding. The organization announced that for marketing purposes it would refer to itself as the World Snooker Association and Ann Yates, who had been on extended leave for medical reasons, resigned. It was all change.

Oliver Reed was on location in Malta, playing Proximo in *Gladiator*, for which he would receive a BAFTA nomination for best actor in a supporting role. On 2 May 1999 he went into The Pub on Archbishop Street in Valletta. After an extended bout of drinking with several members of the British navy, he died there. The death of the apparently indestructible Reed unsettled Higgins. He was a good friend, a drinking partner and a man who could do one-armed push-ups on the bar. He was also someone with whom Higgins had recorded a version of 'Wild Thing' seven years previously.[20] They had shared a lifestyle. The pictures of Higgins caught by the paparazzi as he left St James' Church in Mallow, County Cork were picked up by most of the 'fucking fish and chip' papers. Had he permitted himself a moment of self-reflection he too would have been shocked. Stephen Ford, Reed's great friend, helped him away from the graveside. 'He looked so dreadful,' he winces. 'I couldn't believe it was the same man. I'd noticed him during the service, well I couldn't really help but notice him as his mobile phone went off . . . Ollie would have found that funny, particularly watching him try to turn it off in a panic, but he just seemed so small.' The intensive radiation therapy had made his weight drop to six stone and his eyes seemed to bulge out of his head. His hair was in retreat and his wizened face was perched on top of a scarred and scrawny Modigliani neck. 'I said to Josephine [Reed, Oliver's widow], a bit naughtily I suppose, if we just push him in do you think we'll get two for the price of one? It was just black humour, I like Alex.' Nobody gave him much time.

As a working class man from Belfast in his early fifties, who had smoked eighty a day since his late teenage years and was also a heavy drinker, he was in the highest risk group in Europe. The cancer was, however, in remission. Or so he insisted. On Ulster Television that night he told host Gerry Kelly that he was being looked after by his sisters in Lisburn and denied he had a drink problem. 'I'm a restless cat,' he explained. 'An awful lot of people don't understand that I'm hyperactive.' Nobody really knew what he was talking about, perhaps not even himself, but it showed he was not about to capitulate to the disease. That would be as unnatural as taking responsibility for his own actions. His persistence with the court case against the WPBSA, his decision to become a figurehead for a class action involving 200 people against the tobacco industry (the motivation for appearing on the *Tobacco Wars* documentary) and his insistence that he was preparing to make a comeback were more efficacious than the thirty-eight tablets he had to swallow between 9.30 a.m. and noon every day. There is nobody you would rather put your money on to beat cancer, even if the survival rate after five years is just one in ten. Higgins is a fighter nonpareil. Nobody in the modern era has won two world championships ten years apart. Alex 'Hurricane' Higgins simply refuses to lie down and die, despite the attentions of the WPBSA. If snooker players had cornermen, the towel would have been thrown in years before but he was allowed to carry on. It was not pretty to watch but, like a crime scene in a respectable neighbourhood, it was impossible to ignore.

Higgins had decamped to Dublin and was living the life of an itinerant hustler. His belongings were wherever he left them, he was Belsen-thin and his angular cheekbones looked as though Picasso had allowed his imagination to wander but his sunken eyes peered out from his skull with trademark defiance. He was living between lodging house, pub bedroom and floor-for-the-night. There seemed to be an almost inexhaustible supply of people prepared to give him floor space in exchange for the right to tell their friends that 'Hurricane' Higgins was on his arse, needed somewhere to sleep and they had helped him out. He was a fifty-year-old man who had, probably, earned and spent £3,000,000 with nothing more to show for it than throat cancer, the clothes he stood up in and a couple of carrier bags full of whatever he could rescue from the wreckage of his life. He went back to Manchester. Holly Haise offered to put him up once again. Siobhan Kidd may have been the love of his life but Haise, the woman who stabbed him three times, seemed to love him unconditionally. 'I can't see him sleeping out on the streets, we've been through too much together for that,' she told the *Irish Star*. 'He's a very sick man and will die unless he gets help. I want him to know the spare room is his if he wants it – no strings attached.' Everywhere he went, people wanted to know: 'How did you fuck it all up so badly? You had it all.' It was the same question George Best had to answer at least twenty times a night on the sportsmen's dinner circuit but Higgins lacked the driver, the five-star hotel and the cheque to tell them. Best also had charm enough to deal with the situation, whereas Higgins felt compelled to lash out.

The two men, despite their remarkably proximate upbringing and astonishing talent in their chosen fields, were never close. Best summed-up their relationship in his recent autobiography *Blessed*. He had contracted pneumonia and was in hospital in Belfast. Higgins attempted to arrange a visit. Best was not keen. 'I've never been enamoured of people who use the immortal words, "Do you know who I am?" And I have often heard Alex use them,' he remarked. 'In my experience, he could also be a little aggressive when he's drunk.' Higgins turned up anyway, with a scarf around his neck to hide the scars. 'He looked a lot worse than me,' reflected Best. 'We said "Hello" to each other and he pulled up a chair and sat beside my bed and said, "Give me your hand."' Higgins then affected to read his palm. 'Now, if there's one person I don't need giving me advice or telling me what's going to happen,' wrote Best, 'it's Alex.' Higgins told him he would be out of hospital in a few days, that he would live until he was 80 and that there was nothing wrong with him. Eighteen months later George Best underwent a liver transplant and nearly died on the operating table. [21]

In April 2000 Higgins travelled to the United Arab Emirates to watch the Dubai World Cup horse race. He considered staying in the United Arab Emirates to undertake some coaching work but his medication ran out and Nic Barrow, the official UAE snooker coach, organized a flight back to Belfast. His sister Ann was due to meet him and take him back to the pensioner's bungalow in Lisburn he now called home. As he went through customs at the airport in Dubai he collapsed and was rushed to hospital and 'virtually stopped breathing' twice. Newspapers dusted off his obituary and started chasing pictures. 'It was a tragic waste of a life,' they prepared to say. 'He should have won more than six major titles,' columnists were poised to opine. 'The game should have looked after him,' several sports journalists were about to tell ITN and the BBC. He was a 'genius', he 'revolutionized the game', 'cried when he won the world title in 1982', 'a Jekyll and Hyde character', 'headbutted a tournament official', 'threatened to have Dennis Taylor shot'. All the players who had judged him on the board of the WPBSA were on standby to sentimentalize his departure with an unrecognizable picture. But, not for the first time, Alex Higgins frustrated them all. Two days after his collapse Barrow smiled, 'When I went to see him he was stroppy towards me.' He was soon back in Belfast and helping the lawyer Peter McDonnell to publicize the class action he had put together to win compensation for his clients from the tobacco industry. A week after getting back to Belfast he was seen in Manchester. He could only live life at one pace and there was no compromise. Seven months after collapsing he had beaten cancer after nearly forty sessions of radiotherapy and was fined at Lisburn Magistrates Court for smoking on a train and being drunk and disorderly.

He was soon announcing a twenty-five date tour. Six days later his comeback was confirmed as he was arrested after smashing a window at a pub in Bangor, North Down. 'About five minutes before last orders I noticed a man getting out of a taxi,' Nicola Morrow, the manageress of the Jamaica Inn, told the *Belfast Telegraph*. 'He had been drinking out of a pint glass which he threw at the rocks opposite the bar. He came in and walked over to three people sitting and his language was atrocious . . . He asked me for a drink and I told him we were closed. Then he became abusive to me. He asked me if I knew who he was and when I said no, he said: "I'm Alex Higgins, that's Sir Alex to you."' He was ejected from the premises and a window was broken. Jimmy White paid the bill for the window to prevent the police prosecuting his friend. Before the summer was over, Higgins had flown into Manchester Airport and created mayhem at the Radisson SAS hotel. He called the staff following him with his golf clubs 'fucking idiots'. A white towelling robe was hanging out of his bag as he made his shambolic exit. Later that afternoon he turned up at the home of Holly Haise.

'He first called round at 7.15 p.m. looking like something from the outback, wearing a safari suit and an Australian bush hat,' she said. 'He had clearly been drinking and tried to kick my door in, shouting he wanted money from me . . . I told him to clear off and he eventually went but kept ringing me and leaving incoherent messages on my answer machine. Then he returned about 11.15 p.m. When I answered the door he said something like "you like scarves don't you" then tried to wrap one around my neck.'[22] The local police probably had a separate code for a Higgins–Haise interface. A '147' in progress perhaps. He was warned that he would be arrested if he came back.

Although he was beginning to put on some weight and his cancer was still in remission, when he returned to Northern Ireland he found himself reliant upon the generosity of family and friends. It was certainly a long way from a mansion in Cheshire and a chauffeur-driven ride to Shepherd's Bush to appear on a primetime chat show but , in truth, the 'People's Champion' had travelled less than ten miles from where he was born. The way he lived had not changed at all. He still drank, smoked, gambled and played snooker for money. The quality of his life had arguably improved. The pressure of tournaments had disappeared and there was always the chance of another pay day, as his exhibition matches with Jimmy White across Northern Ireland in the summer of 2002 served to prove.

Within a couple of months he announced a comeback and paid his £30 entry fee for the Benson and Hedges championship, the class action against the tobacco industry notwithstanding. He made an effortless return to the headlines: 'FLAWED STAR HIGGINS ON CUE TO RETURN' (*Daily Mirror*), 'SPORT'S SADDEST COMEBACK EVER' (*Sun*) and 'THE FREAK HURRICANE THAT MUST BE STOPPED' (*Evening Standard*). Dennis Taylor predicted that it could 'turn out to be a bad move.' Ronnie O'Sullivan went on the record to say, 'It has to be good for snooker to have a figure like the Hurricane back putting bums on seats. We need that more than ever in the game.' Higgins' last game in a sanctioned event had been at the Plymouth Pavilions five years previously. His appearance had involved the local police who were compelled to escort him from the premises, and later that same day, the medical staff at Derriford Hospital, who attended to him when he was found lying on the floor outside a nightclub.

The Benson and Hedges championship is an open event staged at the Towers Snooker Club in Mansfield and success in that competition would render him eligible for the Benson and Hedges Masters at Wembley in February, a tournament he had won twice before. He would need to win eight matches to claim a £6,000 cheque and a place in the Masters. Tickets for the satellite event sold out in a matter of hours.

The fact that he had been allowed to register at all was incredible. The catalogue of objections submitted by tournament referees for reported misbehaviour remained, stretching back to the late 1990s, and there were also the outstanding complaints brought by his solicitor, Robin Falvey, against the Association as a result of alleged irregularities during the two disciplinary tribunals in 1992 and 1994. But an accommodation was reached. According to a source inside the WPBSA: 'We have received his application, he has signed the form and been accepted but whether he attends or not is a different matter.' His first game was to be at 10am on 23 October against twenty-two-year-old Lee Spick, a player who was still at nursery school the last time Higgins won the world championship. Spick was understandably concerned: 'I'm not looking forward to it at all,' he said. 'We don't know yet whether he's going to turn up but if he does it won't be a nice atmosphere. Alex used to be a great player and is someone I looked up to and respected. When he was on top form he could do anything. I would rather have played him then than now.' He had no need to worry. Higgins pulled out a few days before the tournament citing, with typically imaginative aplomb, the need for 'extensive dental treatment'.

When I met Alex Higgins in room 271 at the Post House Hotel in August 2001, he was as relaxed as might be realistically expected. He did not know what he was going to do in the short, medium or long term. Actually, he didn't know what he was going to do that night. He was living in and for the moment. He fancied a couple of horses that were running and he knew he wanted a drink. He also suspected that I might be able to fund his desire for instant gratification. As we made our way towards the lift we brushed past a middle-aged couple returning from the three-star restaurant. They looked at the ravaged 'Hurricane' Higgins and then stole another glance before walking ten yards down the corridor and realizing who they had just seen. 'I get that all the time,' he rasped. The lift took an age to arrive. I had already worked out that conversation was a one-way street and decided against small talk.

'Have you enjoyed your life?' I asked him. He looked at me and then up at the illuminated numbers above the lift, adjusted his cravat and said, 'I haven't really had much to do with my life. All I've done is take part in it.'

NOTES

PREFACE

1: *Snookered*, Donald Trelford (Faber, 1986), p. 21
2: When Kean first appeared in *Hamlet* in London he entered the stage to a half-empty auditorium. His performance was such that, during the interval, members of the audience left the theatre to drag their friends in from the various clubs in the environs. Kean finished to a full house.
3: *Wogan*, 23 October 1991
4: BBC Sport, 22 October 2002
5: Oscar Wilde quoted in *Works on Paper: The Craft of Biography and Autobiography*, Michael Holroyd (Little Brown, 2002), p. 4

ONE

1: *Pocket Money*, Gordon Burn (Heinemann, 1986), p. 6
2: Interview with author
3: Interview with author
4: *Snooker – The Records*, Clive Everton (Guinness Books, 1985), p. 13
5: *Alex Through the Looking Glass*, Alex Higgins with Tony Francis (Pelham Books, 1986), p. 5: '[it's] the incorrigible hustler taking a fiver from another ingenu as he did at the Wilmslow Conservative Club one wintry afternoon (in 1985) which sticks in the mind.'
6: Interview with author
7: An auction of *Spitting Image* puppets at Sotheby's in November 2001 saw Lot 52 ('Alex Higgins') realize £220 (plus 17.5 per cent VAT). Other puppets that raised the same figure included Robert Mugabe, Geoffrey Palmer, Jo Brand, 'The Edge', John Harvey Jones, Hugh Laurie and Jimmy Tarbuck.
8: Regarding the Seniors Tour I received the following email from Peter Bainbridge (Seniors Snooker Ltd) on 22 November 2001:

This company has, over the last 2 years, attempted to interest various organisations in the creation of a Seniors circuit or tour for certain qualifying professional players. The key ingredient to such a tour is, as we are sure you will understand, satisfactory coverage by television companies whether terrestrial, satellite or cable. We have so far been unable to obtain such coverage and the development of this aspect of the game is thus on hold until the position changes. We work closely with the governing body of the game . . . and [in response to my question as to whether Higgins would be included] would seek guidance on the eligibility of any senior player. You will appreciate however that, at this stage, it is too early to finally determine who would play in such an event or events.

9: Higgins and Gallagher met when the former world champion lived in Burrage. Years later, Alex Higgins approached Gallagher backstage, after a gig in Blackpool: 'When I get out of it Noel,' he asked, 'can you get me a room?' (*Getting High: The Adventures of Oasis*, Paolo Hewitt, 1997). In response to Higgins' latest request, for a loan of a million pounds, a highly amused Noel Gallagher burst out laughing and issued a wry 'No comment.'

TWO

1: Louis MacNeice, 'Valediction'. *Poems*, selected by Michael Longley (Faber, 2001), p. 11
2: 'Higgins Senior came into our German lesson one morning on the daily ritual of collecting register/absentee details for the school office,' recalls Ian Shuttleworth, another RBAI pupil. 'On his way out he happened to bump against the corner of a desk; given his diminutive stature, the collision seemed to be in, well, let's say the upper thigh area. As soon as the door closed, our teacher muttered, not without sympathy, "Red ball in the side pocket." He then left us a couple of seconds' snigger time before carrying on.' Interview with author
3: Jean Simpson (née Higgins), interviewed for a Sunset + Vine North documentary
4: Ann Brown (née Higgins), interviewed for a Sunset + Vine North documentary
5: www.friendsreunited.co.uk
6: Cecil Mason, interviewed for a Sunset + Vine North documentary
7: Ann Brown and Jean Simpson interviewed for a Sunset + Vine North documentary

8: *'Hurricane' Higgins' Snooker Scrapbook*, Alex Higgins with Angela Patmore (Souvenir Press, 1981), p. 6

9: *A Kestrel for a Knave*, Barry Hines (Penguin, 1969)

10: *'Hurricane' Higgins' Snooker Scrapbook*, p. 6

11: Ibid., p. 8

12: Ibid., p. 8

13: *Alex Through the Looking Glass*, p. 33

14: *This is Your Life*

15: *'Hurricane' Higgins' Snooker Scrapbook*, p. 21

16: Interview with author

17: *Frame by Frame*, Dennis Taylor (Macdonald 1985), pp. 32–34

18: Vince Laverty, interviewed for a Sunset + Vine North documentary

19: *Frame by Frame*, p. 44

20: Interview with author

21: *'Hurricane' Higgins' Snooker Scrapbook*, p. 39

22: *Alex Through the Looking Glass*, p. 43

23: An apprentice or 'probationary' professional had to prove to the governing body that he could earn a living from the game.

24: John McLaughlin and Vince Laverty, interviewed for a Sunset + Vine North documentary

25: Interview with author

26: *Natural Break*, Dennis Taylor, (Macdonald 1985), pp. 19–21

27: Ann Brown (née Higgins), interviewed for a Sunset + Vine North documentary

THREE

1: *Snooker – The Records*, p.56

2: *The American Heritage® Dictionary of the English Language:* Fourth Edition (Houghton Mifflin, 2000)

3: *The Story of Billiards and Snooker*, Clive Everton (Cassell, 1979), p.122

4: *Alex Through the Looking Glass*, p. 46

5: *Pocket Money*, p. 97

6: *Belfast Telegraph*, 24 February 1972

7: *Snooker Scene*, April 1972

8: *Belfast Telegraph*, February 1972

FOUR

1: Mike Langley, *Sunday People*, 5 March 1972

2: Other neutral observers would subsequently arrive at the same conclusion but Morgan and Goddard got there first.

3: Nancy Banks-Smith, *Guardian*

4: *Hurricane Higgins*, a Thames TV documentary, 1972

5: *Higgins, Taylor and Me*, Jim Meadowcroft (Arthur Barker, 1986)

6: *Alex Through the Looking Glass*, p. 57

7: As was twelve-year-old Trevor Morris who was on the same flight. 'I was flying with my sisters to visit my father in Singapore,' recalls Morris, now a professor of political science in North Carolina:

> There were a number of loud, heavy-drinking, rough characters who had obviously chosen that airline since it provided passengers with an open bar. The loudest of these gentlemen periodically walked back [into the economy section] and sat on my armrest, chatted to me and gave me champagne from the bottle he was using to keep his balance. A fellow passenger noted I was a lucky lad to have the world snooker champion, Alex 'Hurricane' Higgins, take such an interest in me. After his third or fourth visit back [to my seat], I was able to match Higgins' weaving gait. Through the fog I realized he was not interested in making my acquaintance but was using me as a ploy to become friendly with my sisters, then aged sixteen and eighteen, who had, as he pointed out, much more interesting chests.

8: *Alex Through the Looking Glass*, p. 59

9: *Daily Mirror*, 3 April 1973

10: *Alex Through the Looking Glass*, pp. 63–4

11: *The Story of Billiards and Snooker* , p. 22

12: *'Hurricane' Higgins' Snooker Scrapbook*, p. 51

13: National Office of Statistics. The average gross weekly earnings of full-time employees whose pay for the survey pay-period was not affected by absence amounted to £36.40 in April 1973. Higgins was set to clear just under £20,000 for the year.

14: 1972 was the worst year of 'The Troubles', embracing 'Bloody Sunday', an IRA bomb in the Abercorn city centre bar and the introduction of direct rule from London. There was a bomb detonated within a few hundred yards of the Higgins family home. The *Belfast Telegraph* reported:

> Donegal Street looked like a battlefield. When the smoke and dust from the blast cleared, injured people were seen lying in pools of blood on the roadway. Some of the casualties lay in agony with glass splinters embedded in their wounds. A body was blown to pieces by

the force of the explosion, which rocked the entire city centre. An old man was comforted on the footpath. As he lay barely conscious, he was unaware that half his leg had been blown off in the explosion.

FIVE

1: *Between Frames*, Ted Lowe with Frank Butler (A & C Black, 1984), p. 49

2: *Ibid.*, p. 51

3: *Pocket Money*, p. 167

4: *Ibid.*

5: It was, in essence, the kind of letter which could have been dictated by his more famous namesake to Joan Greengross, the secretary at Sunshine Desserts, in one of his more inexplicable outbursts.

6: *Hurricane Higgins*, a Thames TV documentary, 1972

7: *The Story of Billiards and Snooker*, p. 23

8: Fred Davis was also one of only two players to win both the World Billards and World Snooker titles. His brother Joe is the other.

9: *Eye of the Hurricane*, John Hennessey (Mainstream, 2000)

10: George Plimpton interviewed for the 1996 documentary *When We Were Kings*, directed by Leon Gast.

11: Interview with author

12: Interview with author

13: 'Push Stroke: A push stroke is made when the tip of the cue remains in contact with the cue-ball (a) after the cue-ball has commenced its forward motion, or (b) as the cue-ball makes contact with an object ball except, where the cue-ball and an object ball are almost touching, it shall not be deemed a push stroke if the cue-ball hits a very fine edge of the object ball.' The Rules of Snooker, www.worldsnooker.com

14: *'Hurricane Higgins' Snooker Scrapbook*, p. 57

15: Interview with author

16: Interview with author

17: *Evil Spirits: The Life of Oliver Reed*, Cliff Goodwin (Virgin Publishing, 2000), p. 174

18: Interview with author

19: Interview with author

20: *The Story of Billiards and Snooker*, p.126

21: *Griff: The Autobiography of Terry Griffiths* (Pelham Books, 1989), p. 42

22: Interview with author

23: Ray Reardon, interviewed for a Sunset + Vine North documentary

24: *Playing for Keeps*, Cliff Thorburn with Clive Everton (Partridge Press, 1987), p. 39

SIX

1: *The Story of Billards and Snooker*, p. 136
2: *Behind the White Ball*, Jimmy White (Hutchinson, 1998), p. 478
3: Interview with author
4: It was not until an Extraordinary General Meeting of the WPBSA in the late 1970s voted to end the practice of two qualifiers joining the top fourteen in favour of eight qualifers joining the highest ranking eight professionals in the all-important top sixteen that some measure of balance was brought to the process.
5: Ted Lowe has always held that players should conform to certain sartorial codes. He noted with disdain that '[Higgins] was not the least embarrassed in 1972 to be interviewed on television in shirt and braces', *Between Frames*, p. 119
6: *'Hurricane' Higgins' Snooker Scrapbook*, p. 66
7: *Daily Mirror*, 26 September 1979

SEVEN

1: 'Although later on I did sneak off during the lunch periods to go to the local snooker club . . . I did not miss school to play. I was by now beginning to grow up mentally and took a more responsible attitude to life', *Griff*, p. 10
2: *Pocket Money*, p. 24
3: *Griff*, p. 69
4: *Alex Through the Looking Glass*, p. 93
5: In June 1999, the temporary curate of St Bartholomew's Church, David Leaver, wrote a farewell in the parish newsletter which concluded with his observation that thirty- and fortysomethings in Wilmslow were 'as pagan as any group of people I have ever met'. Despite protestations to the contrary, they were no different twenty years earlier.
6: Interview with author
7: *Frame by Frame*, p. 96
8: Angela Patmore, 'Death by Miscue', *Snooker Scene*, 1981
9: William Shakespeare, *Twelfth Night*. Act ii, Sc. 4

EIGHT

1: Steve Davis, interviewed for a Sunset + Vine North documentary.

2: 'So now I moved over [to Britain in 1980] . . . About four days after we'd moved into the house, we're stood by the front door and I'm off to play and I said to [my wife]: "What the hell have we done here?"' *Playing for Keeps*, p. 83

3: *Alex Through the Looking Glass*, p. 98

4: 'When I played Alex in the 1981 Benson and Hedges final we were very much in the same position at the interval (as we had been in the final in 1980). He did not ask me to share the money. And when I mentioned this to him later, he said, "Oh, I fancied beating you . . ." Well, I learnt a lesson there.' *Griff*, p. 93

5: *Alex Through the Looking Glass*, p. 96

6: Interview with author

7: *Frame and Fortune*, Steve Davis (Arthur Barker, 1982), p. 41

8: *Is It Me?*, Terry Wogan (BBC Worldwide, 2001), p. 102

9: Interview with author

NINE

1: Dave Martin finished English Amateur Snooker Champion runner-up twice.

2: Almost inevitably, Steve Davis retained the first of his major titles a few days later by whitewashing Jimmy White and then treating Terry Griffiths with a similar disregard to win 16–3. *Snooker Scene* described him as winning it with 'ludicrous ease'.

3: *Daily Mirror*, 14 December 1981

4: Steve Davis, interviewed for a Sunset + Vine North documentary

5: Noreen Taylor, *Daily Mirror*, 15 December, 1981

6: *Alex Through the Looking Glass*, p. 117

7: Barry Hearn, interviewed for a Sunset + Vine North documentary

8: The seedings were, at this time, calculated on the basis of performances in the last three world championships.

9: Patmore wrote or co-wrote *Leading From The Front* (the autobiography of Mike Gatting); *Sportsmen Under Stress*; *Playing on Their Nerves: the Sport Experiment* (both general but definitive works) and *The Giants of Sumo*.

10: Interview with author

TEN

1: Ray Reardon, interviewed for a Sunset + Vine North documentary

2: Ibid.

3: Ibid.

4: *Alex Through the Looking Glass*, p. 104

5: Repeated attempts by the author to access the WPBSA disciplinary files have met with a polite but defiant refusal. As Clive Everton, the editor of *Snooker Scene* predicted, 'You won't get them. Simply because they will have to divulge information about themselves.'

6: *News of the World*, January 1986

7: Ray Reardon interviewed for a Sunset + Vine documentary. After the introduction and liberal imbibing of free champagne during this AGM, an alcohol ban was introduced.

8: Terry Griffiths was also on the WPBSA committee in 1982. 'At the time I felt you had to be tough with him – whether that involved a fine or a ban. But it never happened properly . . . someone said, "You can't ban the World Champion. He wouldn't be in the tournaments. What are the sponsors going to say?" So he was let off. The board was too weak. They failed to [stamp their authority]. And the problems continued.' *Griff*, pp. 89–90

9: Alan Hart used to be the captain of the darts team at the Kenilworth. 'I'd been playing darts with Alex all afternoon and he decided he wanted to stay on. I explained that we had a darts match that evening against another pub team and that it would not be possible. He badgered me but I was not about to drop a regular player for him. In the end I told him that he couldn't play as he was not registered. He asked if he could play under an assumed name. I had to tell him that as he was one of the most famous men in the country there was little chance of him getting away with it.'

10: 'One Four Seven', music and lyrics by Sammes & Swain

11: *Behind the White Ball*, p. 4

12: Ibid., p. 7

13: *Alex Through the Looking Glass*, p. 105

14: Interview with author

15: In the piece, Ted Corbett (the journalist credited with the story) wrote, 'Was it a gesture of despair or a full blooded "get lost" gesture? Only Higgins knows.' Corbett subsequently told *Snooker Scene*: 'My copy was changed so drastically that I feel it was an affront to my professional attitude to my work. I was not consulted in any way.' It seems, in this instance, that Higgins may have been the innocent victim of an opportunist subeditor at the *Daily Star*.

16: Watterson was able to concentrate on his snooker. He had received a letter from the WPBSA that informed him he was not promoting the next world champion-ships. Del Simmons had been appointed contract negotiator for the governing body two months previously while Paul Hatherell, a former employee of W. D. and H.O. Wills, became tournament director. Higgins was shortly to come into contact with Hatherell.

ELEVEN

1: *Alex Through the Looking Glass*, p. 110–11
2: Ibid.
3: Clive Everton, *Guardian*, 5 December 1983
4: 'The banning of Alex Higgins from snooker tournaments in Sydney and Auckland this summer raises fundamental questions for sport, in general, to answer. Higgins' personal 'style' is difficult to defend but . . . more pertinent, though, was the reaction of sponsors, Phillip Morris, the cigarette company. If the ban on Higgins remains after his appeal, sport will immediately be left to ponder: What actual rights should a sponsor have to dictate who plays and who does not?' *Sunday Telegraph*, February 1984.
5: As reported by John Wilde, during an interview for 'Impure Genius', *Loaded*, January 1998
6: *Pocket Money*, p. 5
7: *Playing for Keeps*, p. 112
8: *Frame by Frame*, pp. 94–8
9: *Alex Through The Looking Glass*, p. 129
10: *Pocket Money*, p. 6
11: The £150,000 Goya Matchroom event was essentially put together by Barry Hearn to help promote the range of male toiletries his players were now endorsing. It was now possible to smell like Tony Meo.

TWELVE

1: Dudley Doust, *Sunday Times*, 24 November 1985
2: *Pocket Money*, pp. 152–53
3: *Alex Through the Looking Glass*, p. 166
4: *Pocket Money*, pp. 163–4
5: *Snooker Scene*, April 1986
6: Guinness had withdrawn their sponsorship. No other sponsor could match the £125,000 prize-money fund or seemed prepared to pay the rate the WPBSA, through Del Simmons, was asking to have their name associated with the event. With a fortnight to go he

secured a £50,000 contribution to the prize-money fund from Car Care Plan. It worked out at £3,100 per hour of coverage on national television, which was, by sponsorship standards, a bargain.

7: 'Snooker Loopy,' music and lyrics by Hodges & Peacock

8: *Behind the White Ball*, p. 199

9: *Playing for Keeps*, p. 129

10: Ibid., p. 45

11: 'I am sorry to say that Oscar drinks far more that he ought,' wrote Beerbohm to Reggie Turner in April 1893. 'Indeed the first time I saw him, after all that long period of distant adoration and reverence, he was in a hopeless state of intoxication . . .' *Max Beerbohm's Letters to Reggie Turner*, ed. Rupert Hart-Davis (Rupert Hart-Davis, 1964)

12: *Playing for Keeps*, p. 93

13: Ann Yates, inteviewed for a Sunset + Vine North documentary

THIRTEEN

1: Ann Yates, interviewed for a Sunset & Vine North documentary

2: The referees were John Street, John Smyth and Alan Chamberlain.

3: '"Deadeye Dick" was an honorific often accorded to a person who was a virtuoso with firearms. So it is a sort of lungfish of a nickname. It was born in the ocean, but it adapted to life ashore.' *Deadeye Dick*, Kurt Vonnegut (Delacourte, 1982)

4: Theodore Millon, Disorders of Personality DSM – III: Axis II (Wiley, 1981)

5: *Pocket Money*, p. 123

6: The use of beta blockers was a burning issue for the sport in the late 1980s. The Minister for Sport announced that taking such a drug was 'tantamount to cheating'. The feeling was that they should be proscribed as they were able inhibit the signs of stress which can affect the performance of a player in a crucial match. Factors such as: an increased heartbeat, perspiration and feelings of anxiety. The Sports Council (a government-funded body) were keen to ban their use in line with International Olympic Committee rules. However, snooker was keen to permit their use when prescribed for a genuine medicinal purpose. All information taken from *Snooker Scene*.

7: Pat Hammond, interviewed for a Sunset + Vine North documentary

8: *Behind the White Ball*, p. 199

9: Steve Davis, interviewed for a Sunset + Vine North documentary

FOURTEEN

1: National Office of Statistics

2: 'Gone To Pot', *Total Sport*

3: *Snooker Scene*, December 1989

4: Rowan Simons, an Englishman who works for ODC Media in Beijing, worked on the 1988 Kent Cup but when contacted was reluctant to talk about the event.

5: Cf. Reginald Perrin (Chapter 5). This kind of thing cannot be invented.

6: *Snooker Scene*, March 1990, p. 3

7: Taylor has never publicly confirmed or denied that Higgins insulted his mother, preferring instead to say, 'He insulted a member of my family.' It is, however, generally accepted by the snooker fraternity that it was his mother. Taylor has never made clear the precise nature of the comments made by Higgins.

8: *Snooker Scene*, March 1990

9: *When Snooker Ruled the World*, a BBC Manchester documentary, April 2002

10: Higgins had previously been placed on a charge by the WPBSA and made the tabloids when he revealed the label on the inside of another jacket for the benefit of the cameras. The charge was subsequently dropped when it became apparent that the clothes were part of a successful range that was available everywhere.

11: *Sunday People*, 9 November 1997

12: *Faithfull*, Marianne Faithfull (Penguin, 1984), pp. 415–6

13: Ann Yates, interviewed for Sunset + Vine North documentary

FIFTEEN

1: To view the portrait of Higgins go to: www.edgallery.com/rodney/

2: *Encyclopaedia Britannica* (www.britannica.com/eb/article?eu=16759)

3: *News of the World*, 27 February 1994

4: *Today*, 28 February 1994

5: *Snooker Scene*

6: *Sunday Mirror*, 27 November 1994

7: Interview with author

8: www.yearsofgold.org.uk

9: *Daily Record*, 27 February 1996

10: *Sunday Mirror*, 11 August 1996

11: William Shakespeare, *Hamlet*. Act iv, Sc.5

12: *Daily Record*, 4 May 1997

13: *Frame by Frame*, p. 99

14: Ann Yates, interviewed for Sunset + Vine North documentary

15: *Sunday People*, August 1997

16: *The Abusive Personality*, D. G. Dutton (Guilford Press, 1998), p. 58

17: *Daily Mirror*, 25 August 1997

18: *Daily Mail*, 8 January 1998. Except, perhaps, for Manchester University student Pete Hackleton and his friend Toby in 1997. Pete was in a bar called Robinski's near the University campus when his attention was drawn to a 'grizzled old man in a big black cowboy hat.' Higgins was playing pool for £10 a game. Hackleton sauntered across. 'He was quite amenable,' he remembers, 'but hammered.' Naturally, there were a number of challengers lined up to play the former world snooker champion. 'It was clear I wasn't going to get a game, so I was starting to make excuses for myself . . . when Toby entered stage right.' The hapless interloper was a first year student from the West Country: 'Oh Alex. I can't believe that I've actually met you. Are you really the real Alex Higgins?' Hackleton concludes: 'Alex looked at us, as if weighing up his options, then looked back at Toby. He took a step towards him, so that they were face-to-face, grabbed hold of his balls and squeezed for all he was worth. "Are these really your real bollocks?" asked Alex, holding on tight.'

19: *Snooker Scene*, August 1998

20: Higgins and Reed duetted on a reworking of 'Wild Thing' with the Troggs in 1992. Bass guitarist Chris Britton recalls: 'Our manager at the time was a chap called Stan Green and he was also involved with Keith Floyd who was a mate of Ollie's and the whole thing got kicked around and just happened . . . it took a weekend in the studio and it was hilarious fun. The one time we did a TV show [to promote the single], we did it in Ireland. Ollie turned up but Alex decided to go off somewhere else.' Interview with author

21: *Blessed*, George Best with Roy Collins (Ebury Press, 2001), pp. 355–6

22: *Daily Mirror*, 10 August 2001

INDEX

ACKNOWLEDGEMENTS

The author and publisher wish to thank the following for permission to quote from copyrighted material:

A & C Black (Publishers) Ltd for *Between Frames* by Ted Lowe; Gillon Aitken Associates Ltd for *Pocket Money* © 1986 Gordon Burn; Arthur Barker Ltd for *Frame and Fortune* by Steve Davis and *Higgins, Taylor and Me* by Jim Meadowcroft; Book of Dreams Music Ltd for 'One Four Seven' by Sammes & Swain; Clive Everton for *The Story of Billiards and Snooker* and extracts from *Snooker Scene* magazine; Faber & Faber Ltd for *Reservoir Dogs* by Quentin Tarantino; David Higham Associates for 'Valediction' by Louis MacNeice and 'Do Not Go Gentle Into That Good Night' by Dylan Thomas; Mainstream Publishing for *Eye of the Hurricane* by John Hennessey; Music Sales Ltd for 'Mars Bars' by O'Neill & Bradley © West Bank Songs Ltd (Universal/MCA Music Ltd); Palan Music Ltd for 'Snooker Loopy' by Hodges & Peacock © 1995; Penguin Books (UK) Ltd for *Griff* by Terry Griffiths, published by Pelham Books © 1989 Matchroom Ltd; *Private Eye* magazine for 'New Higgins Sensation' (Issue 740); Random House Group Ltd for *Playing for Keeps* by Cliff Thorburn published by Partridge Press and *Behind the White Ball* by Jimmy White, published by Hutchinson; Rondor Music (London) Ltd for 'Up the Junction' by Difford & Tilbrook © 1979; Virgin Publishing Ltd for *Evil Spirits* © Cliff Goodwin 2000.